My Girlfriend's a GEEK

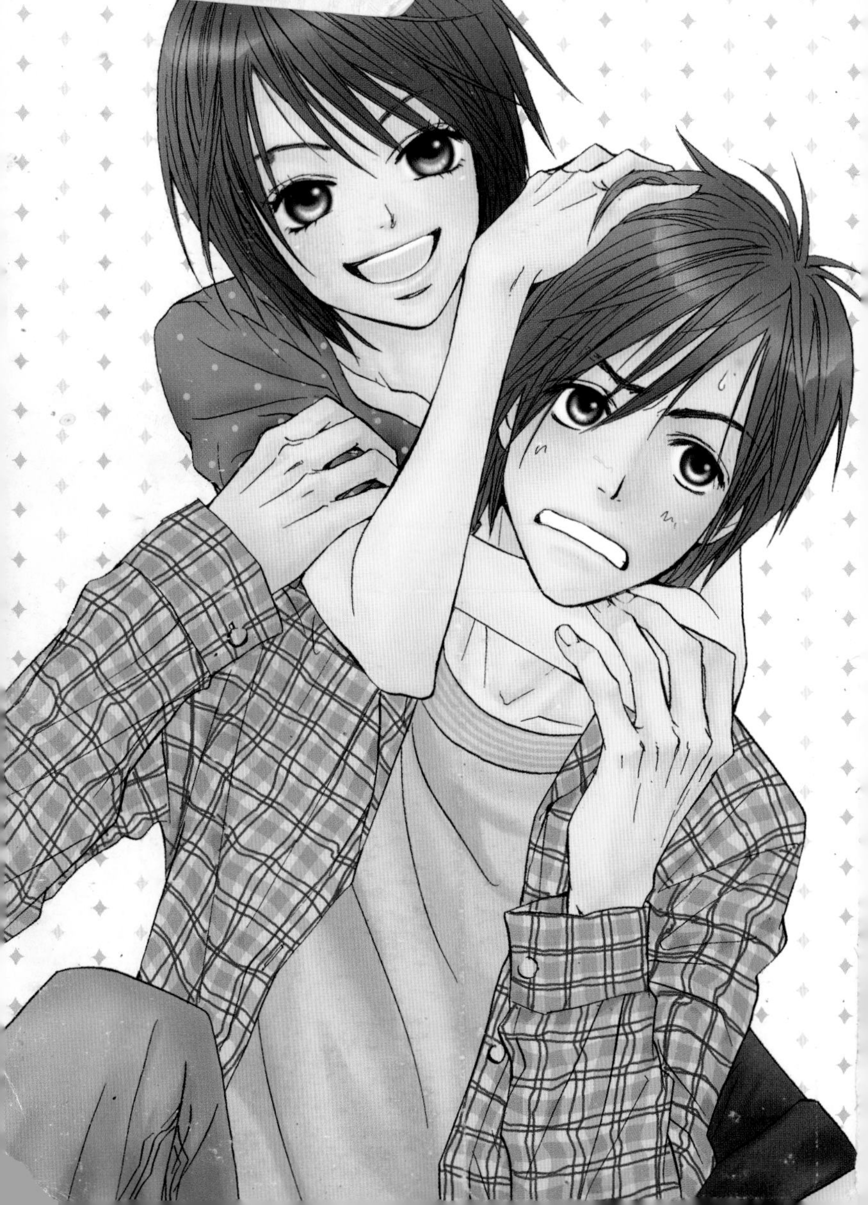

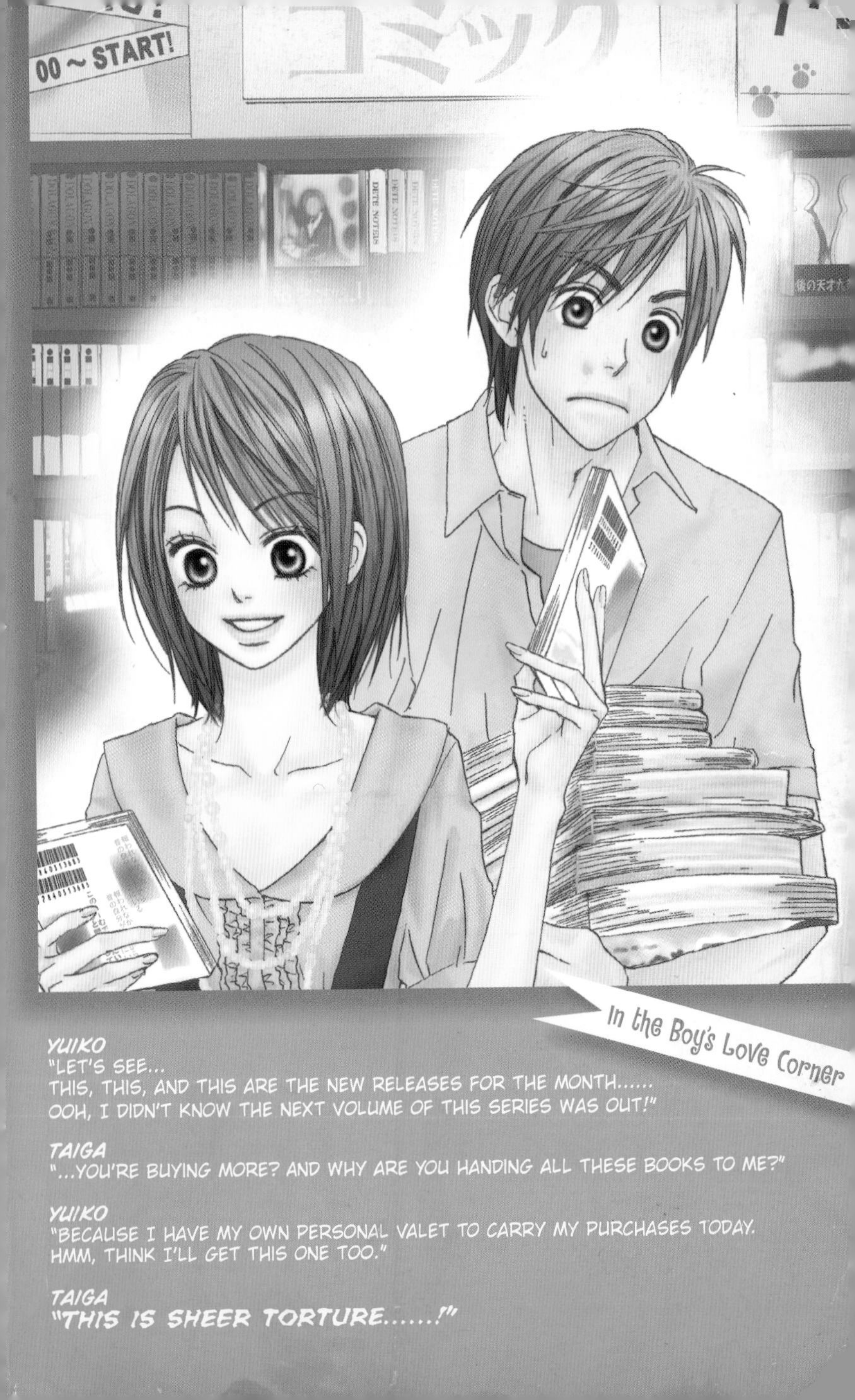
00 ~ START!
コミック
DETE NOTES

In the Boy's Love Corner

YUIKO
"LET'S SEE...
THIS, THIS, AND THIS ARE THE NEW RELEASES FOR THE MONTH......
OOH, I DIDN'T KNOW THE NEXT VOLUME OF THIS SERIES WAS OUT!"

TAIGA
"...YOU'RE BUYING MORE? AND WHY ARE YOU HANDING ALL THESE BOOKS TO ME?"

YUIKO
"BECAUSE I HAVE MY OWN PERSONAL VALET TO CARRY MY PURCHASES TODAY.
HMM, THINK I'LL GET THIS ONE TOO."

TAIGA
"THIS IS SHEER TORTURE......!"

My Girlfriend's a GEEK

1

RIZE SHINBA
STORY: PENTABU

CONTENTS

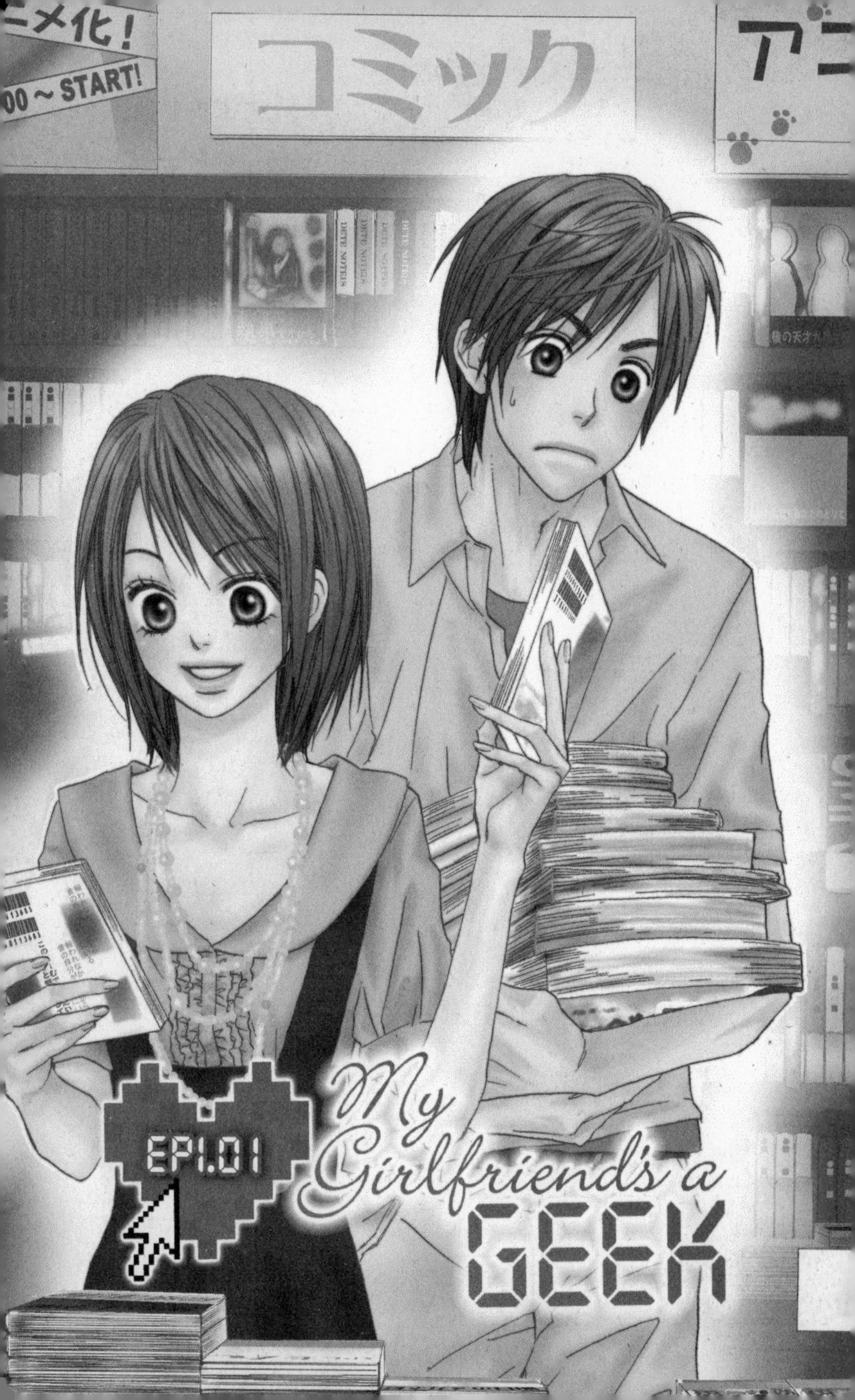
コミック
EP1.01
My Girlfriend's a
GEEK

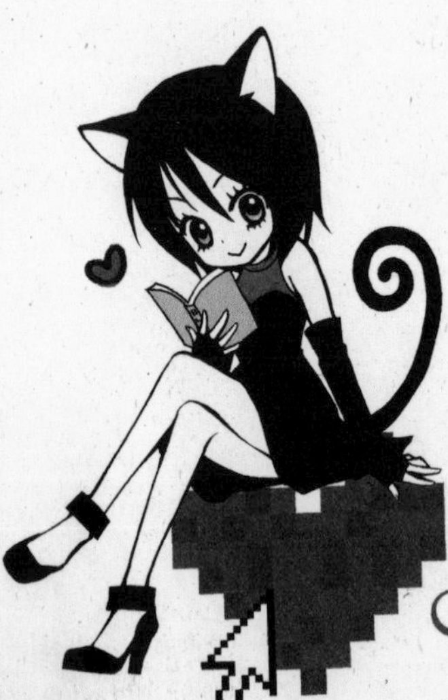

My Girlfriend's a GEEK

* This manga is a work of fiction based upon *My Girlfriend's a Geek*," Volumes 1 and 2, by Pentabu.

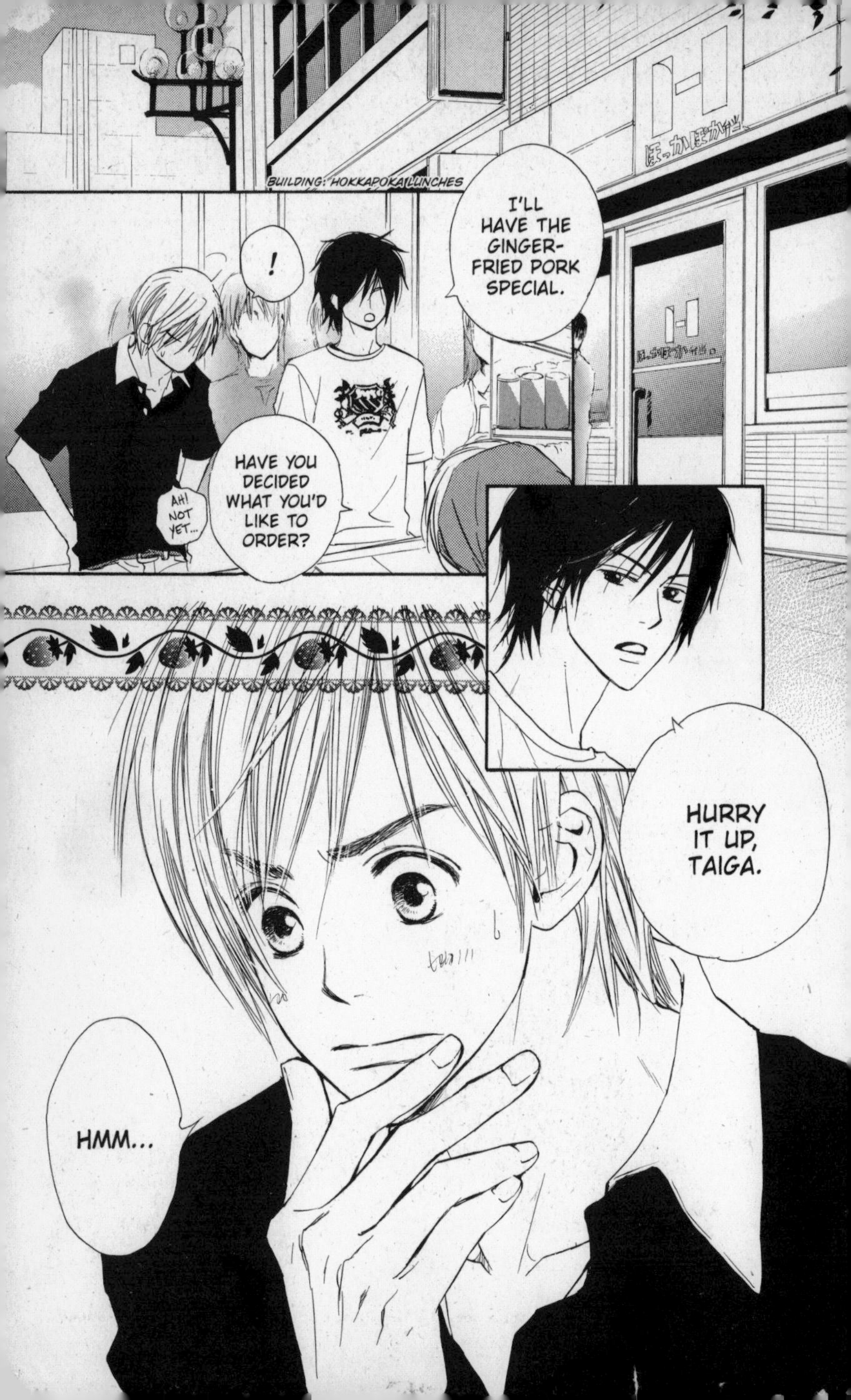
BUILDING: HOKKAPOKA LUNCHES
I'LL HAVE THE GINGER-FRIED PORK SPECIAL.
!
HAVE YOU DECIDED WHAT YOU'D LIKE TO ORDER?
AH! NOT YET...
HURRY IT UP, TAIGA.
HMM...

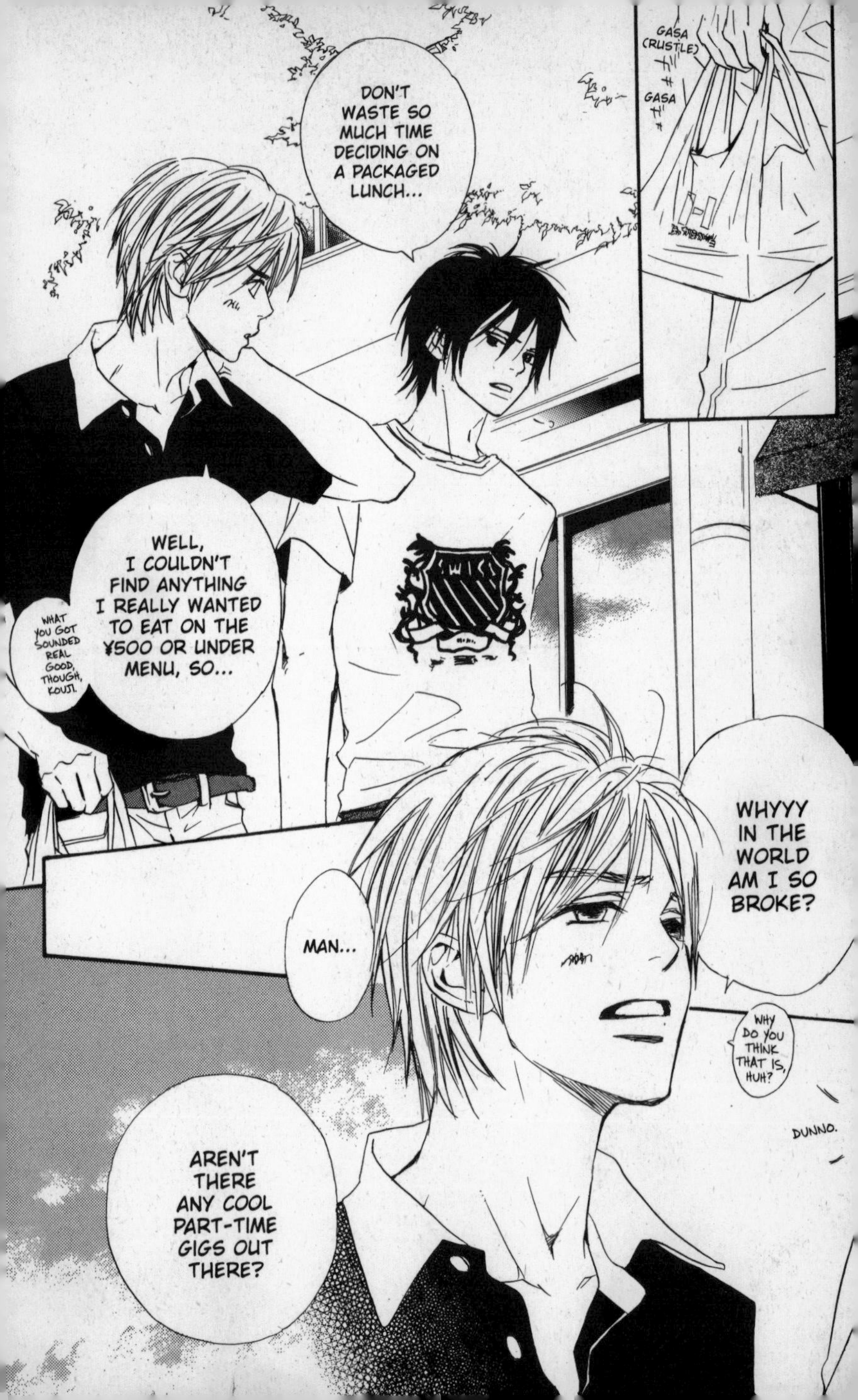
GASA (RUSTLE)
GASA
DON'T WASTE SO MUCH TIME DECIDING ON A PACKAGED LUNCH...
WELL, I COULDN'T FIND ANYTHING I REALLY WANTED TO EAT ON THE ¥500 OR UNDER MENU, SO...
WHAT YOU GOT SOUNDED REAL GOOD, THOUGH, KOUJI.
WHYYY IN THE WORLD AM I SO BROKE?
MAN...
WHY DO YOU THINK THAT IS, HUH?
DUNNO.
AREN'T THERE ANY COOL PART-TIME GIGS OUT THERE?

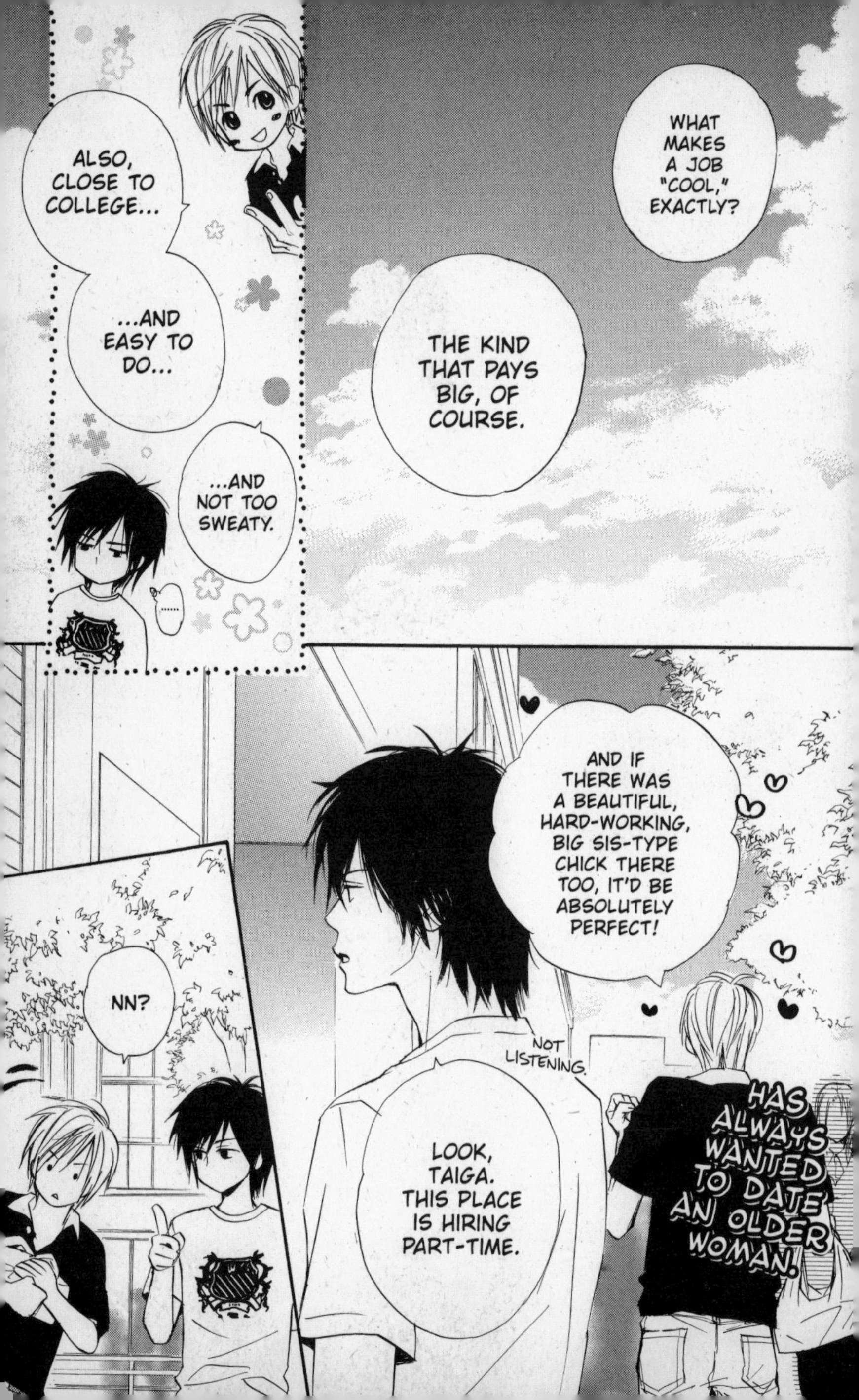
WHAT MAKES A JOB "COOL," EXACTLY?
THE KIND THAT PAYS BIG, OF COURSE.
ALSO, CLOSE TO COLLEGE...
...AND EASY TO DO...
...AND NOT TOO SWEATY.
......
AND IF THERE WAS A BEAUTIFUL, HARD-WORKING, BIG SIS-TYPE CHICK THERE TOO, IT'D BE ABSOLUTELY PERFECT!
HAS ALWAYS WANTED TO DATE AN OLDER WOMAN.
NOT LISTENING.
LOOK, TAIGA. THIS PLACE IS HIRING PART-TIME.
NN?

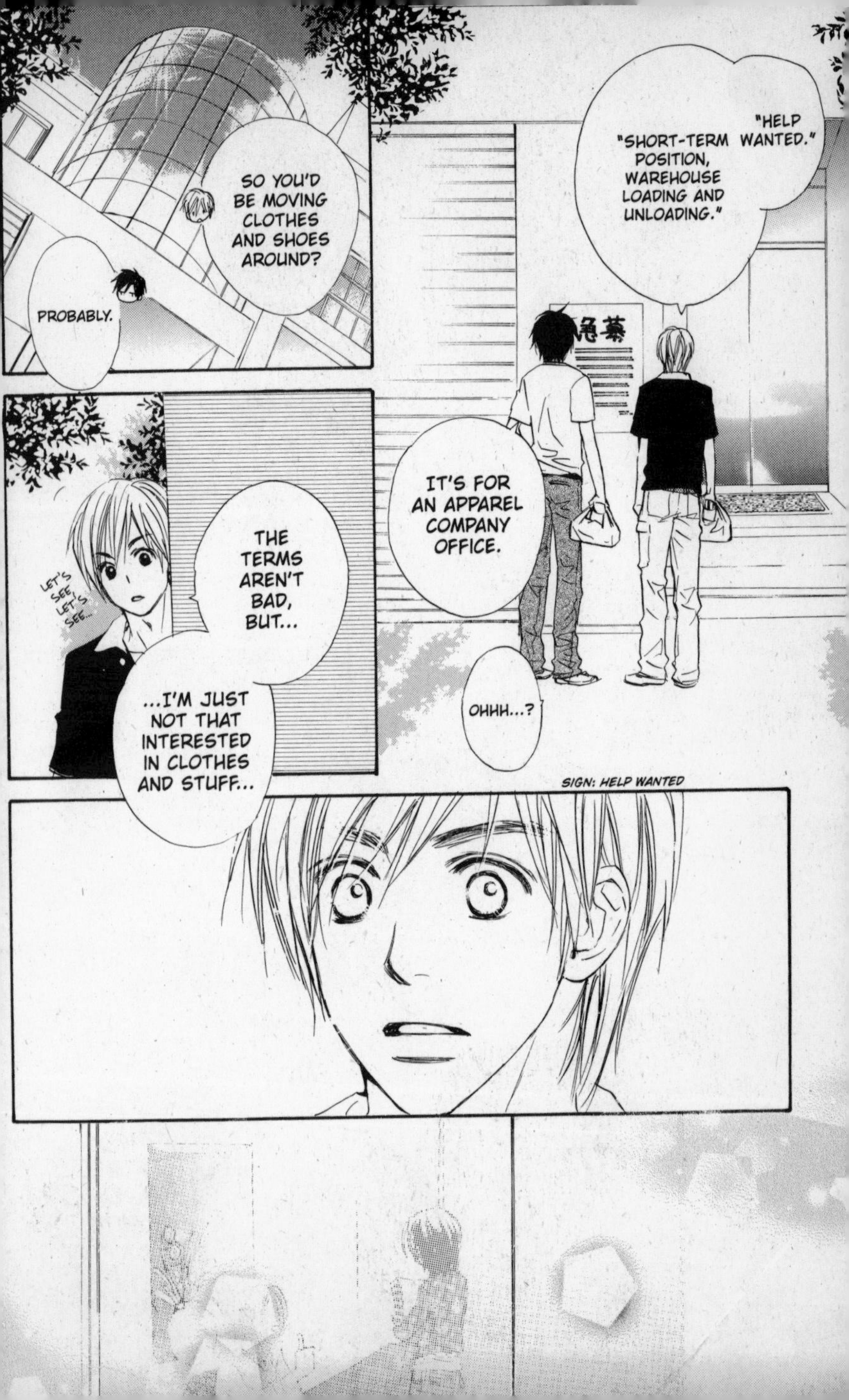
"HELP WANTED."
"SHORT-TERM POSITION, WAREHOUSE LOADING AND UNLOADING."
IT'S FOR AN APPAREL COMPANY OFFICE.
OHHH...?
SIGN: HELP WANTED
SO YOU'D BE MOVING CLOTHES AND SHOES AROUND?
PROBABLY.
LET'S SEE LET'S SEE...
THE TERMS AREN'T BAD, BUT...
...I'M JUST NOT THAT INTERESTED IN CLOTHES AND STUFF...

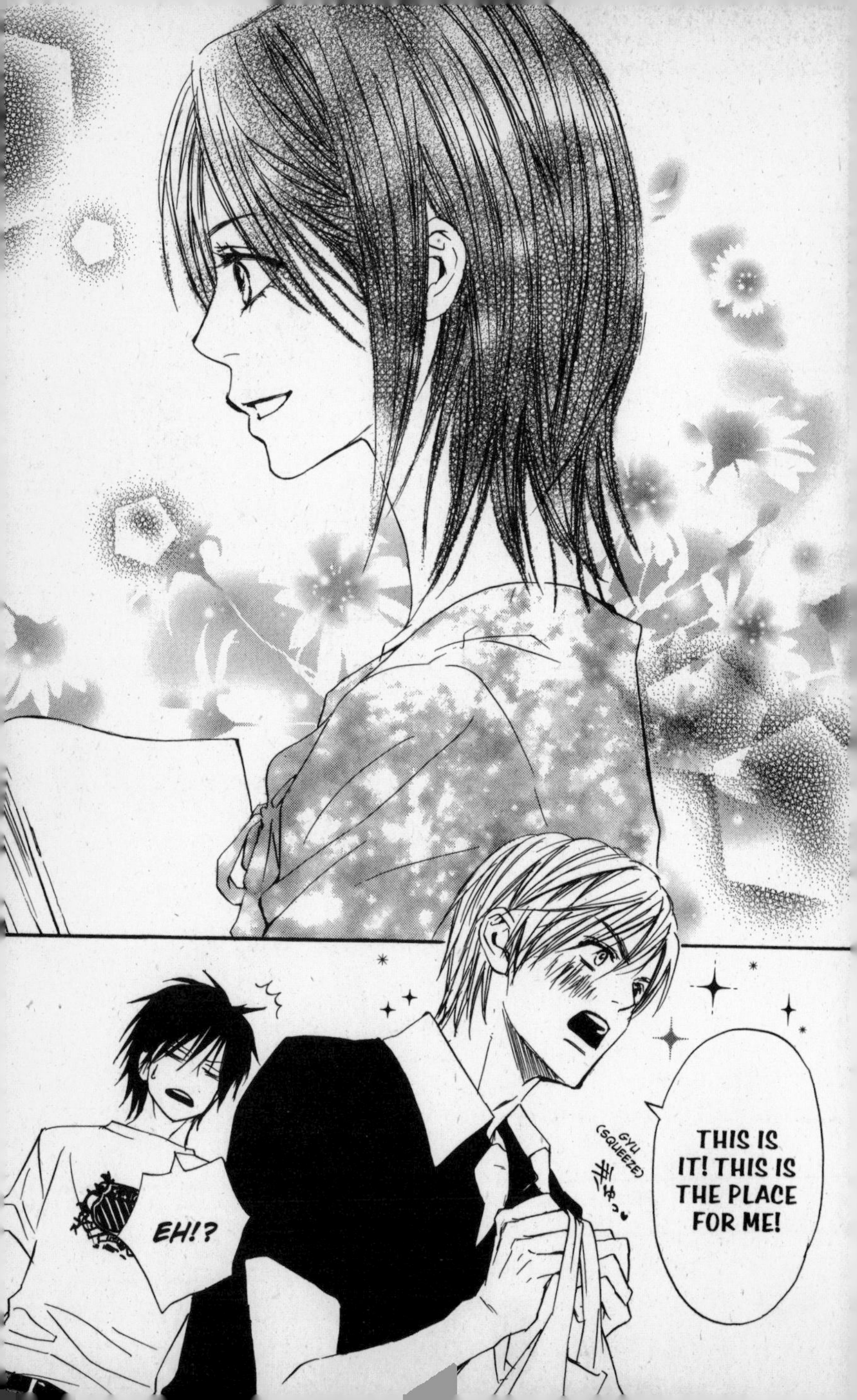
THIS IS IT! THIS IS THE PLACE FOR ME!
GYU (SQUEEZE)
EH!?

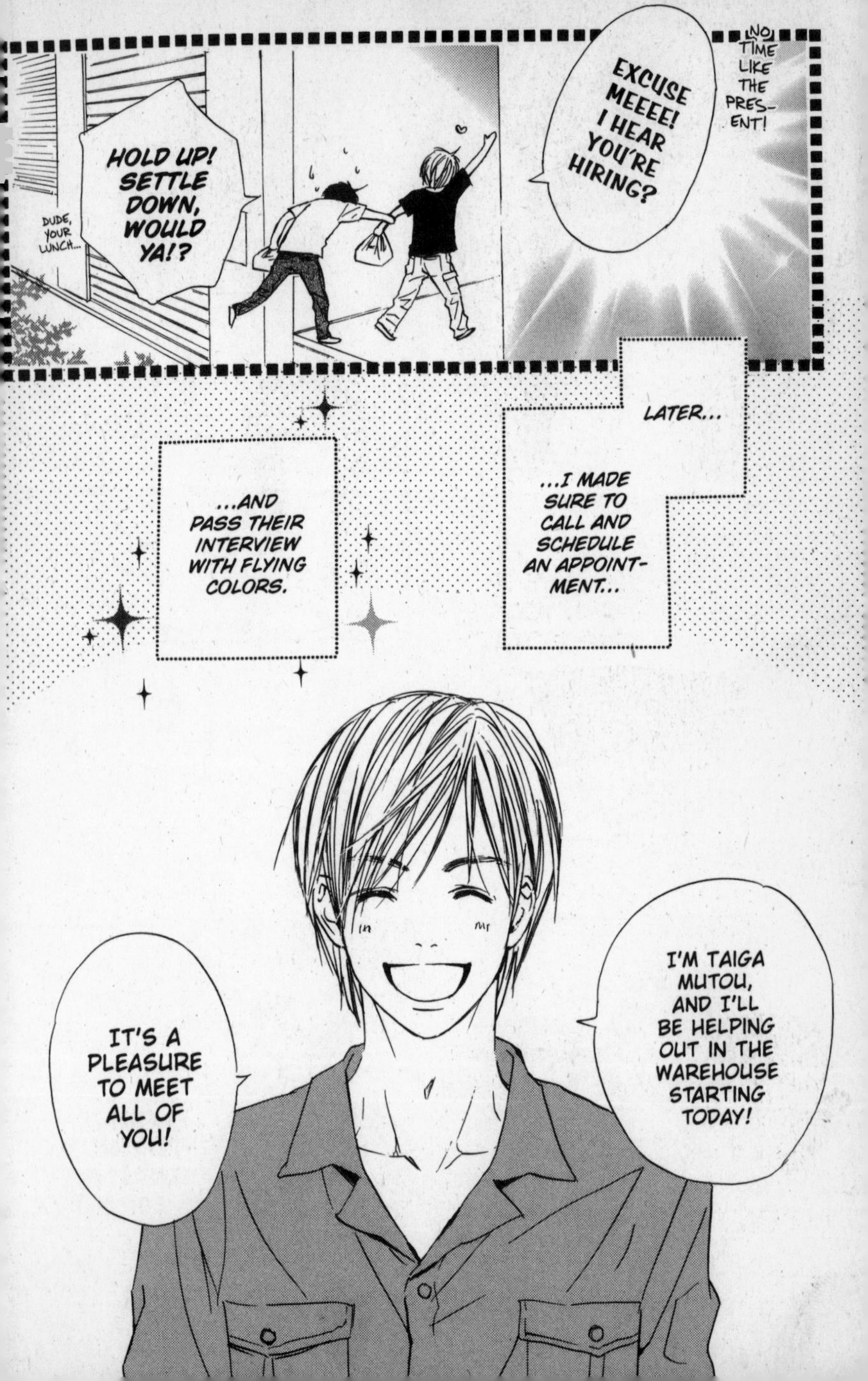
NO TIME LIKE THE PRES- ENT!
EXCUSE MEEEE! I HEAR YOU'RE HIRING?
HOLD UP! SETTLE DOWN, WOULD YA!?
DUDE, YOUR LUNCH...
LATER...
...I MADE SURE TO CALL AND SCHEDULE AN APPOINT- MENT...
...AND PASS THEIR INTERVIEW WITH FLYING COLORS.
I'M TAIGA MUTOU, AND I'LL BE HELPING OUT IN THE WAREHOUSE STARTING TODAY!
IT'S A PLEASURE TO MEET ALL OF YOU!

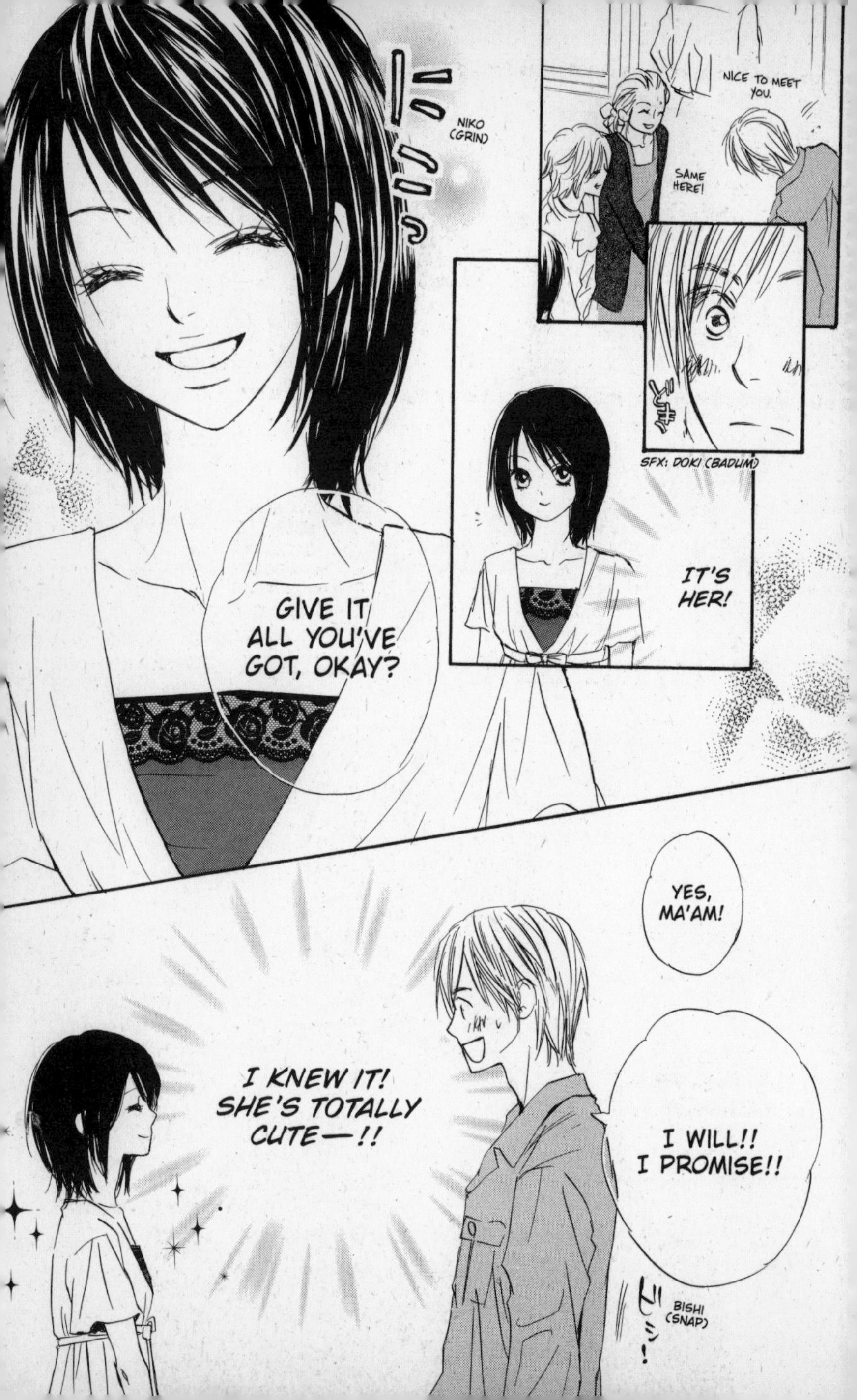
NICE TO MEET YOU.
SAME HERE!
SFX: DOKI (BADUM)
IT'S HER!
NIKO (GRIN)
GIVE IT ALL YOU'VE GOT, OKAY?
YES, MA'AM!
I WILL!! I PROMISE!!
BISHI (SNAP)
I KNEW IT! SHE'S TOTALLY CUTE—!!

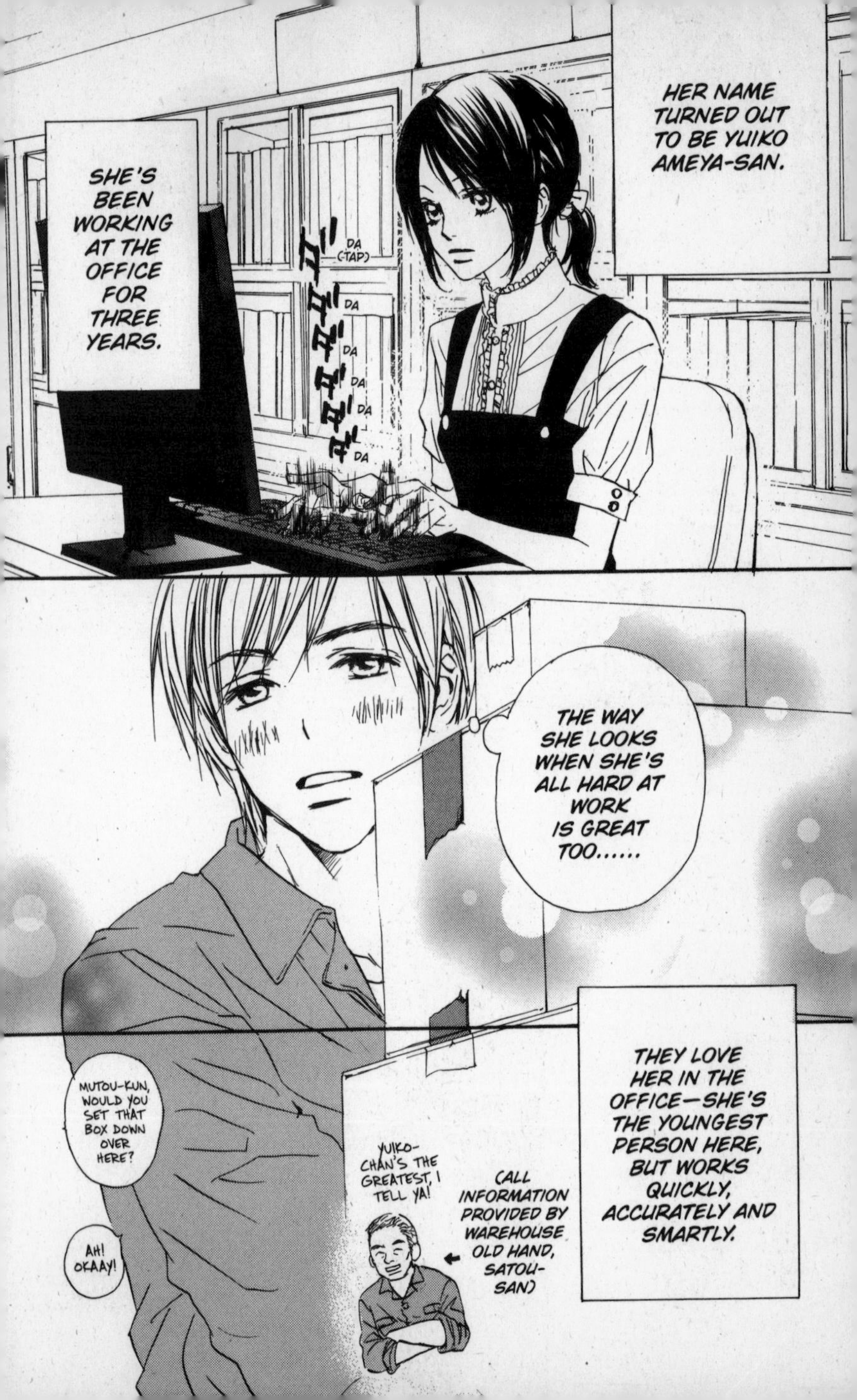
HER NAME TURNED OUT TO BE YUIKO AMEYA-SAN.
SHE'S BEEN WORKING AT THE OFFICE FOR THREE YEARS.
DA (TAP)
DA
DA
DA
DA
DA
THE WAY SHE LOOKS WHEN SHE'S ALL HARD AT WORK IS GREAT TOO......
THEY LOVE HER IN THE OFFICE—SHE'S THE YOUNGEST PERSON HERE, BUT WORKS QUICKLY, ACCURATELY AND SMARTLY.
YUIKO-CHAN'S THE GREATEST, I TELL YA!
(ALL INFORMATION PROVIDED BY WAREHOUSE OLD HAND, SATOU-SAN)
MUTOU-KUN, WOULD YOU SET THAT BOX DOWN OVER HERE?
AH! OKAAY!

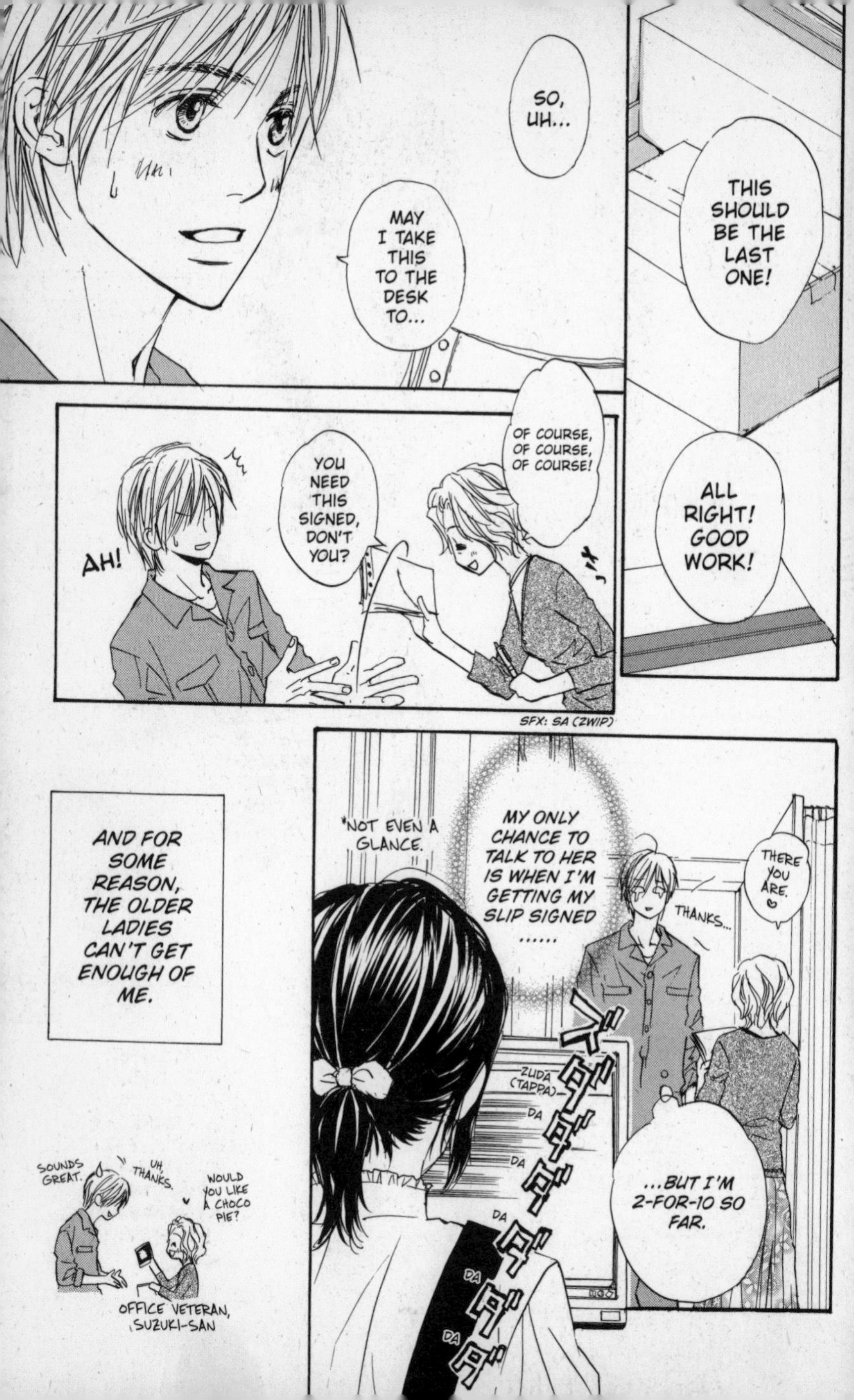
THIS SHOULD BE THE LAST ONE!
ALL RIGHT! GOOD WORK!
SO, UH...
MAY I TAKE THIS TO THE DESK TO...
OF COURSE, OF COURSE, OF COURSE!
YOU NEED THIS SIGNED, DON'T YOU?
AH!
SFX: SA (ZWIP)
THERE YOU ARE.
THANKS...
MY ONLY CHANCE TO TALK TO HER IS WHEN I'M GETTING MY SLIP SIGNED ......
*NOT EVEN A GLANCE.
ZUDA (TAPPA)
DA
DA
DA
DA
DA
...BUT I'M 2-FOR-10 SO FAR.
AND FOR SOME REASON, THE OLDER LADIES CAN'T GET ENOUGH OF ME.
WOULD YOU LIKE A CHOCO PIE?
UH, THANKS.
SOUNDS GREAT.
OFFICE VETERAN, SUZUKI-SAN

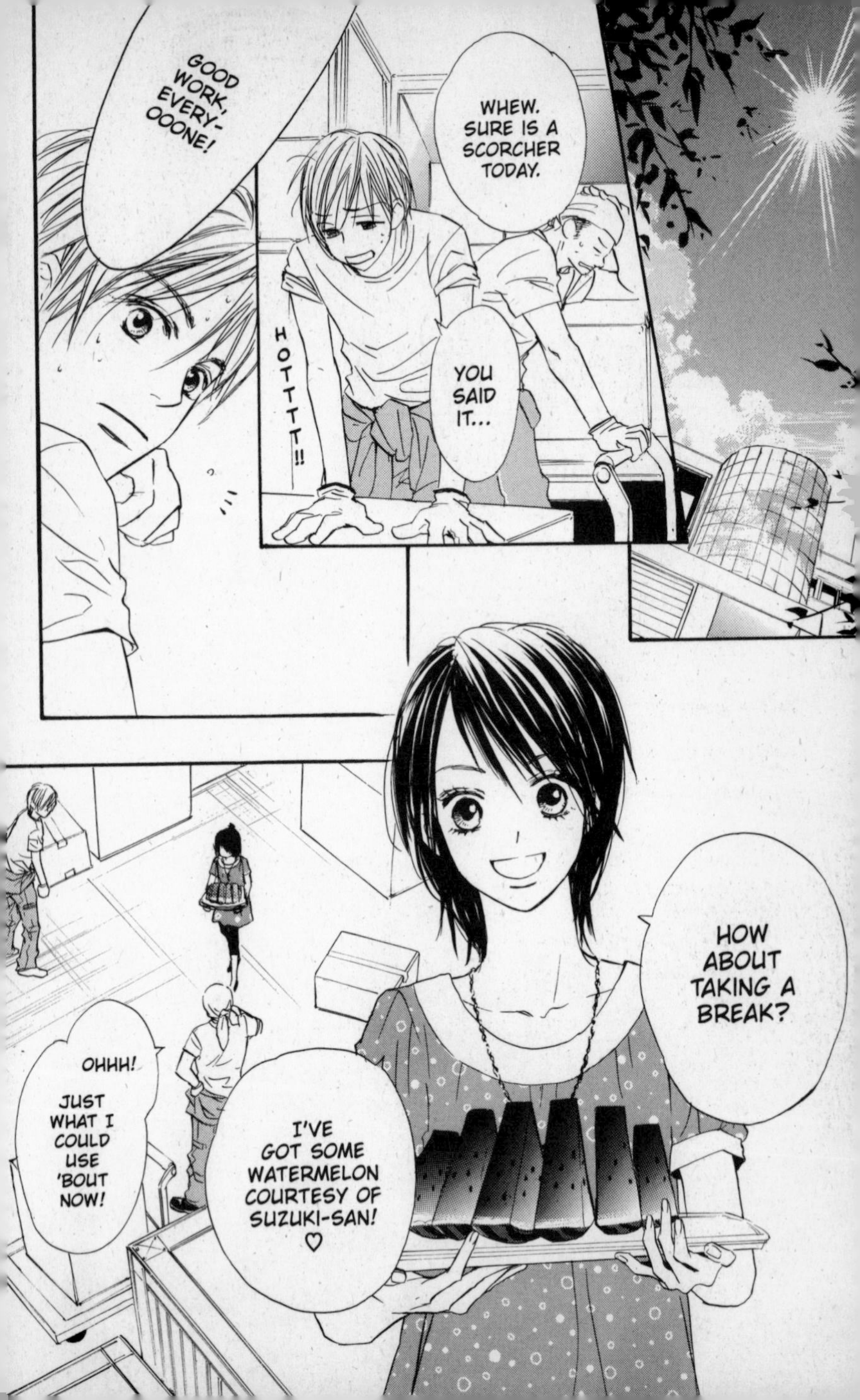
WHEW. SURE IS A SCORCHER TODAY.
YOU SAID IT...
HOTTTTT!!
GOOD WORK, EVERY-OOONE!
HOW ABOUT TAKING A BREAK?
I'VE GOT SOME WATERMELON COURTESY OF SUZUKI-SAN! ♡
OHHH!
JUST WHAT I COULD USE 'BOUT NOW!

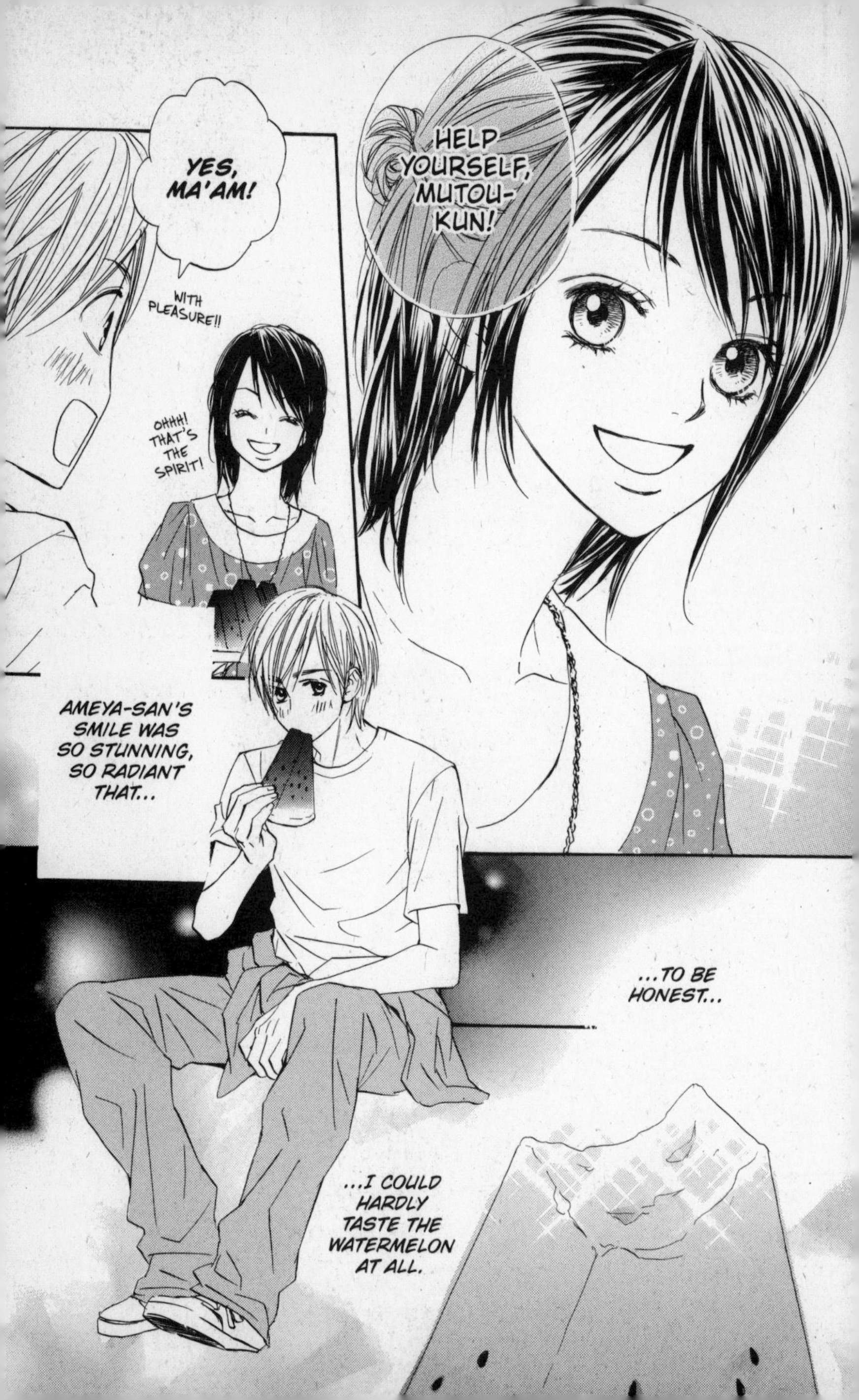
HELP YOURSELF, MUTOU-KUN!
YES, MA'AM!
WITH PLEASURE!!
OHHH! THAT'S THE SPIRIT!
AMEYA-SAN'S SMILE WAS SO STUNNING, SO RADIANT THAT...
...TO BE HONEST...
...I COULD HARDLY TASTE THE WATERMELON AT ALL.

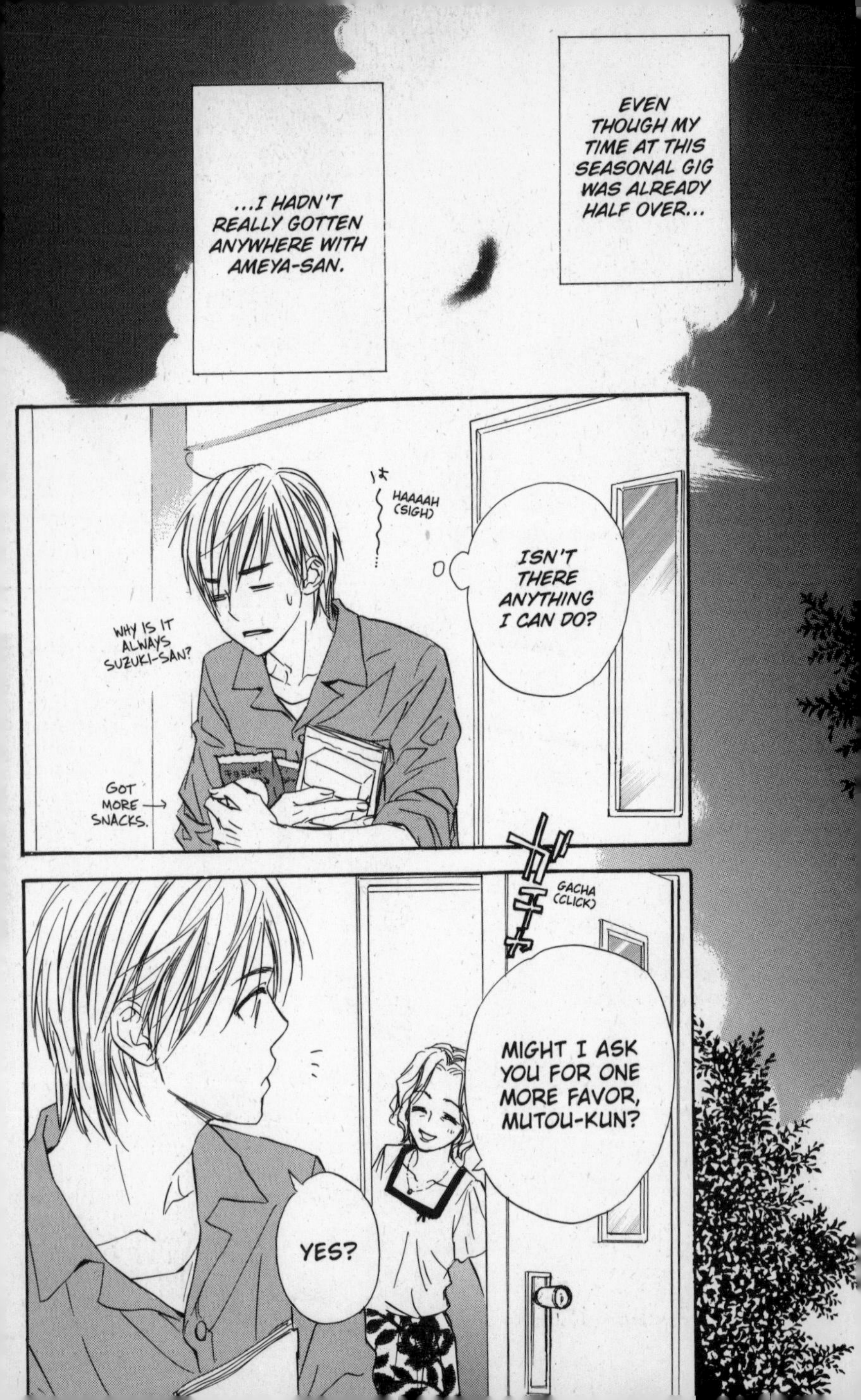
EVEN THOUGH MY TIME AT THIS SEASONAL GIG WAS ALREADY HALF OVER...
...I HADN'T REALLY GOTTEN ANYWHERE WITH AMEYA-SAN.
ISN'T THERE ANYTHING I CAN DO?
HAAAAH (SIGH)
WHY IS IT ALWAYS SUZUKI-SAN?
GOT MORE SNACKS.
GACHA (CLICK)
MIGHT I ASK YOU FOR ONE MORE FAVOR, MUTOU-KUN?
YES?

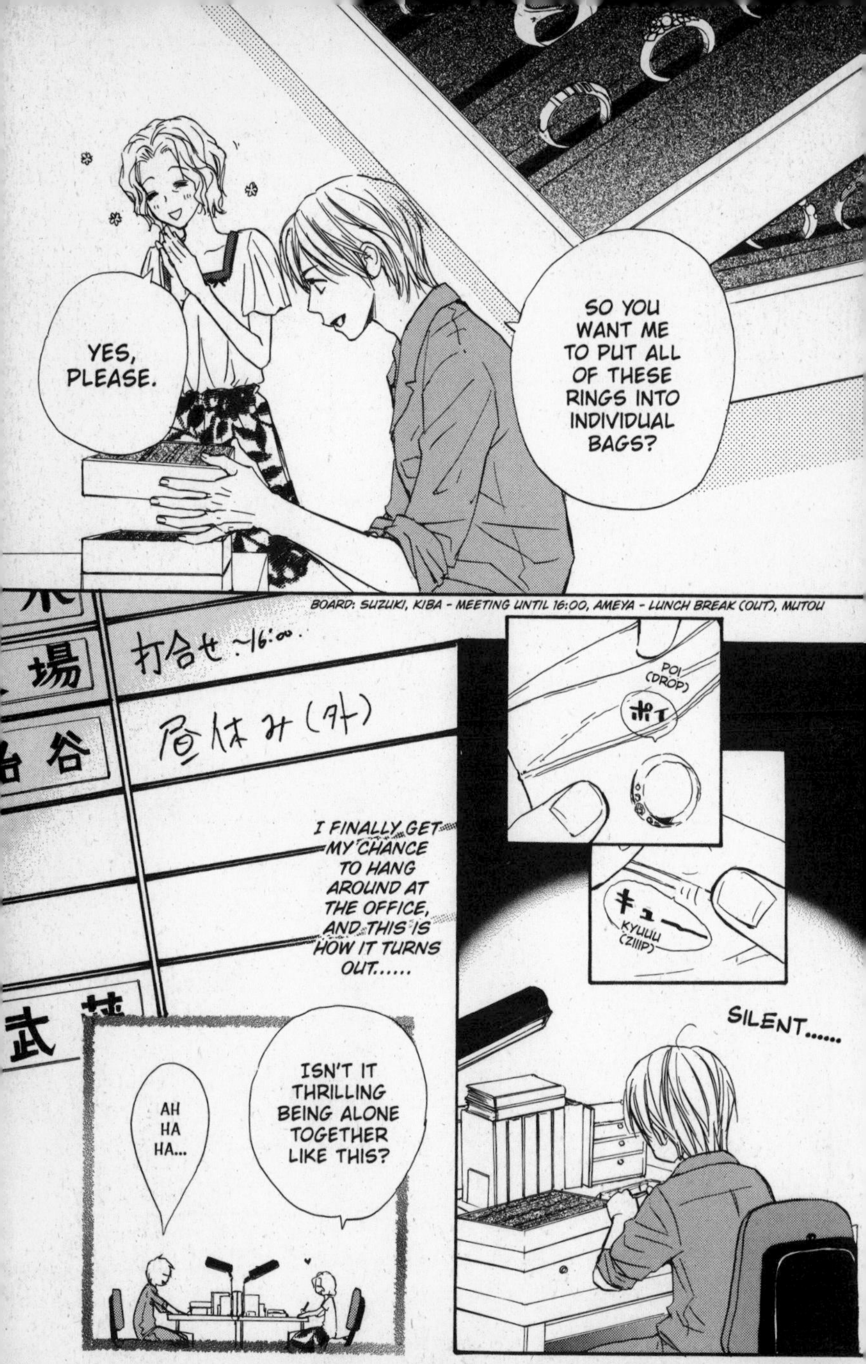
SO YOU WANT ME TO PUT ALL OF THESE RINGS INTO INDIVIDUAL BAGS?
YES, PLEASE.
BOARD: SUZUKI, KIBA - MEETING UNTIL 16:00, AMEYA - LUNCH BREAK (OUT), MUTOU
ポイ
POI (DROP)
キュー
KYUUU (ZIIIP)
SILENT......
打合せ ~16:00
昼休み (外)
I FINALLY GET MY CHANCE TO HANG AROUND AT THE OFFICE, AND THIS IS HOW IT TURNS OUT......
ISN'T IT THRILLING BEING ALONE TOGETHER LIKE THIS?
AH HA HA...

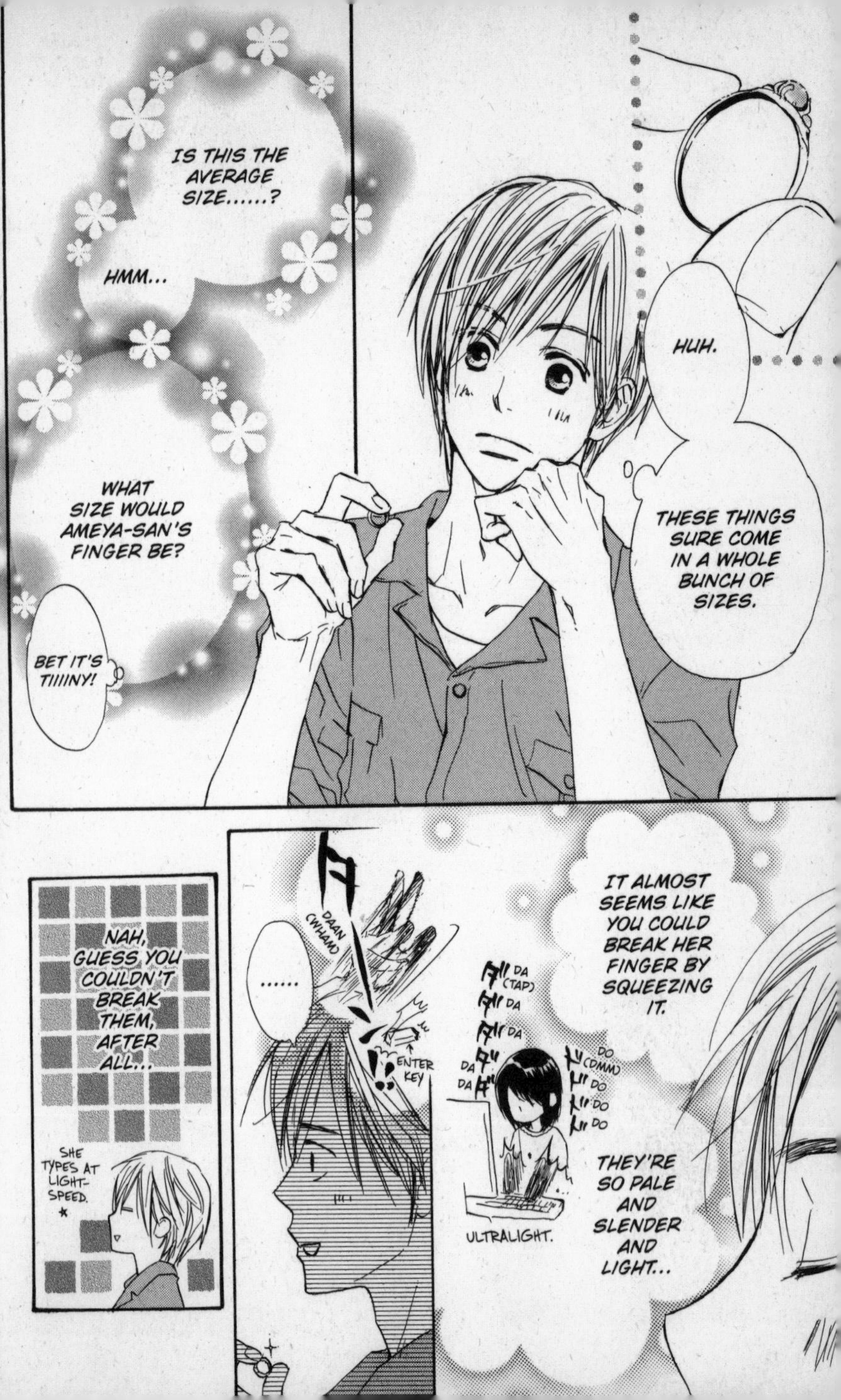
HUH.
THESE THINGS SURE COME IN A WHOLE BUNCH OF SIZES.
IS THIS THE AVERAGE SIZE......?
HMM...
WHAT SIZE WOULD AMEYA-SAN'S FINGER BE?
BET IT'S TIIIINY!
IT ALMOST SEEMS LIKE YOU COULD BREAK HER FINGER BY SQUEEZING IT.
THEY'RE SO PALE AND SLENDER AND LIGHT...
DO (DMM) DO DO DO
DA (TAP) DA DA DA DA
ULTRALIGHT.
DAAN (WHAM)
ENTER KEY
......
NAH, GUESS YOU COULDN'T BREAK THEM, AFTER ALL...
SHE TYPES AT LIGHT-SPEED. ★

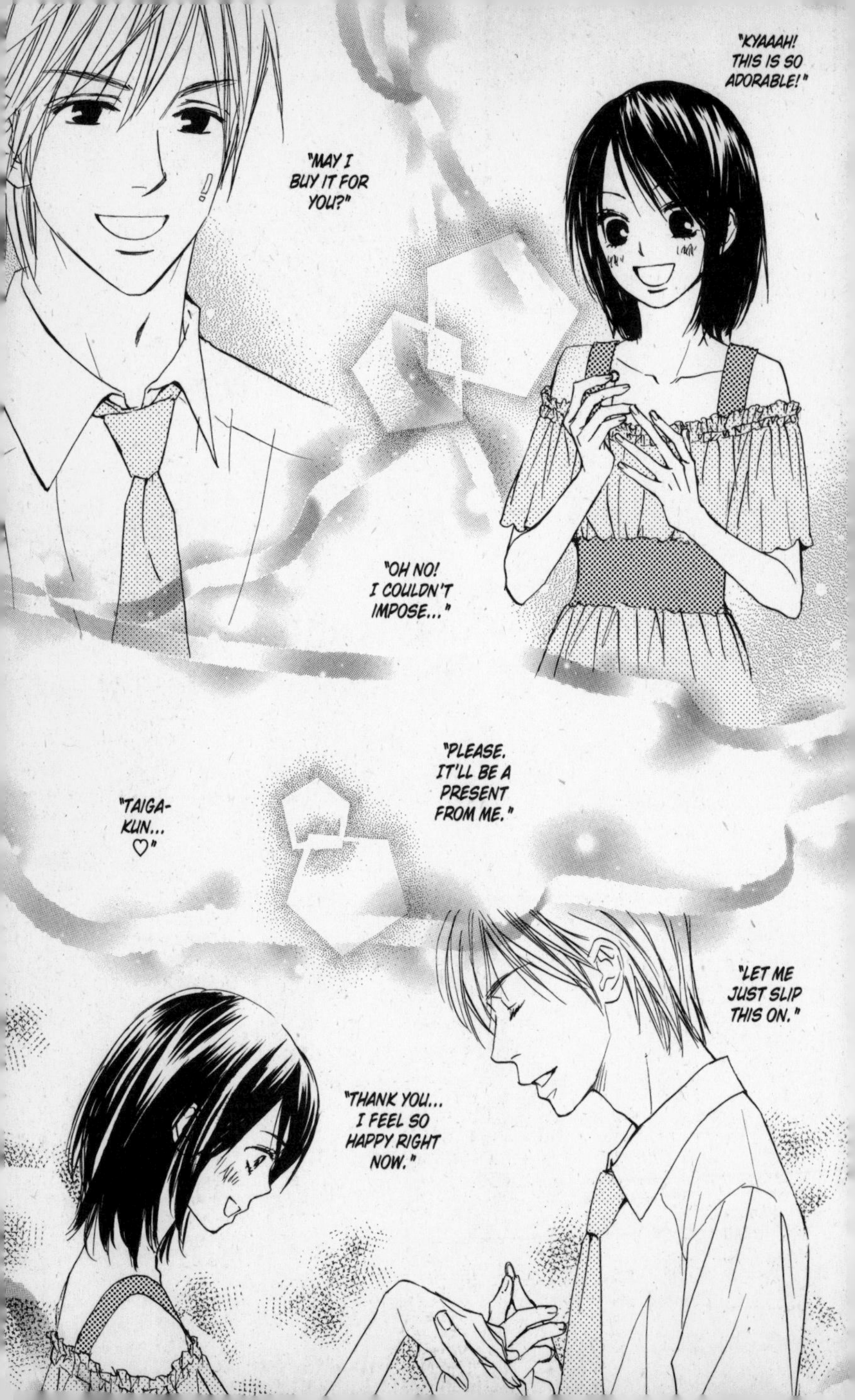
"KYAAAH! THIS IS SO ADORABLE!"
"MAY I BUY IT FOR YOU?"
"OH NO! I COULDN'T IMPOSE..."
"PLEASE. IT'LL BE A PRESENT FROM ME."
"TAIGA-KUN... ♡"
"LET ME JUST SLIP THIS ON."
"THANK YOU... I FEEL SO HAPPY RIGHT NOW."

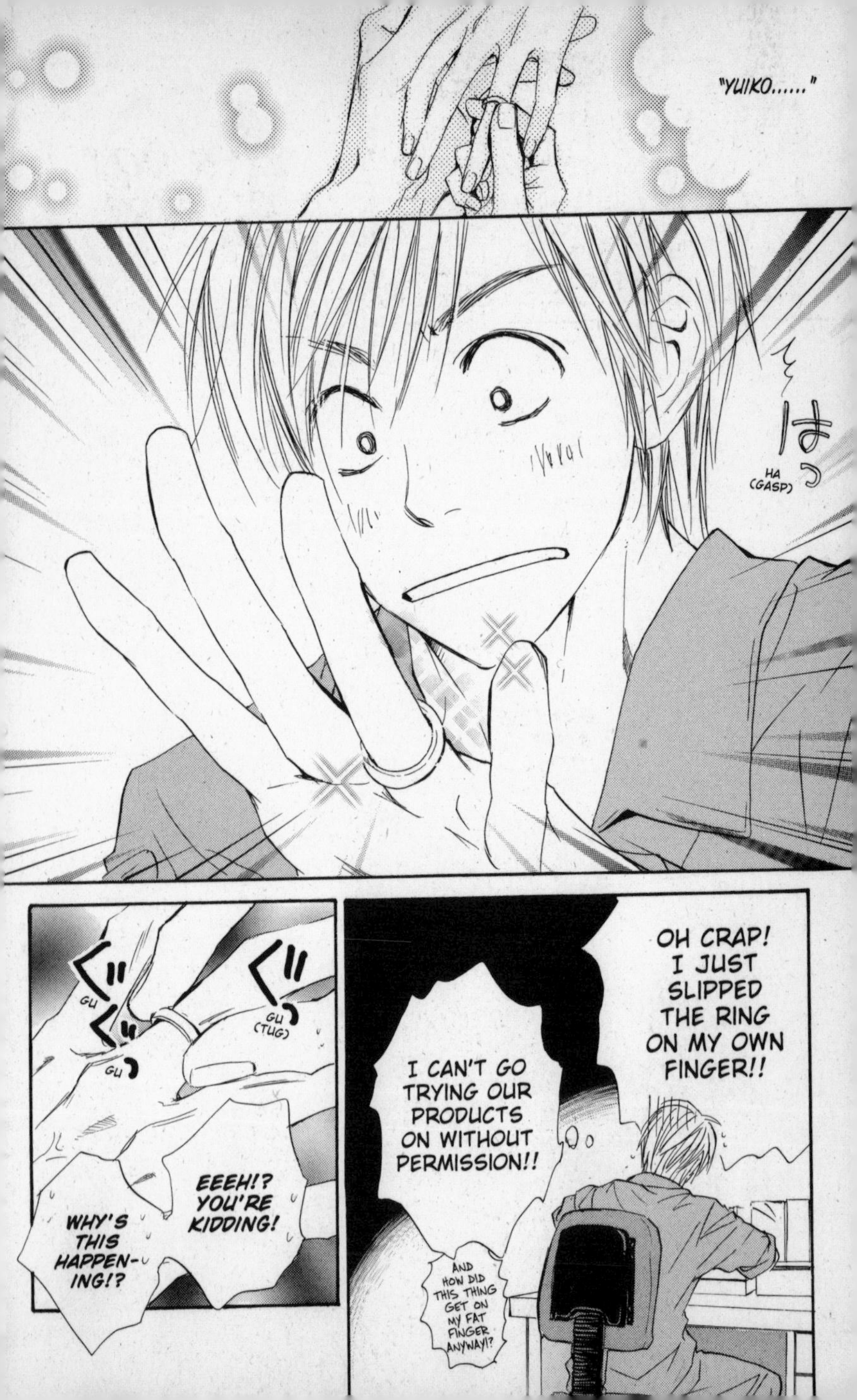
"YUIKO......"
はっ
HA (GASP)
OH CRAP! I JUST SLIPPED THE RING ON MY OWN FINGER!!
I CAN'T GO TRYING OUR PRODUCTS ON WITHOUT PERMISSION!!
AND HOW DID THIS THING GET ON MY FAT FINGER ANYWAY!?
ぐいっ
GU (TUG)
ぐいっ
GU
ぐいっ
GU
EEEH!? YOU'RE KIDDING!
WHY'S THIS HAPPEN-ING!?

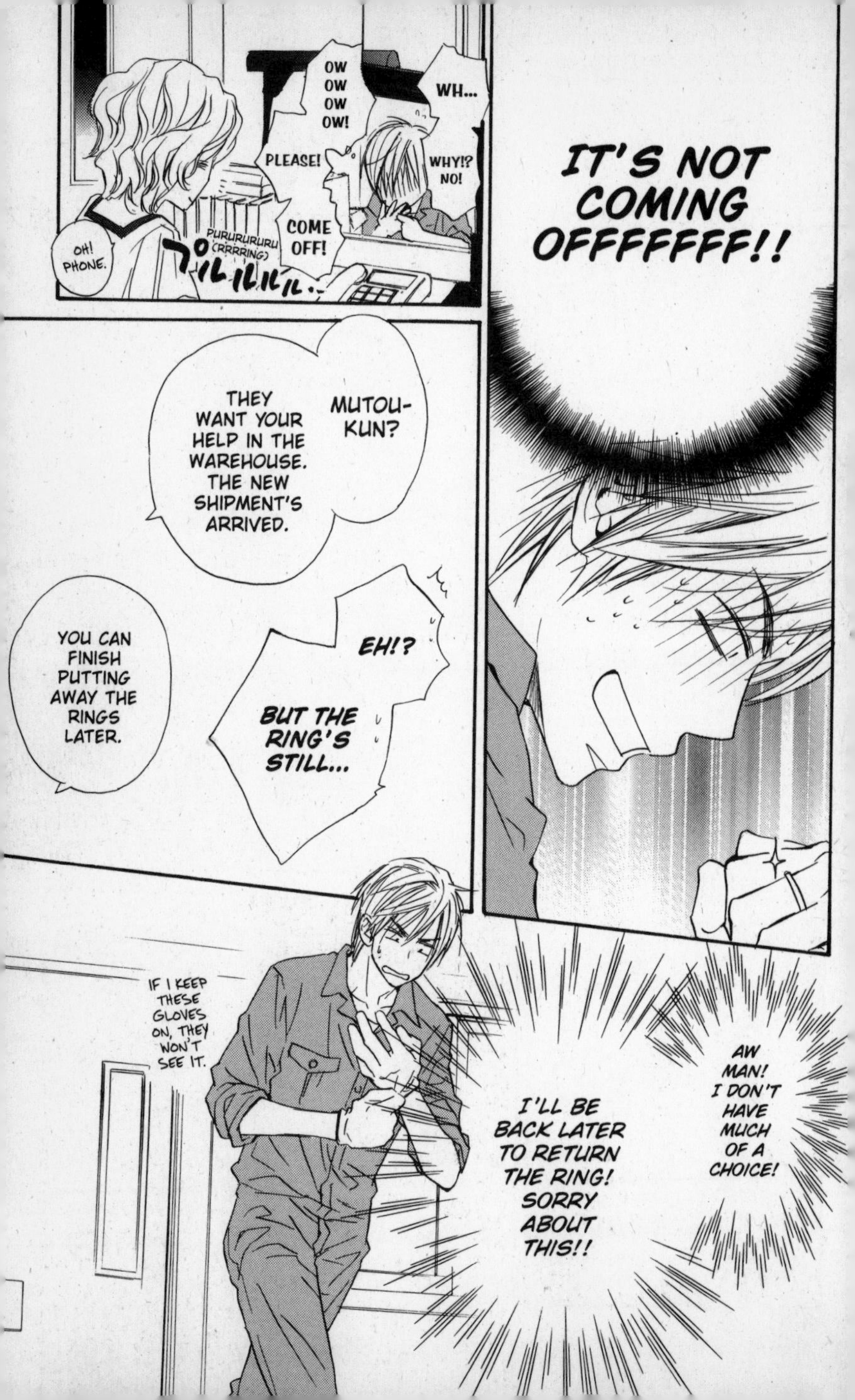
IT'S NOT COMING OFFFFFFF!!
WH...
OW OW OW OW!
WHY!? NO!
PLEASE!
COME OFF!
PURURURURU (RRRRING)
OH! PHONE.
MUTOU-KUN?
THEY WANT YOUR HELP IN THE WAREHOUSE. THE NEW SHIPMENT'S ARRIVED.
EH!?
BUT THE RING'S STILL...
YOU CAN FINISH PUTTING AWAY THE RINGS LATER.
AW MAN! I DON'T HAVE MUCH OF A CHOICE!
I'LL BE BACK LATER TO RETURN THE RING! SORRY ABOUT THIS!!
IF I KEEP THESE GLOVES ON, THEY WON'T SEE IT.

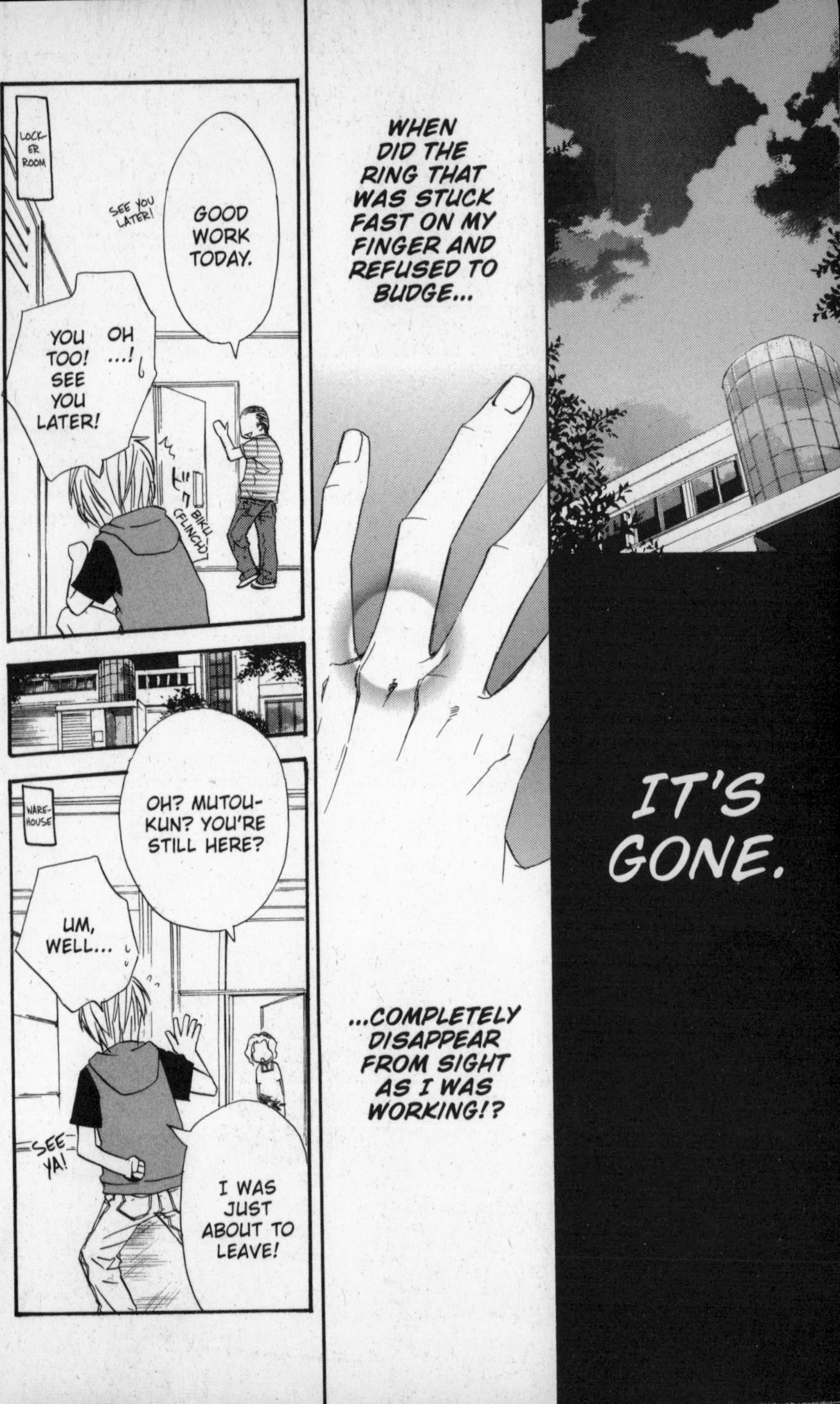
IT'S GONE.
WHEN DID THE RING THAT WAS STUCK FAST ON MY FINGER AND REFUSED TO BUDGE...
...COMPLETELY DISAPPEAR FROM SIGHT AS I WAS WORKING!?
LOCKER ROOM
GOOD WORK TODAY.
SEE YOU LATER!
OH ...!
YOU TOO! SEE YOU LATER!
BIKU (FLINCH)
WAREHOUSE
OH? MUTOU-KUN? YOU'RE STILL HERE?
UM, WELL...
I WAS JUST ABOUT TO LEAVE!
SEE-YA!

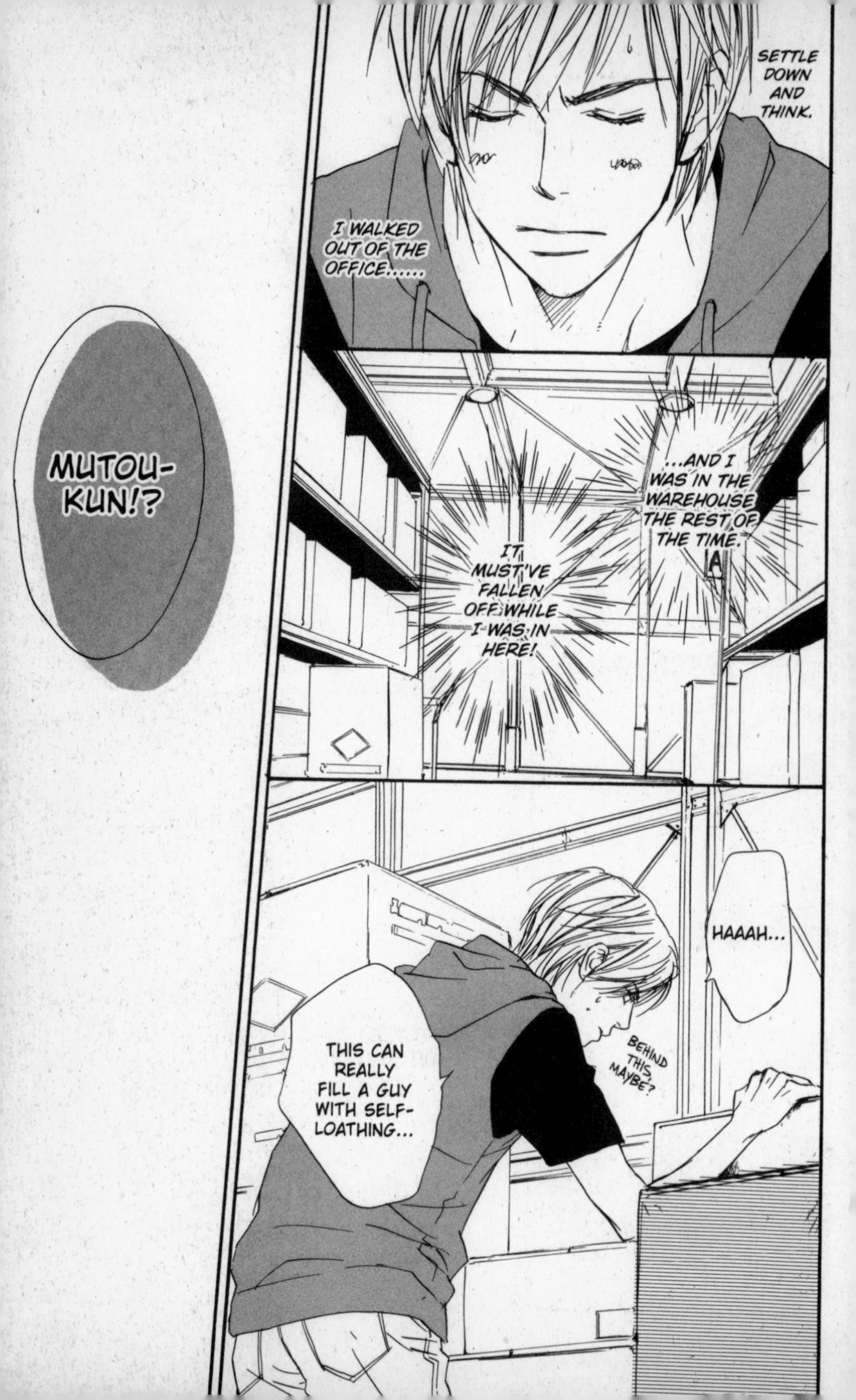

SETTLE DOWN AND THINK.
I WALKED OUT OF THE OFFICE......
...AND I WAS IN THE WAREHOUSE THE REST OF THE TIME.
IT MUST'VE FALLEN OFF WHILE I WAS IN HERE!
HAAAH...
BEHIND THIS, MAYBE?
THIS CAN REALLY FILL A GUY WITH SELF-LOATHING...
MUTOU-KUN!?

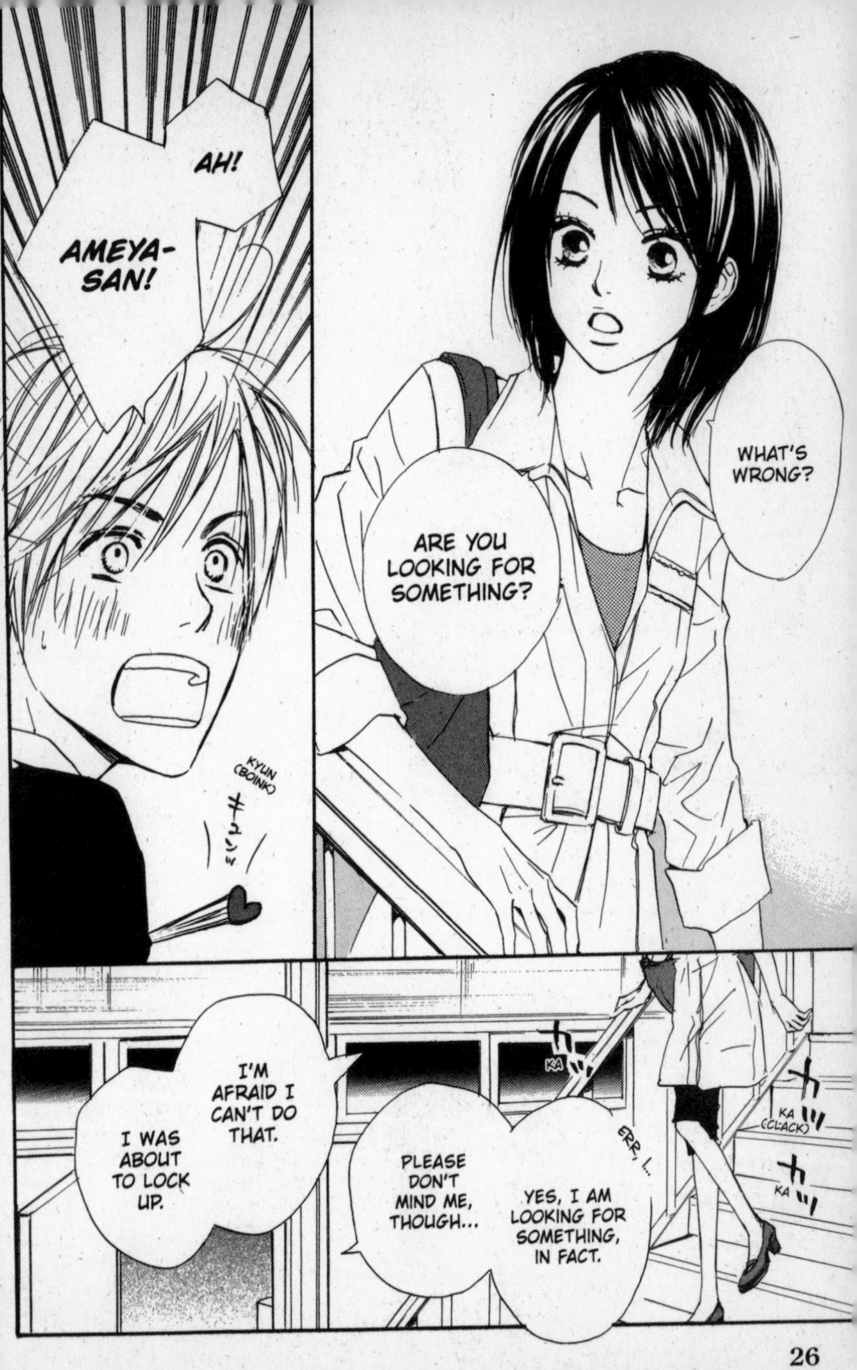
WHAT'S WRONG?
ARE YOU LOOKING FOR SOMETHING?
AH!
AMEYA-SAN!
KYUN (BOINK)
KA (CLACK)
KA
KA
ERR, I...
YES, I AM LOOKING FOR SOMETHING, IN FACT.
PLEASE DON'T MIND ME, THOUGH...
I'M AFRAID I CAN'T DO THAT.
I WAS ABOUT TO LOCK UP.

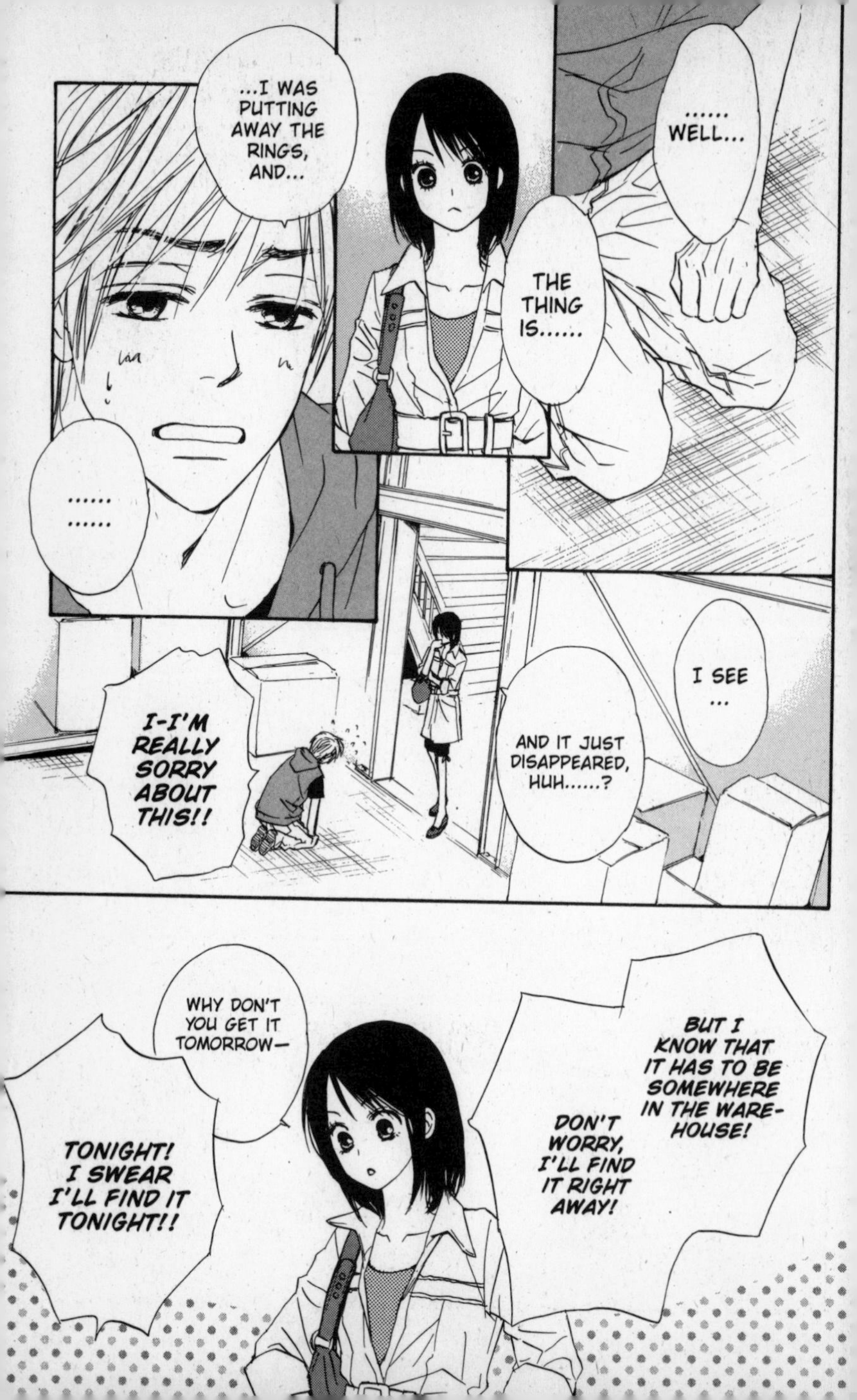
...... WELL...
THE THING IS......
...I WAS PUTTING AWAY THE RINGS, AND...
....
I SEE ...
AND IT JUST DISAPPEARED, HUH......?
I-I'M REALLY SORRY ABOUT THIS!!
BUT I KNOW THAT IT HAS TO BE SOMEWHERE IN THE WARE-HOUSE!
DON'T WORRY, I'LL FIND IT RIGHT AWAY!
WHY DON'T YOU GET IT TOMORROW—
TONIGHT! I SWEAR I'LL FIND IT TONIGHT!!

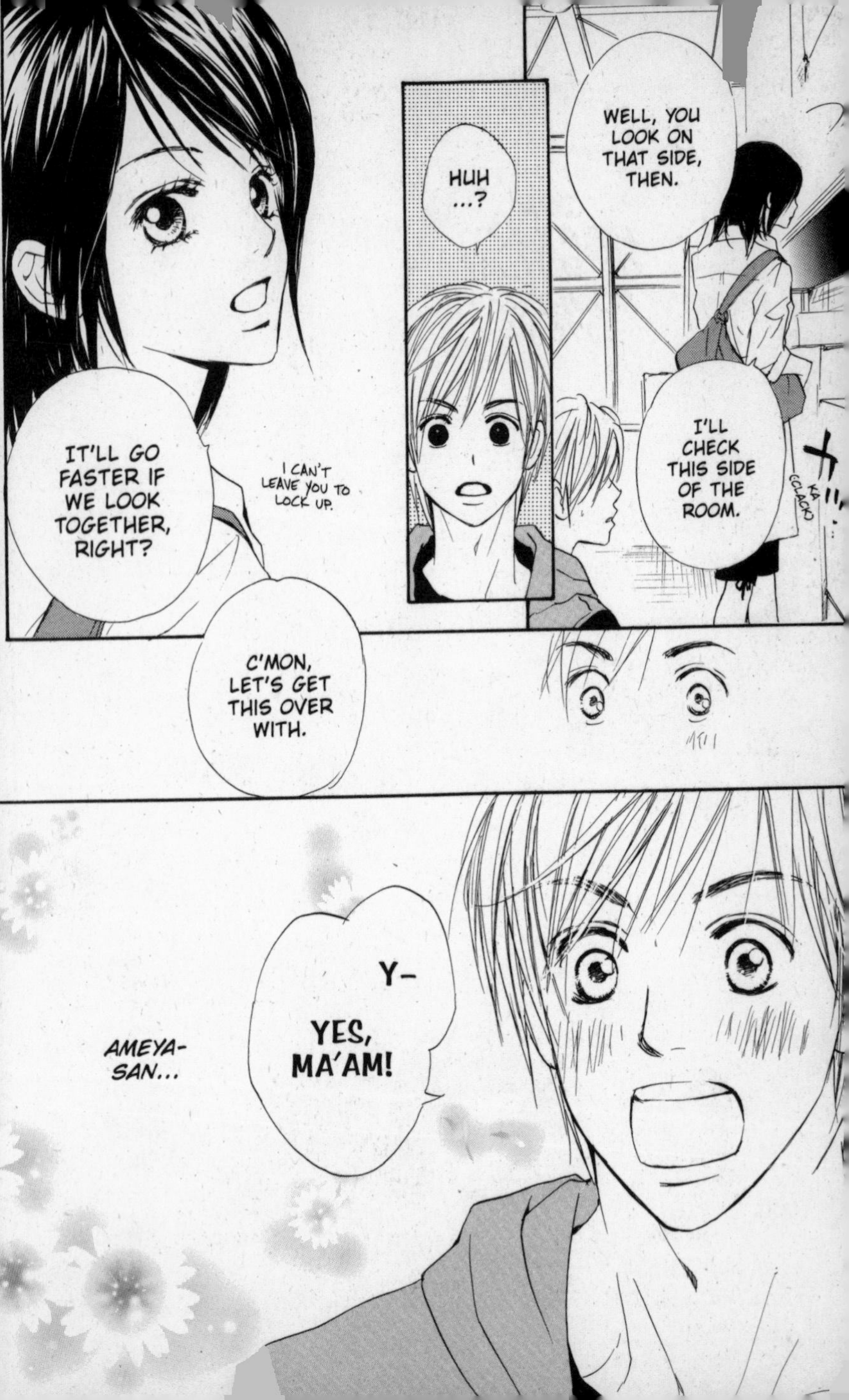
WELL, YOU LOOK ON THAT SIDE, THEN.
I'LL CHECK THIS SIDE OF THE ROOM.
KA (CLACK)
HUH ...?
IT'LL GO FASTER IF WE LOOK TOGETHER, RIGHT?
I CAN'T LEAVE YOU TO LOCK UP.
C'MON, LET'S GET THIS OVER WITH.
Y-
YES, MA'AM!
AMEYA-SAN...

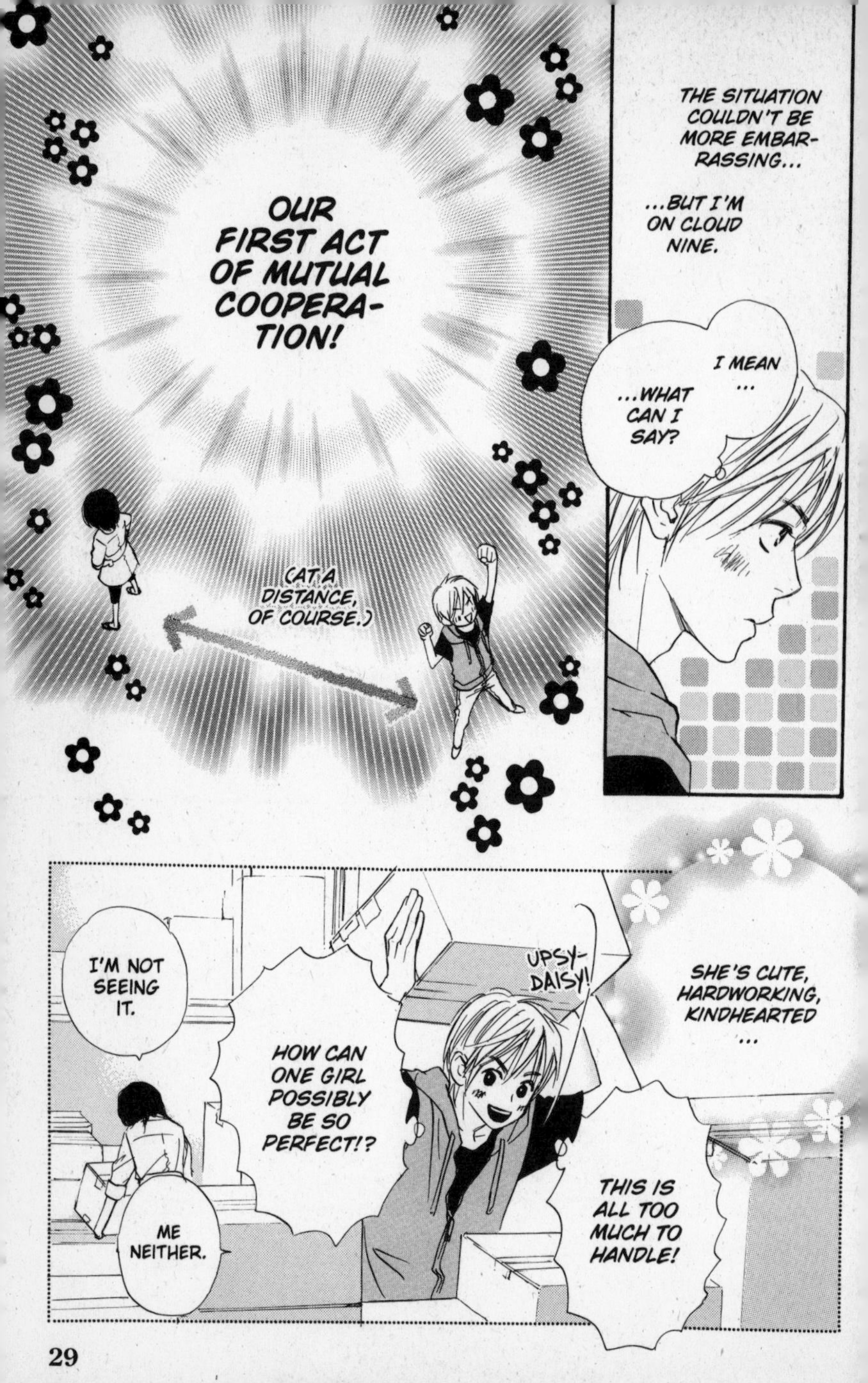
THE SITUATION COULDN'T BE MORE EMBARRASSING...
...BUT I'M ON CLOUD NINE.
I MEAN ...
...WHAT CAN I SAY?
OUR FIRST ACT OF MUTUAL COOPERATION!
(AT A DISTANCE, OF COURSE.)
SHE'S CUTE, HARDWORKING, KINDHEARTED ...
THIS IS ALL TOO MUCH TO HANDLE!
UPSY-DAISY!
HOW CAN ONE GIRL POSSIBLY BE SO PERFECT!?
I'M NOT SEEING IT.
ME NEITHER.

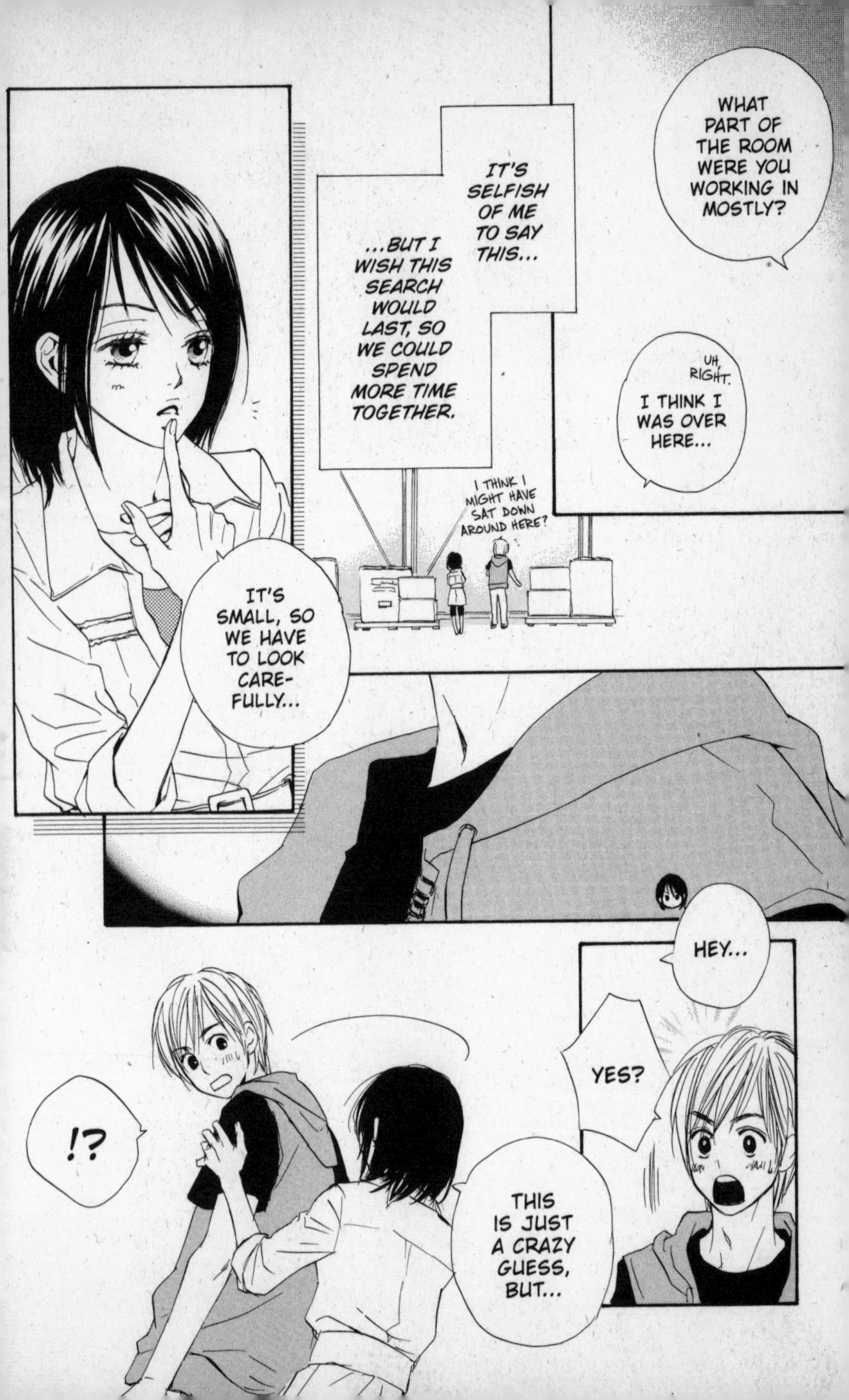
WHAT PART OF THE ROOM WERE YOU WORKING IN MOSTLY?
UH, RIGHT.
I THINK I WAS OVER HERE...
IT'S SELFISH OF ME TO SAY THIS...
...BUT I WISH THIS SEARCH WOULD LAST, SO WE COULD SPEND MORE TIME TOGETHER.
I THINK I MIGHT HAVE SAT DOWN AROUND HERE?
IT'S SMALL, SO WE HAVE TO LOOK CAREFULLY...
HEY...
YES?
THIS IS JUST A CRAZY GUESS, BUT...
!?

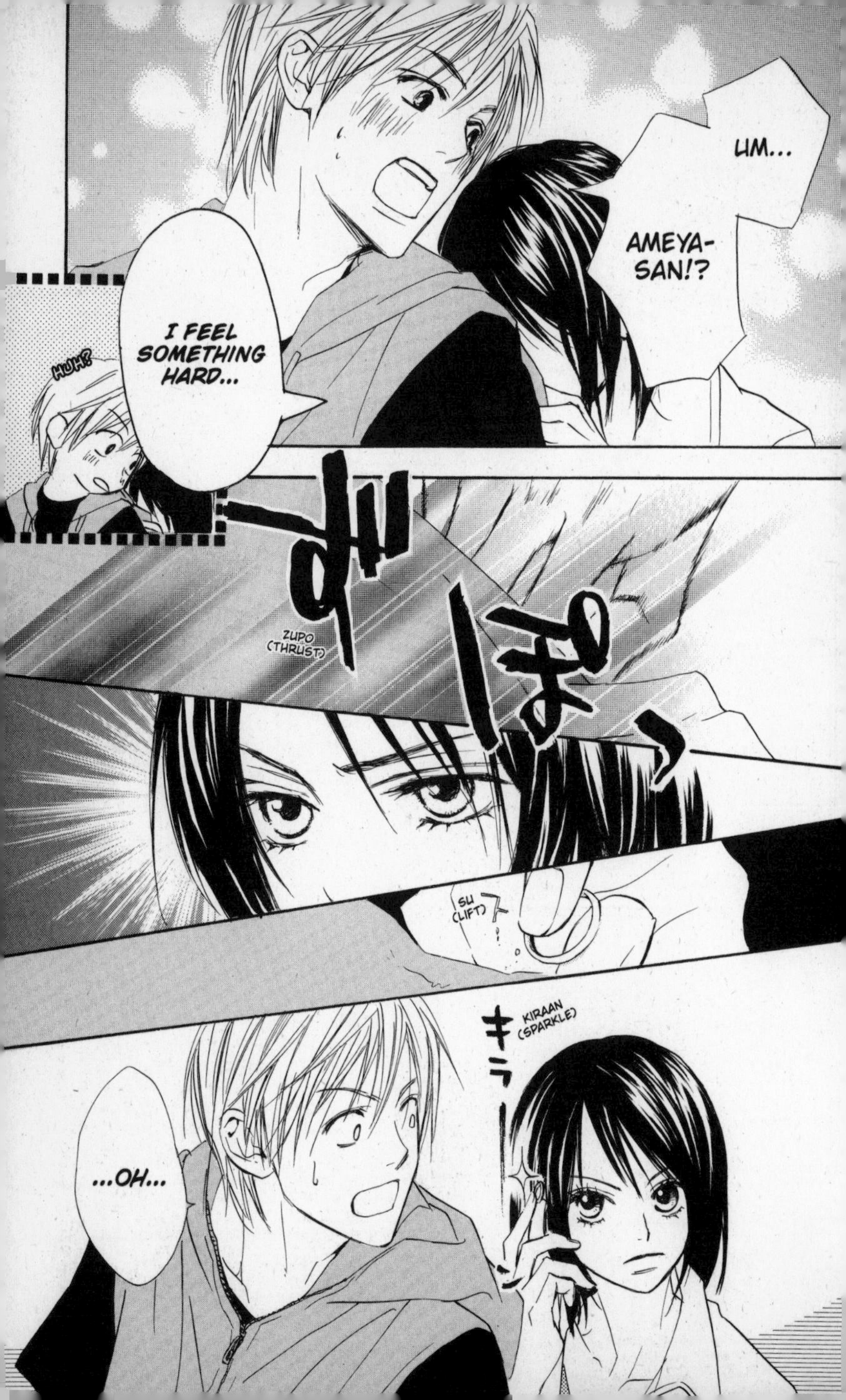
UM...
AMEYA-SAN!?
I FEEL SOMETHING HARD...
HUH?
ZUPO (THRUST)
SU (LIFT)
KIRAAN (SPARKLE)
...OH...

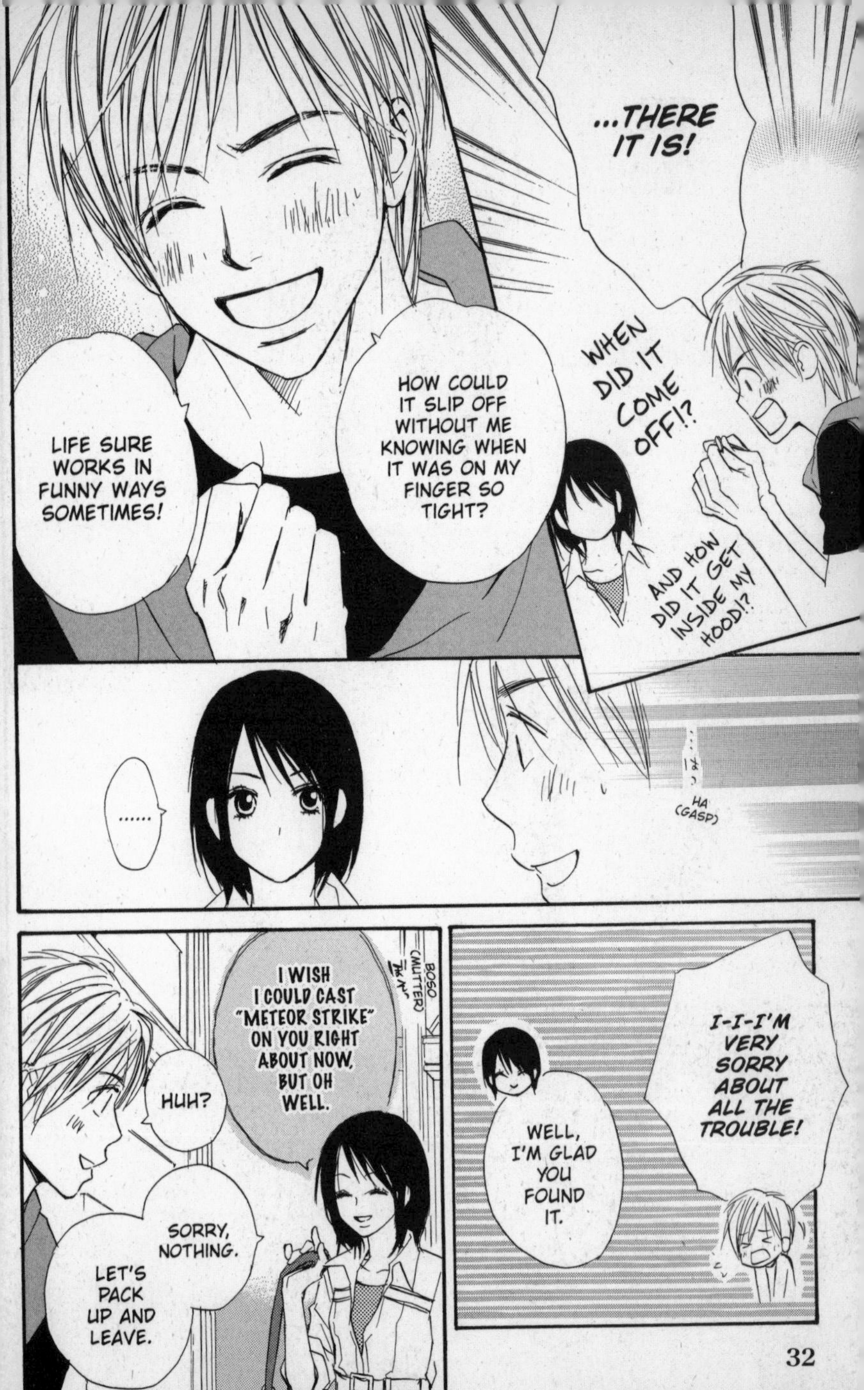
...THERE IT IS!
WHEN DID IT COME OFF!?
AND HOW DID IT GET INSIDE MY HOOD!?
HOW COULD IT SLIP OFF WITHOUT ME KNOWING WHEN IT WAS ON MY FINGER SO TIGHT?
LIFE SURE WORKS IN FUNNY WAYS SOMETIMES!
HA (GASP)
......
I-I-I'M VERY SORRY ABOUT ALL THE TROUBLE!
WELL, I'M GLAD YOU FOUND IT.
BOSO (MUTTER)
I WISH I COULD CAST "METEOR STRIKE" ON YOU RIGHT ABOUT NOW, BUT OH WELL.
HUH?
SORRY, NOTHING.
LET'S PACK UP AND LEAVE.

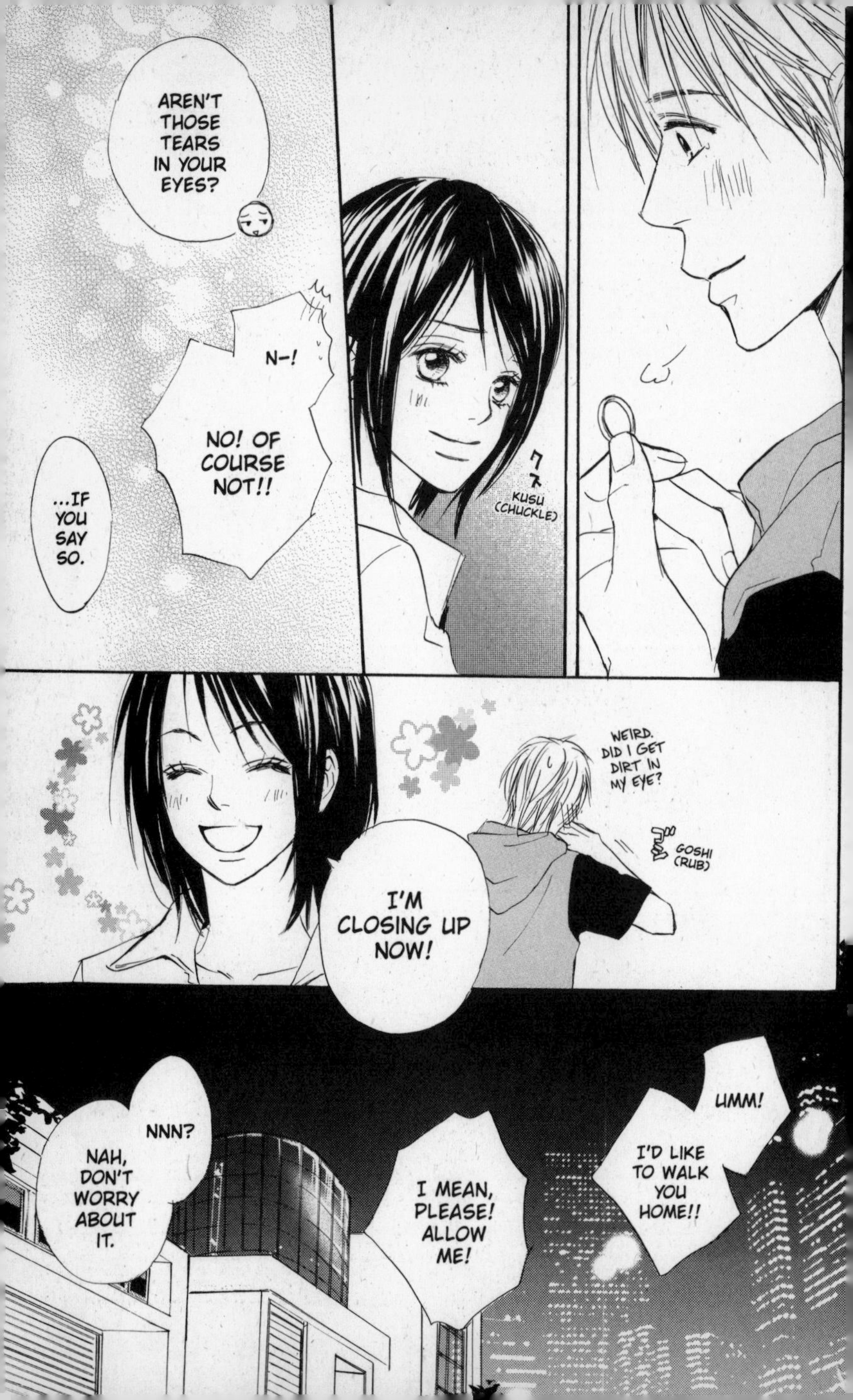
KUSU (CHUCKLE)
AREN'T THOSE TEARS IN YOUR EYES?
N-!
NO! OF COURSE NOT!!
...IF YOU SAY SO.
WEIRD. DID I GET DIRT IN MY EYE?
GOSHI (RUB)
I'M CLOSING UP NOW!
UMM!
I'D LIKE TO WALK YOU HOME!!
I MEAN, PLEASE! ALLOW ME!
NNN?
NAH, DON'T WORRY ABOUT IT.

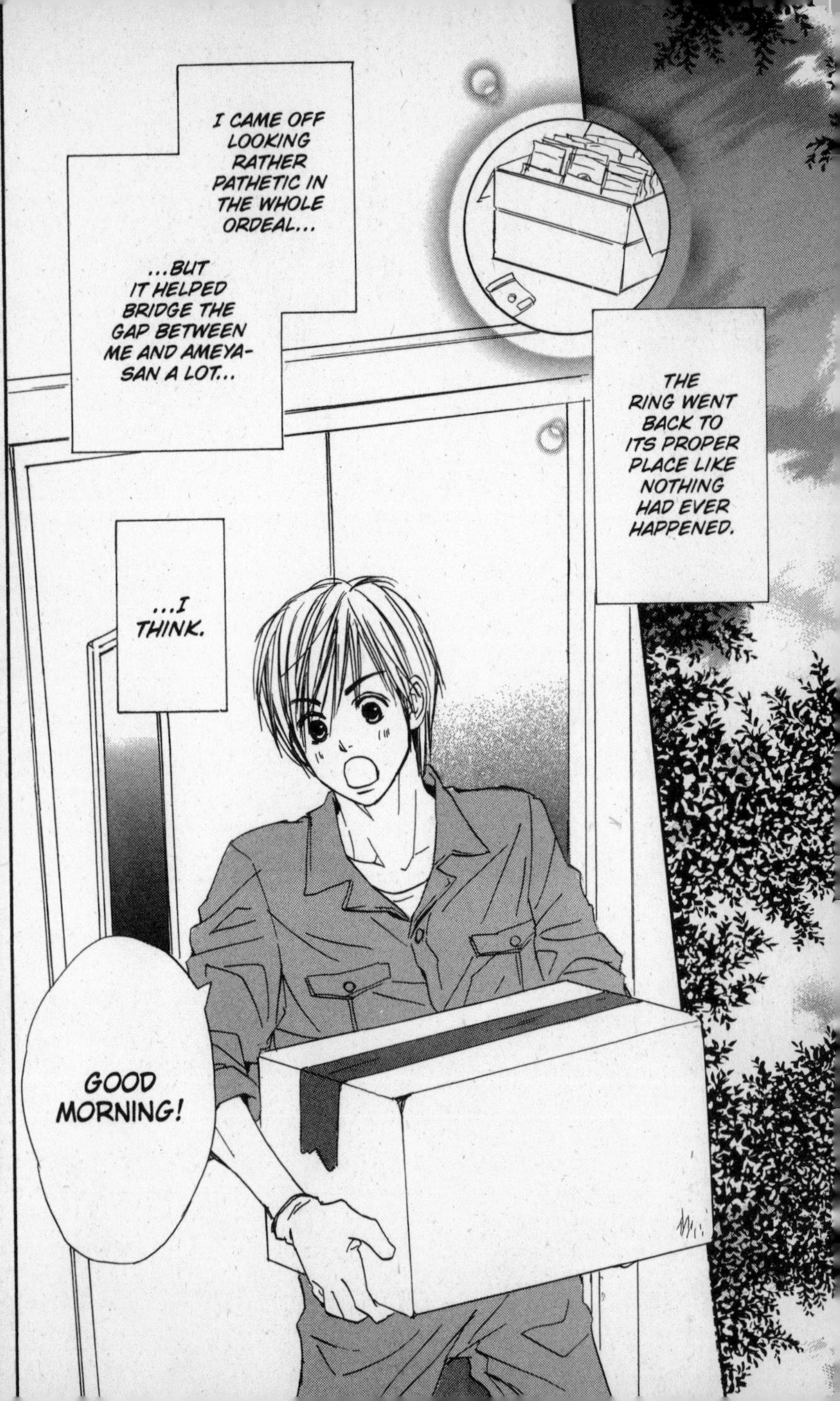
THE RING WENT BACK TO ITS PROPER PLACE LIKE NOTHING HAD EVER HAPPENED.
I CAME OFF LOOKING RATHER PATHETIC IN THE WHOLE ORDEAL...
...BUT IT HELPED BRIDGE THE GAP BETWEEN ME AND AMEYA-SAN A LOT...
...I THINK.
GOOD MORNING!

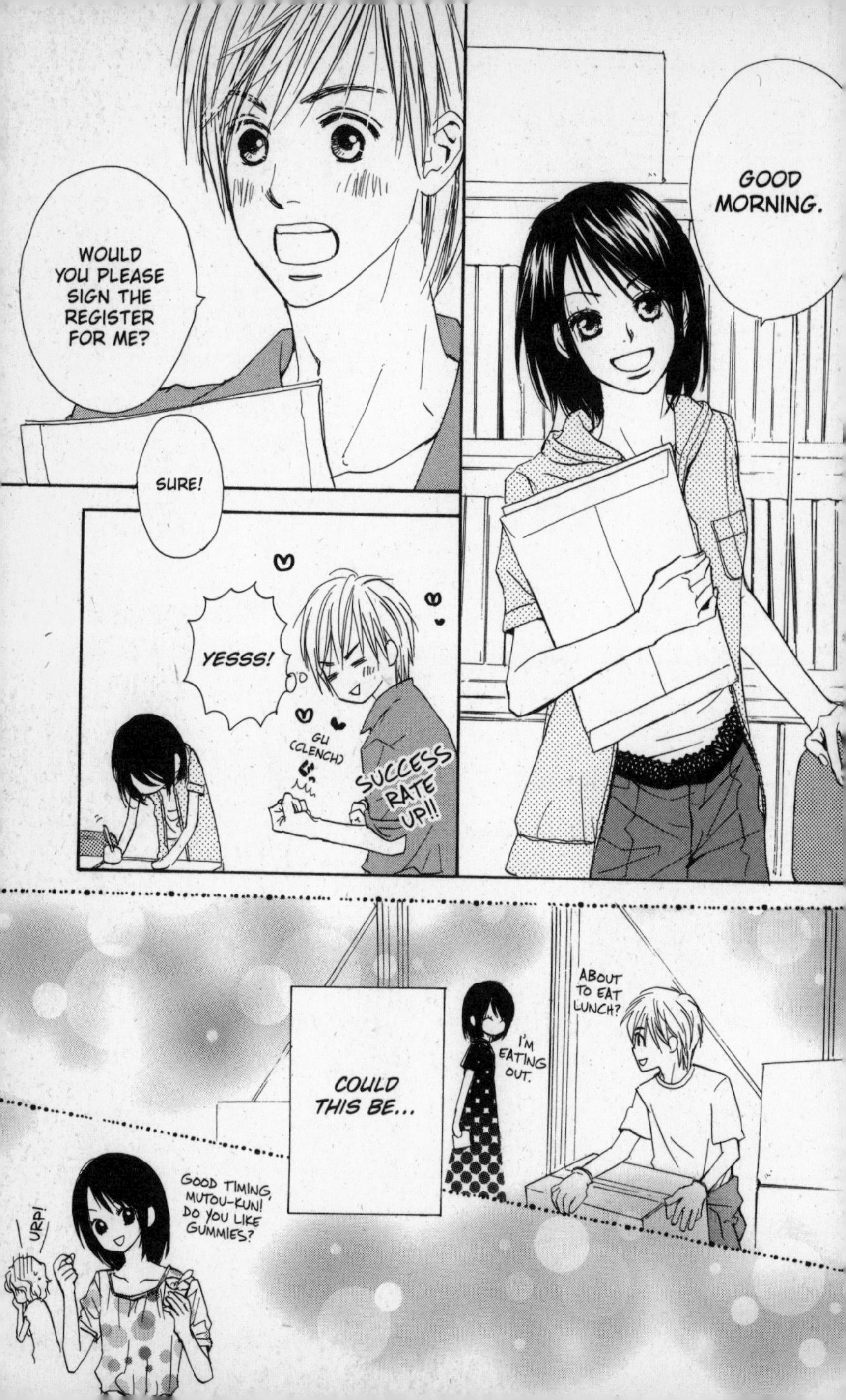
GOOD MORNING.
WOULD YOU PLEASE SIGN THE REGISTER FOR ME?
SURE!
YESSS!
GU (CLENCH)
SUCCESS RATE UP!!
ABOUT TO EAT LUNCH?
I'M EATING OUT.
COULD THIS BE...
GOOD TIMING, MUTOU-KUN! DO YOU LIKE GUMMIES?
URP!

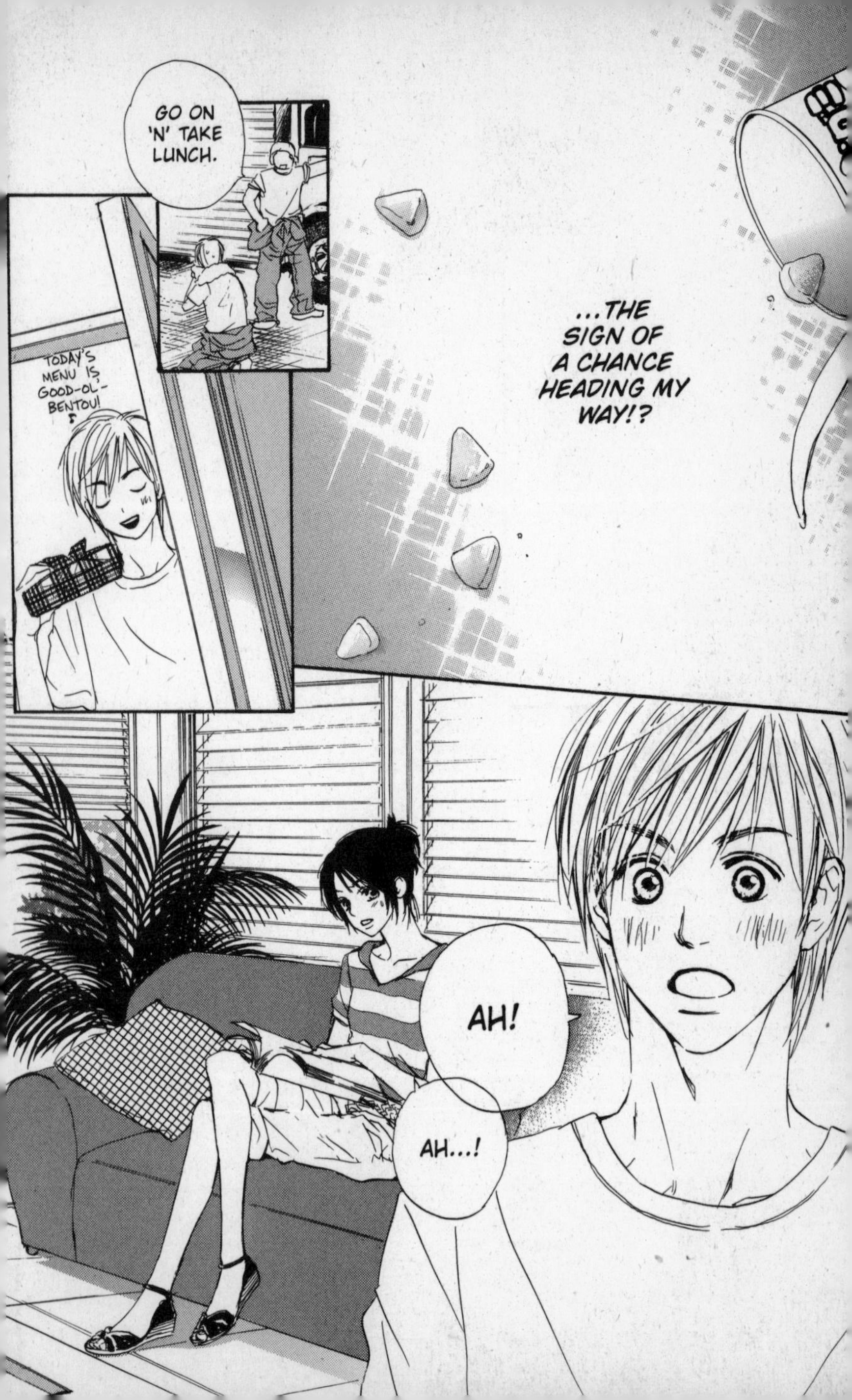
...THE SIGN OF A CHANCE HEADING MY WAY!?
GO ON 'N' TAKE LUNCH.
TODAY'S MENU IS GOOD-OL-BENTOU! ♪
AH!
AH...!

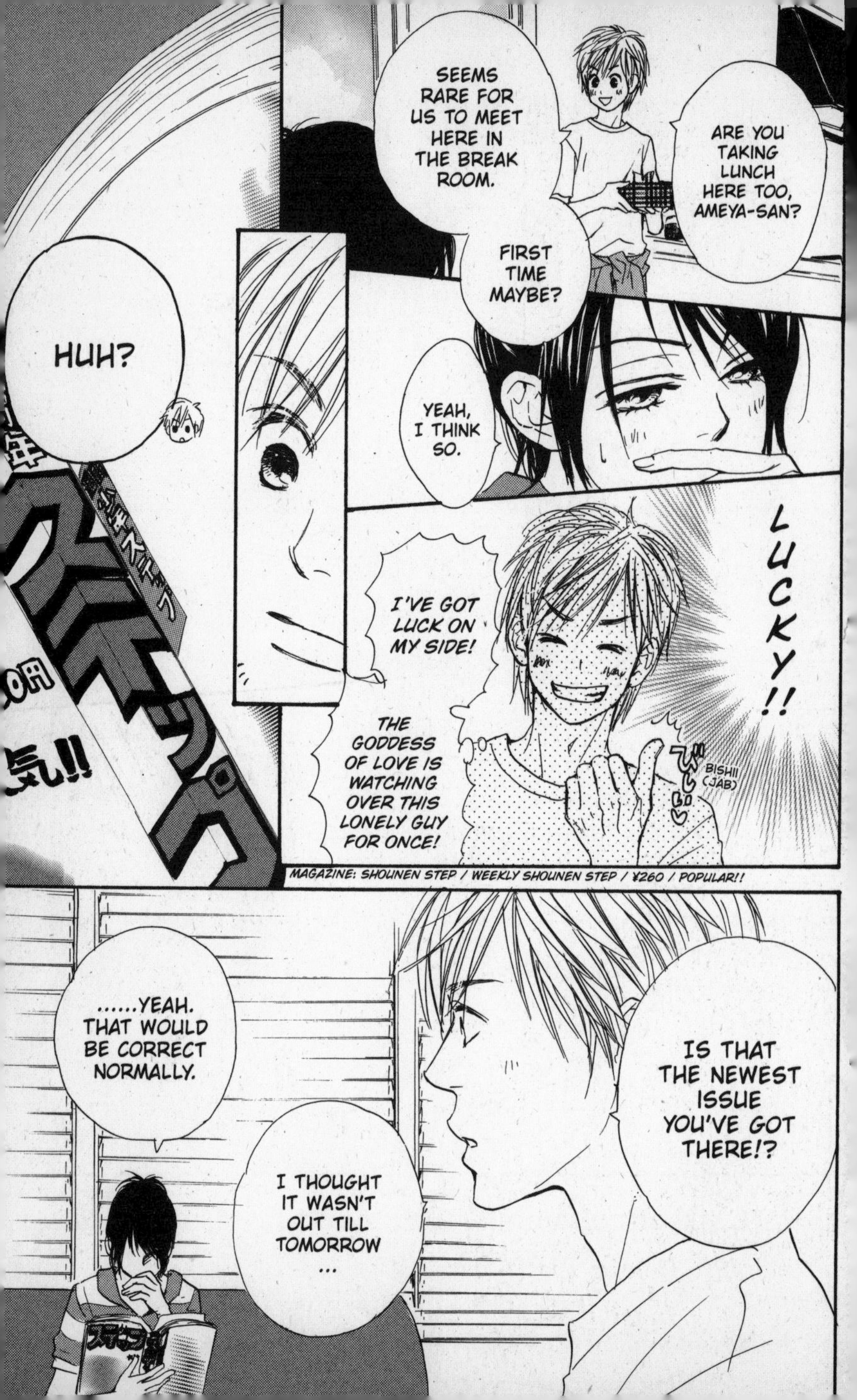
ARE YOU TAKING LUNCH HERE TOO, AMEYA-SAN?
SEEMS RARE FOR US TO MEET HERE IN THE BREAK ROOM.
FIRST TIME MAYBE?
YEAH, I THINK SO.
LUCKY!!
I'VE GOT LUCK ON MY SIDE!
THE GODDESS OF LOVE IS WATCHING OVER THIS LONELY GUY FOR ONCE!
BISHII (JAB)
HUH?
MAGAZINE: SHOUNEN STEP / WEEKLY SHOUNEN STEP / ¥260 / POPULAR!!
IS THAT THE NEWEST ISSUE YOU'VE GOT THERE!?
I THOUGHT IT WASN'T OUT TILL TOMORROW ...
......YEAH. THAT WOULD BE CORRECT NORMALLY.

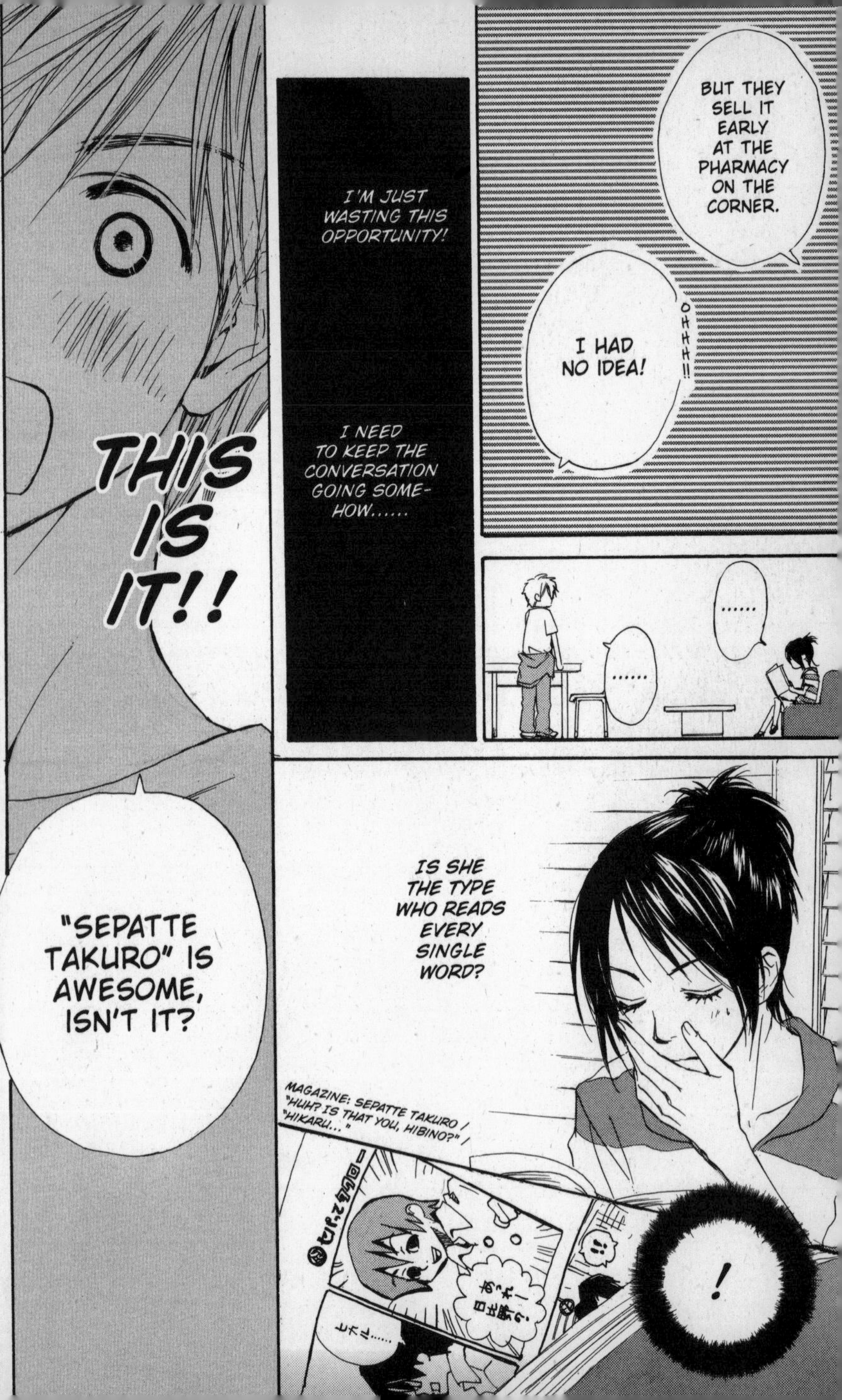

BUT THEY SELL IT EARLY AT THE PHARMACY ON THE CORNER.
I HAD NO IDEA!
OHHH!!
......
......
I'M JUST WASTING THIS OPPORTUNITY!
I NEED TO KEEP THE CONVERSATION GOING SOME-HOW......
IS SHE THE TYPE WHO READS EVERY SINGLE WORD?
MAGAZINE: SEPATTE TAKURO / "HUH? IS THAT YOU, HIBINO?" / "HIKARU..."
!
THIS IS IT!!
"SEPATTE TAKURO" IS AWESOME, ISN'T IT?

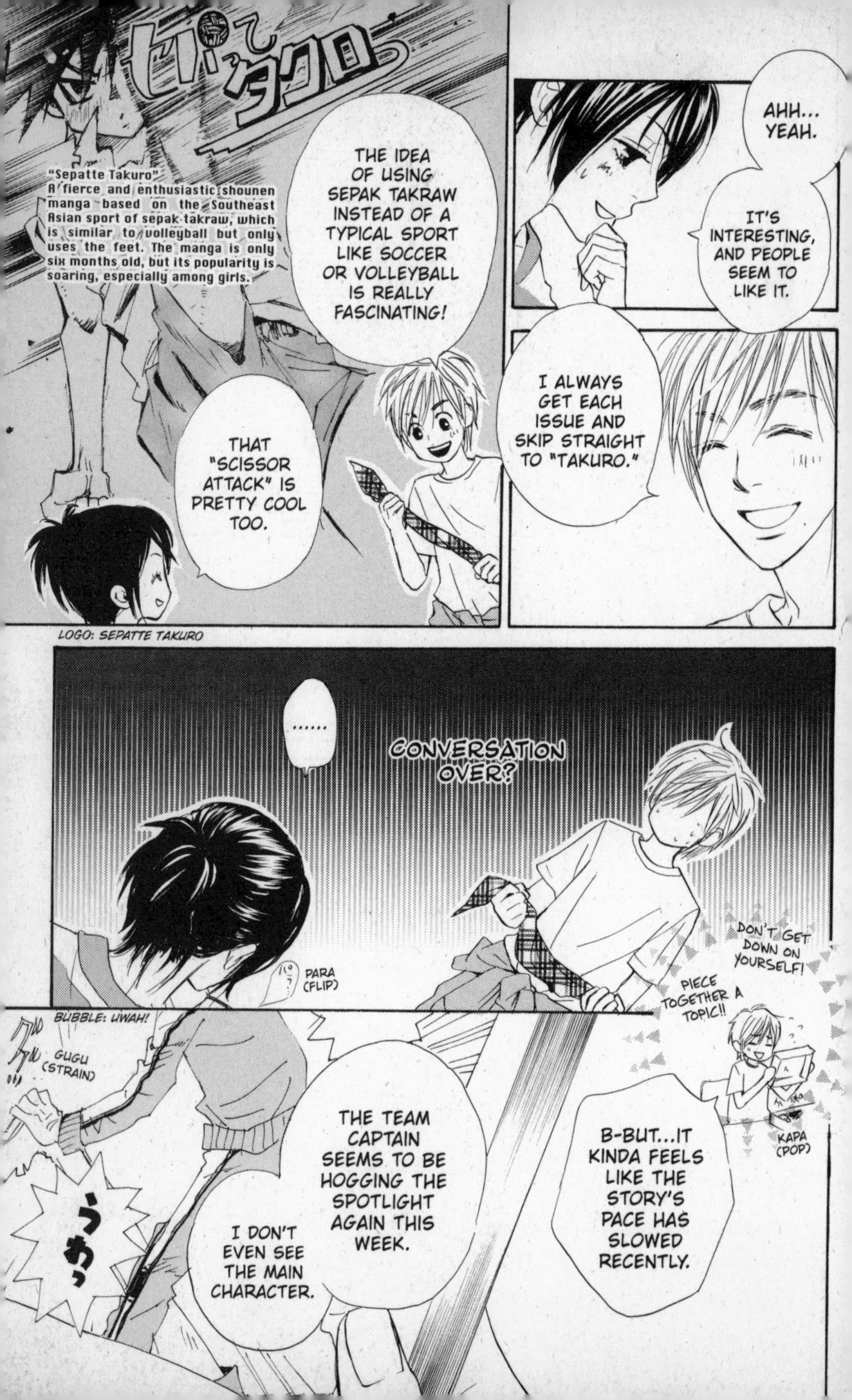
AHH... YEAH.
IT'S INTERESTING, AND PEOPLE SEEM TO LIKE IT.
I ALWAYS GET EACH ISSUE AND SKIP STRAIGHT TO "TAKURO."
"Sepatte Takuro" A fierce and enthusiastic shounen manga based on the Southeast Asian sport of sepak takraw, which is similar to volleyball but only uses the feet. The manga is only six months old, but its popularity is soaring, especially among girls.
THE IDEA OF USING SEPAK TAKRAW INSTEAD OF A TYPICAL SPORT LIKE SOCCER OR VOLLEYBALL IS REALLY FASCINATING!
THAT "SCISSOR ATTACK" IS PRETTY COOL TOO.
LOGO: SEPATTE TAKURO
......
CONVERSATION OVER?
PARA (FLIP)
DON'T GET DOWN ON YOURSELF!
PIECE TOGETHER A TOPIC!!
KAPA (POP)
B-BUT...IT KINDA FEELS LIKE THE STORY'S PACE HAS SLOWED RECENTLY.
THE TEAM CAPTAIN SEEMS TO BE HOGGING THE SPOTLIGHT AGAIN THIS WEEK.
I DON'T EVEN SEE THE MAIN CHARACTER.
BUBBLE: UWAH!
うわっ
GUGU (STRAIN)

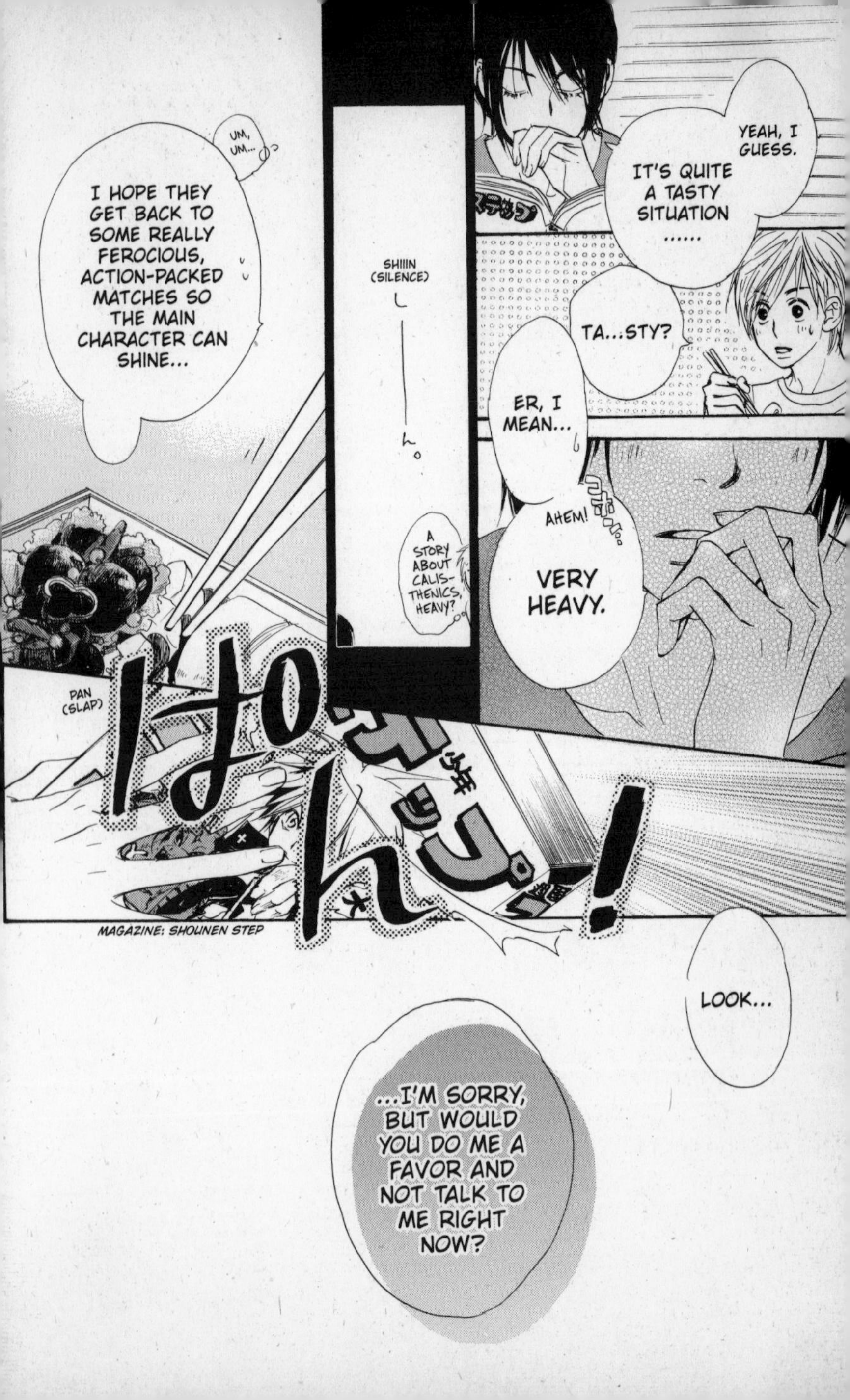

YEAH, I GUESS.
IT'S QUITE A TASTY SITUATION ......
TA...STY?
ER, I MEAN...
AHEM!
VERY HEAVY.
SHIIIN (SILENCE)
A STORY ABOUT CALISTHENICS, HEAVY?
UM, UM...
I HOPE THEY GET BACK TO SOME REALLY FEROCIOUS, ACTION-PACKED MATCHES SO THE MAIN CHARACTER CAN SHINE...
PAN (SLAP)
MAGAZINE: SHOUNEN STEP
LOOK...
...I'M SORRY, BUT WOULD YOU DO ME A FAVOR AND NOT TALK TO ME RIGHT NOW?

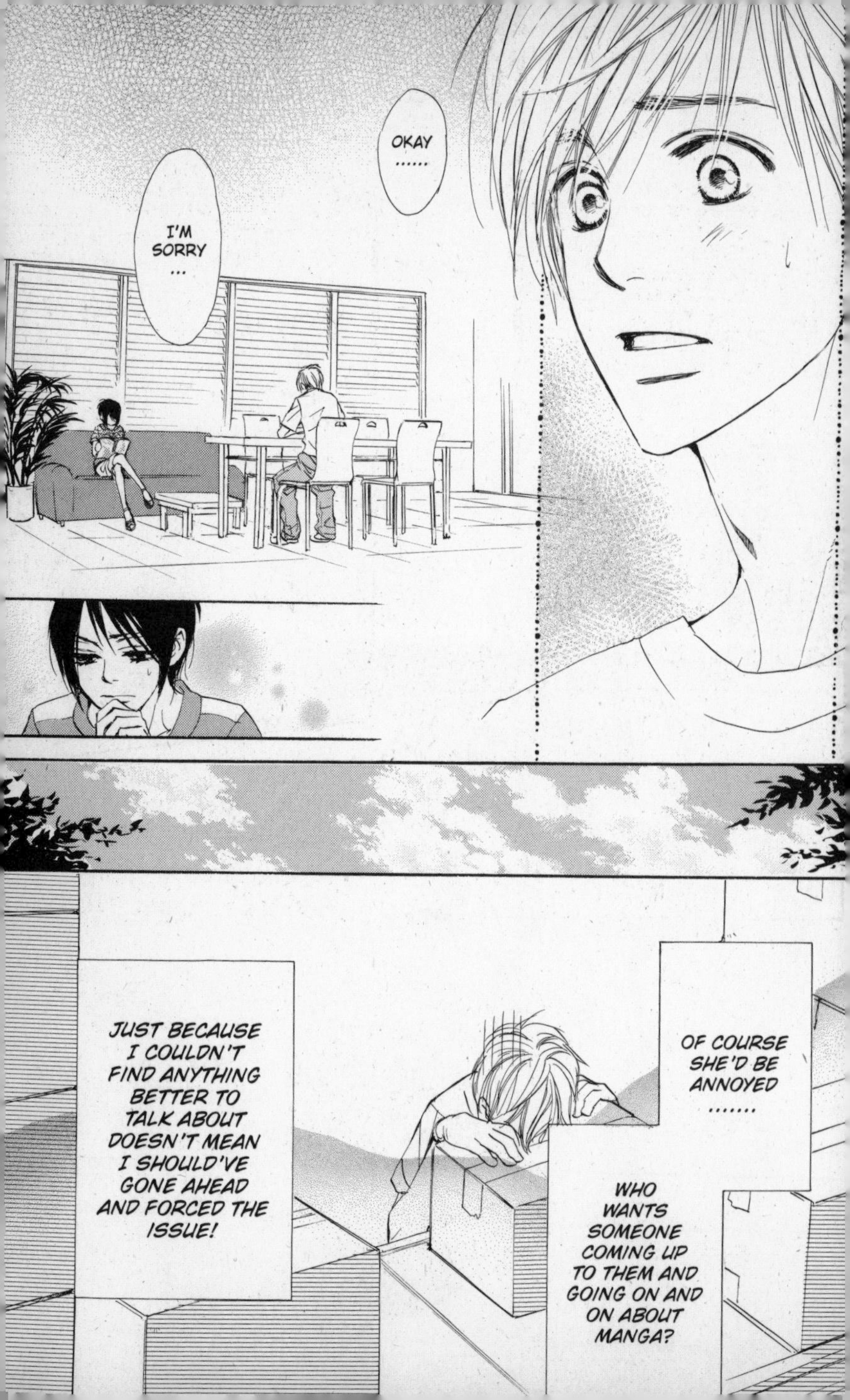
OKAY ......
I'M SORRY ...
OF COURSE SHE'D BE ANNOYED ....
WHO WANTS SOMEONE COMING UP TO THEM AND GOING ON AND ON ABOUT MANGA?
JUST BECAUSE I COULDN'T FIND ANYTHING BETTER TO TALK ABOUT DOESN'T MEAN I SHOULD'VE GONE AHEAD AND FORCED THE ISSUE!

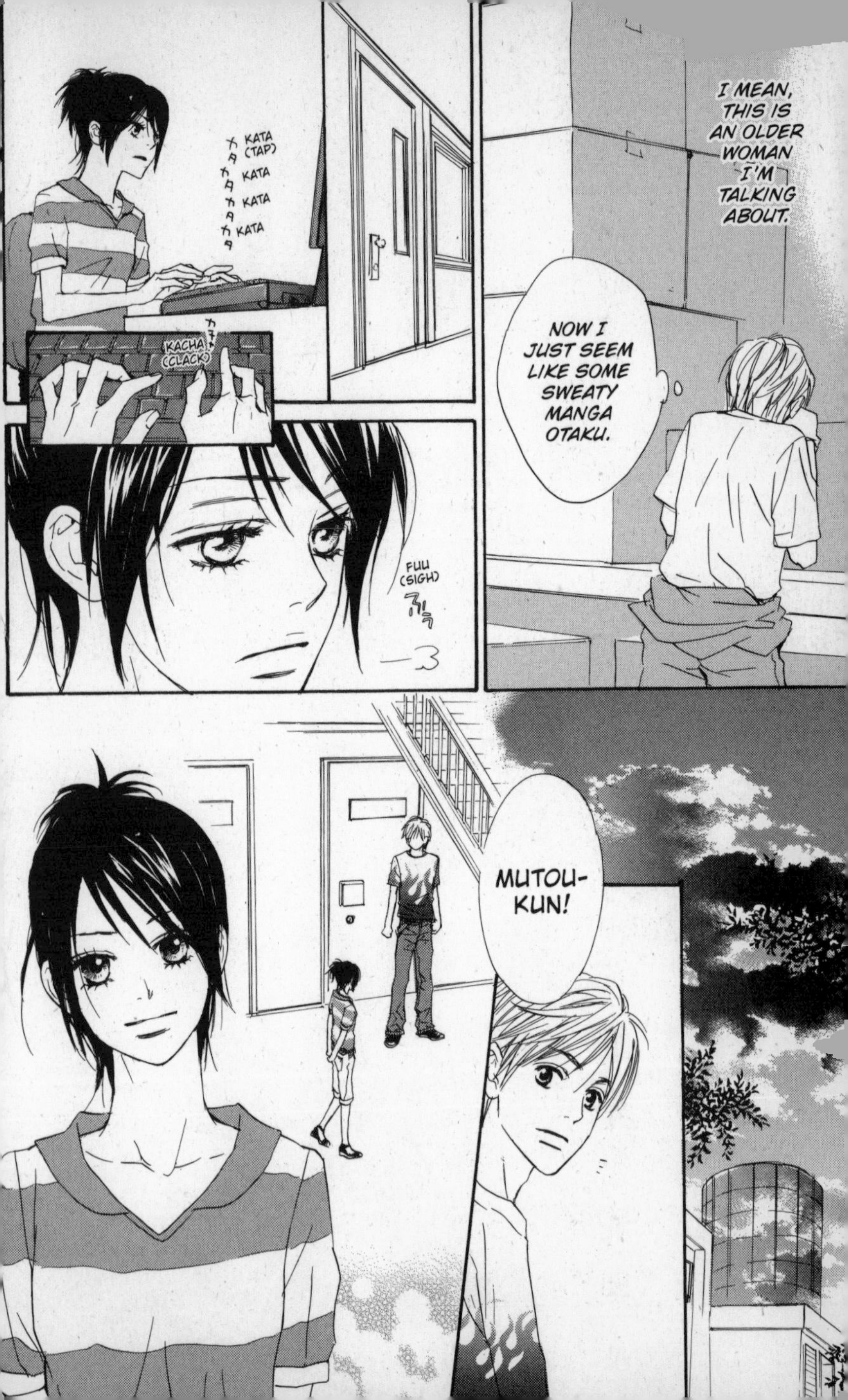
I MEAN, THIS IS AN OLDER WOMAN I'M TALKING ABOUT.
NOW I JUST SEEM LIKE SOME SWEATY MANGA OTAKU.
KATA (TAP)
KATA
KATA
KATA
KACHA (CLACK)
FUU (SIGH)
MUTOU-KUN!

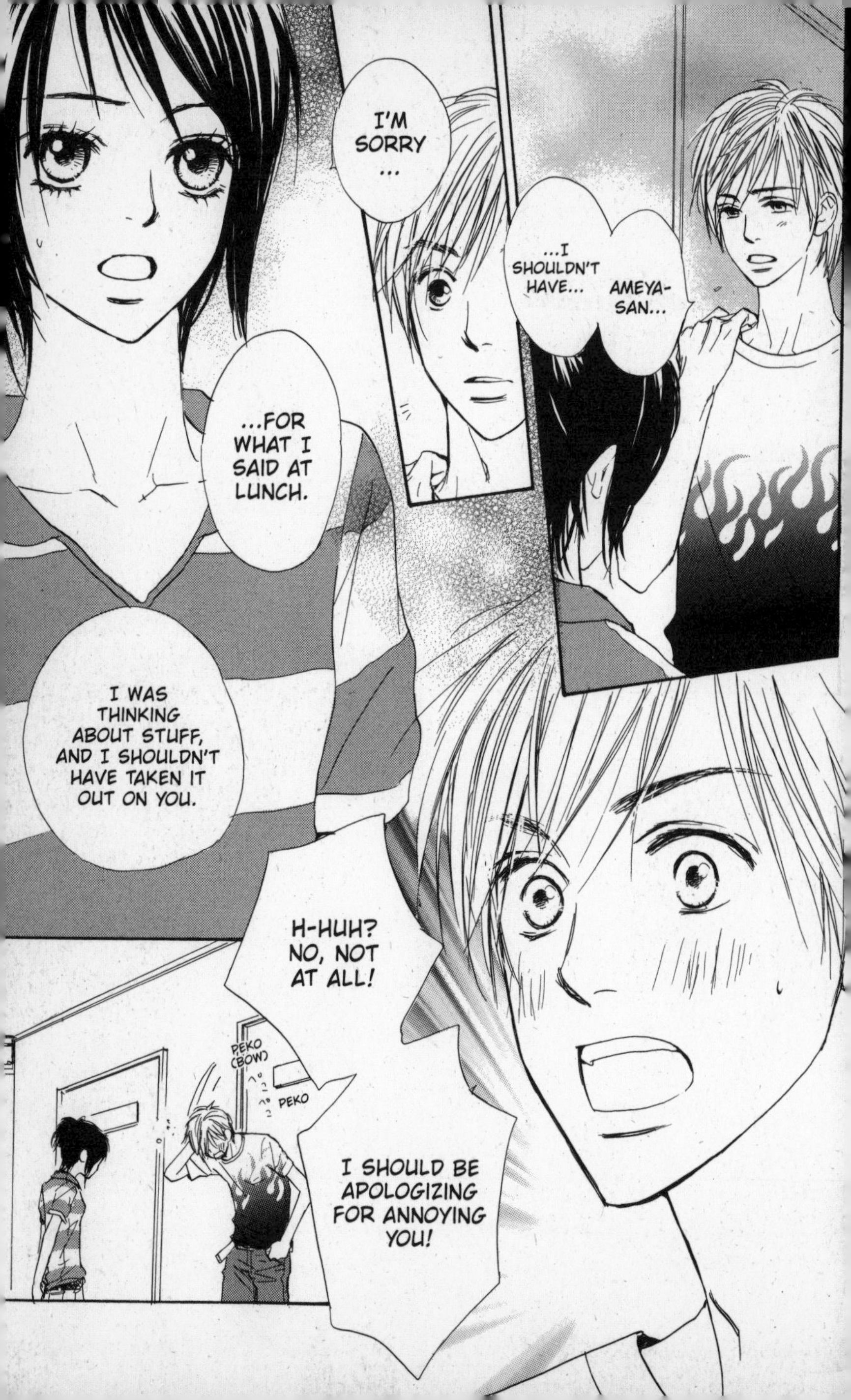
AMEYA-SAN...
...I SHOULDN'T HAVE...
I'M SORRY ...
...FOR WHAT I SAID AT LUNCH.
I WAS THINKING ABOUT STUFF, AND I SHOULDN'T HAVE TAKEN IT OUT ON YOU.
H-HUH? NO, NOT AT ALL!
I SHOULD BE APOLOGIZING FOR ANNOYING YOU!
PEKO (BOW)
PEKO

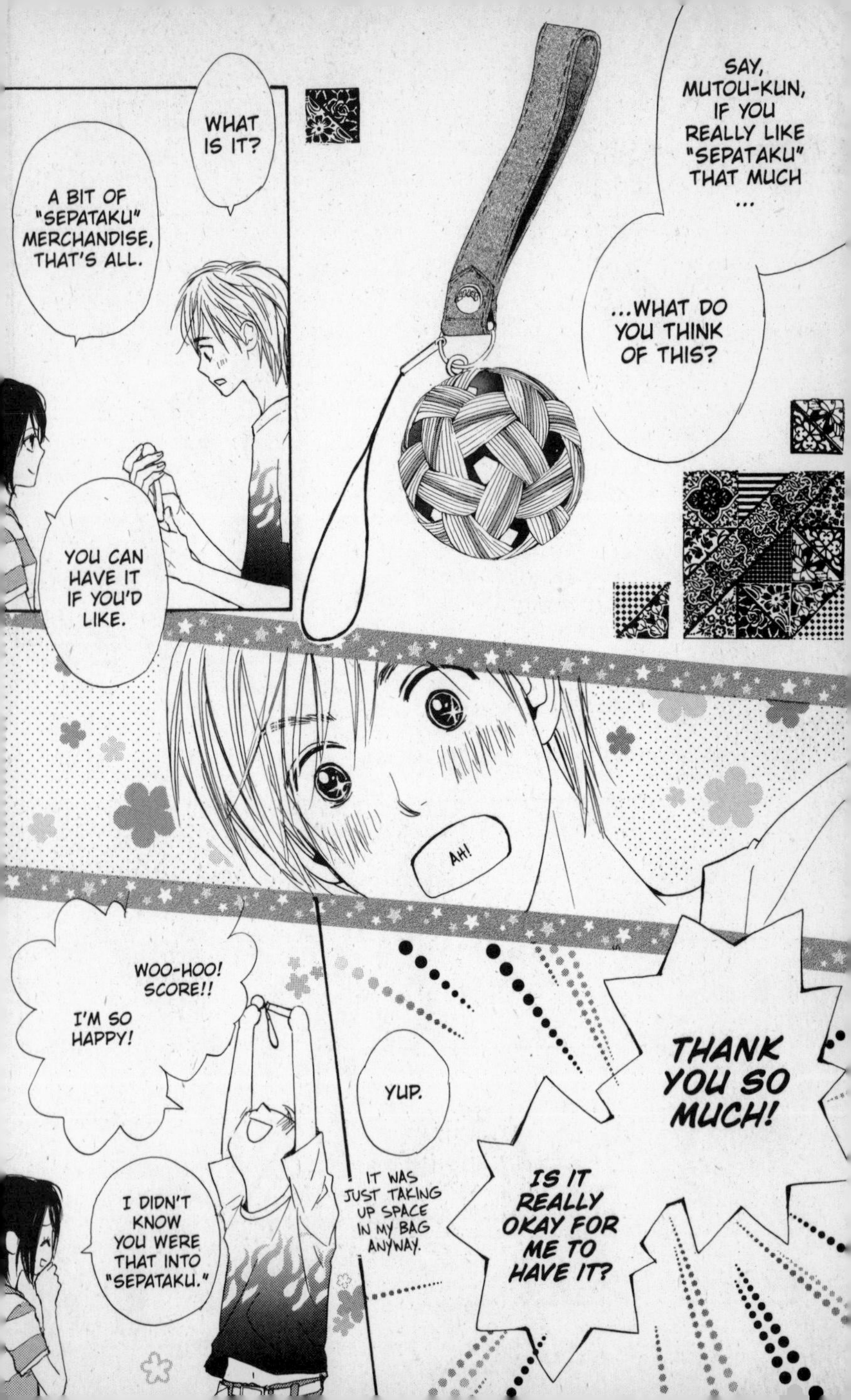
SAY, MUTOU-KUN, IF YOU REALLY LIKE "SEPATAKU" THAT MUCH ...
...WHAT DO YOU THINK OF THIS?
WHAT IS IT?
A BIT OF "SEPATAKU" MERCHANDISE, THAT'S ALL.
YOU CAN HAVE IT IF YOU'D LIKE.
AH!
THANK YOU SO MUCH!
IS IT REALLY OKAY FOR ME TO HAVE IT?
YUP.
IT WAS JUST TAKING UP SPACE IN MY BAG ANYWAY.
WOO-HOO! SCORE!!
I'M SO HAPPY!
I DIDN'T KNOW YOU WERE THAT INTO "SEPATAKU."

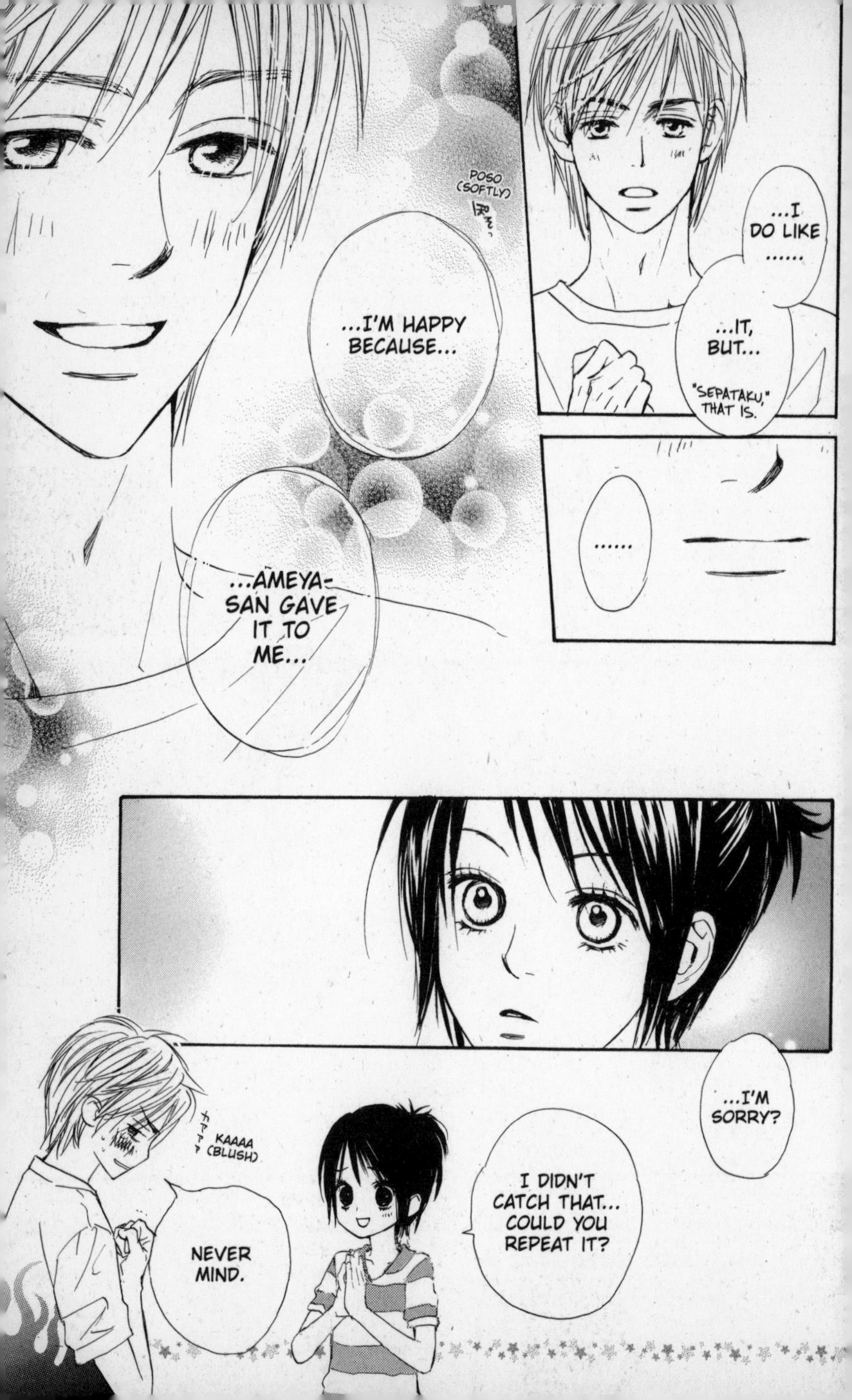
...I DO LIKE ......
...IT, BUT...
"SEPATAKU," THAT IS.
......
POSO (SOFTLY)
...I'M HAPPY BECAUSE...
...AMEYA-SAN GAVE IT TO ME...
...I'M SORRY?
I DIDN'T CATCH THAT... COULD YOU REPEAT IT?
KAAAA (BLUSH)
NEVER MIND.

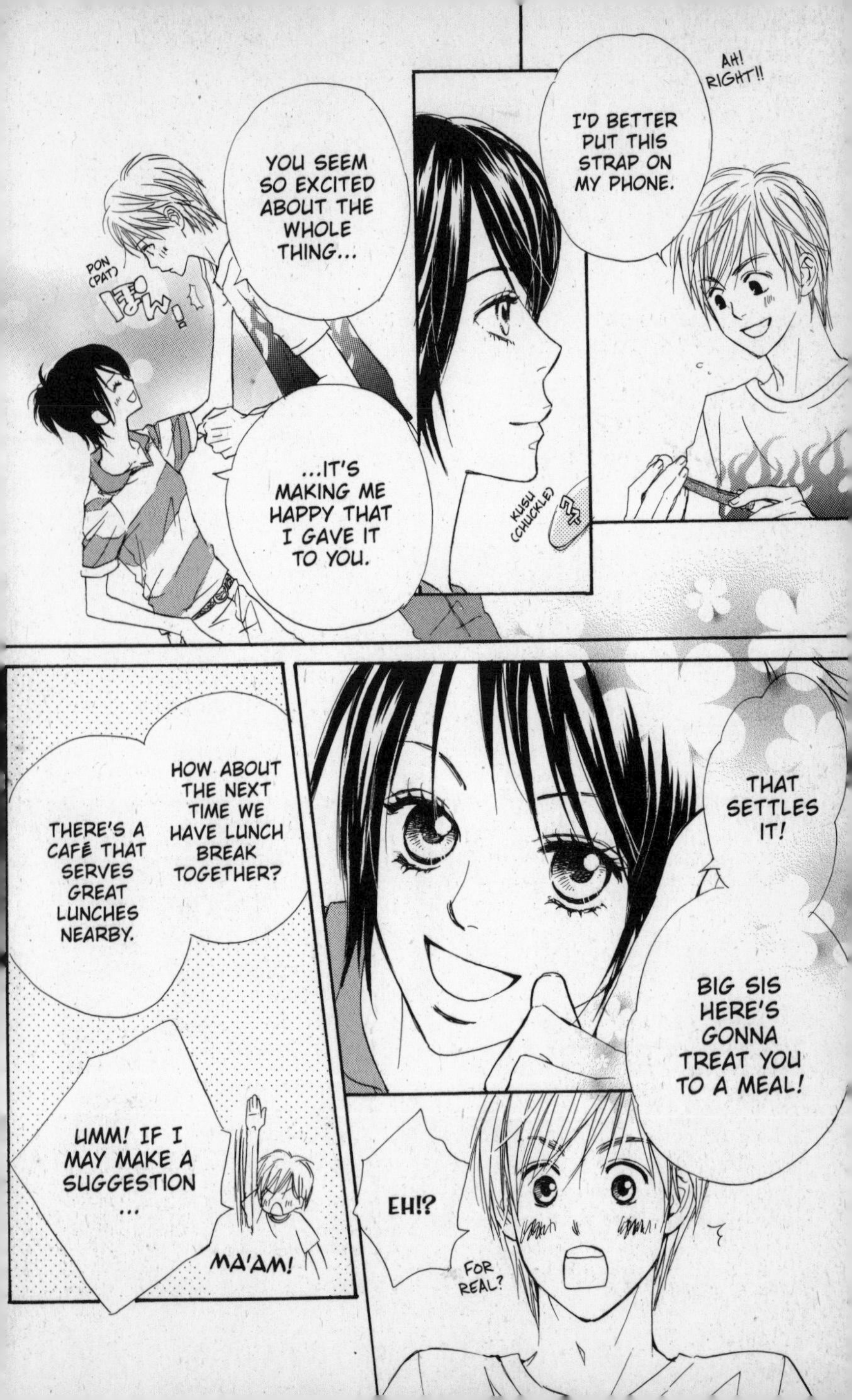
AH! RIGHT!!
I'D BETTER PUT THIS STRAP ON MY PHONE.
KUSU (CHUCKLE)
YOU SEEM SO EXCITED ABOUT THE WHOLE THING...
...IT'S MAKING ME HAPPY THAT I GAVE IT TO YOU.
PON (PAT)
THAT SETTLES IT!
BIG SIS HERE'S GONNA TREAT YOU TO A MEAL!
EH!?
FOR REAL?
HOW ABOUT THE NEXT TIME WE HAVE LUNCH BREAK TOGETHER?
THERE'S A CAFÉ THAT SERVES GREAT LUNCHES NEARBY.
UMM! IF I MAY MAKE A SUGGESTION ...
MA'AM!

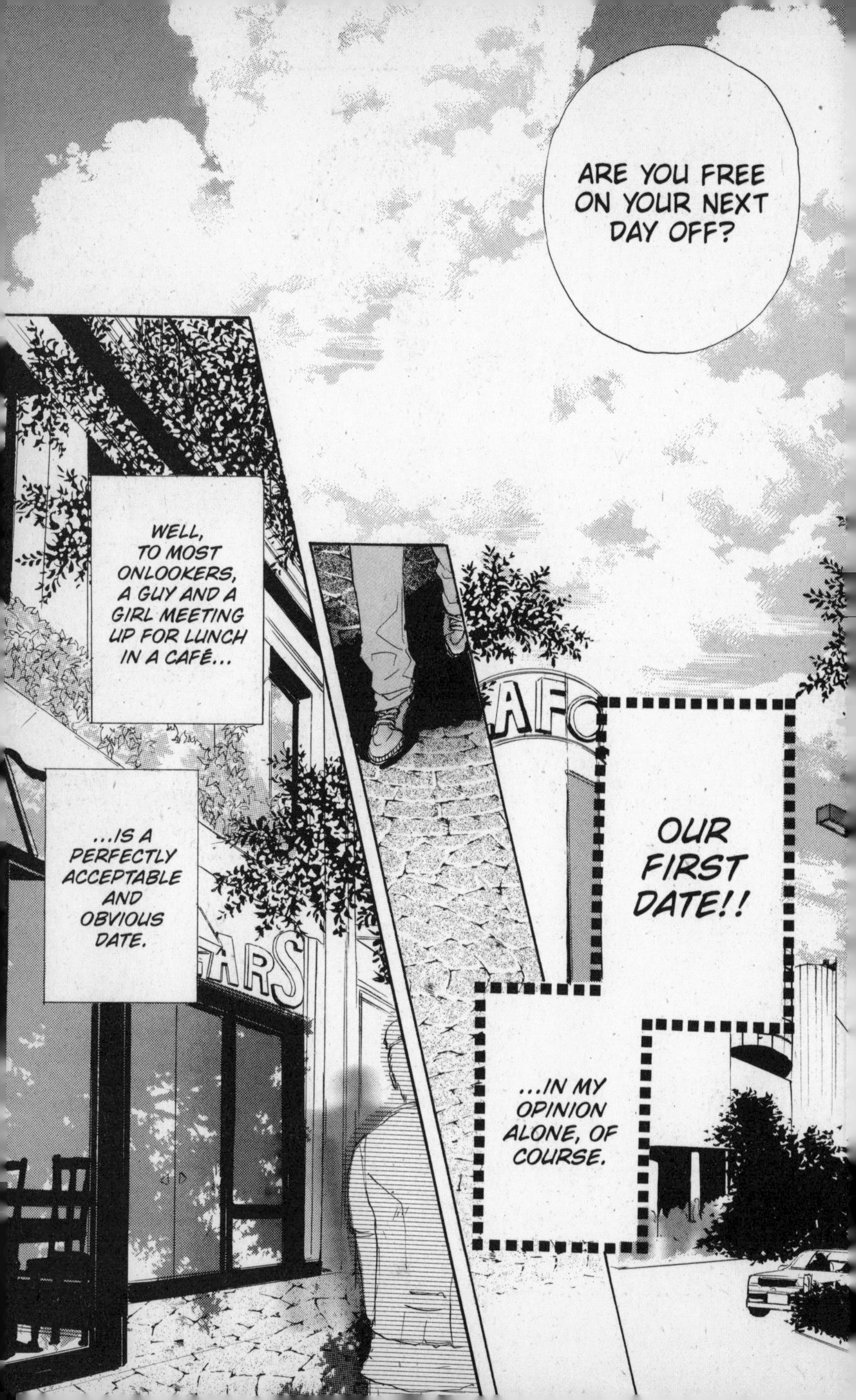

ARE YOU FREE ON YOUR NEXT DAY OFF?
OUR FIRST DATE!!
...IN MY OPINION ALONE, OF COURSE.
WELL, TO MOST ONLOOKERS, A GUY AND A GIRL MEETING UP FOR LUNCH IN A CAFÉ...
...IS A PERFECTLY ACCEPTABLE AND OBVIOUS DATE.

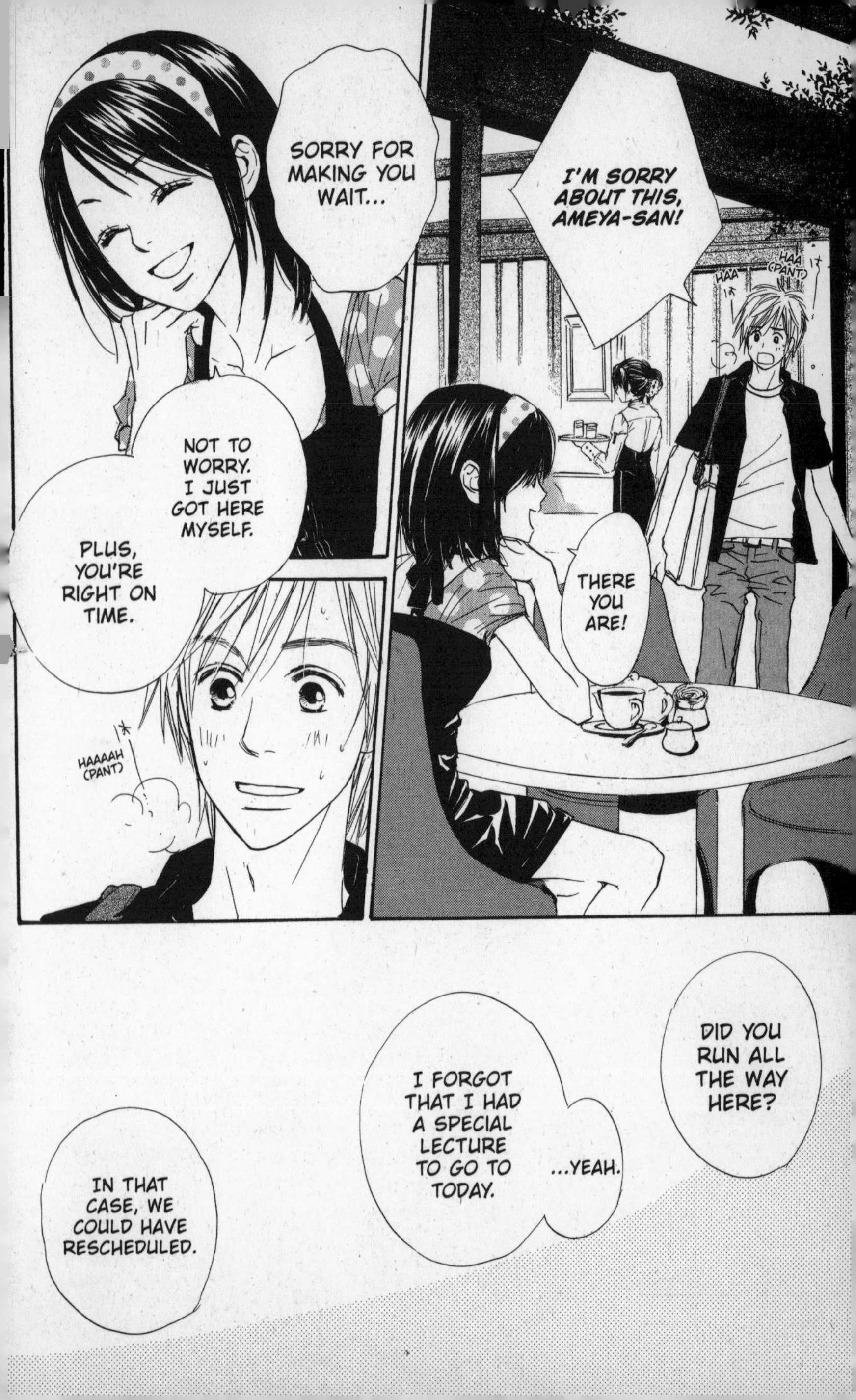
I'M SORRY ABOUT THIS, AMEYA-SAN!
HAA (PANT)
HAA
THERE YOU ARE!
SORRY FOR MAKING YOU WAIT...
NOT TO WORRY. I JUST GOT HERE MYSELF.
PLUS, YOU'RE RIGHT ON TIME.
HAAAAH (PANT)
DID YOU RUN ALL THE WAY HERE?
...YEAH.
I FORGOT THAT I HAD A SPECIAL LECTURE TO GO TO TODAY.
IN THAT CASE, WE COULD HAVE RESCHEDULED.

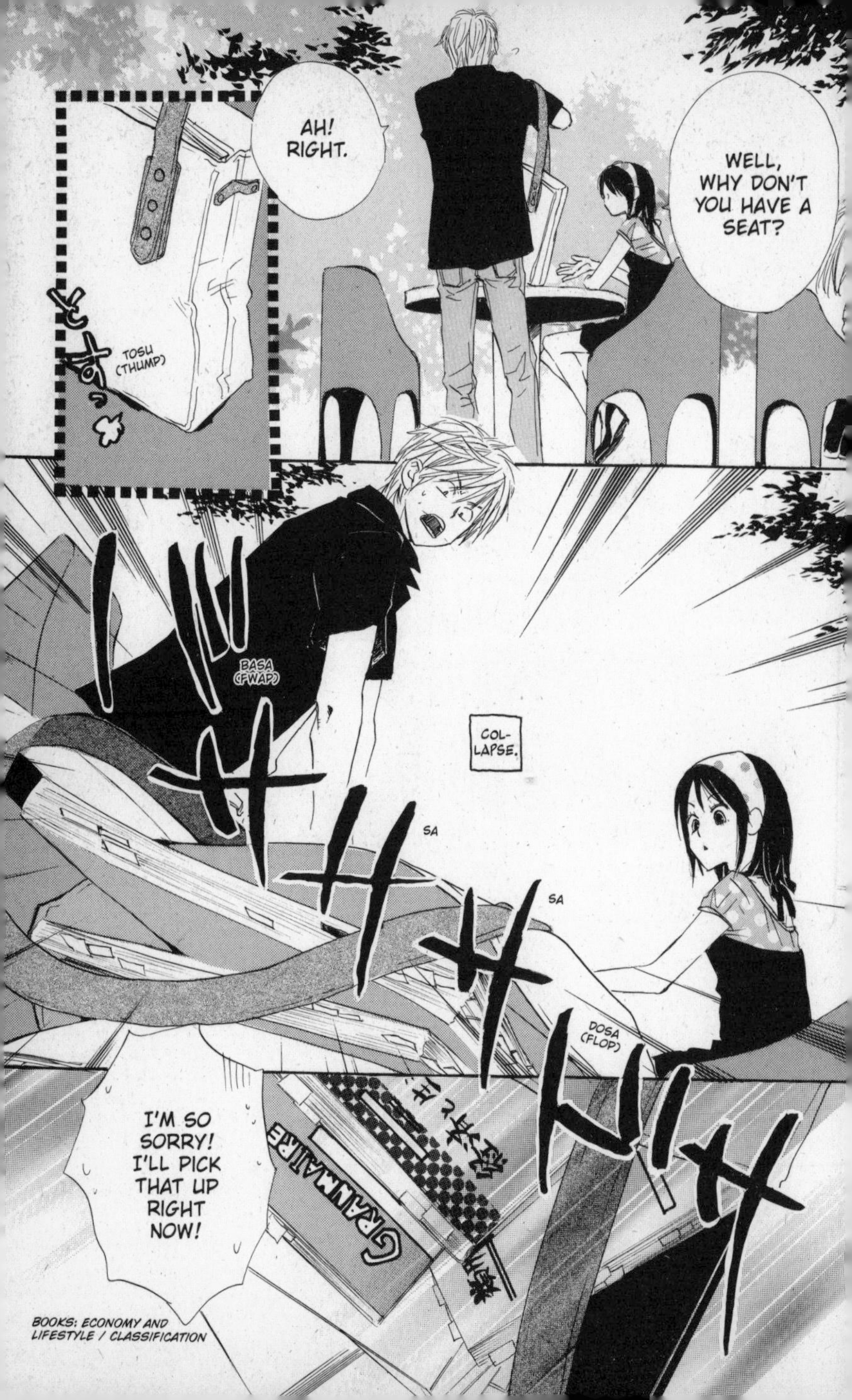
WELL, WHY DON'T YOU HAVE A SEAT?
AH! RIGHT.
TOSU (THUMP)
COL-LAPSE.
BASA (FWAP)
SA
SA
DOSA (FLOP)
I'M SO SORRY! I'LL PICK THAT UP RIGHT NOW!
BOOKS: ECONOMY AND LIFESTYLE / CLASSIFICATION

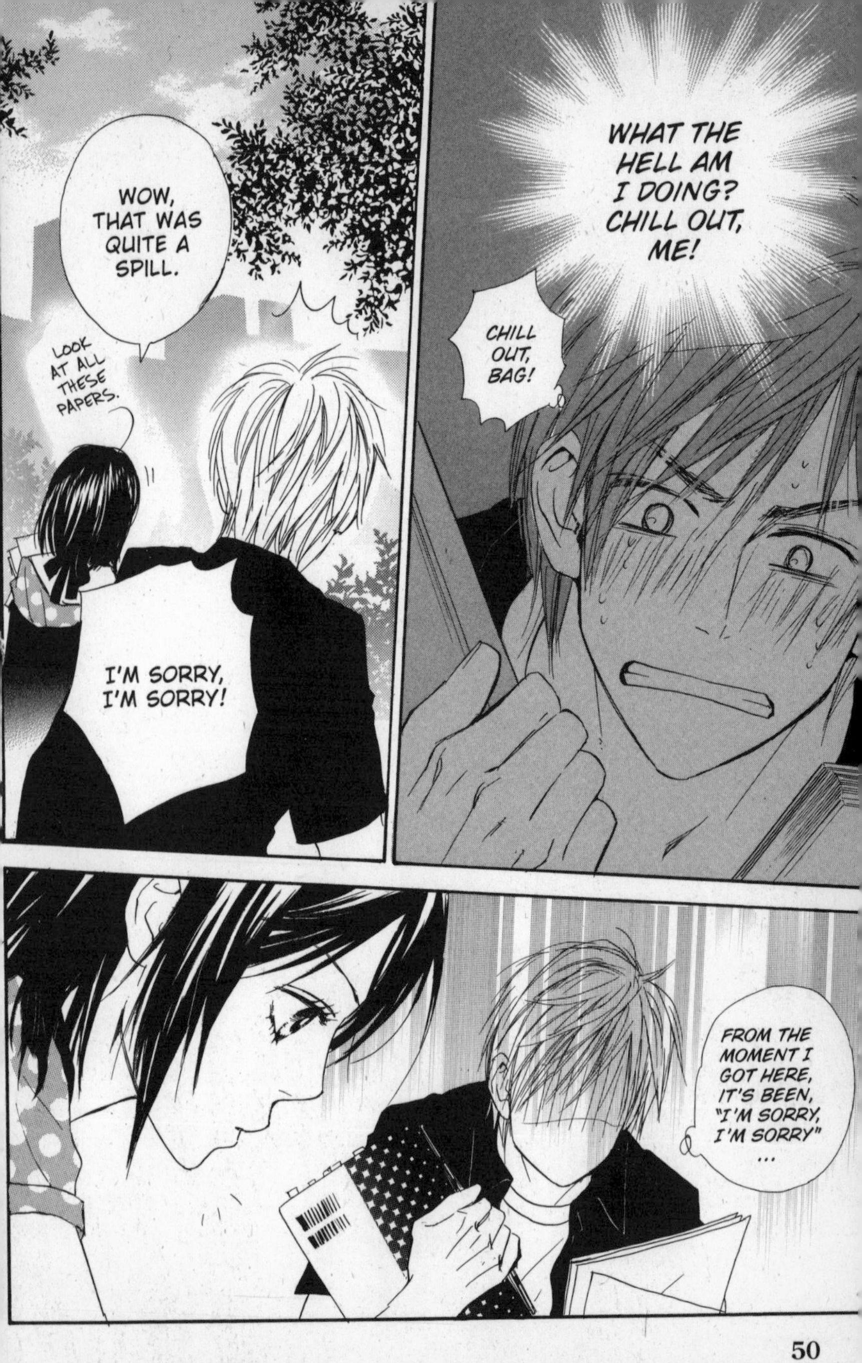
WHAT THE HELL AM I DOING? CHILL OUT, ME!
CHILL OUT, BAG!
WOW, THAT WAS QUITE A SPILL.
LOOK AT ALL THESE PAPERS.
I'M SORRY, I'M SORRY!
FROM THE MOMENT I GOT HERE, IT'S BEEN, "I'M SORRY, I'M SORRY" ...

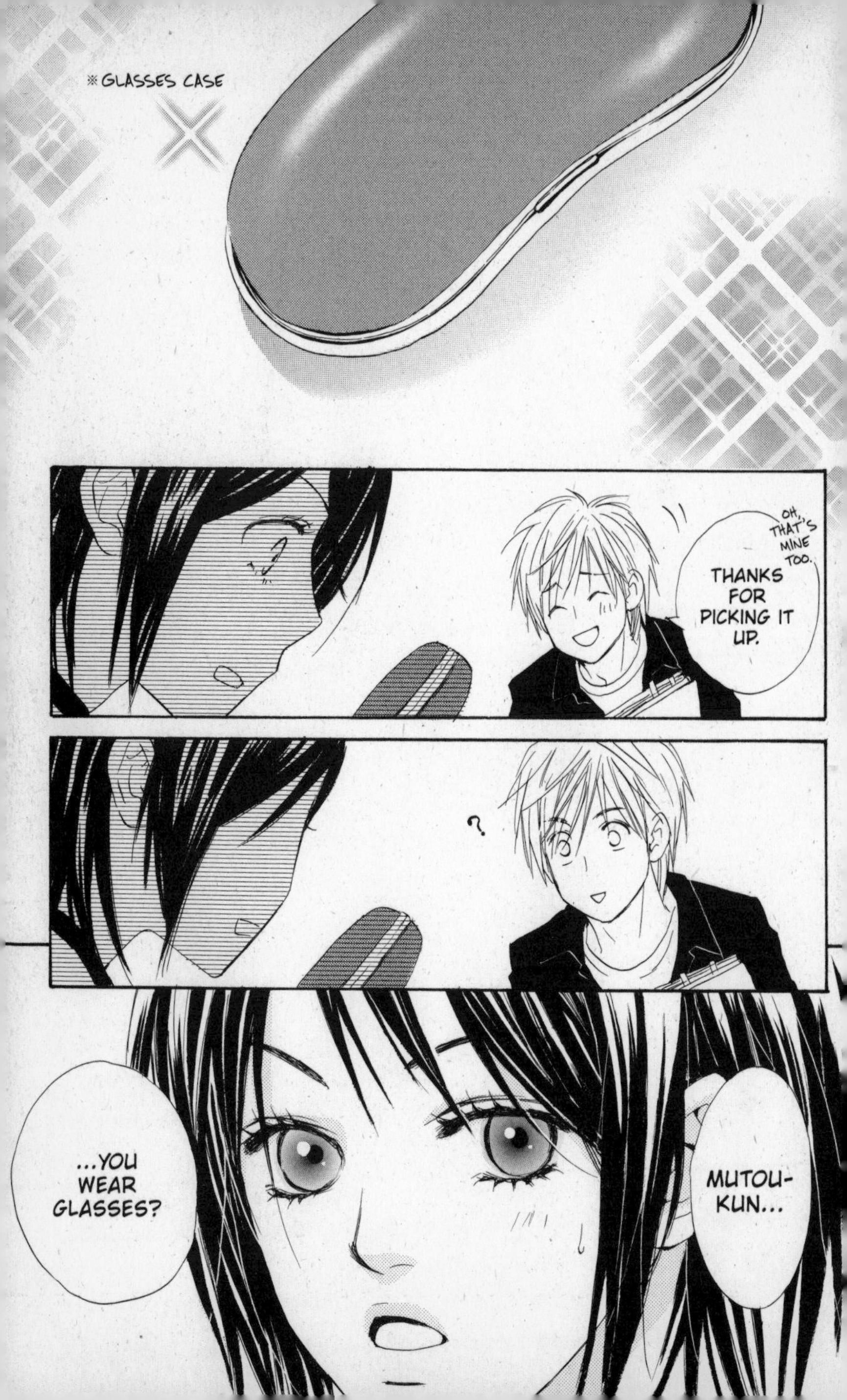
※GLASSES CASE
OH, THAT'S MINE TOO.
THANKS FOR PICKING IT UP.
?
MUTOU-KUN...
...YOU WEAR GLASSES?

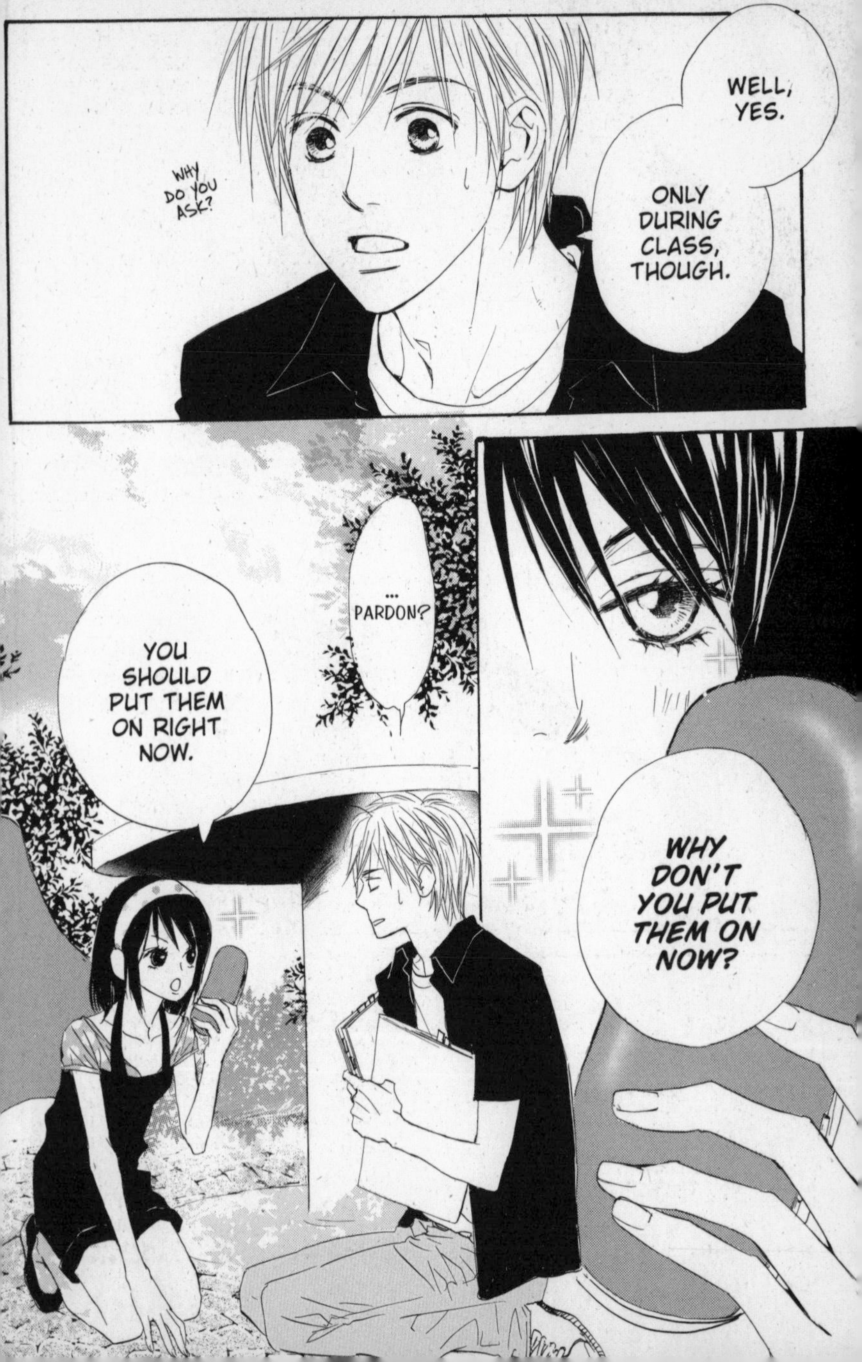
WELL, YES.
ONLY DURING CLASS, THOUGH.
WHY DO YOU ASK?
WHY DON'T YOU PUT THEM ON NOW?
... PARDON?
YOU SHOULD PUT THEM ON RIGHT NOW.

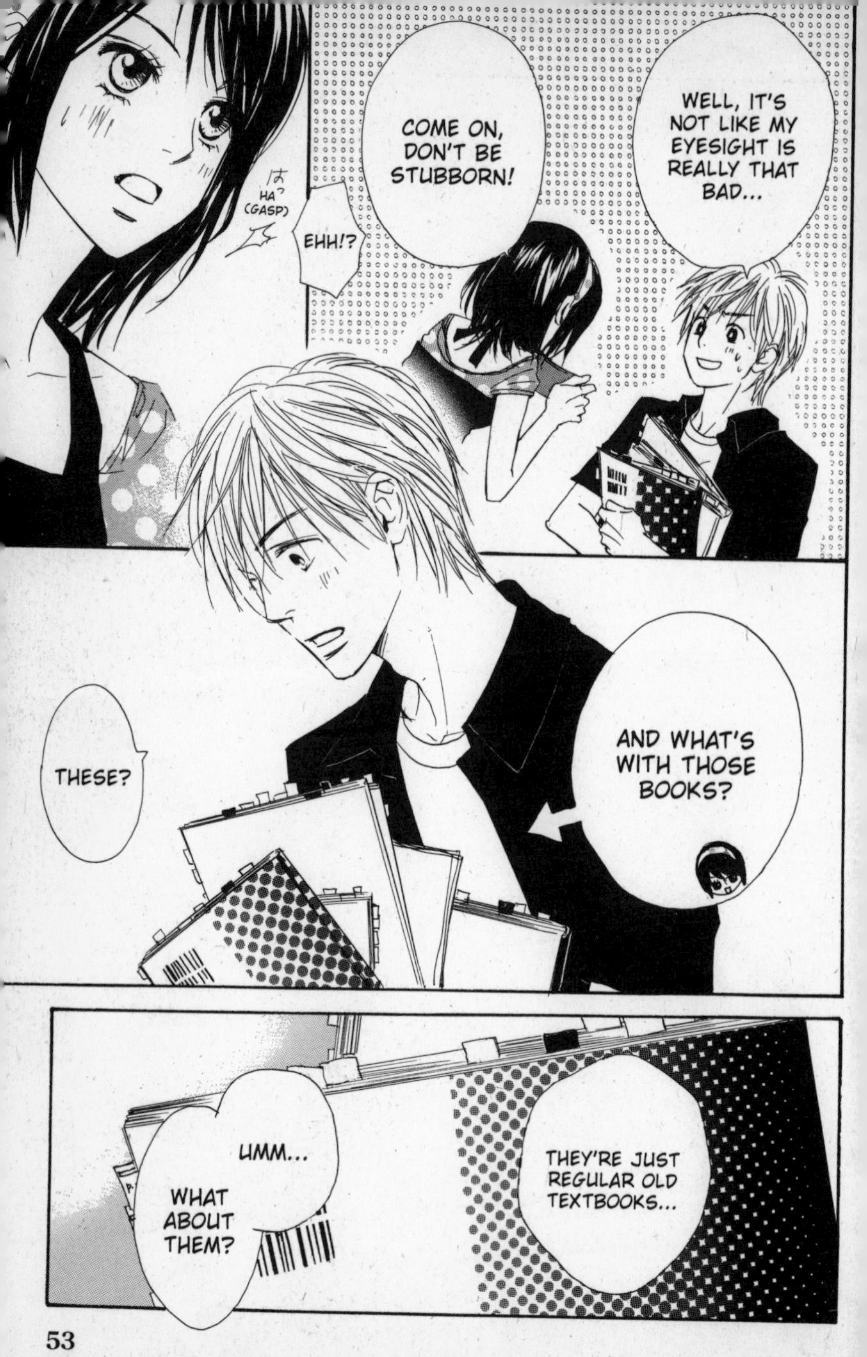

WELL, IT'S NOT LIKE MY EYESIGHT IS REALLY THAT BAD...
COME ON, DON'T BE STUBBORN!
EHH!?
は HA? (GASP)
AND WHAT'S WITH THOSE BOOKS?
THESE?
THEY'RE JUST REGULAR OLD TEXTBOOKS...
UMM... WHAT ABOUT THEM?

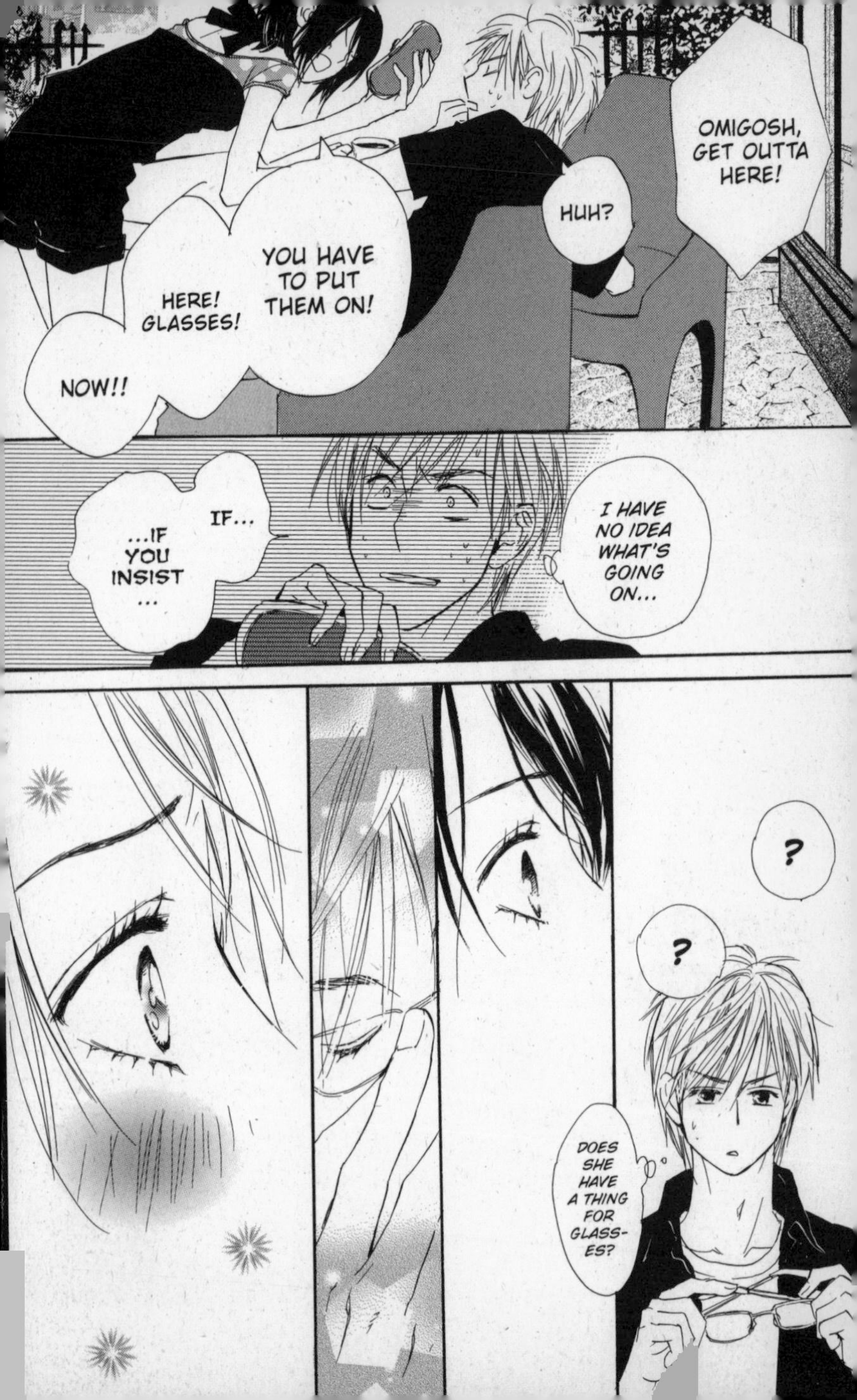
OMIGOSH, GET OUTTA HERE!
HUH?
YOU HAVE TO PUT THEM ON!
HERE! GLASSES!
NOW!!
I HAVE NO IDEA WHAT'S GOING ON...
IF...
...IF YOU INSIST ...
?
?
DOES SHE HAVE A THING FOR GLASS-ES?

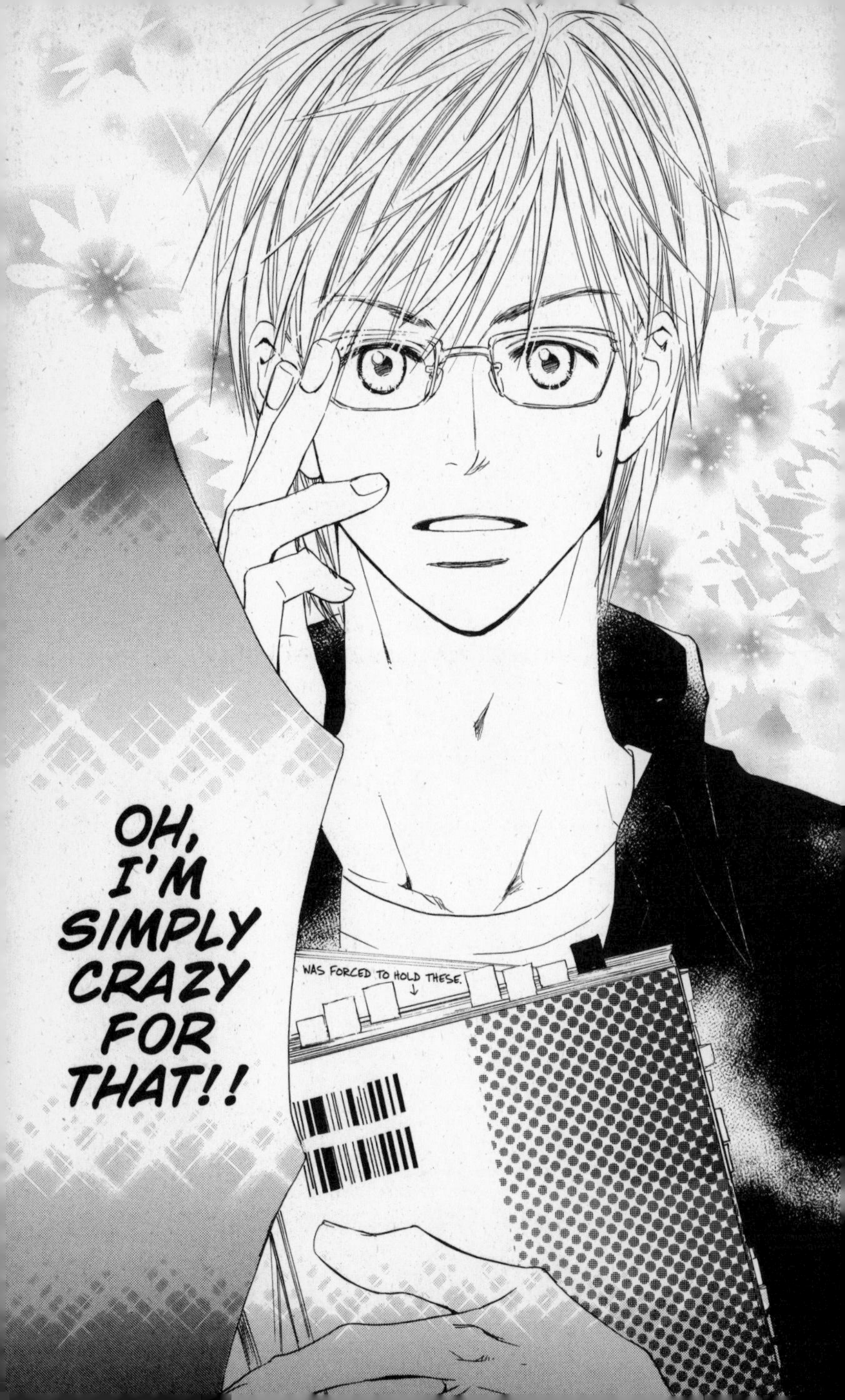
OH, I'M SIMPLY CRAZY FOR THAT!!
WAS FORCED TO HOLD THESE.

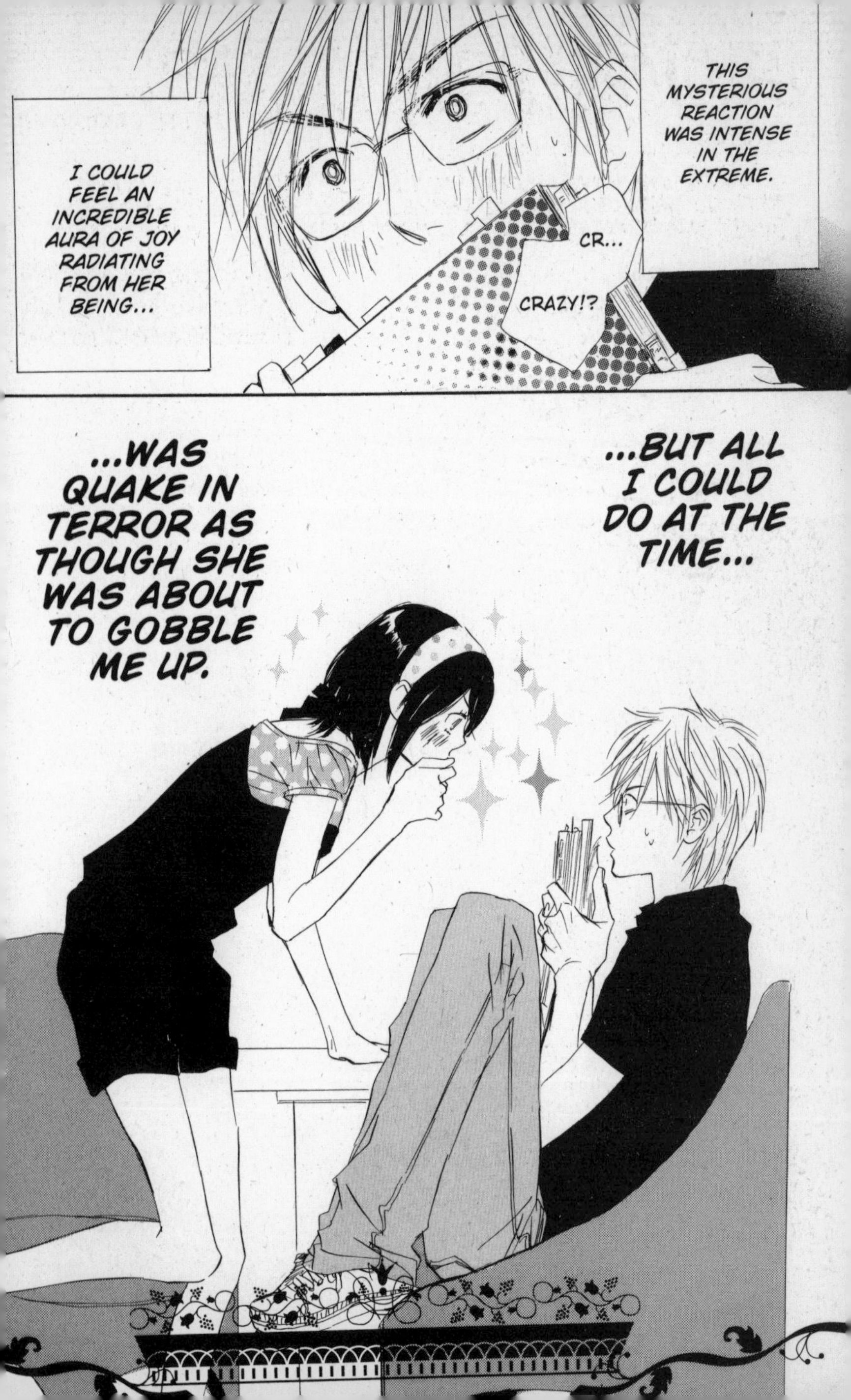
THIS MYSTERIOUS REACTION WAS INTENSE IN THE EXTREME.
CR...
CRAZY!?
I COULD FEEL AN INCREDIBLE AURA OF JOY RADIATING FROM HER BEING...
...BUT ALL I COULD DO AT THE TIME...
...WAS QUAKE IN TERROR AS THOUGH SHE WAS ABOUT TO GOBBLE ME UP.

FUJOSHI NEWS

vol.01
SECRETS OF "SEPATTE TAKURO" (1)

YUIKO-SAN LOVES "SEPATTE TAKURO" SO MUCH, SHE BUYS "WEEKLY SHOUNEN STEP" BEFORE IT GOES ON SALE EVERY WEEK. WHAT KIND OF MANGA IS IT, ANYWAY? LET'S TAKE A LITTLE PEEK!♥

LOGO: "SEPATTE TAKURO"

SEPATTE TAKURO
AUTHOR: FIGHT OOYAMA-SENSEI

STORY:

LONELY AND GLOOMY TAKURO SEBA JUST STARTED ATTENDING MAYA MIDDLE SCHOOL. HE WAS HOPING TO JOIN A CLUB TO WHICH HE COULD DEDICATE HIMSELF AND FIND A PURPOSE, BUT HIS LACK OF COURAGE KEPT HIM FROM SPEAKING UP.

ONE DAY, TAKURO PICKED UP A MYSTERIOUS BALL OFF THE GROUND. SUDDENLY, A STRANGE SPIRIT EMERGED FROM THE BALL. IT SAID, "I AM THE SPIRIT OF SEPAK. YOU ARE NOW CURSED! IF YOU WANT TO UNDO THIS CURSE, YOU MUST DEDICATE YOURSELF TO SEPAK TAKRAW AND WIN!"

THE NEXT DAY, TAKURO FOUND HIMSELF WALKING STRAIGHT TO THE GYM AS IF GUIDED BY AN INVISIBLE HAND. THERE HE FOUND THE SEPAK TAKRAW CLUB'S CAPTAIN AND ITS ACE PLAYER, HIBINO AND HIKARU, TRADING FEROCIOUS VOLLEYS WITH THE BALL!!

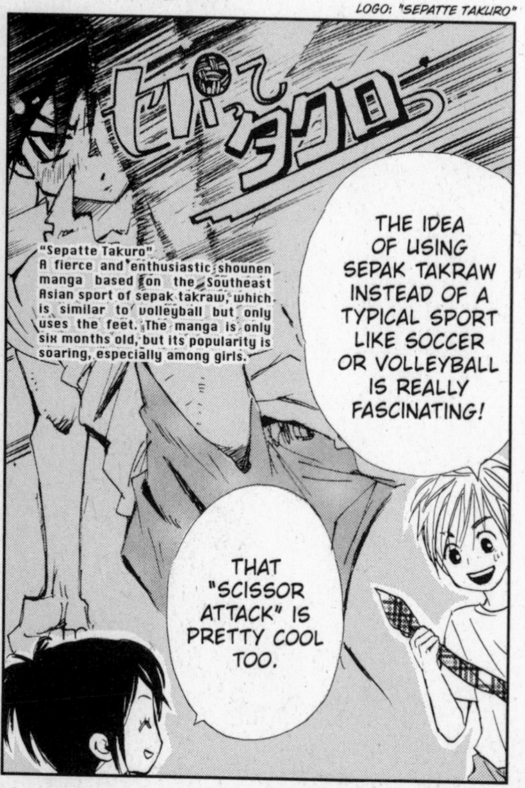
THE IDEA OF USING SEPAK TAKRAW INSTEAD OF A TYPICAL SPORT LIKE SOCCER OR VOLLEYBALL IS REALLY FASCINATING!
"Sepatte Takuro" A fierce and enthusiastic shounen manga based on the Southeast Asian sport of sepak takraw, which is similar to volleyball but only uses the feet. The manga is only six months old, but its popularity is soaring, especially among girls.
THAT "SCISSOR ATTACK" IS PRETTY COOL TOO.

OFFICIAL "SEPATTE TAKURO" CELL PHONE STRAP. THERE ARE SIX KINDS IN ALL (INCLUDING SECRET VARIETIES). YUIKO-SAN HAS THE COMPLETE COLLECTION, OF COURSE.

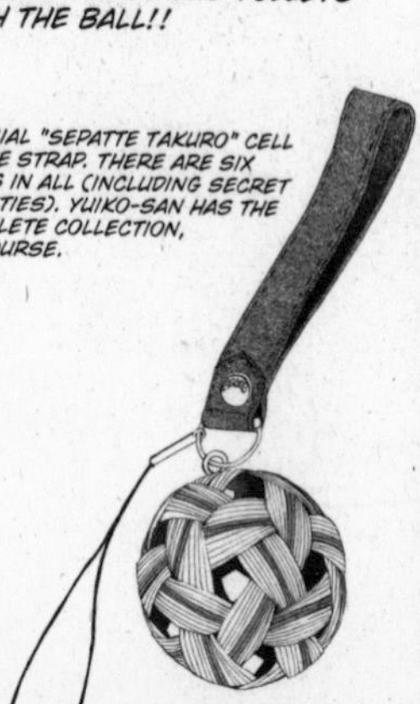

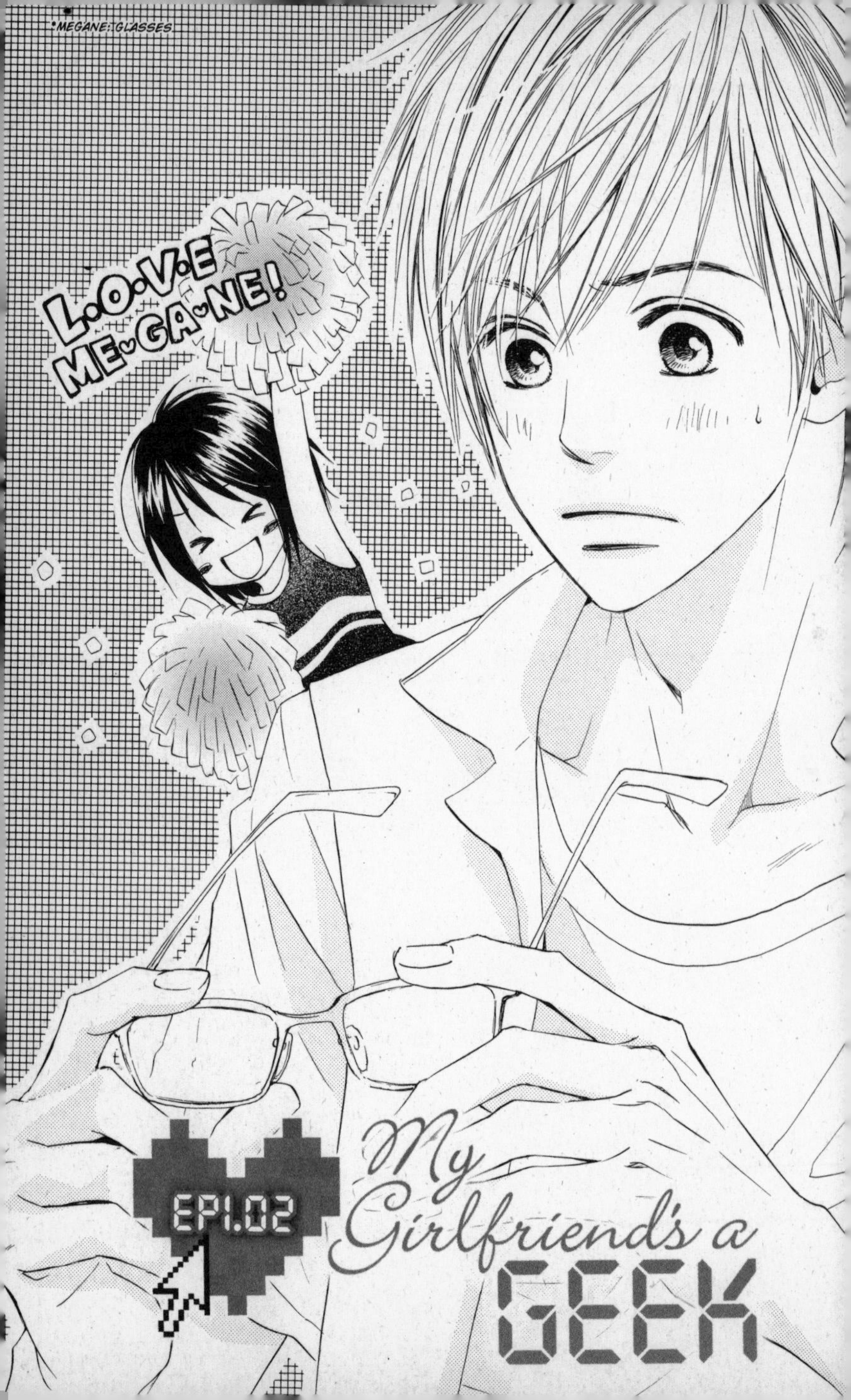

*MEGANE: GLASSES
L·O·V·E
ME·GA·NE!
EP1.02
My Girlfriend's a
GEEK

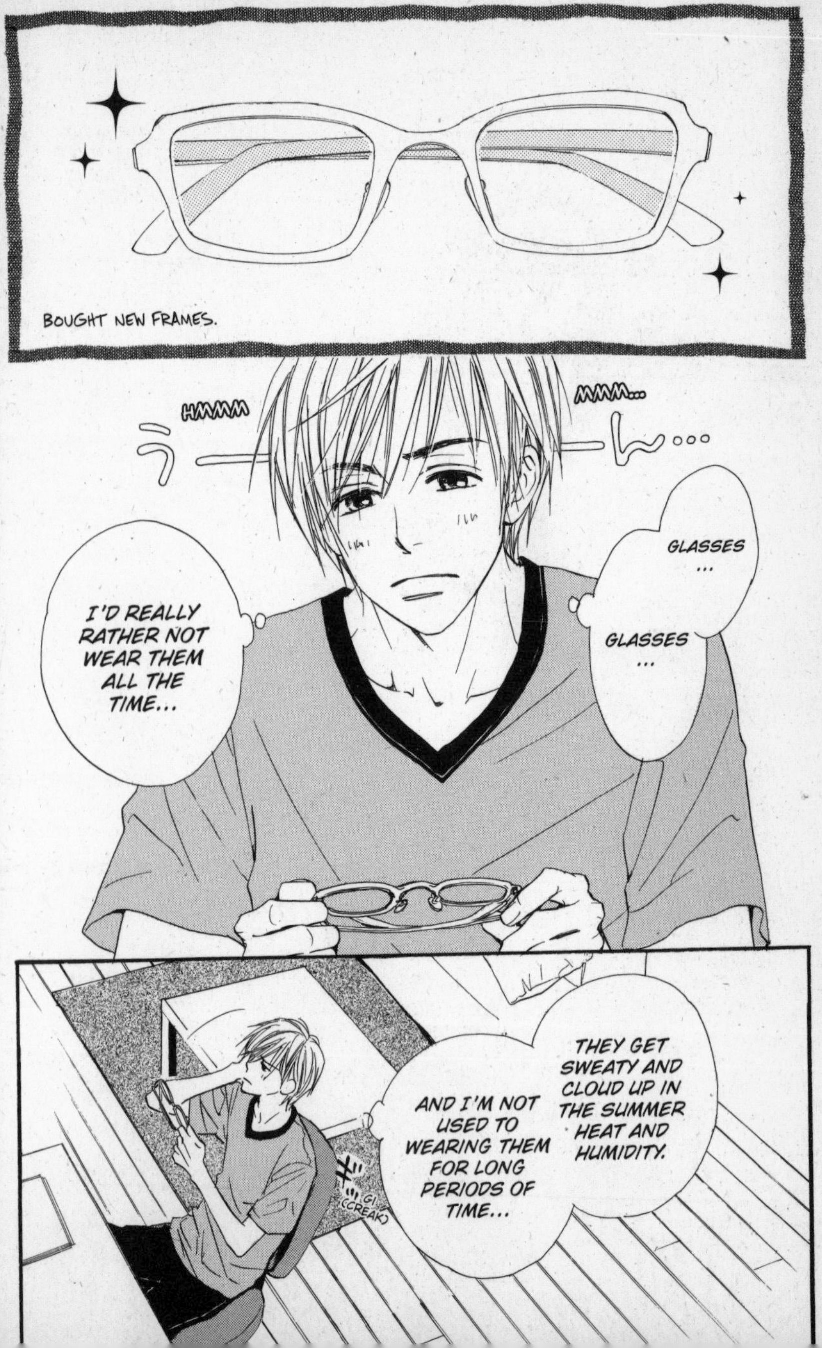
BOUGHT NEW FRAMES.
MMM...
HMMM
うーーん…
GLASSES ... GLASSES ...
I'D REALLY RATHER NOT WEAR THEM ALL THE TIME...
THEY GET SWEATY AND CLOUD UP IN THE SUMMER HEAT AND HUMIDITY.
AND I'M NOT USED TO WEARING THEM FOR LONG PERIODS OF TIME...
GI (CREAK)

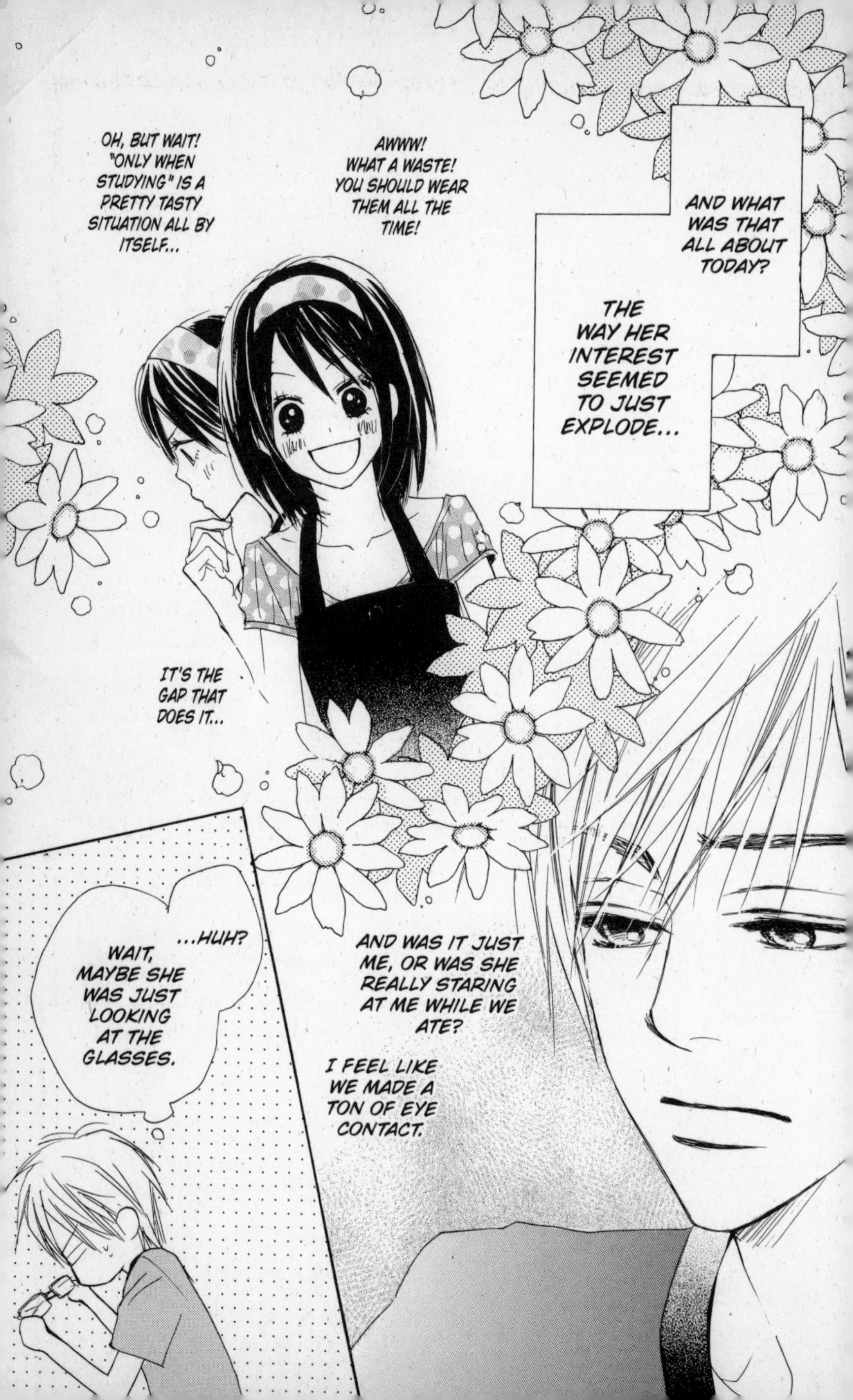
AND WHAT WAS THAT ALL ABOUT TODAY?
THE WAY HER INTEREST SEEMED TO JUST EXPLODE...
AWWW! WHAT A WASTE! YOU SHOULD WEAR THEM ALL THE TIME!
OH, BUT WAIT! "ONLY WHEN STUDYING" IS A PRETTY TASTY SITUATION ALL BY ITSELF...
IT'S THE GAP THAT DOES IT...
AND WAS IT JUST ME, OR WAS SHE REALLY STARING AT ME WHILE WE ATE?
I FEEL LIKE WE MADE A TON OF EYE CONTACT.
...HUH?
WAIT, MAYBE SHE WAS JUST LOOKING AT THE GLASSES.

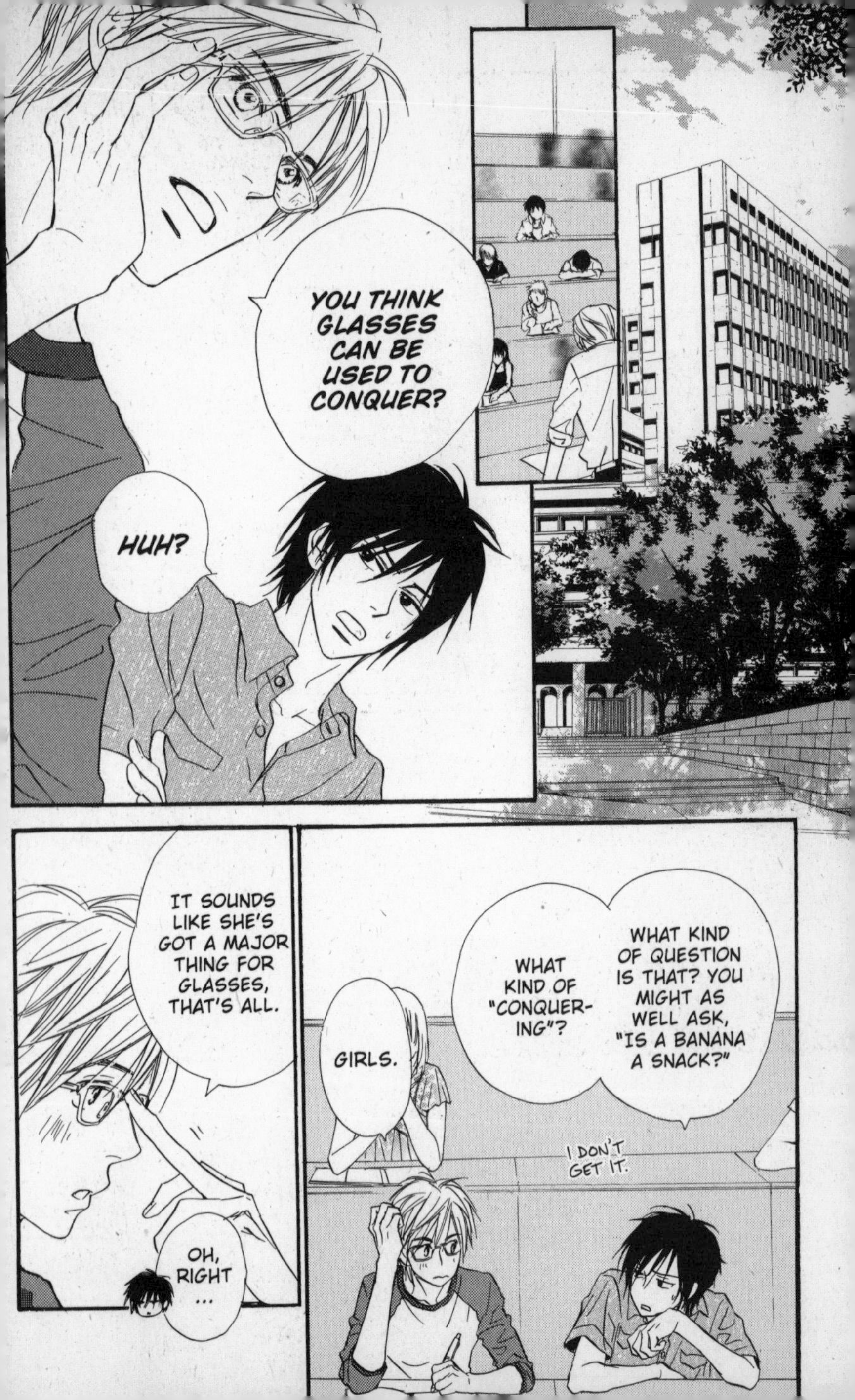
YOU THINK GLASSES CAN BE USED TO CONQUER?
HUH?
WHAT KIND OF QUESTION IS THAT? YOU MIGHT AS WELL ASK, "IS A BANANA A SNACK?"
WHAT KIND OF "CONQUER-ING"?
GIRLS.
I DON'T GET IT.
IT SOUNDS LIKE SHE'S GOT A MAJOR THING FOR GLASSES, THAT'S ALL.
OH, RIGHT ...

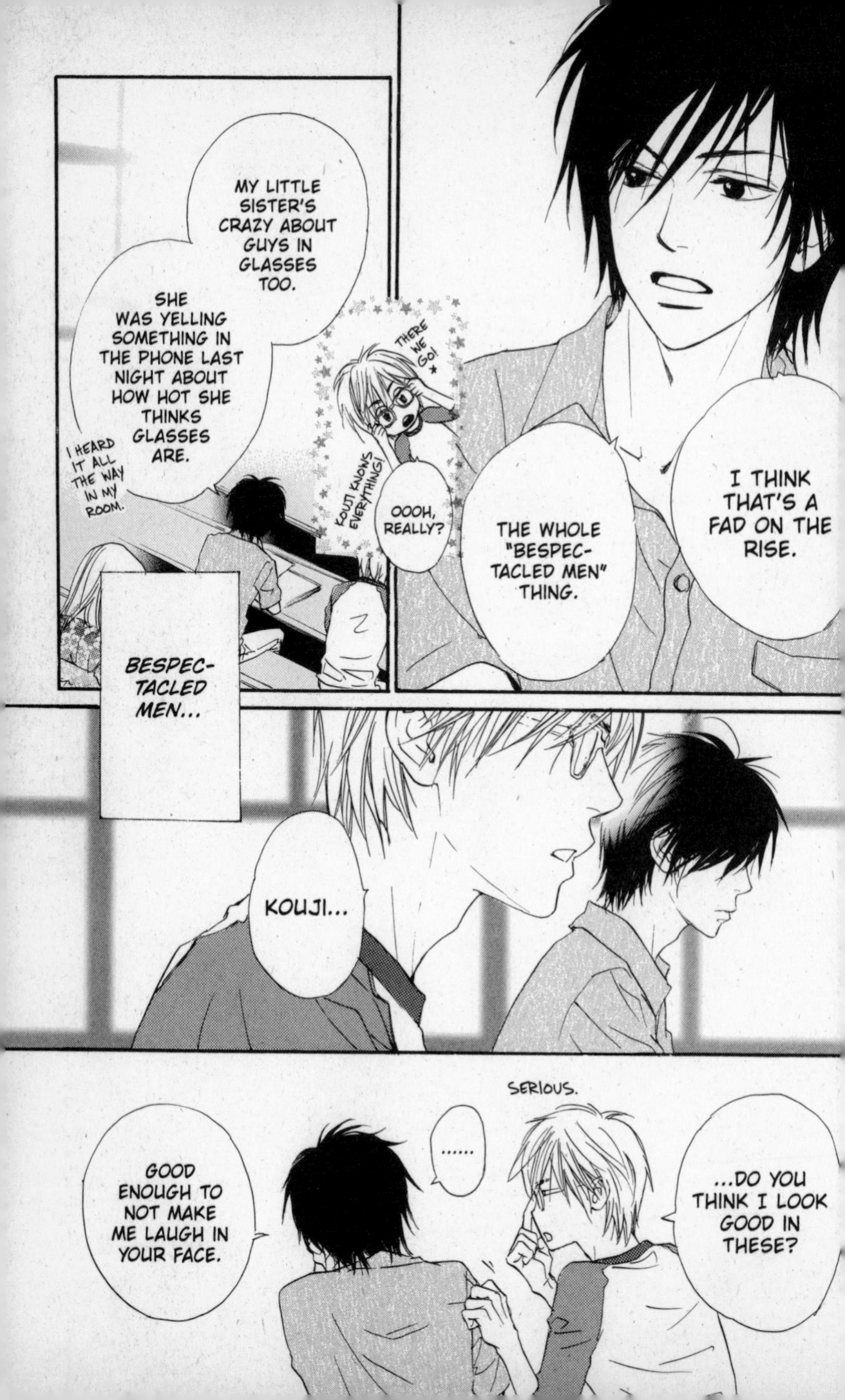
I THINK THAT'S A FAD ON THE RISE.
THE WHOLE "BESPEC-TACLED MEN" THING.
THERE WE GO! ★
OOOH, REALLY?
KOUJI KNOWS EVERYTHING!
MY LITTLE SISTER'S CRAZY ABOUT GUYS IN GLASSES TOO.
SHE WAS YELLING SOMETHING IN THE PHONE LAST NIGHT ABOUT HOW HOT SHE THINKS GLASSES ARE.
I HEARD IT ALL THE WAY IN MY ROOM.
BESPEC-TACLED MEN...
KOUJI...
SERIOUS.
...DO YOU THINK I LOOK GOOD IN THESE?
......
GOOD ENOUGH TO NOT MAKE ME LAUGH IN YOUR FACE.

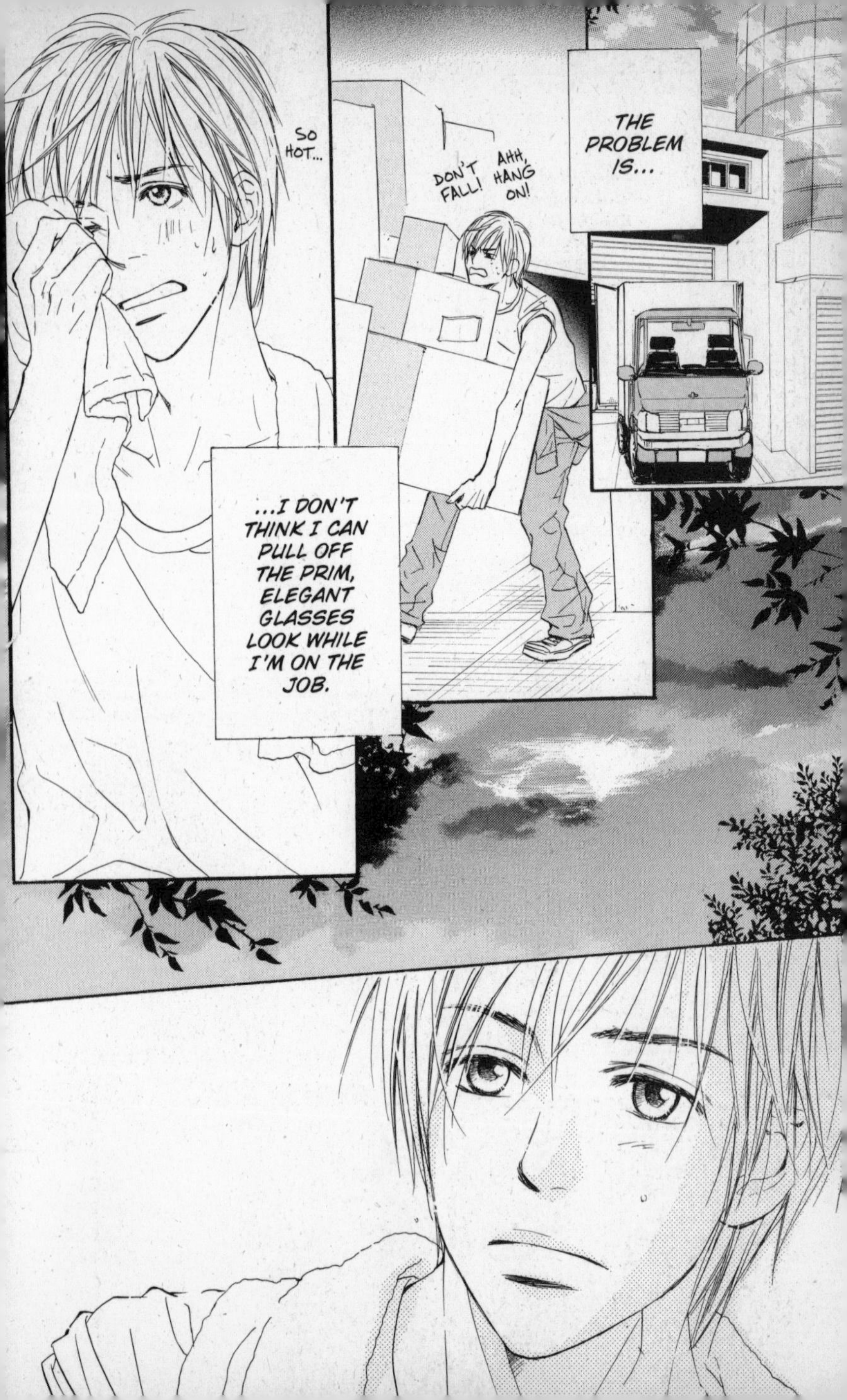
THE PROBLEM IS...
AHH, HANG ON!
DON'T FALL!
SO HOT...
...I DON'T THINK I CAN PULL OFF THE PRIM, ELEGANT GLASSES LOOK WHILE I'M ON THE JOB.

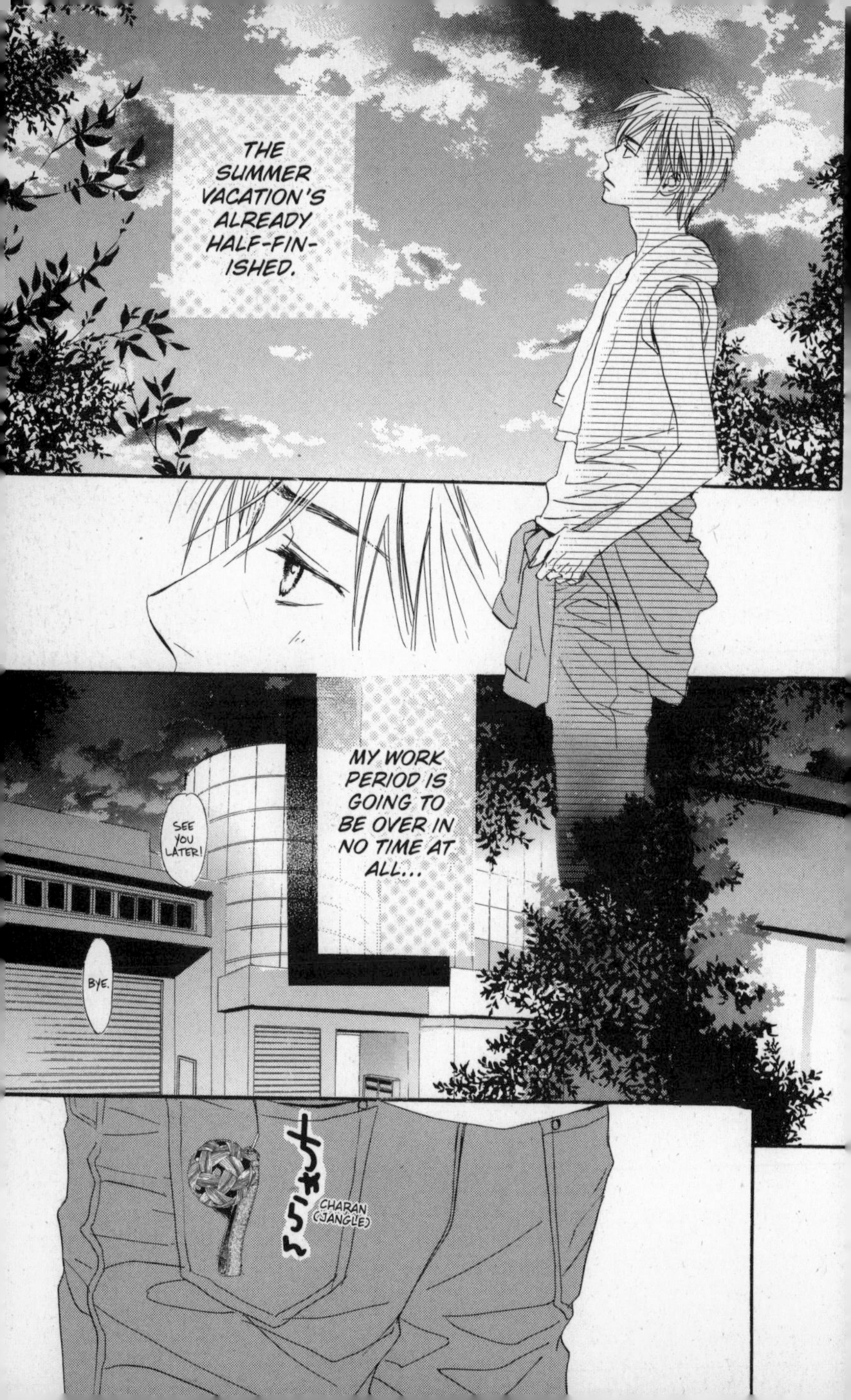
THE SUMMER VACATION'S ALREADY HALF-FIN-ISHED.
MY WORK PERIOD IS GOING TO BE OVER IN NO TIME AT ALL...
SEE YOU LATER!
BYE.
ちゃらん
CHARAN (JANGLE)

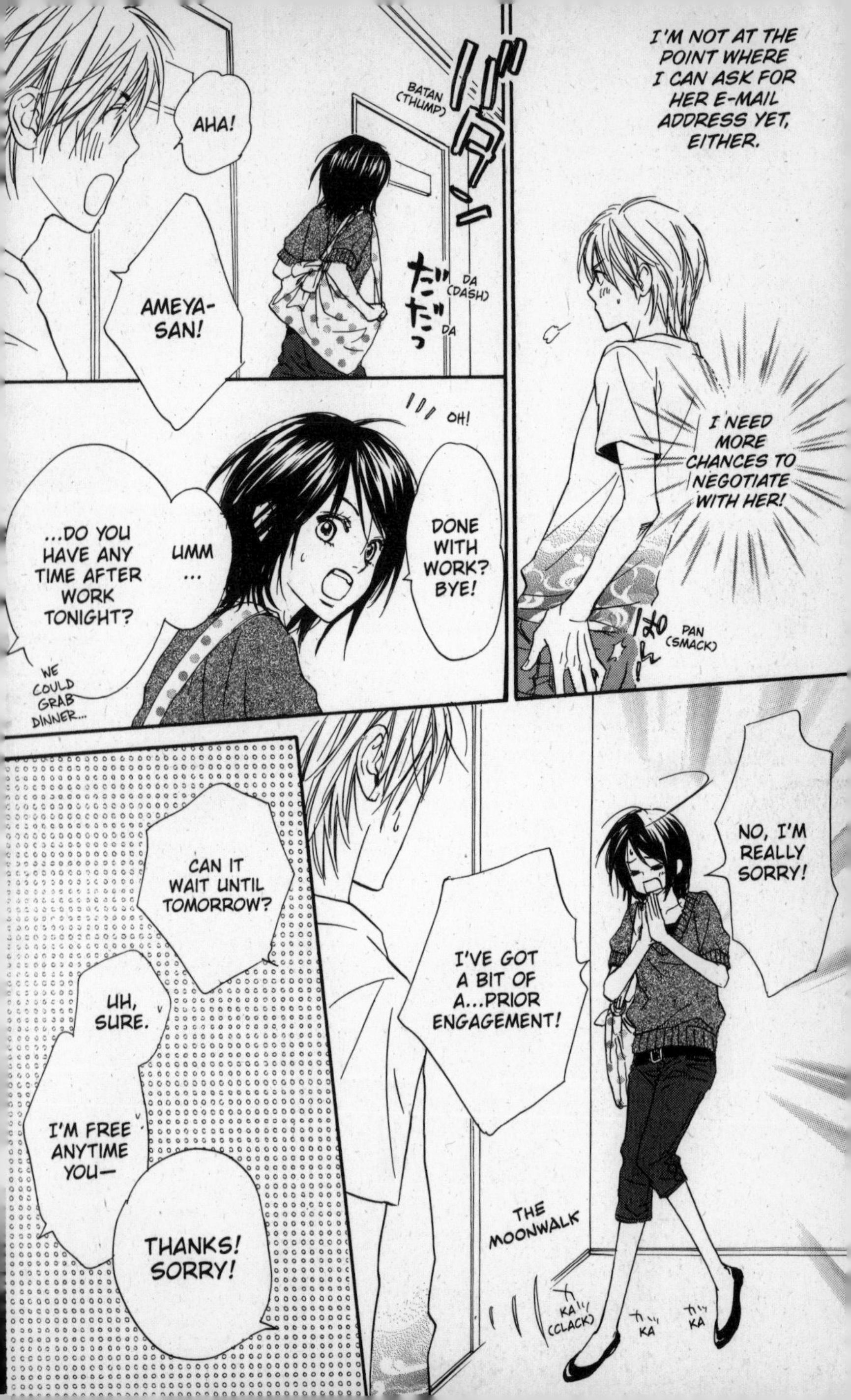
I'M NOT AT THE POINT WHERE I CAN ASK FOR HER E-MAIL ADDRESS YET, EITHER.
I NEED MORE CHANCES TO NEGOTIATE WITH HER!
PAN (SMACK)
BATAN (THUMP)
DA (DASH) DA
AHA!
AMEYA-SAN!
OH!
DONE WITH WORK? BYE!
UMM ...
...DO YOU HAVE ANY TIME AFTER WORK TONIGHT?
WE COULD GRAB DINNER...
NO, I'M REALLY SORRY!
I'VE GOT A BIT OF A...PRIOR ENGAGEMENT!
THE MOONWALK
KA (CLACK)
KA
KA
CAN IT WAIT UNTIL TOMORROW?
UH, SURE.
I'M FREE ANYTIME YOU—
THANKS! SORRY!

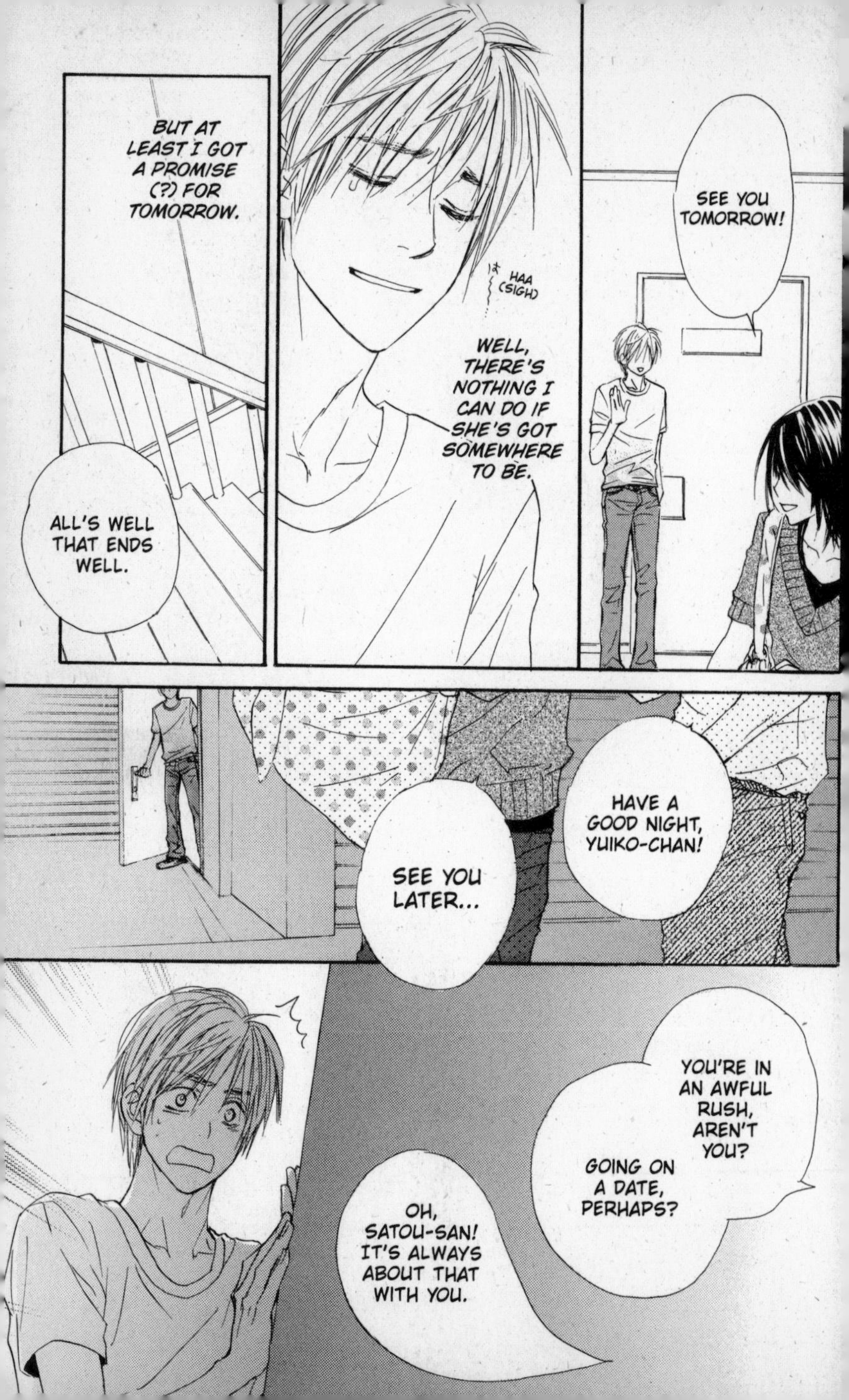
SEE YOU TOMORROW!
は HAA (SIGH)
WELL, THERE'S NOTHING I CAN DO IF SHE'S GOT SOMEWHERE TO BE.
BUT AT LEAST I GOT A PROMISE (?) FOR TOMORROW.
ALL'S WELL THAT ENDS WELL.
HAVE A GOOD NIGHT, YUIKO-CHAN!
SEE YOU LATER...
YOU'RE IN AN AWFUL RUSH, AREN'T YOU?
GOING ON A DATE, PERHAPS?
OH, SATOU-SAN! IT'S ALWAYS ABOUT THAT WITH YOU.

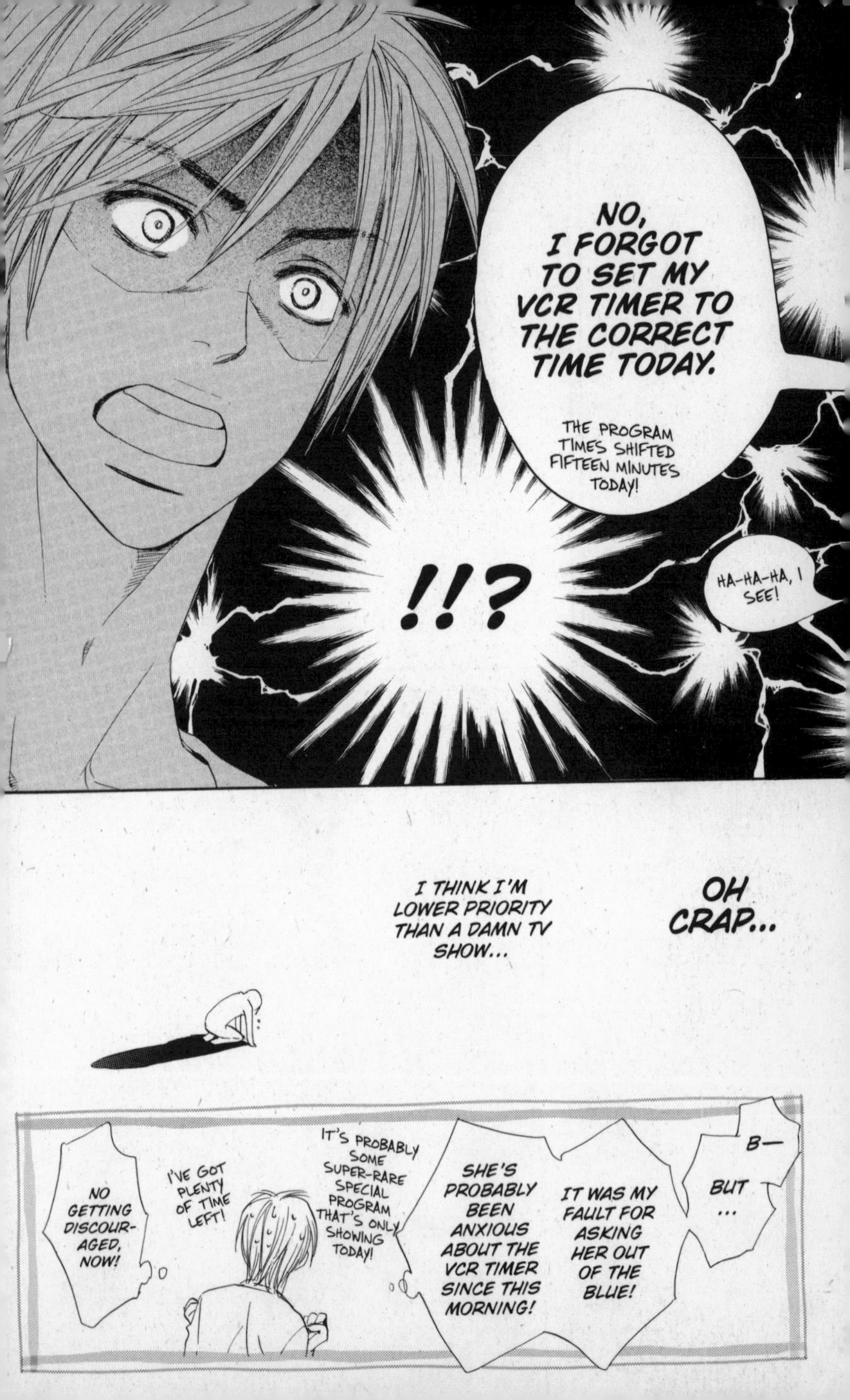
NO, I FORGOT TO SET MY VCR TIMER TO THE CORRECT TIME TODAY.
THE PROGRAM TIMES SHIFTED FIFTEEN MINUTES TODAY!
HA-HA-HA, I SEE!
!!?
OH CRAP...
I THINK I'M LOWER PRIORITY THAN A DAMN TV SHOW...
B— BUT ...
IT WAS MY FAULT FOR ASKING HER OUT OF THE BLUE!
SHE'S PROBABLY BEEN ANXIOUS ABOUT THE VCR TIMER SINCE THIS MORNING!
IT'S PROBABLY SOME SUPER-RARE SPECIAL PROGRAM THAT'S ONLY SHOWING TODAY!
I'VE GOT PLENTY OF TIME LEFT!
NO GETTING DISCOURAGED, NOW!

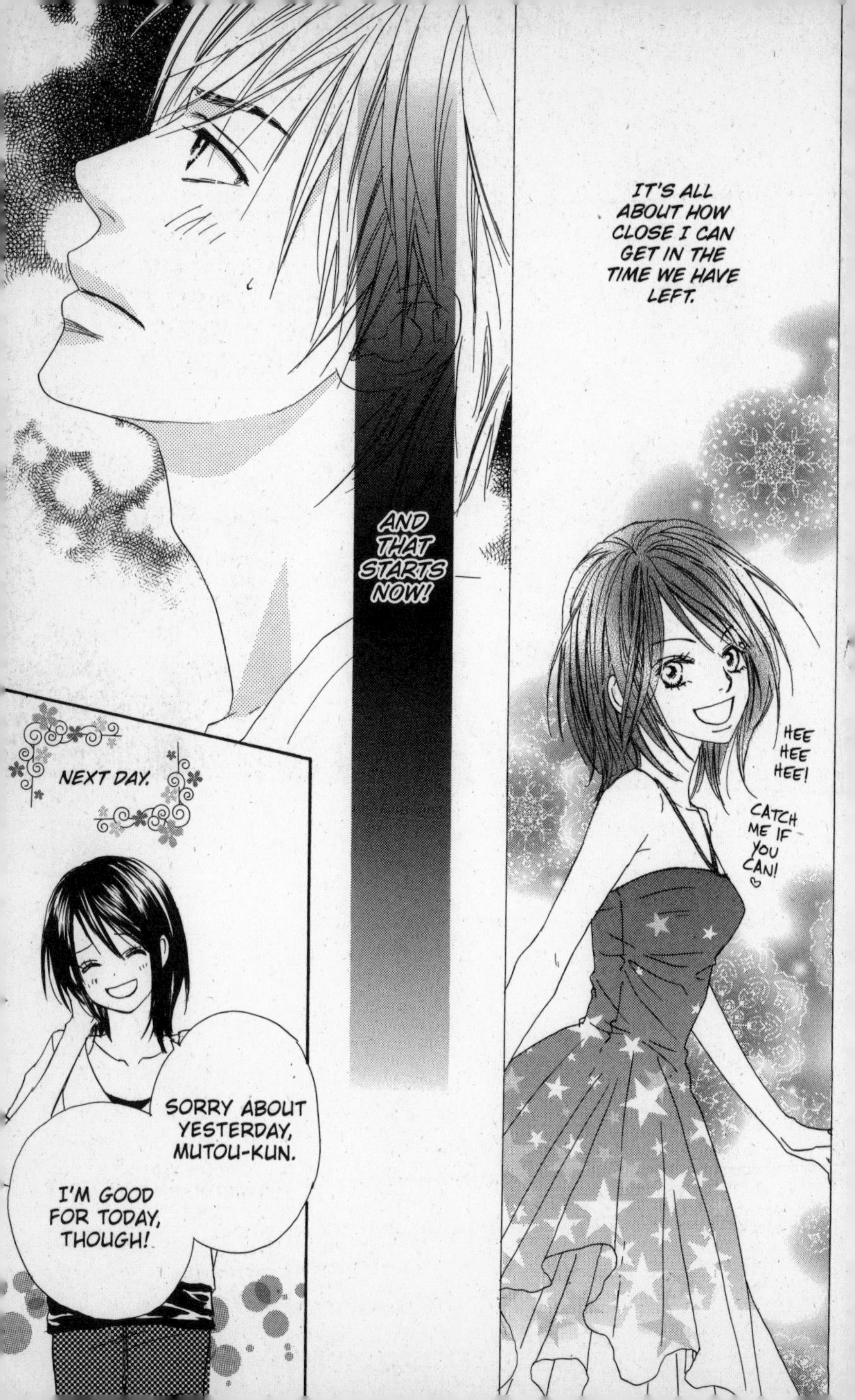
IT'S ALL ABOUT HOW CLOSE I CAN GET IN THE TIME WE HAVE LEFT.
HEE HEE HEE!
CATCH ME IF YOU CAN! ♡
AND THAT STARTS NOW!
NEXT DAY.
SORRY ABOUT YESTERDAY, MUTOU-KUN.
I'M GOOD FOR TODAY, THOUGH!

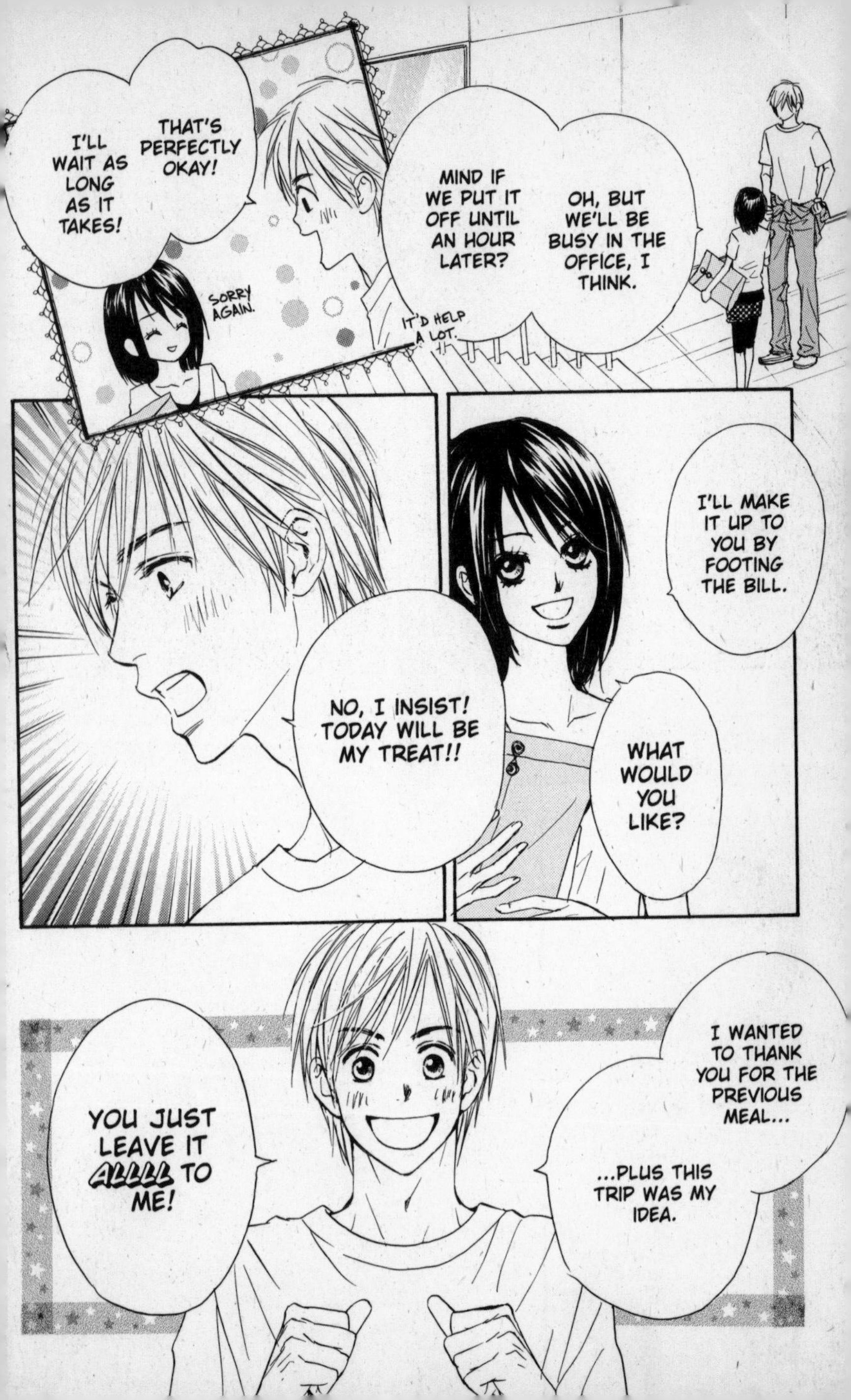
OH, BUT WE'LL BE BUSY IN THE OFFICE, I THINK.
MIND IF WE PUT IT OFF UNTIL AN HOUR LATER?
IT'D HELP A LOT.
THAT'S PERFECTLY OKAY!
I'LL WAIT AS LONG AS IT TAKES!
SORRY AGAIN.
I'LL MAKE IT UP TO YOU BY FOOTING THE BILL.
WHAT WOULD YOU LIKE?
NO, I INSIST! TODAY WILL BE MY TREAT!!
I WANTED TO THANK YOU FOR THE PREVIOUS MEAL...
...PLUS THIS TRIP WAS MY IDEA.
YOU JUST LEAVE IT ALLLL TO ME!

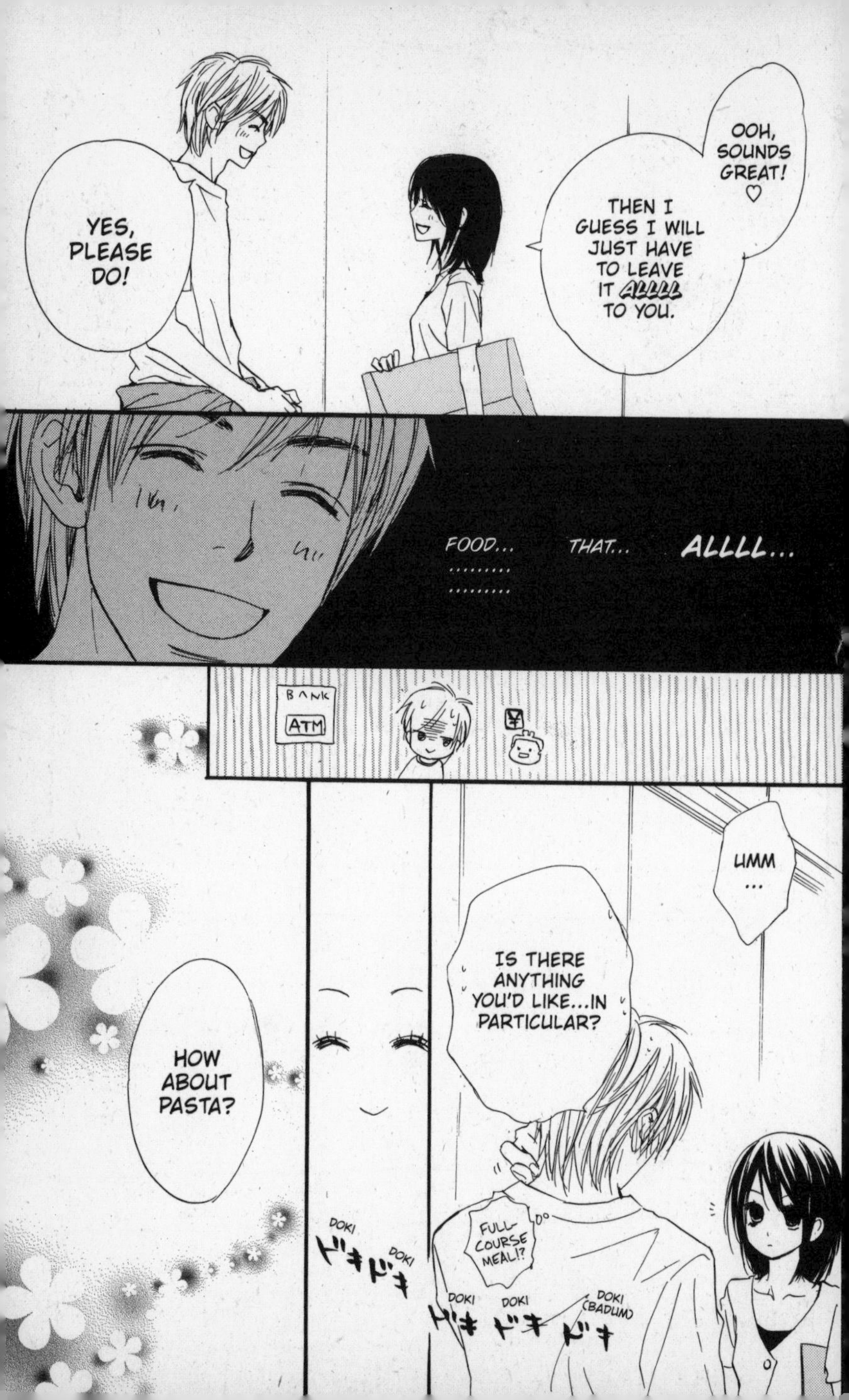
OOH, SOUNDS GREAT! ♡
THEN I GUESS I WILL JUST HAVE TO LEAVE IT ALLLL TO YOU.
YES, PLEASE DO!
FOOD... THAT... ALLLL...
....
....
BANK
ATM
¥
UMM...
IS THERE ANYTHING YOU'D LIKE...IN PARTICULAR?
FULL-COURSE MEAL!?
DOKI ドキ DOKI ドキ DOKI (BADUM) ドキ
DOKI ドキ DOKI ドキ
HOW ABOUT PASTA?

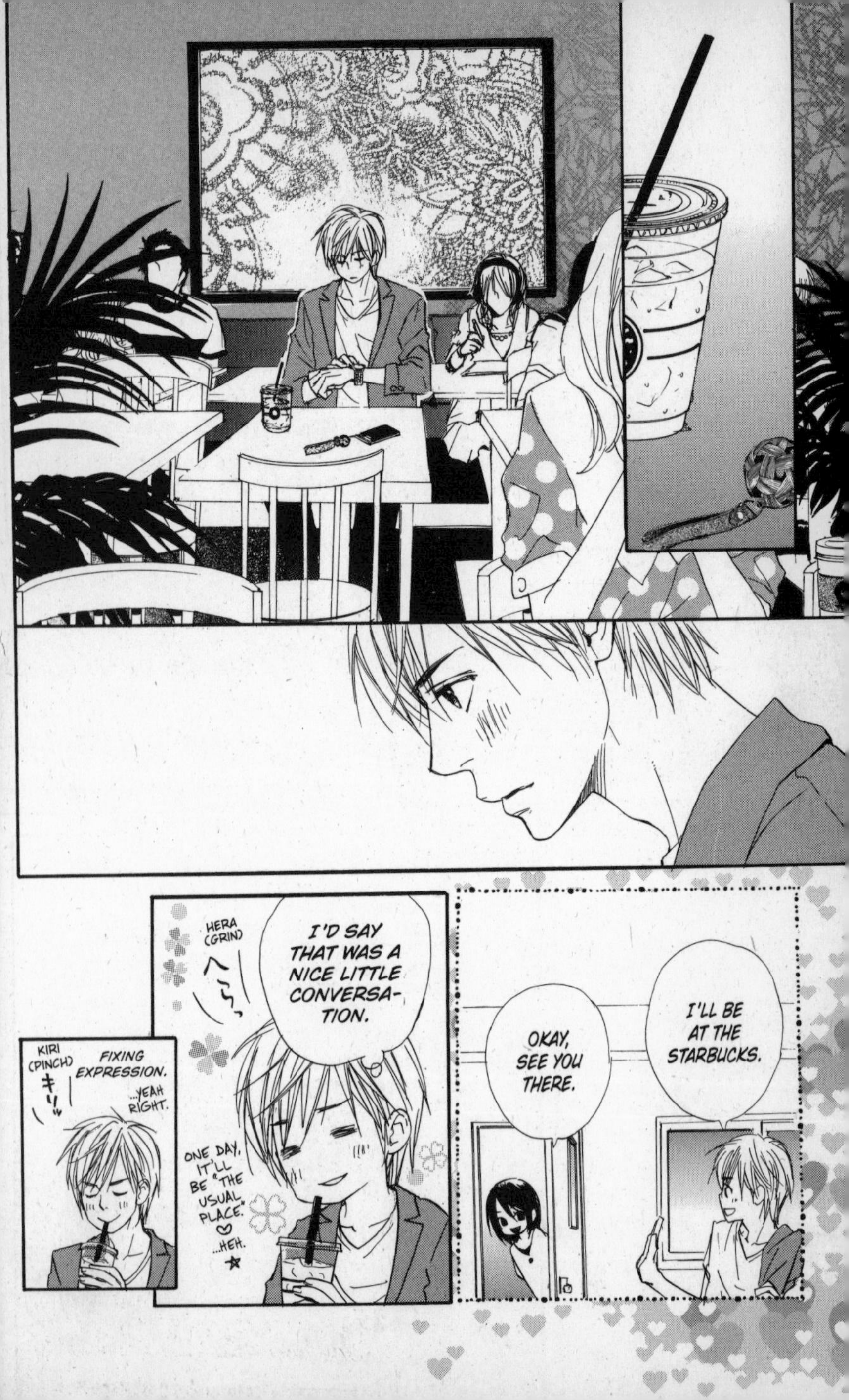
I'LL BE AT THE STARBUCKS.
OKAY, SEE YOU THERE.
I'D SAY THAT WAS A NICE LITTLE CONVERSA-TION.
HERA (GRIN)
ONE DAY, IT'LL BE "THE USUAL PLACE." ...HEH.
FIXING EXPRESSION.
KIRI (PINCH)
...YEAH RIGHT.

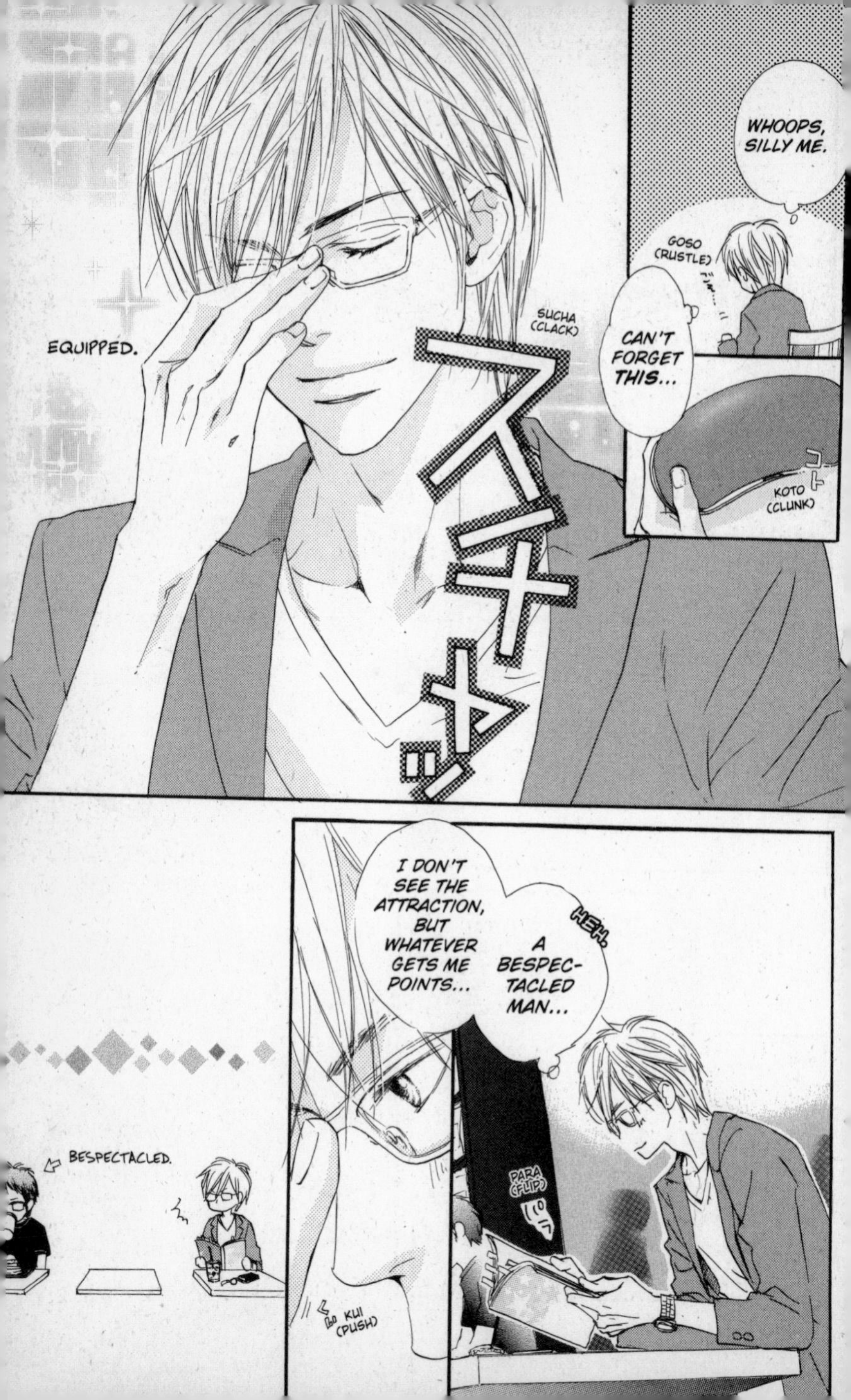
WHOOPS, SILLY ME.
GOSO (RUSTLE)
CAN'T FORGET THIS...
KOTO (CLUNK)
スチャッ
SUCHA (CLACK)
EQUIPPED.
I DON'T SEE THE ATTRACTION, BUT WHATEVER GETS ME POINTS...
A BESPECTACLED MAN...
HEH.
PARA (FLIP)
KUI (PUSH)
BESPECTACLED.

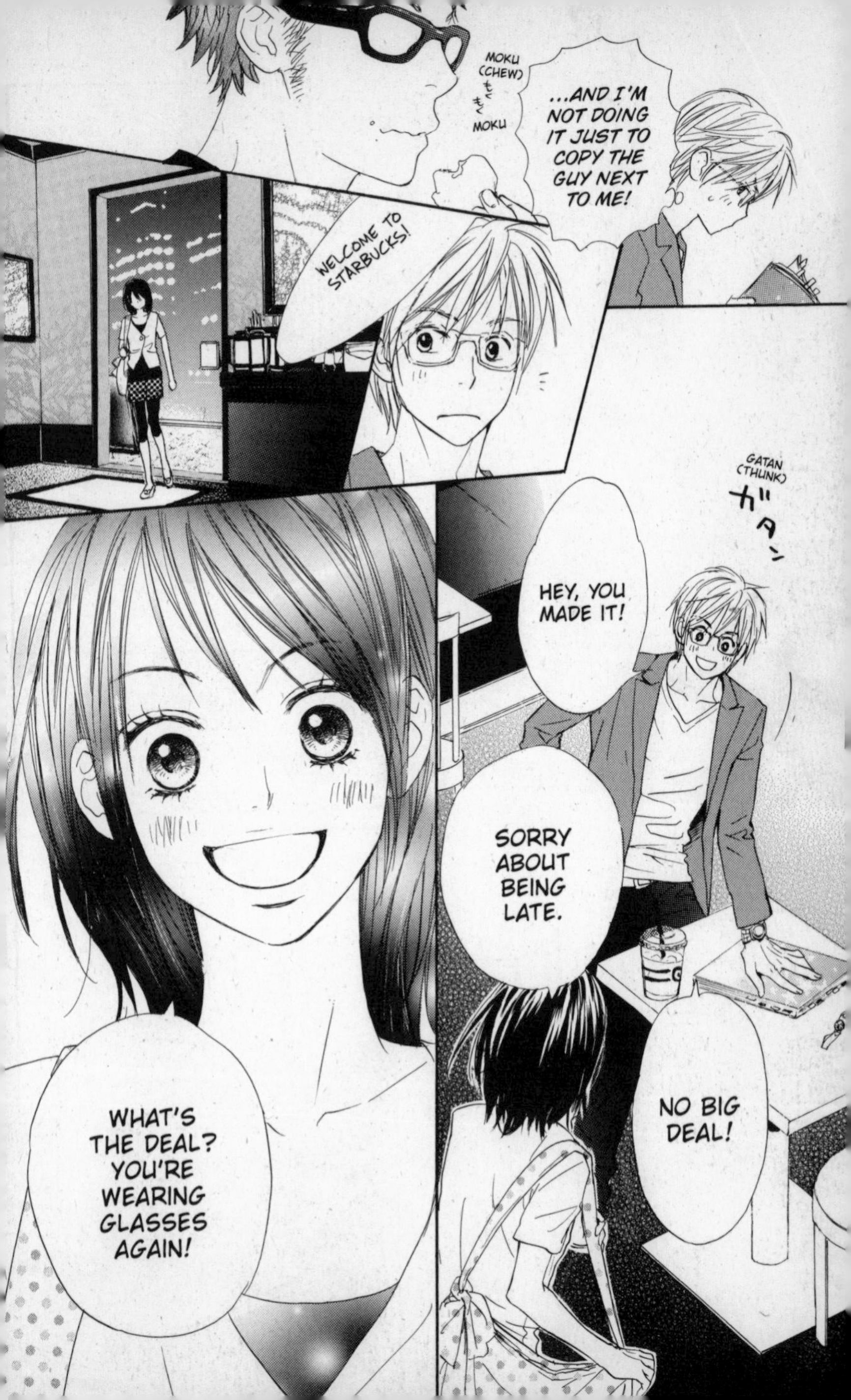
...AND I'M NOT DOING IT JUST TO COPY THE GUY NEXT TO ME!
MOKU (CHEW) MOKU
WELCOME TO STARBUCKS!
GATAN (THUNK)
HEY, YOU MADE IT!
SORRY ABOUT BEING LATE.
NO BIG DEAL!
WHAT'S THE DEAL? YOU'RE WEARING GLASSES AGAIN!

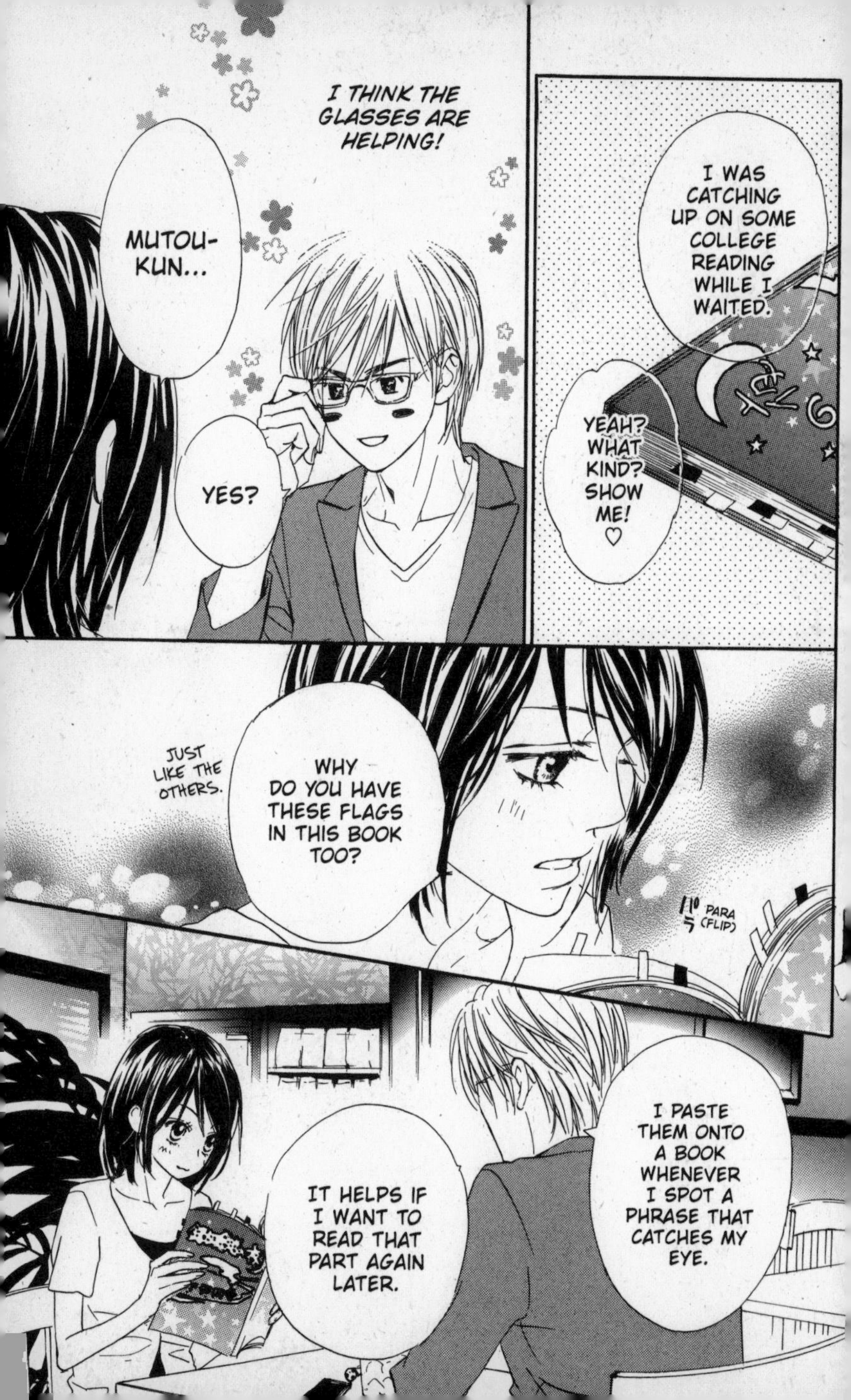

I WAS CATCHING UP ON SOME COLLEGE READING WHILE I WAITED.
YEAH? WHAT KIND? SHOW ME! ♡
I THINK THE GLASSES ARE HELPING!
MUTOU-KUN...
YES?
パラ PARA (FLIP)
WHY DO YOU HAVE THESE FLAGS IN THIS BOOK TOO?
JUST LIKE THE OTHERS.
I PASTE THEM ONTO A BOOK WHENEVER I SPOT A PHRASE THAT CATCHES MY EYE.
IT HELPS IF I WANT TO READ THAT PART AGAIN LATER.

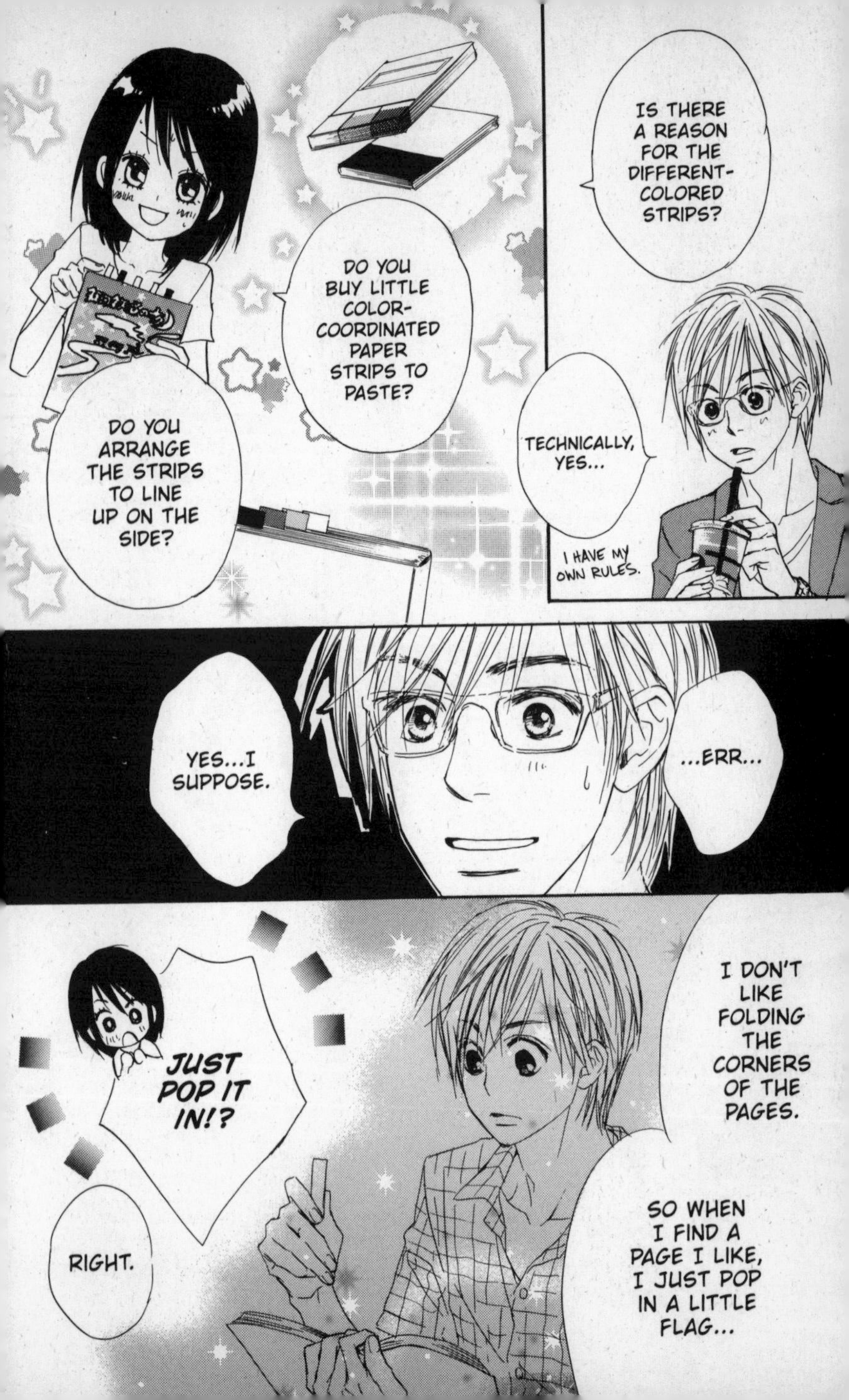
IS THERE A REASON FOR THE DIFFERENT-COLORED STRIPS?
TECHNICALLY, YES...
I HAVE MY OWN RULES.
DO YOU BUY LITTLE COLOR-COORDINATED PAPER STRIPS TO PASTE?
DO YOU ARRANGE THE STRIPS TO LINE UP ON THE SIDE?
...ERR...
YES...I SUPPOSE.
I DON'T LIKE FOLDING THE CORNERS OF THE PAGES.
SO WHEN I FIND A PAGE I LIKE, I JUST POP IN A LITTLE FLAG...
JUST POP IT IN!?
RIGHT.

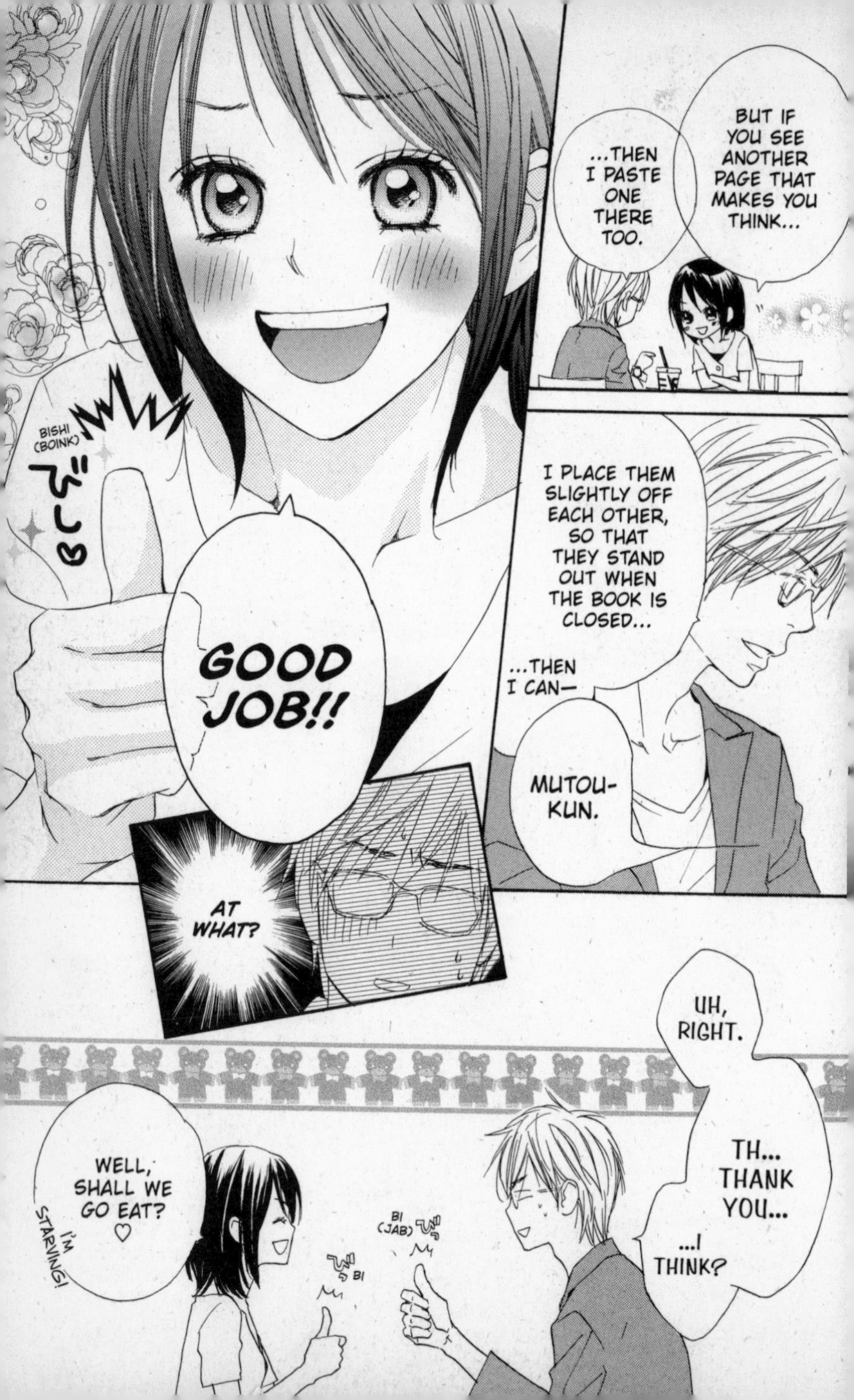
BUT IF YOU SEE ANOTHER PAGE THAT MAKES YOU THINK...
...THEN I PASTE ONE THERE TOO.
I PLACE THEM SLIGHTLY OFF EACH OTHER, SO THAT THEY STAND OUT WHEN THE BOOK IS CLOSED...
...THEN I CAN—
MUTOU-KUN.
BISHI (BOINK)
びしっ
GOOD JOB!!
AT WHAT?
UH, RIGHT.
TH... THANK YOU...
...I THINK?
BI (JAB)
WELL, SHALL WE GO EAT? ♡
I'M STARVING!
BI

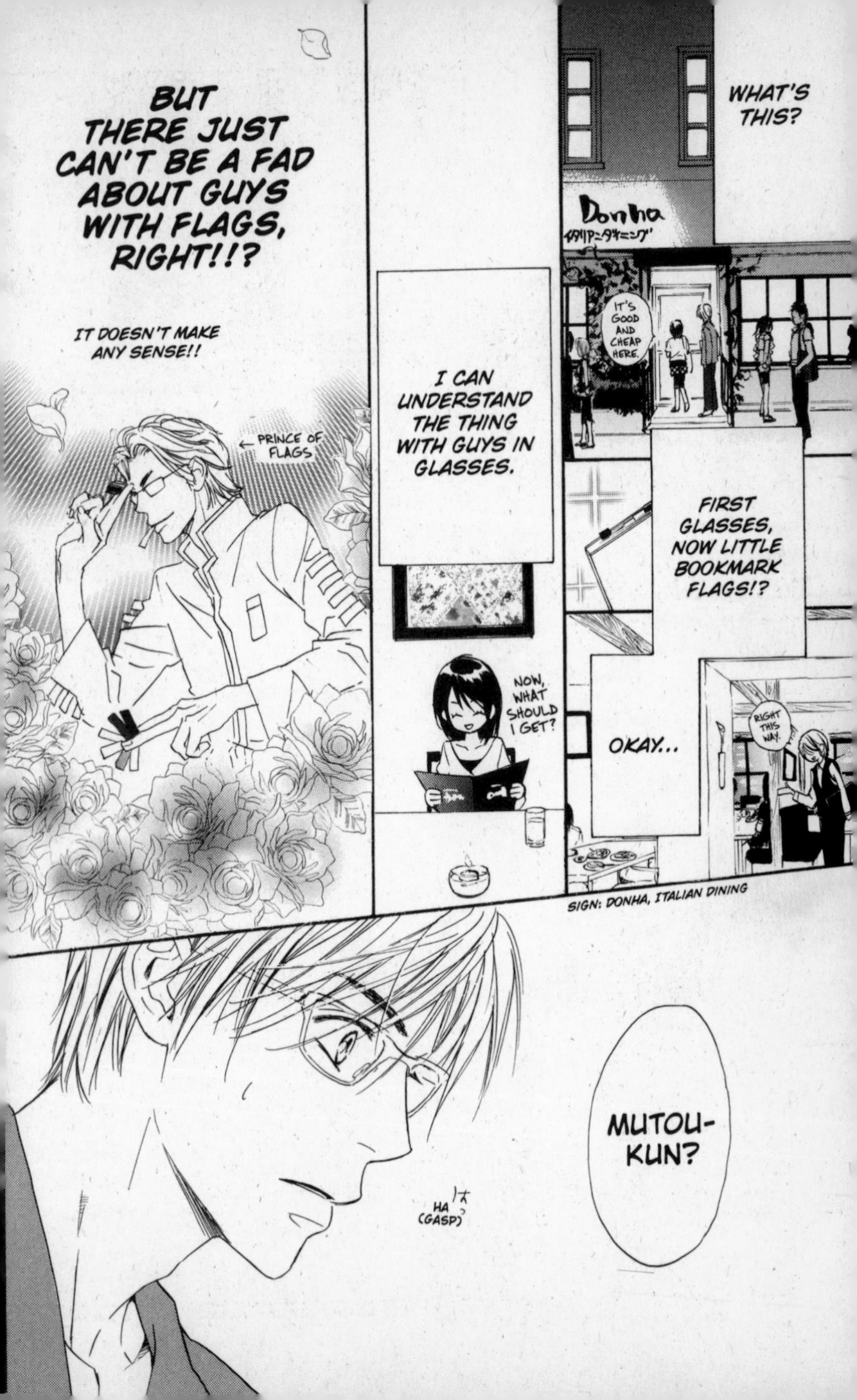
WHAT'S THIS?
Donha
イタリアンダイニング
IT'S GOOD AND CHEAP HERE.
FIRST GLASSES, NOW LITTLE BOOKMARK FLAGS!?
RIGHT THIS WAY.
OKAY...
SIGN: DONHA, ITALIAN DINING
I CAN UNDERSTAND THE THING WITH GUYS IN GLASSES.
NOW, WHAT SHOULD I GET?
BUT THERE JUST CAN'T BE A FAD ABOUT GUYS WITH FLAGS, RIGHT!!?
IT DOESN'T MAKE ANY SENSE!!
← PRINCE OF FLAGS
MUTOU-KUN?
はっ
HA (GASP)

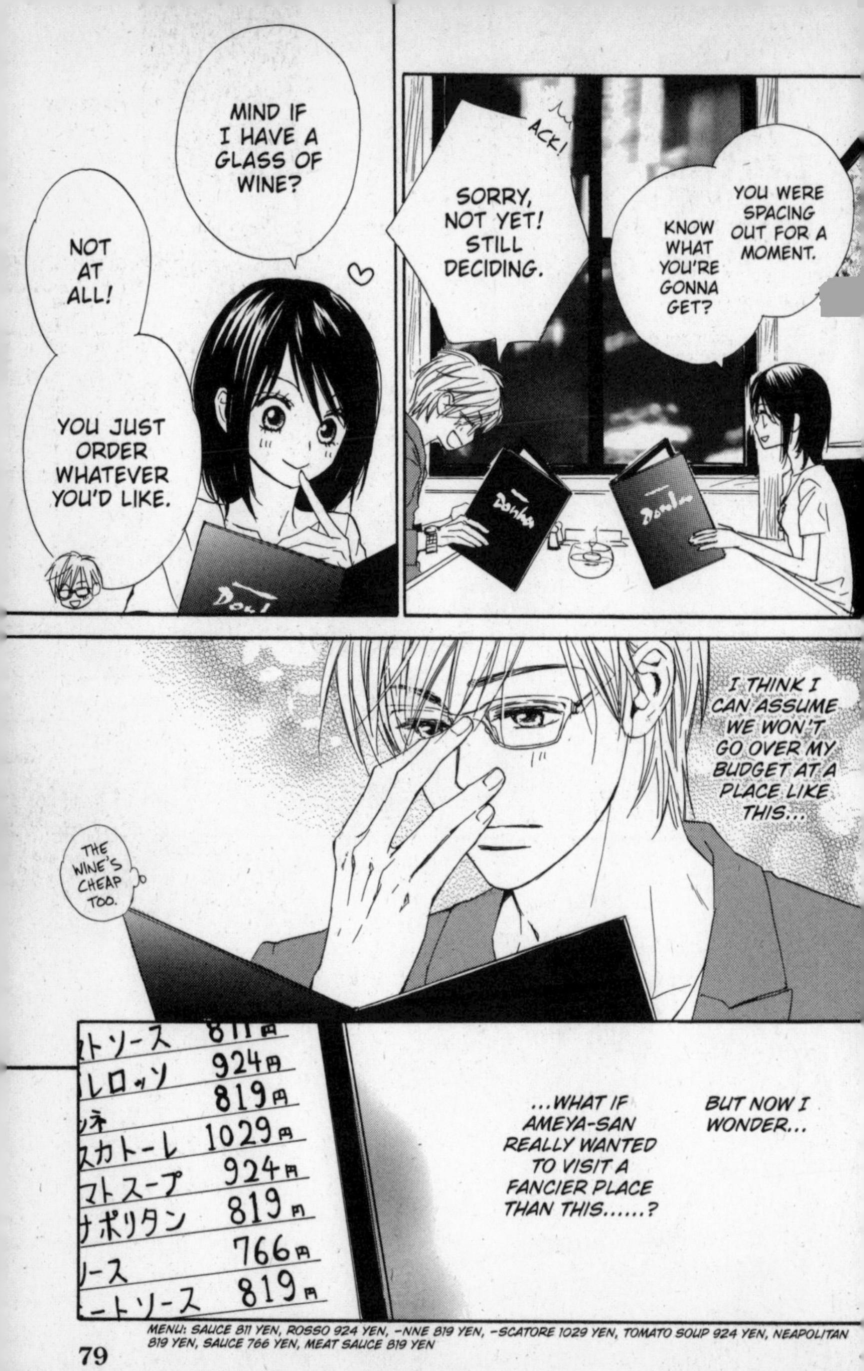
YOU WERE SPACING OUT FOR A MOMENT.
KNOW WHAT YOU'RE GONNA GET?
ACK!
SORRY, NOT YET! STILL DECIDING.
MIND IF I HAVE A GLASS OF WINE?
NOT AT ALL!
YOU JUST ORDER WHATEVER YOU'D LIKE.
I THINK I CAN ASSUME WE WON'T GO OVER MY BUDGET AT A PLACE LIKE THIS...
THE WINE'S CHEAP TOO.
BUT NOW I WONDER...
...WHAT IF AMEYA-SAN REALLY WANTED TO VISIT A FANCIER PLACE THAN THIS......?
ルロッソ 924円
819円
ッネ
スカトーレ 1029円
マトスープ 924円
ナポリタン 819円
766円
ース
ートソース 819円
MENU: SAUCE 811 YEN, ROSSO 924 YEN, -NNE 819 YEN, -SCATORE 1029 YEN, TOMATO SOUP 924 YEN, NEAPOLITAN 819 YEN, SAUCE 766 YEN, MEAT SAUCE 819 YEN

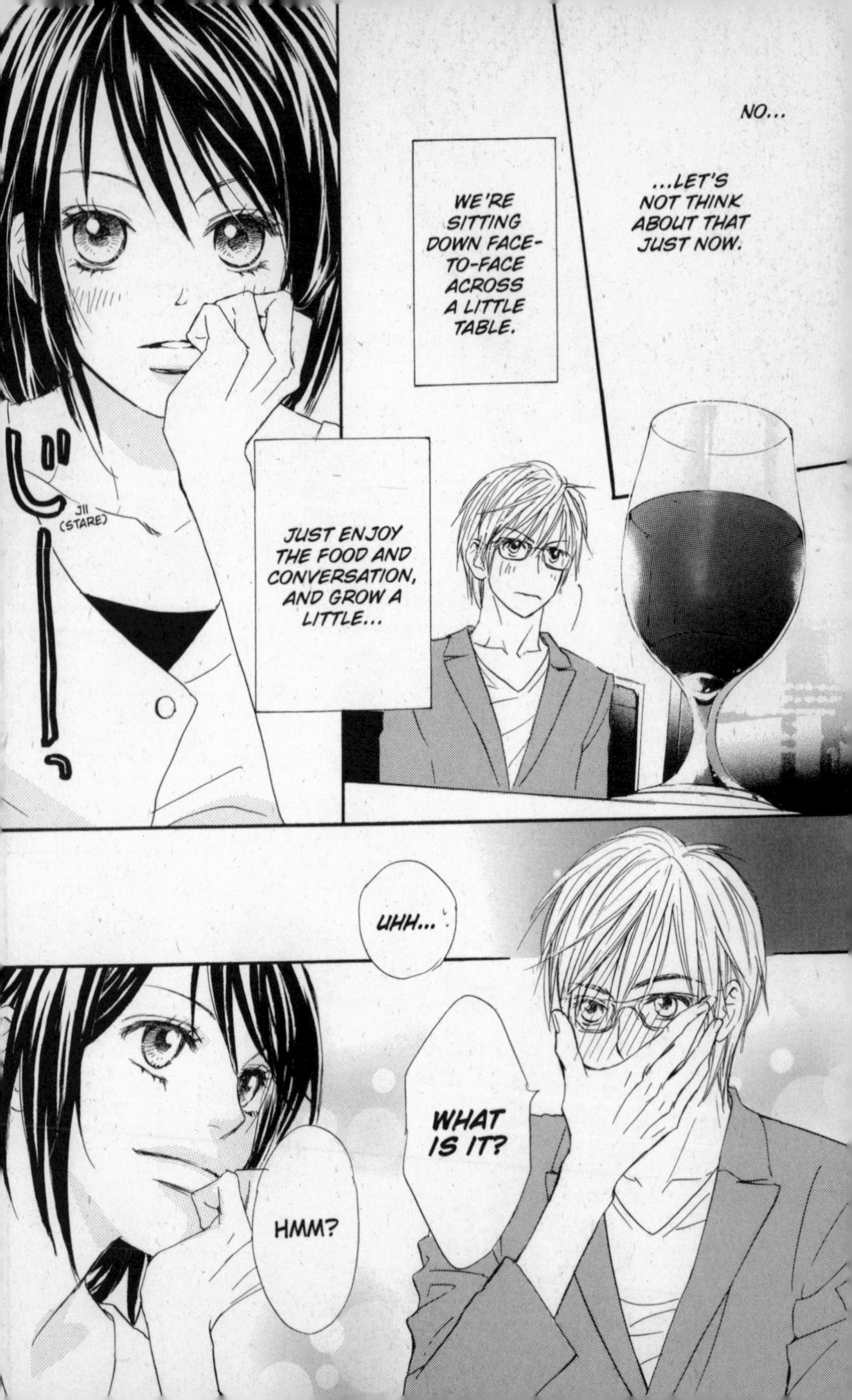
NO...
...LET'S NOT THINK ABOUT THAT JUST NOW.
WE'RE SITTING DOWN FACE-TO-FACE ACROSS A LITTLE TABLE.
JUST ENJOY THE FOOD AND CONVERSATION, AND GROW A LITTLE...
JII (STARE)
UHH...
WHAT IS IT?
HMM?

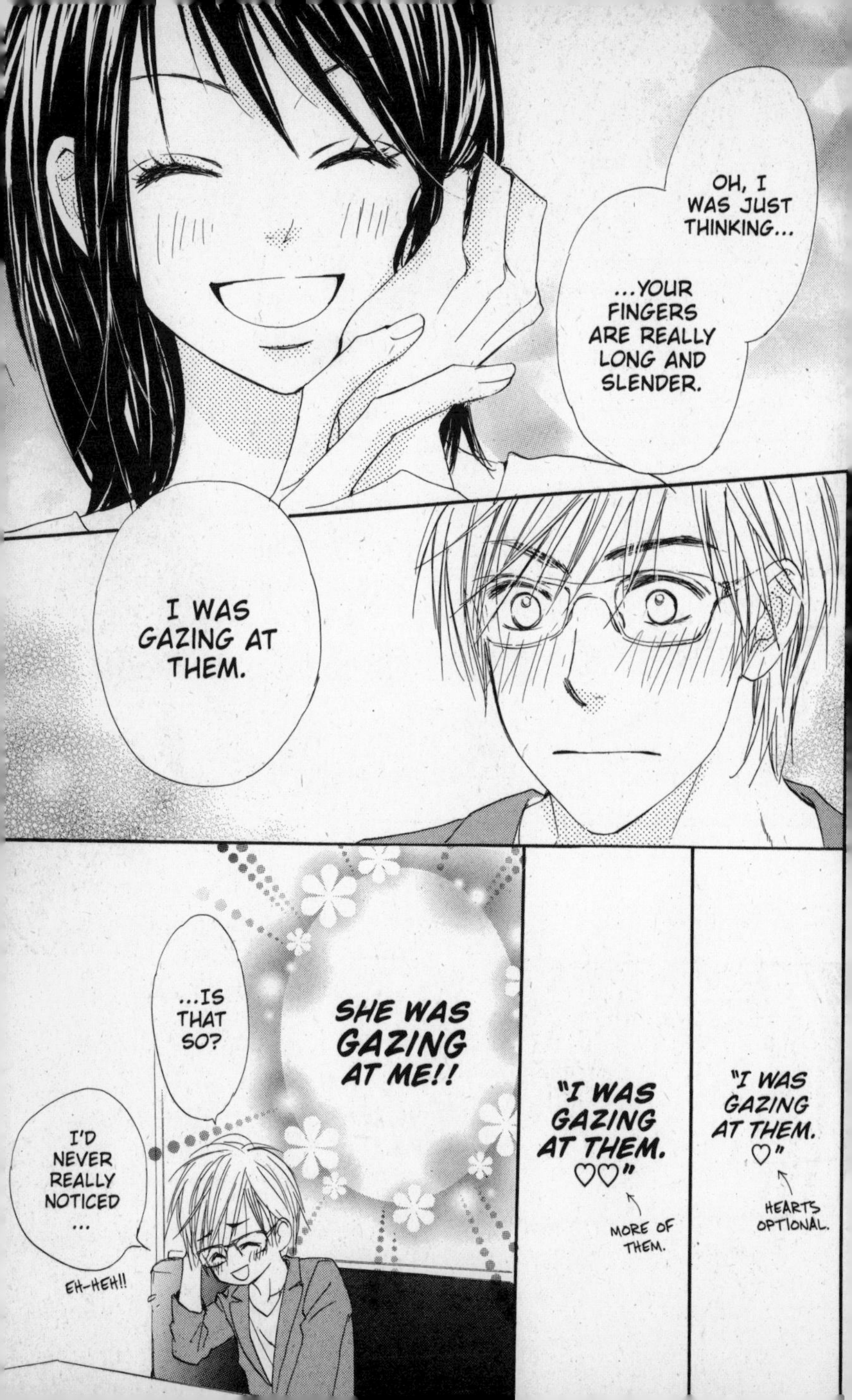
OH, I WAS JUST THINKING...
...YOUR FINGERS ARE REALLY LONG AND SLENDER.
I WAS GAZING AT THEM.
"I WAS GAZING AT THEM. ♡"
HEARTS OPTIONAL.
"I WAS GAZING AT THEM. ♡♡"
MORE OF THEM.
SHE WAS GAZING AT ME!!
...IS THAT SO?
I'D NEVER REALLY NOTICED...
EH-HEH!!

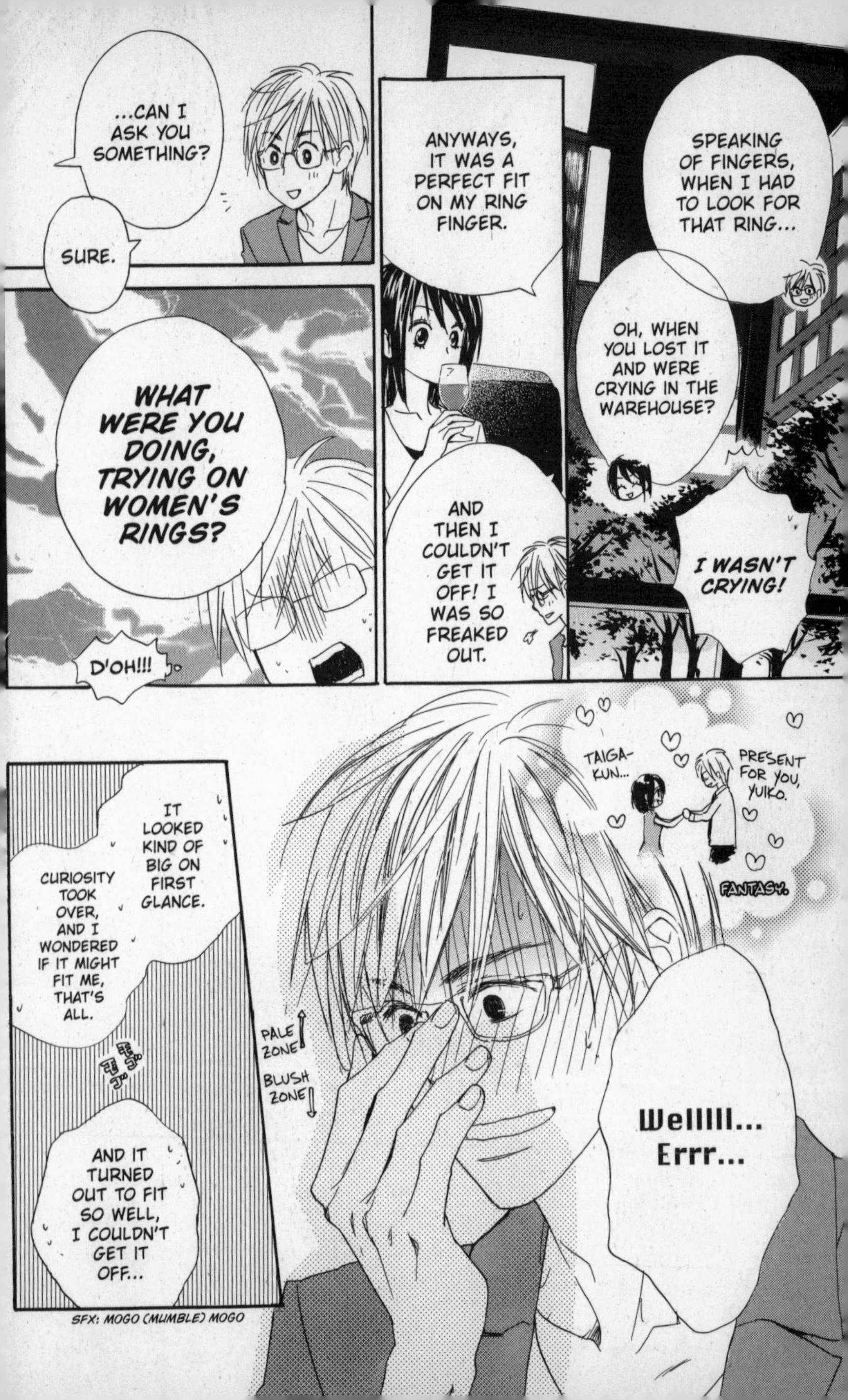
SPEAKING OF FINGERS, WHEN I HAD TO LOOK FOR THAT RING...
OH, WHEN YOU LOST IT AND WERE CRYING IN THE WAREHOUSE?
I WASN'T CRYING!
ANYWAYS, IT WAS A PERFECT FIT ON MY RING FINGER.
AND THEN I COULDN'T GET IT OFF! I WAS SO FREAKED OUT.
...CAN I ASK YOU SOMETHING?
SURE.
WHAT WERE YOU DOING, TRYING ON WOMEN'S RINGS?
D'OH!!!
PRESENT FOR YOU, YUIKO.
TAIGA-KUN...
FANTASY.
Wellllll... Errr...
PALE ZONE
BLUSH ZONE
IT LOOKED KIND OF BIG ON FIRST GLANCE.
CURIOSITY TOOK OVER, AND I WONDERED IF IT MIGHT FIT ME, THAT'S ALL.
AND IT TURNED OUT TO FIT SO WELL, I COULDN'T GET IT OFF...
SFX: MOGO (MUMBLE) MOGO

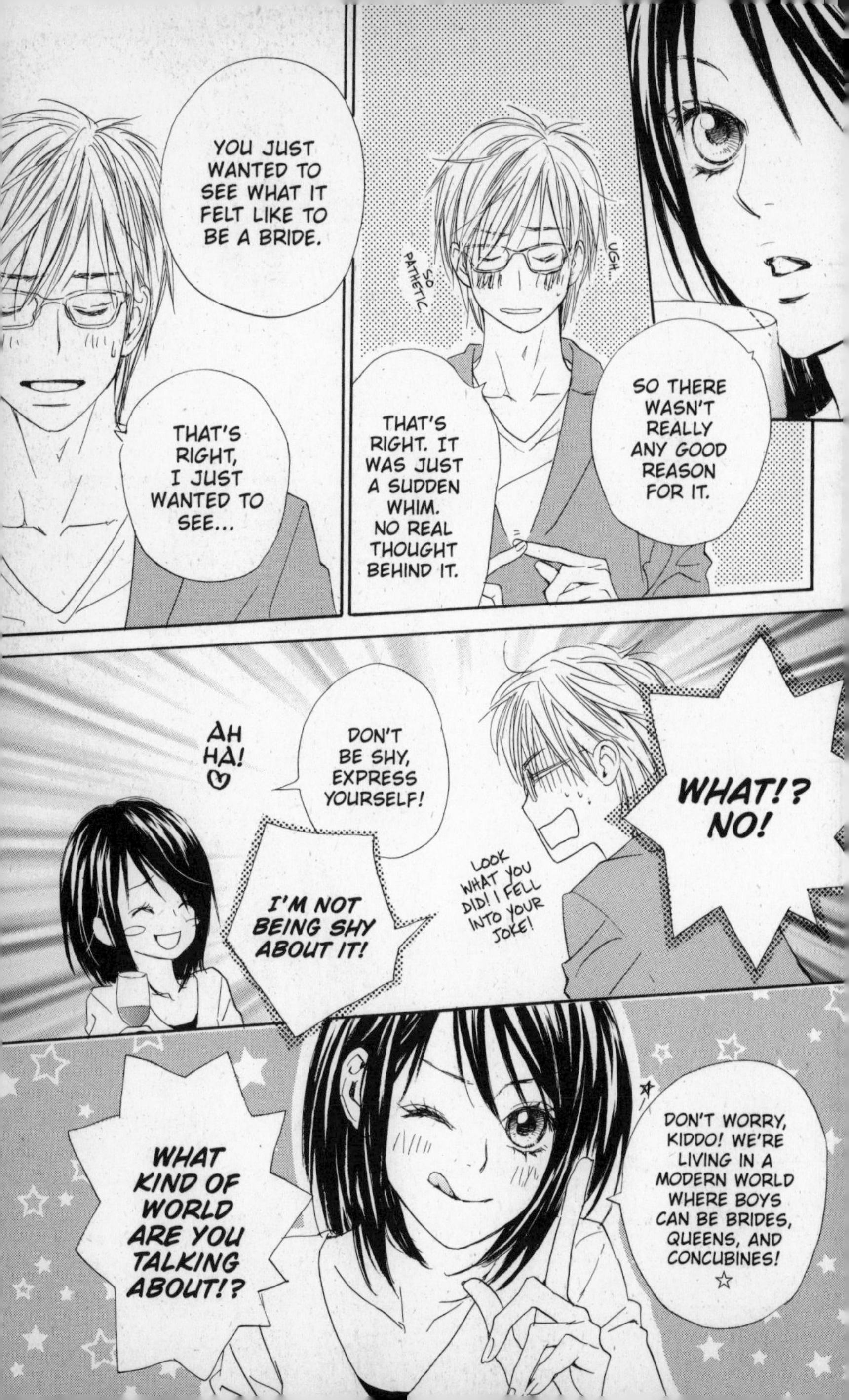
SO THERE WASN'T REALLY ANY GOOD REASON FOR IT.
UGH...
SO PATHETIC
THAT'S RIGHT. IT WAS JUST A SUDDEN WHIM. NO REAL THOUGHT BEHIND IT.
YOU JUST WANTED TO SEE WHAT IT FELT LIKE TO BE A BRIDE.
THAT'S RIGHT, I JUST WANTED TO SEE...
WHAT!? NO!
LOOK WHAT YOU DID! I FELL INTO YOUR JOKE!
DON'T BE SHY, EXPRESS YOURSELF!
AH HA!
I'M NOT BEING SHY ABOUT IT!
DON'T WORRY, KIDDO! WE'RE LIVING IN A MODERN WORLD WHERE BOYS CAN BE BRIDES, QUEENS, AND CONCUBINES! ☆
WHAT KIND OF WORLD ARE YOU TALKING ABOUT!?

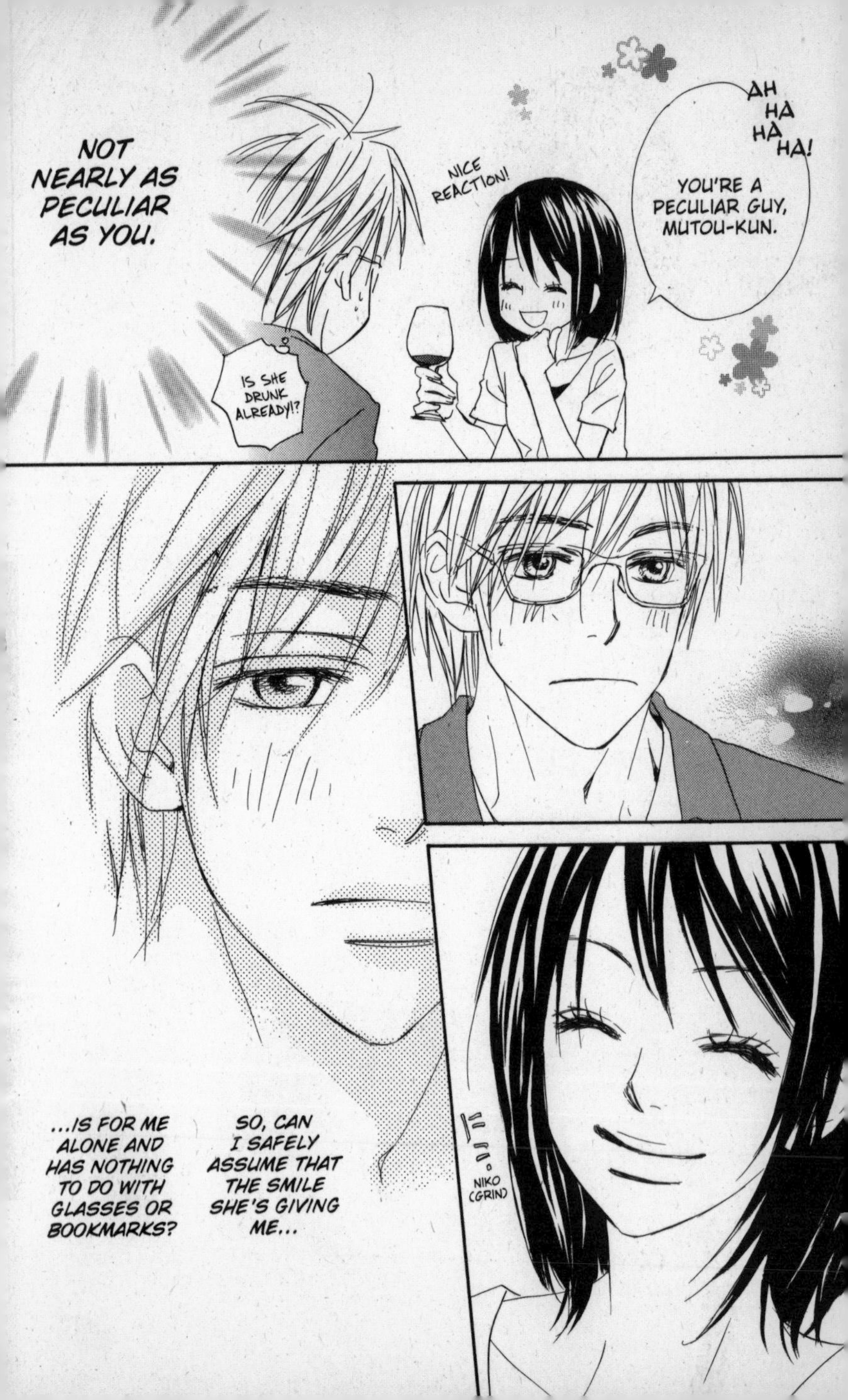
AH HA HA HA!
YOU'RE A PECULIAR GUY, MUTOU-KUN.
NICE REACTION!
IS SHE DRUNK ALREADY!?
NOT NEARLY AS PECULIAR AS YOU.
NIKO (GRIN)
SO, CAN I SAFELY ASSUME THAT THE SMILE SHE'S GIVING ME...
...IS FOR ME ALONE AND HAS NOTHING TO DO WITH GLASSES OR BOOKMARKS?

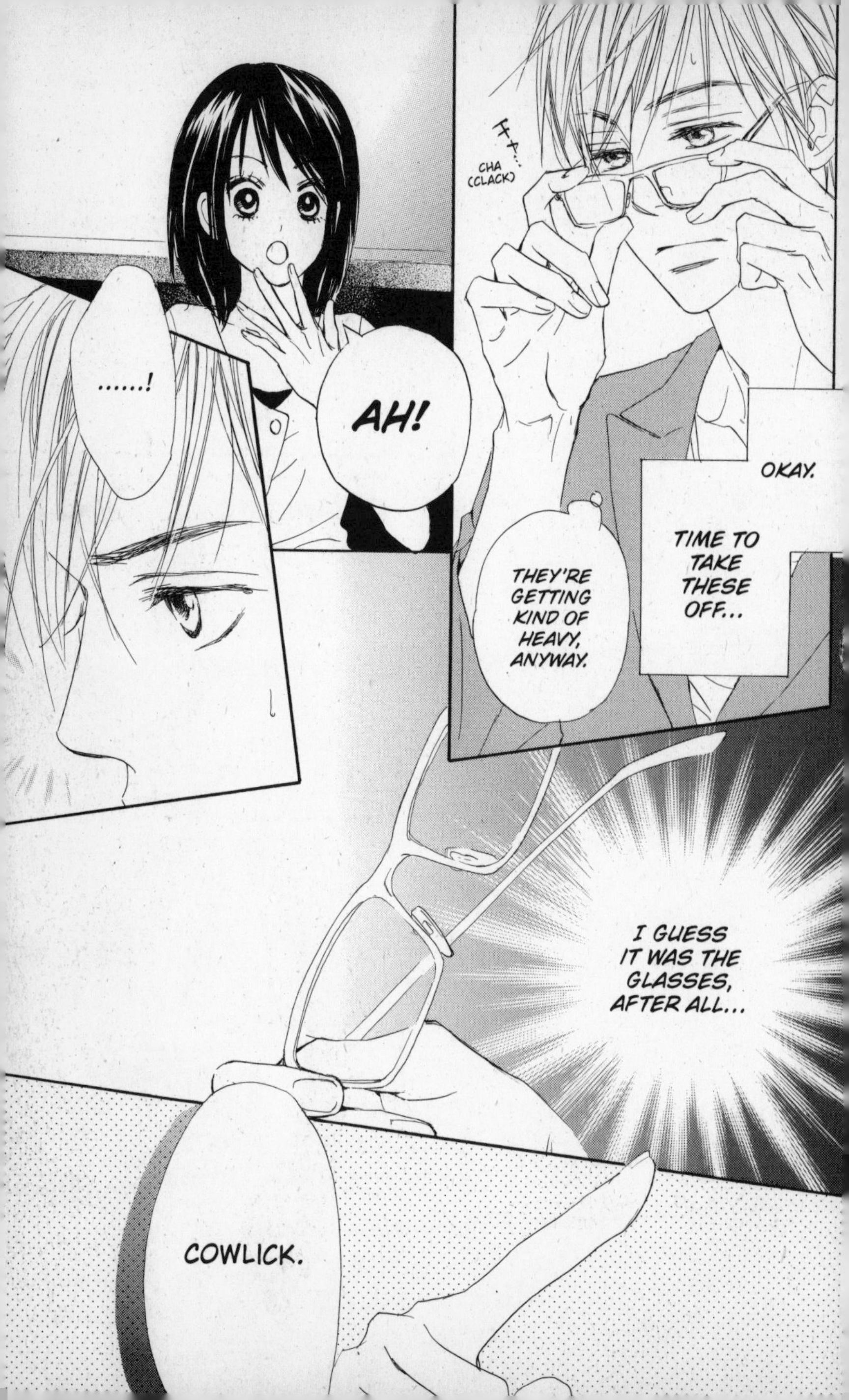
CHA (CLACK)
OKAY.
TIME TO TAKE THESE OFF...
THEY'RE GETTING KIND OF HEAVY, ANYWAY.
AH!
......!
I GUESS IT WAS THE GLASSES, AFTER ALL...
COWLICK.

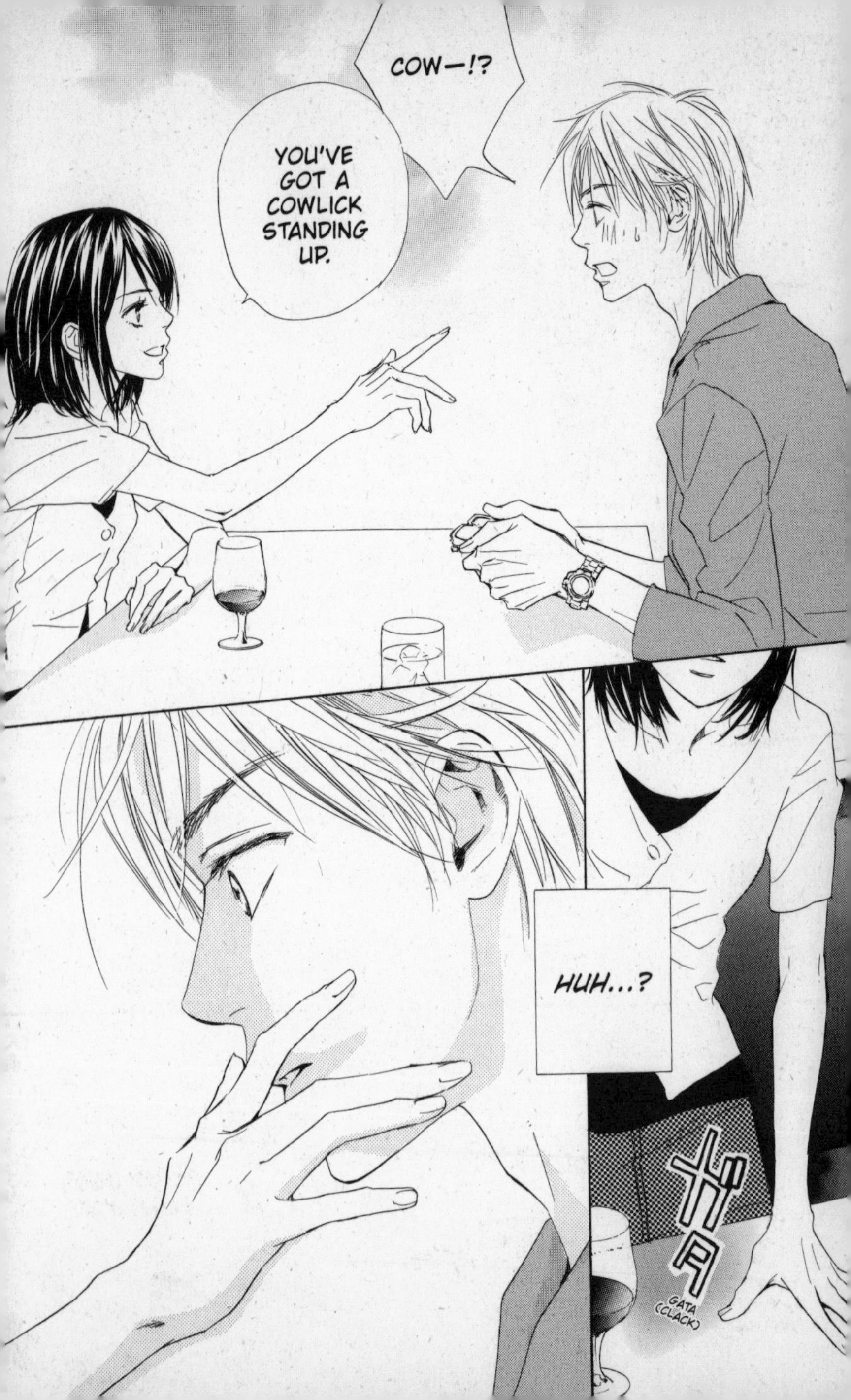
YOU'VE GOT A COWLICK STANDING UP.
COW—!?
HUH...?
GATA (CLACK)

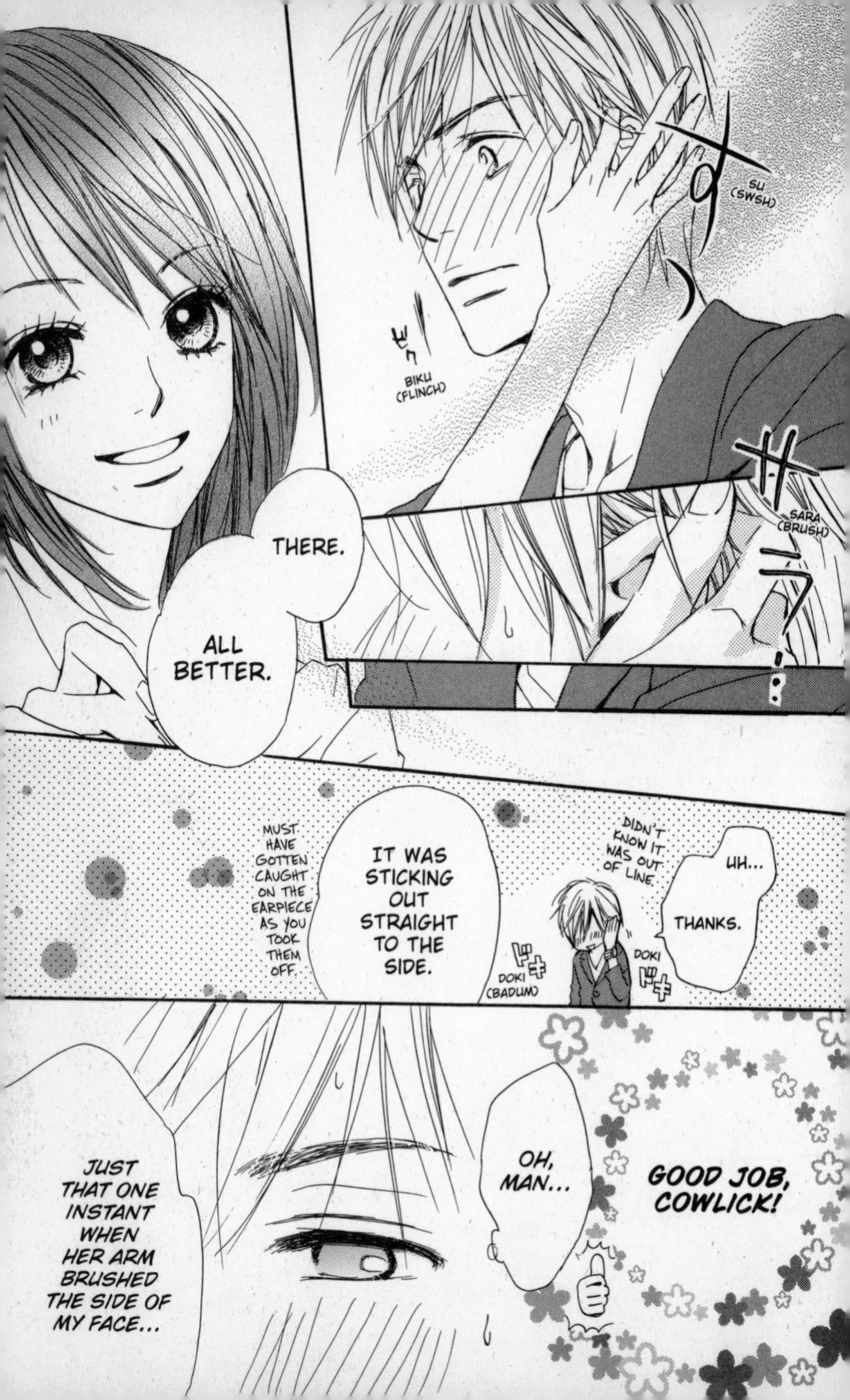
SU (SWSH)
BIKU (FLINCH)
SARA (BRUSH)
THERE.
ALL BETTER.
UH... THANKS.
DIDN'T KNOW IT WAS OUT OF LINE.
DOKI
DOKI (BADUM)
IT WAS STICKING OUT STRAIGHT TO THE SIDE.
MUST HAVE GOTTEN CAUGHT ON THE EARPIECE AS YOU TOOK THEM OFF.
GOOD JOB, COWLICK!
OH, MAN...
JUST THAT ONE INSTANT WHEN HER ARM BRUSHED THE SIDE OF MY FACE...

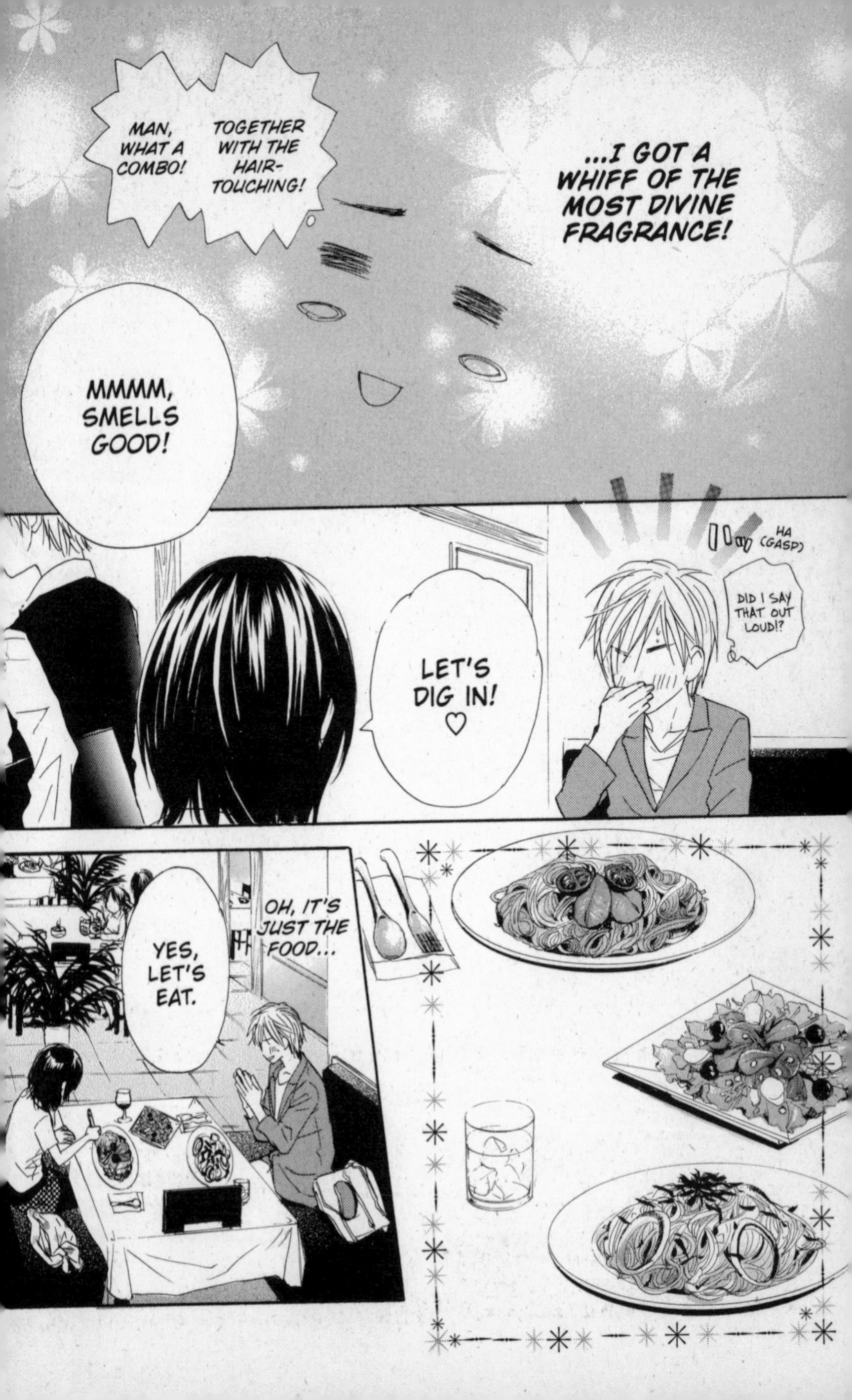
...I GOT A WHIFF OF THE MOST DIVINE FRAGRANCE!
TOGETHER WITH THE HAIR-TOUCHING!
MAN, WHAT A COMBO!
MMMM, SMELLS GOOD!
HA (GASP)
DID I SAY THAT OUT LOUD!?
LET'S DIG IN! ♡
OH, IT'S JUST THE FOOD...
YES, LET'S EAT.

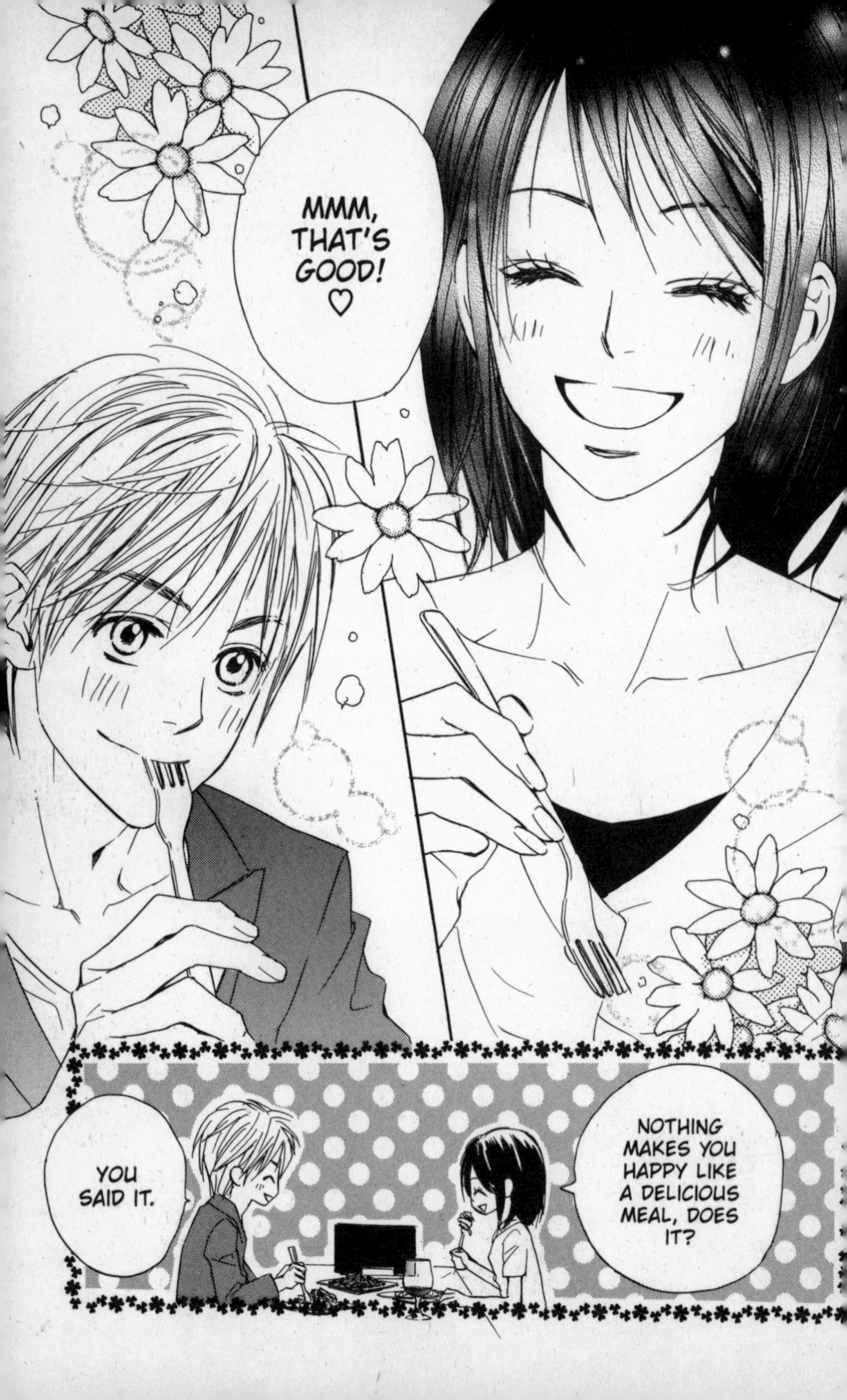
MMM, THAT'S GOOD! ♡
NOTHING MAKES YOU HAPPY LIKE A DELICIOUS MEAL, DOES IT?
YOU SAID IT.

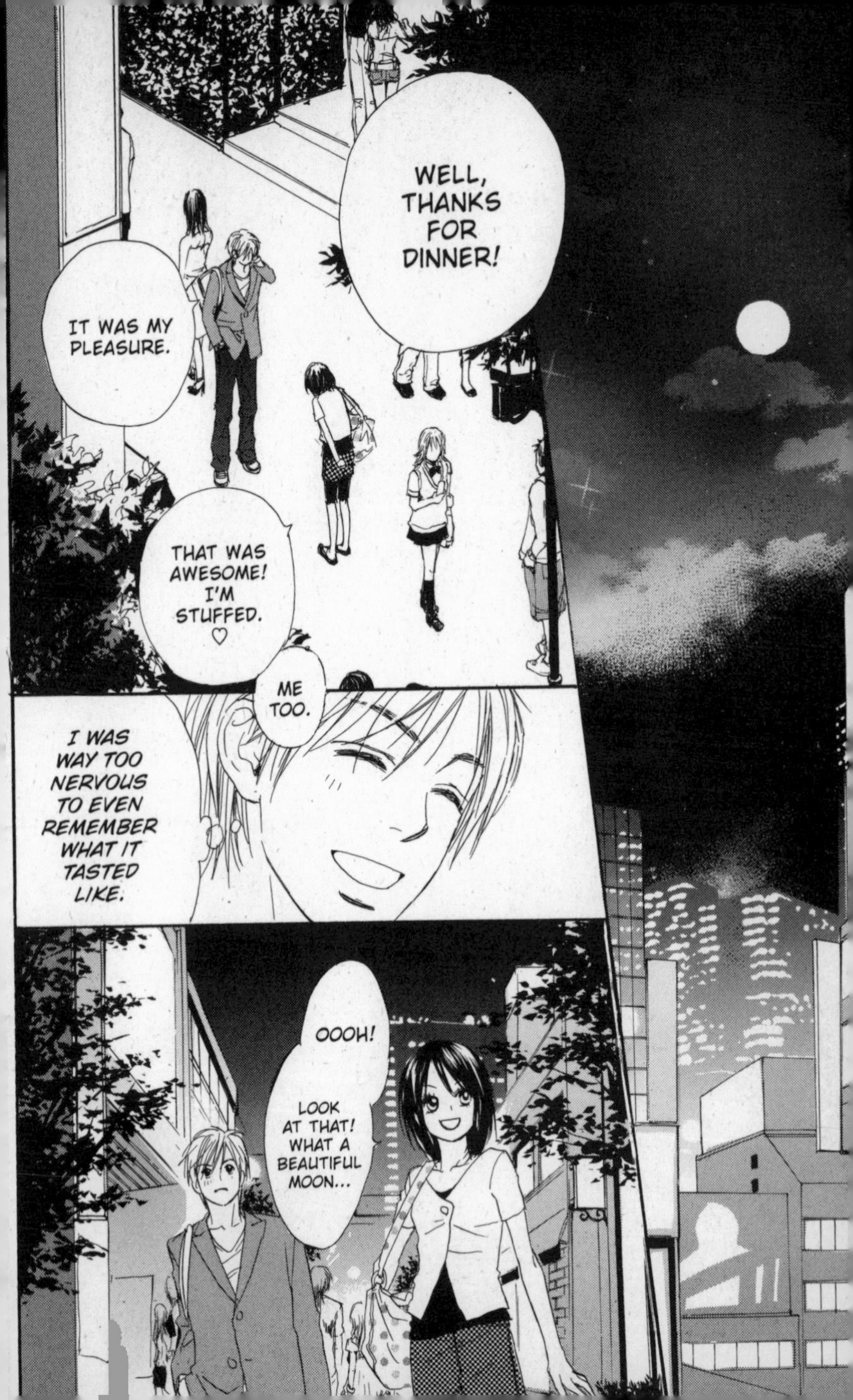
WELL, THANKS FOR DINNER!
IT WAS MY PLEASURE.
THAT WAS AWESOME! I'M STUFFED. ♡
ME TOO.
I WAS WAY TOO NERVOUS TO EVEN REMEMBER WHAT IT TASTED LIKE.
OOOH!
LOOK AT THAT! WHAT A BEAUTIFUL MOON...

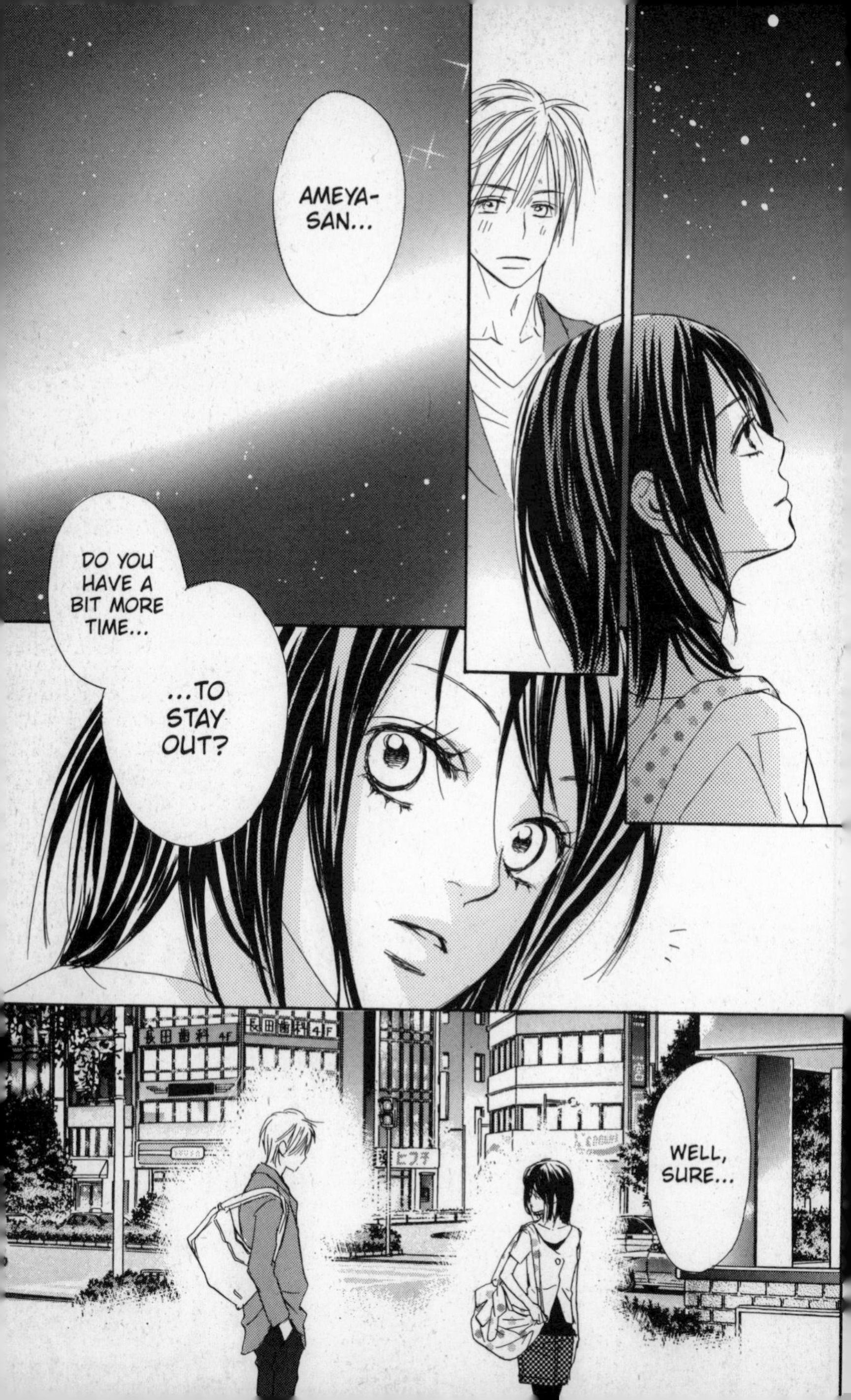
AMEYA-SAN...
DO YOU HAVE A BIT MORE TIME...
...TO STAY OUT?
WELL, SURE...

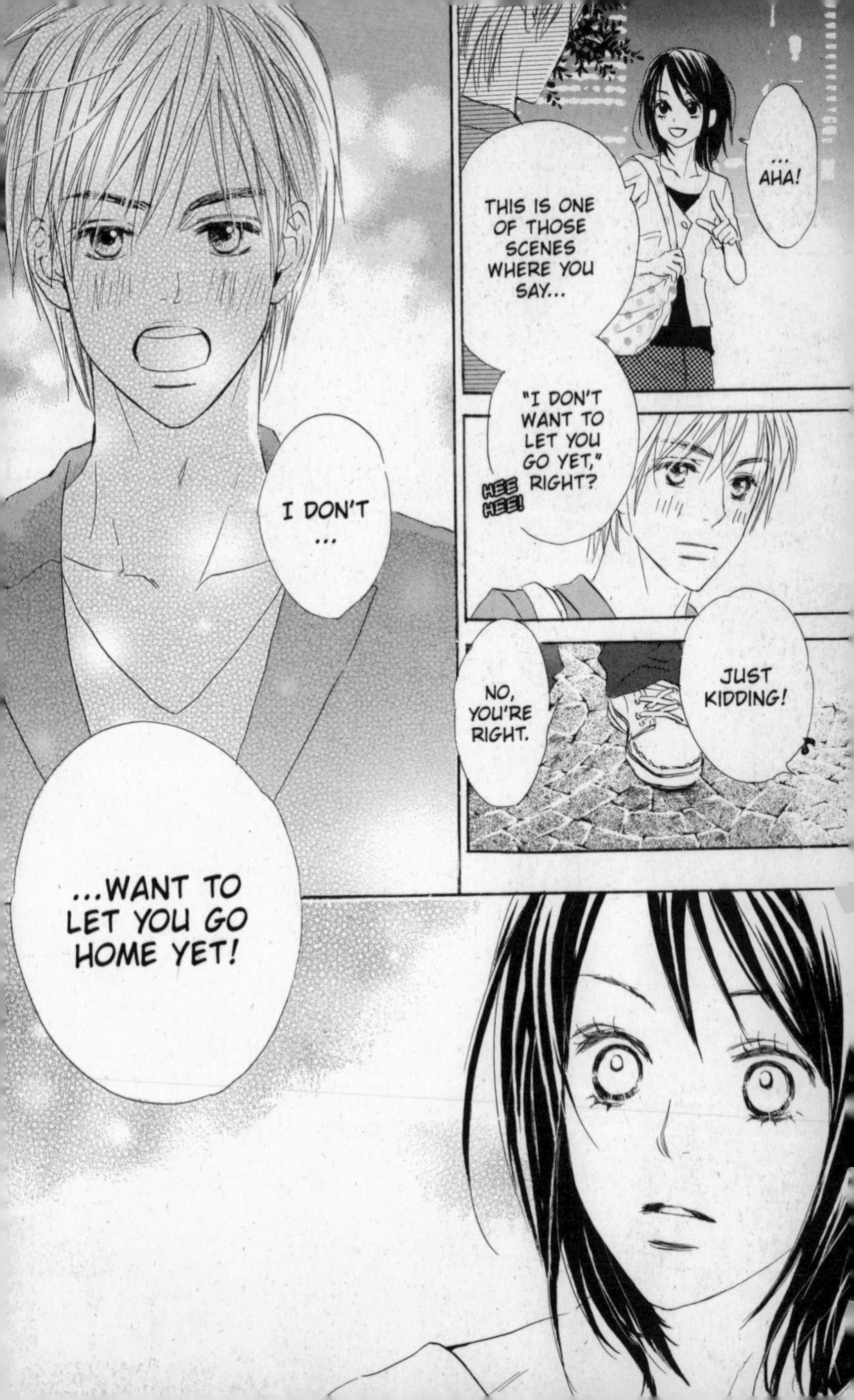
...AHA!
THIS IS ONE OF THOSE SCENES WHERE YOU SAY...
"I DON'T WANT TO LET YOU GO YET," RIGHT?
HEE HEE!
JUST KIDDING!
NO, YOU'RE RIGHT.
I DON'T ...
...WANT TO LET YOU GO HOME YET!

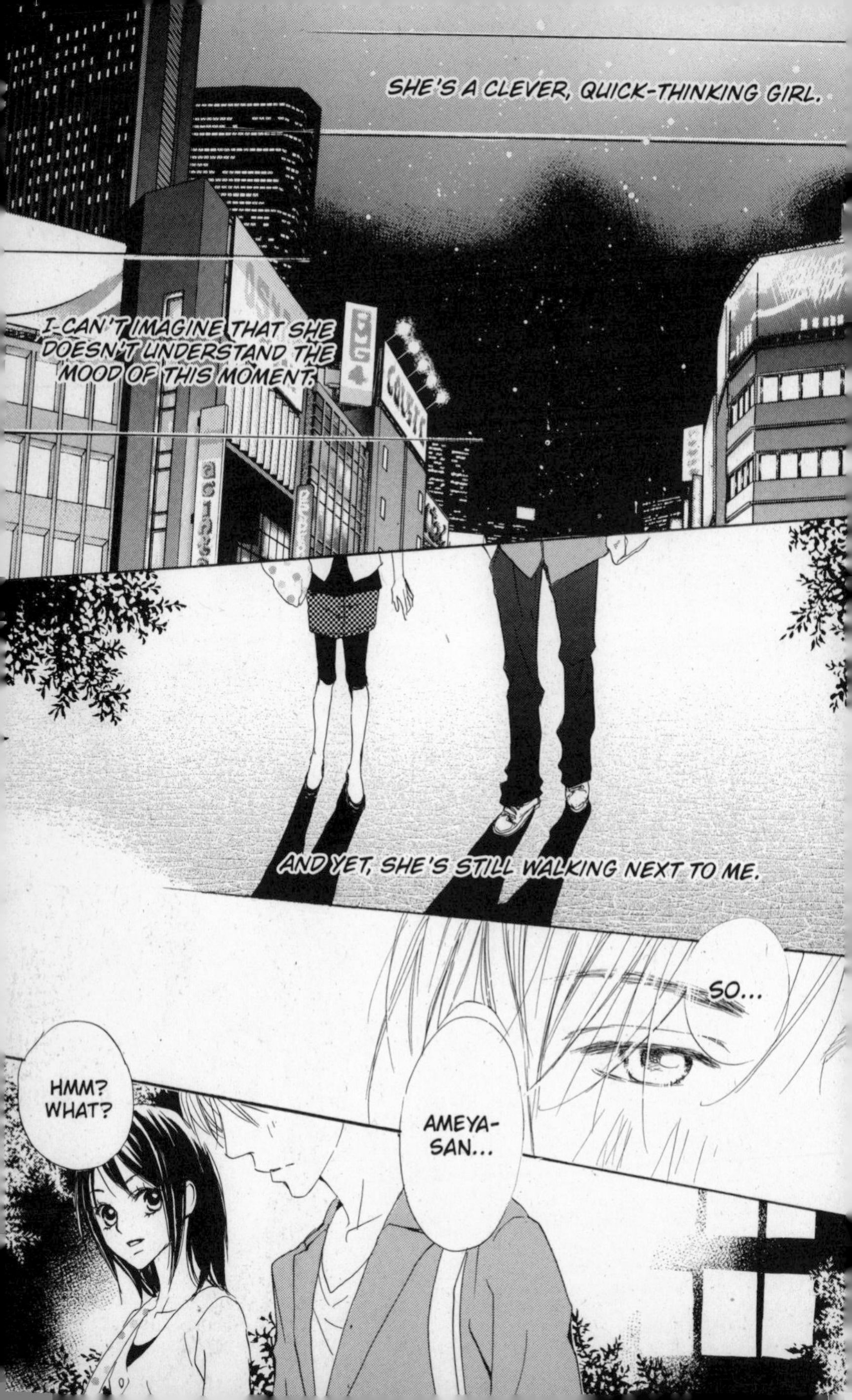
SHE'S A CLEVER, QUICK-THINKING GIRL.
I CAN'T IMAGINE THAT SHE DOESN'T UNDERSTAND THE MOOD OF THIS MOMENT.
AND YET, SHE'S STILL WALKING NEXT TO ME.
SO...
AMEYA-SAN...
HMM? WHAT?

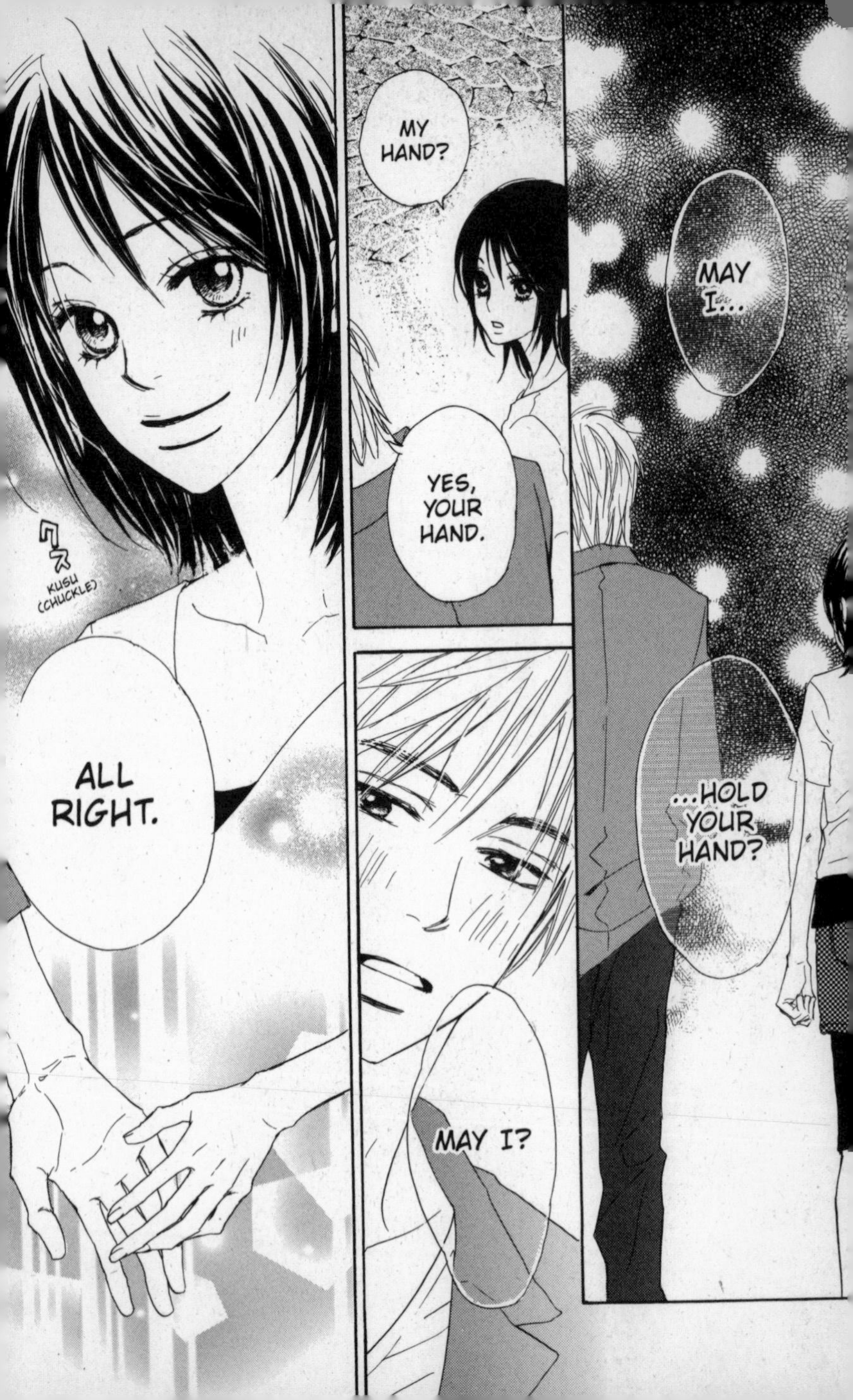
MAY I...
...HOLD YOUR HAND?
MY HAND?
YES, YOUR HAND.
MAY I?
クス
KUSU (CHUCKLE)
ALL RIGHT.

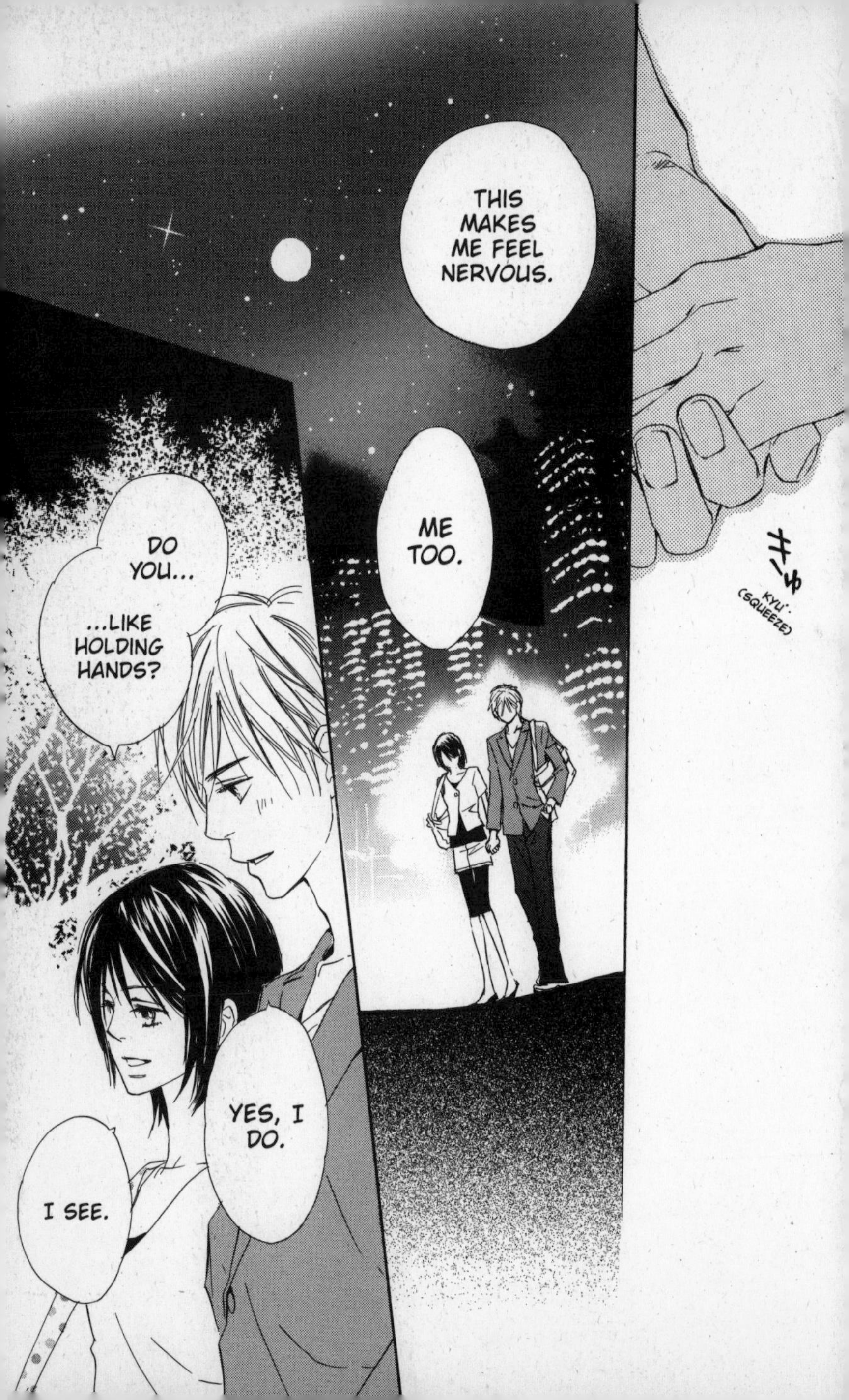
KYU'
(SQUEEZE)
THIS MAKES ME FEEL NERVOUS.
ME TOO.
DO YOU...
...LIKE HOLDING HANDS?
YES, I DO.
I SEE.

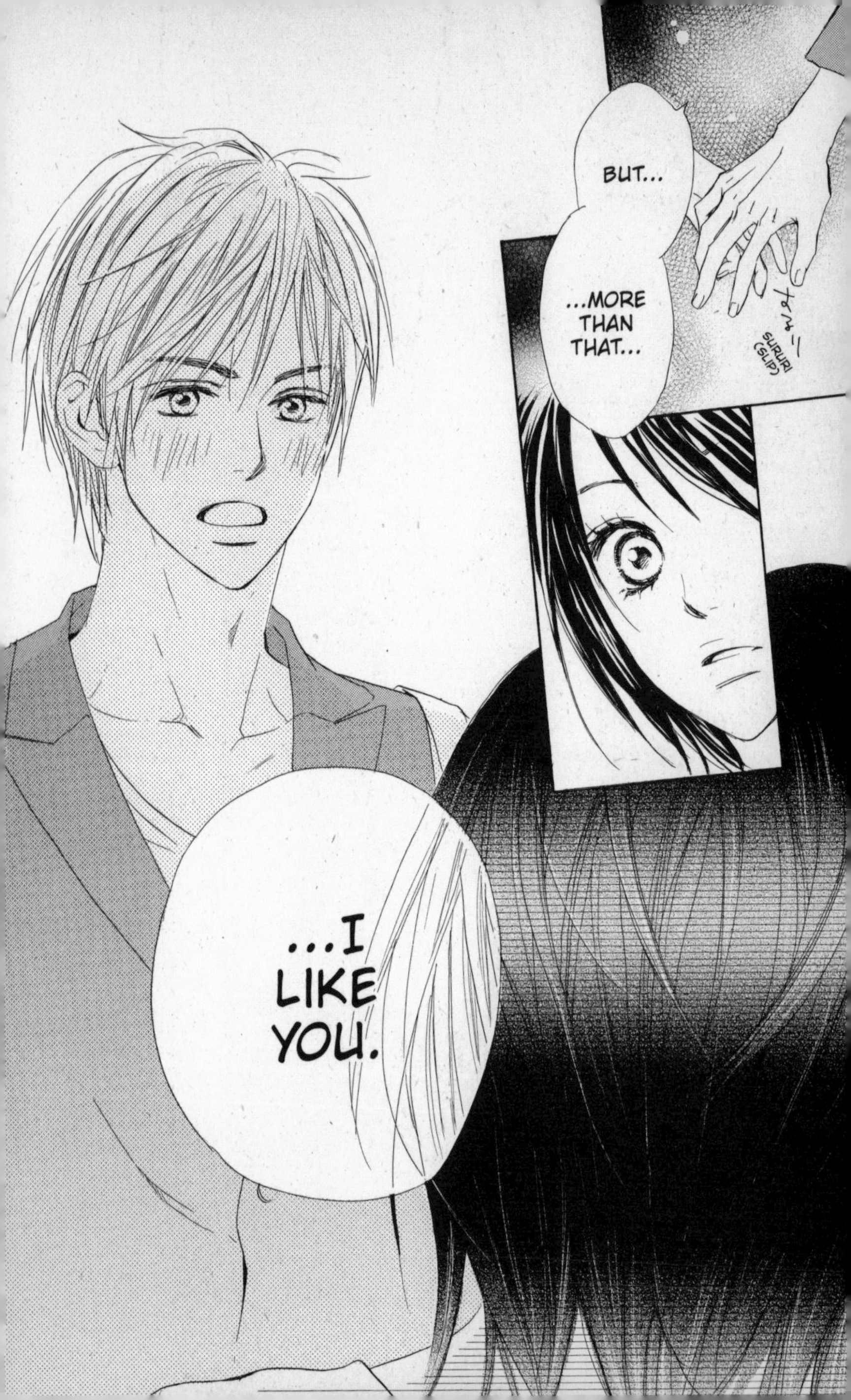
BUT...
SURURI (SLIP)
...MORE THAN THAT...
...I LIKE YOU.

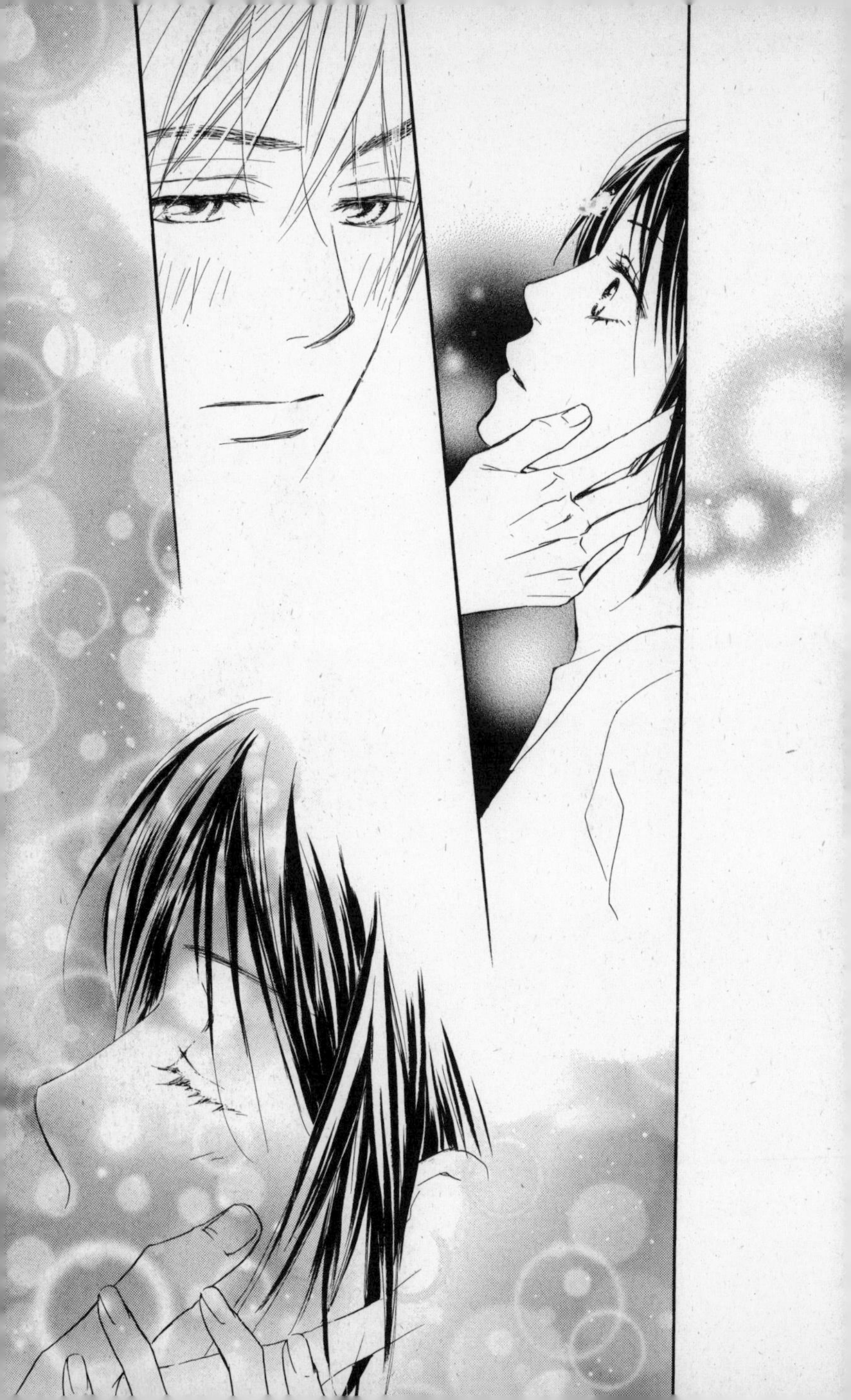

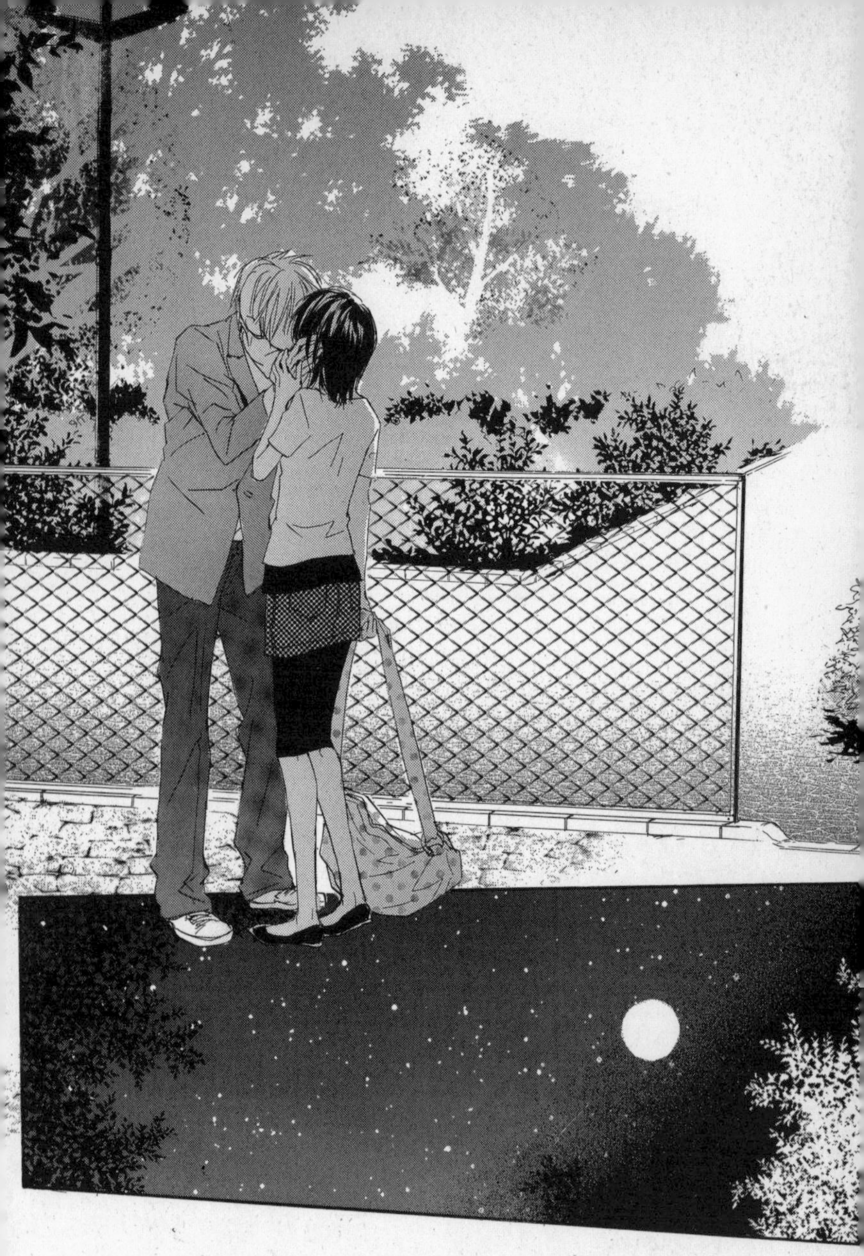

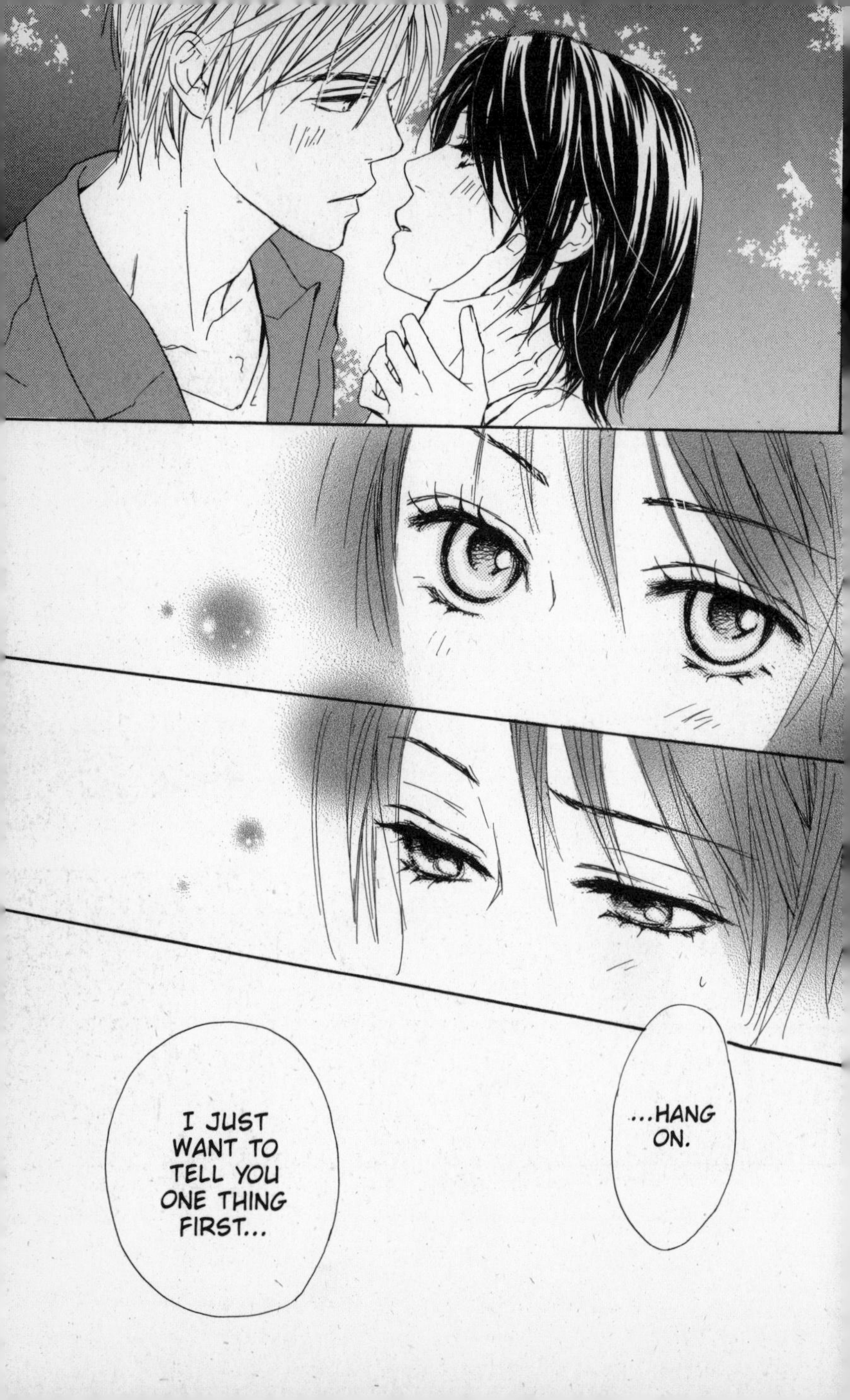
...HANG ON.
I JUST WANT TO TELL YOU ONE THING FIRST...

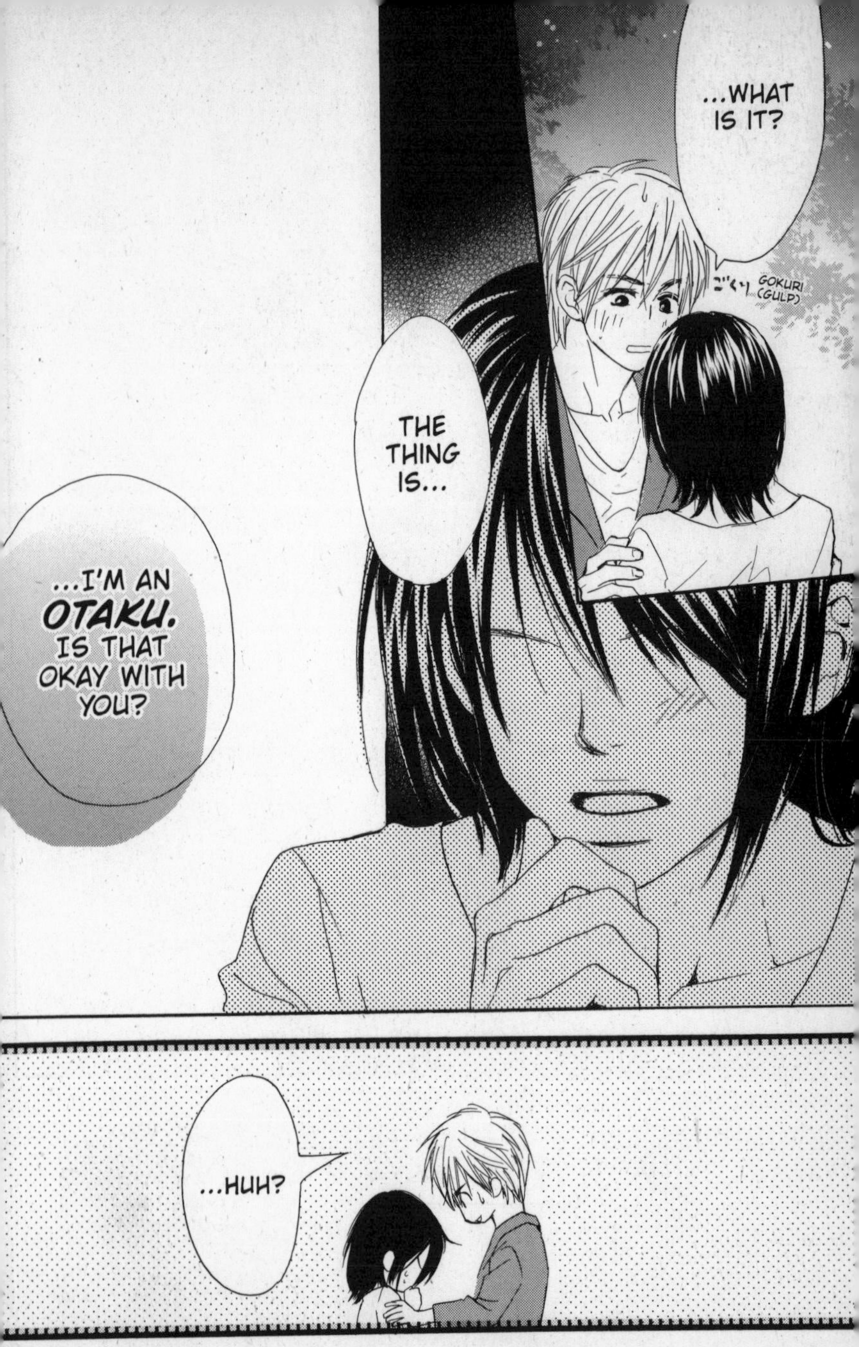
...WHAT IS IT?
ごくり GOKURI (GULP)
THE THING IS...
...I'M AN *OTAKU.* IS THAT OKAY WITH YOU?
...HUH?

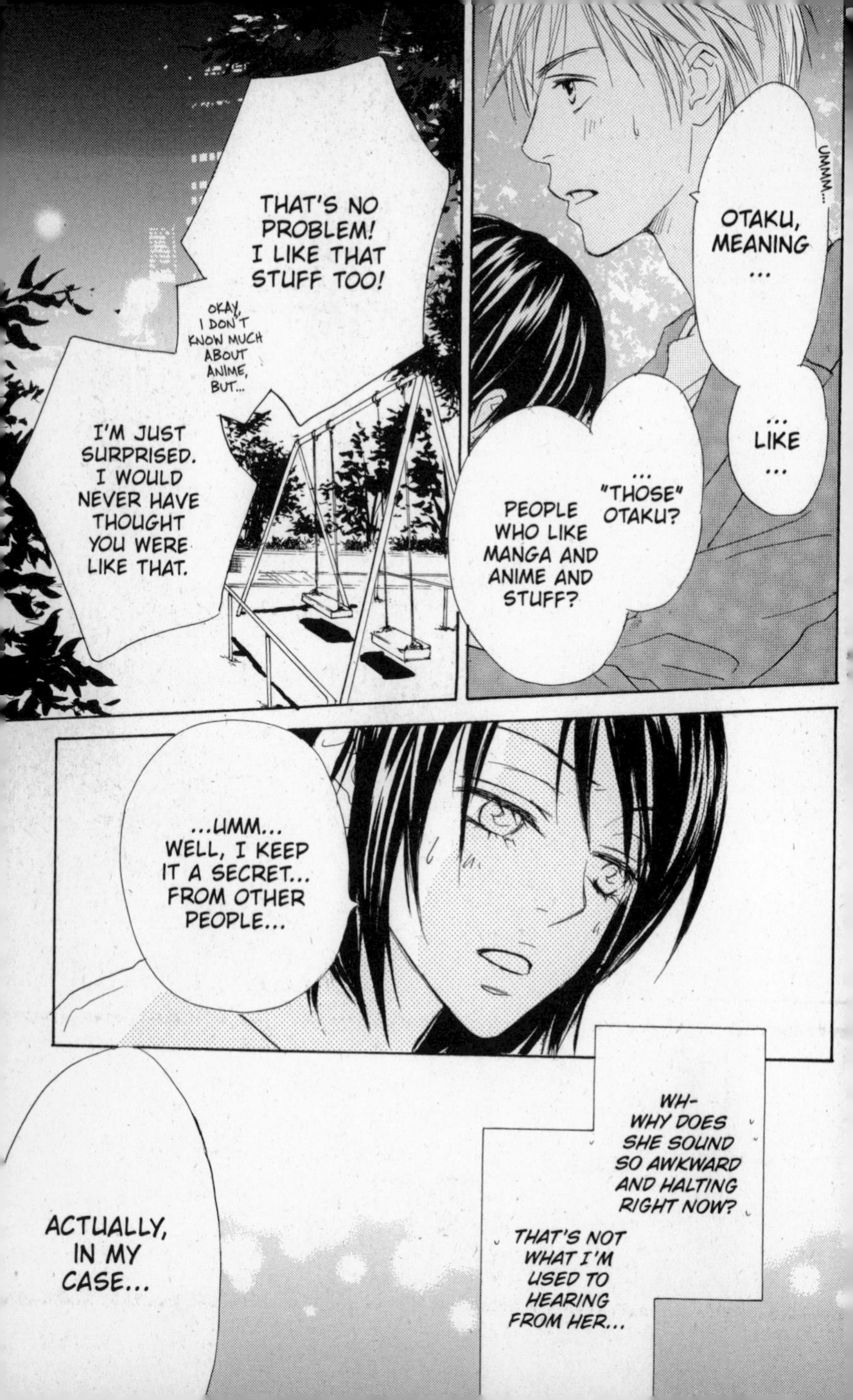
UMMM...
OTAKU, MEANING ...
... LIKE ...
... "THOSE" OTAKU?
PEOPLE WHO LIKE MANGA AND ANIME AND STUFF?
THAT'S NO PROBLEM! I LIKE THAT STUFF TOO!
OKAY, I DON'T KNOW MUCH ABOUT ANIME, BUT...
I'M JUST SURPRISED. I WOULD NEVER HAVE THOUGHT YOU WERE LIKE THAT.
...UMM... WELL, I KEEP IT A SECRET... FROM OTHER PEOPLE...
WH- WHY DOES SHE SOUND SO AWKWARD AND HALTING RIGHT NOW?
THAT'S NOT WHAT I'M USED TO HEARING FROM HER...
ACTUALLY, IN MY CASE...

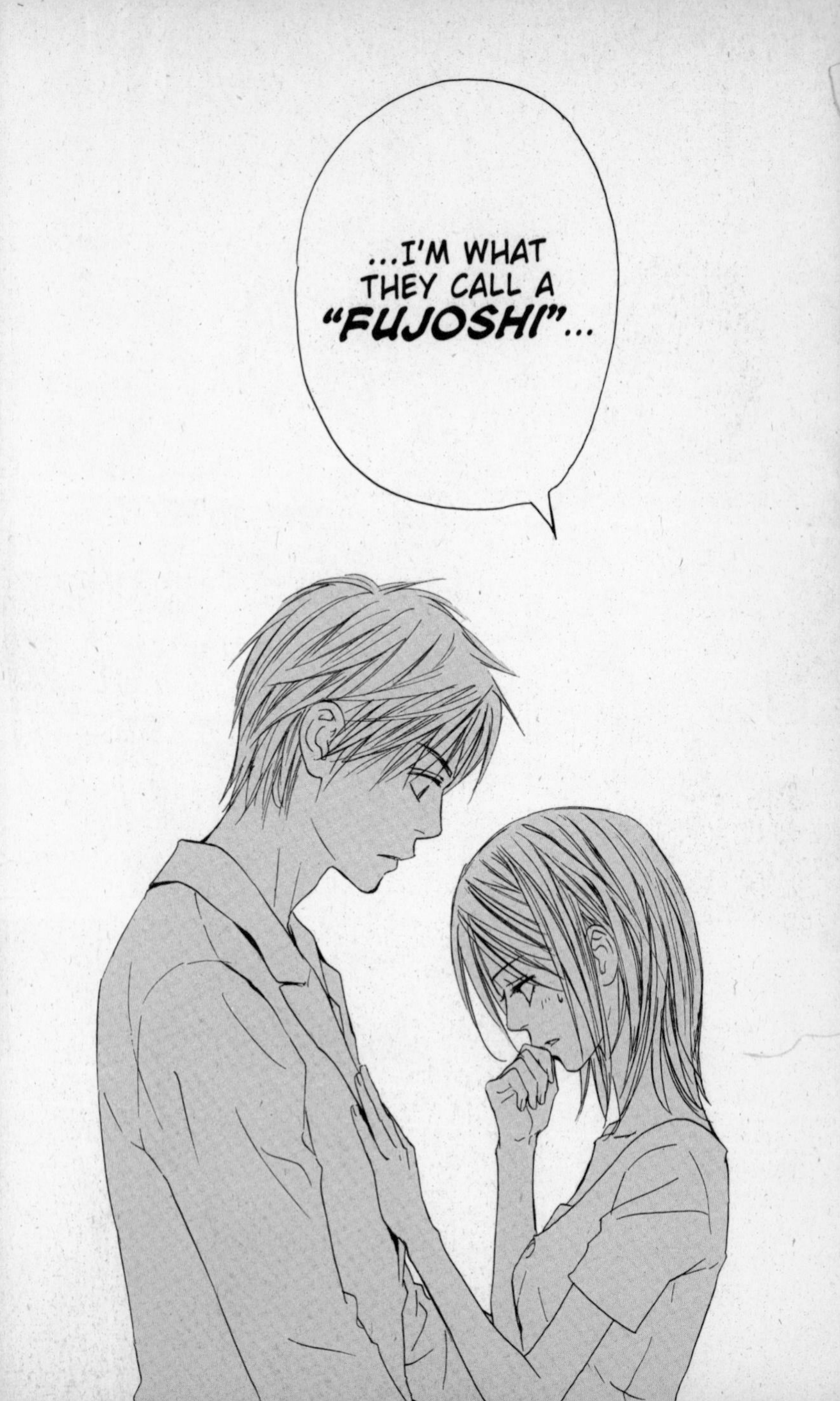
...I'M WHAT THEY CALL A "FUJOSHI"...

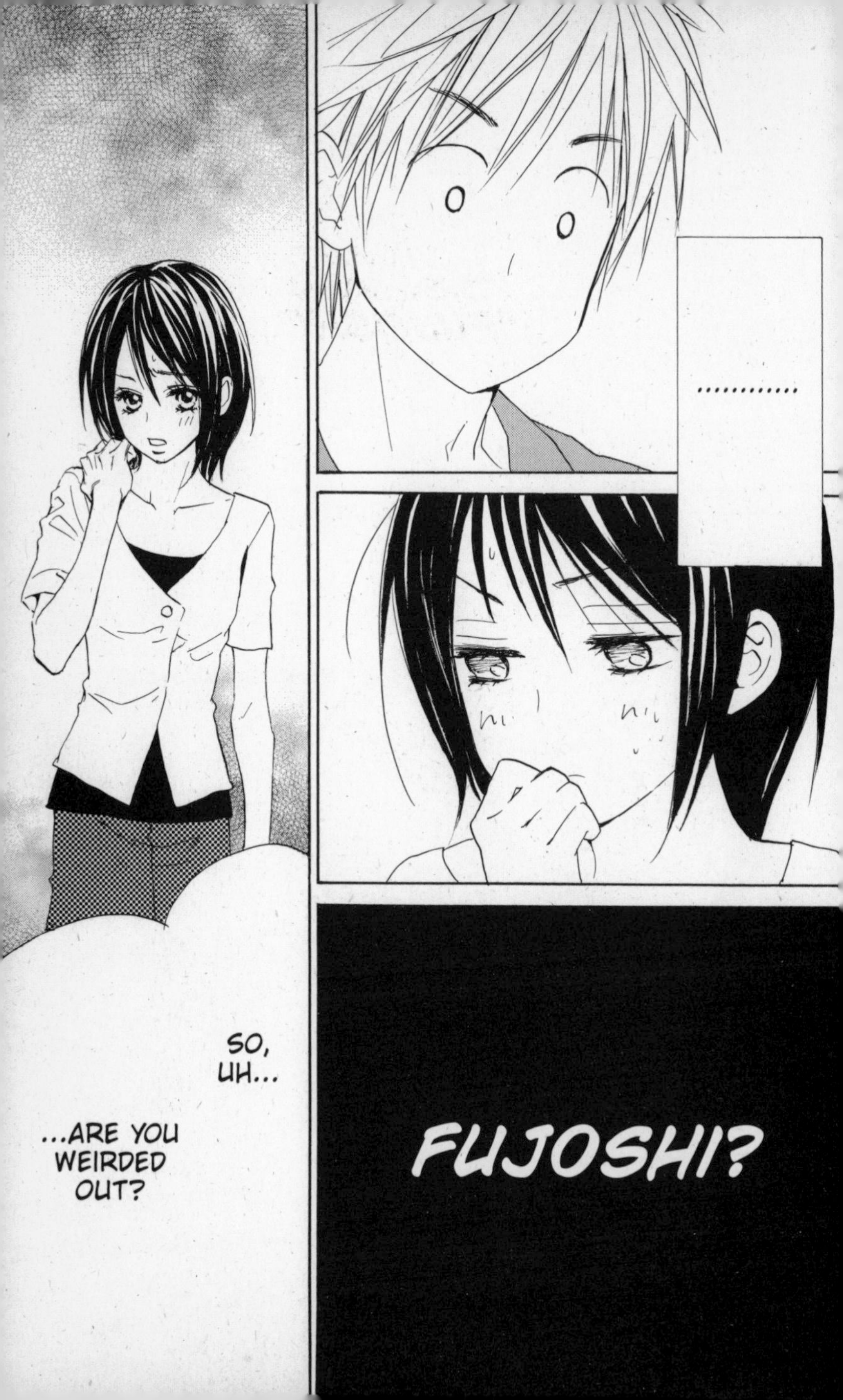

....
FUJOSHI?
SO, UH...
...ARE YOU WEIRDED OUT?

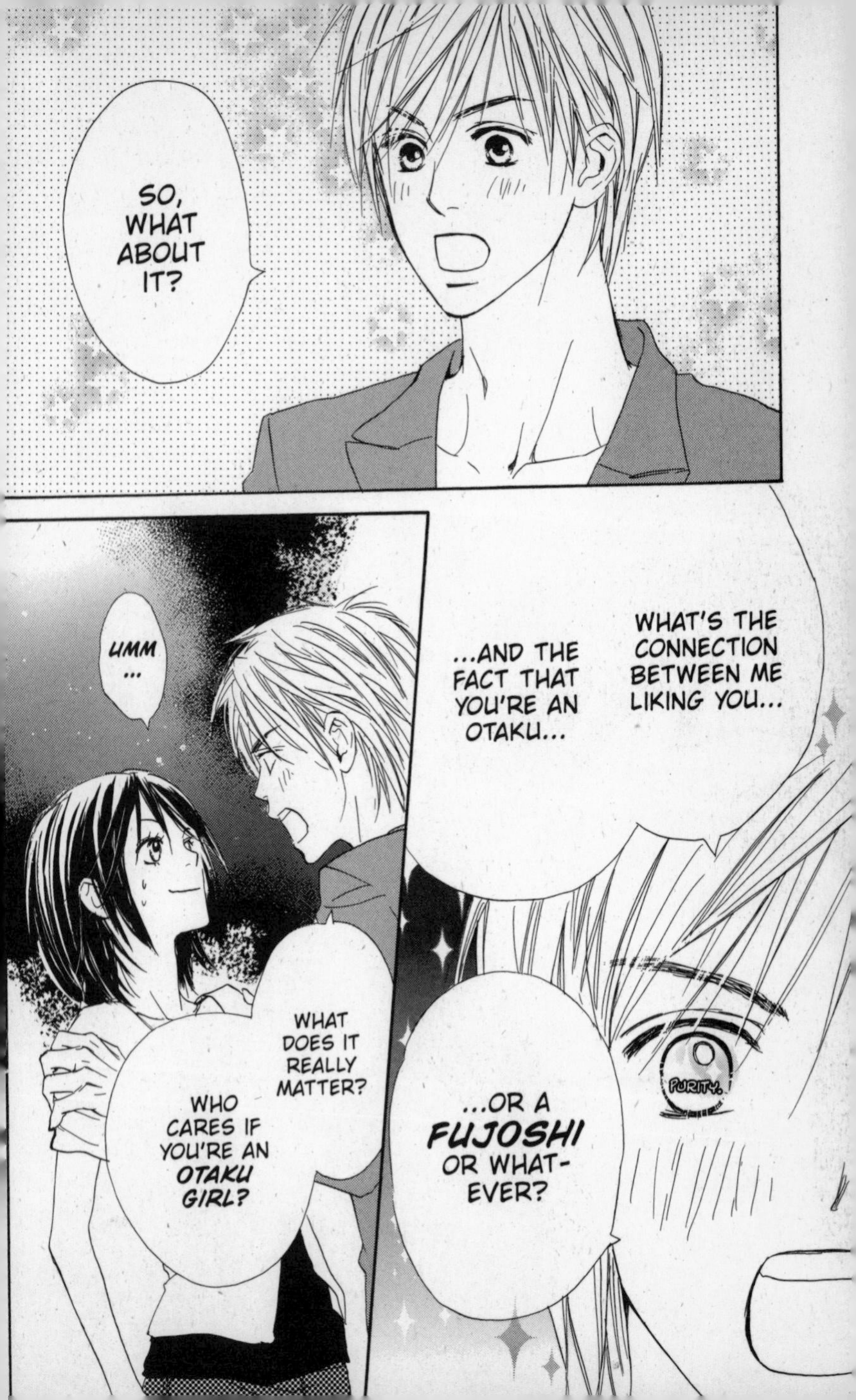
SO, WHAT ABOUT IT?
WHAT'S THE CONNECTION BETWEEN ME LIKING YOU...
...AND THE FACT THAT YOU'RE AN OTAKU...
...OR A FUJOSHI OR WHAT-EVER?
PURITY.
UMM...
WHAT DOES IT REALLY MATTER?
WHO CARES IF YOU'RE AN OTAKU GIRL?

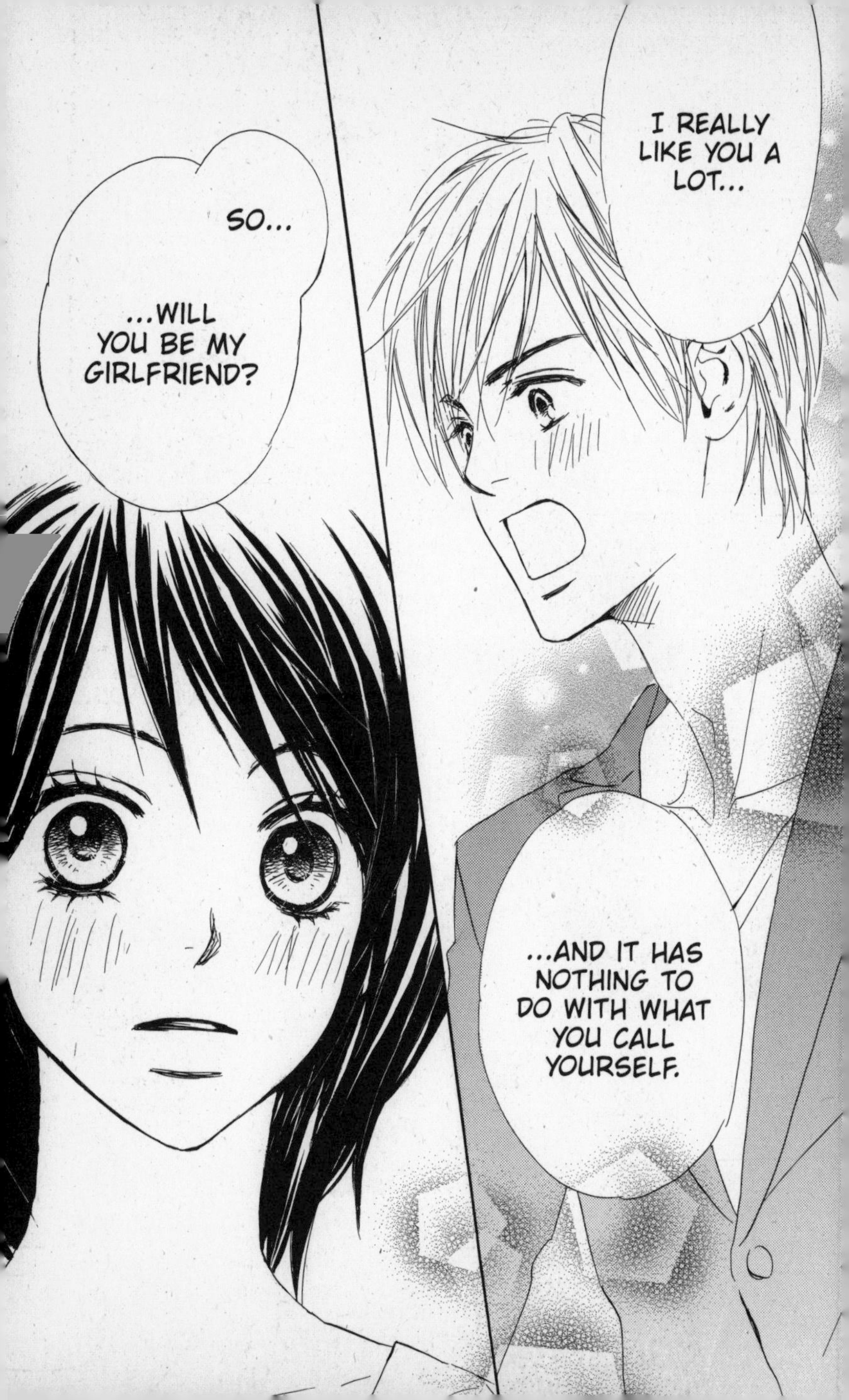
I REALLY LIKE YOU A LOT...
...AND IT HAS NOTHING TO DO WITH WHAT YOU CALL YOURSELF.
SO...
...WILL YOU BE MY GIRLFRIEND?

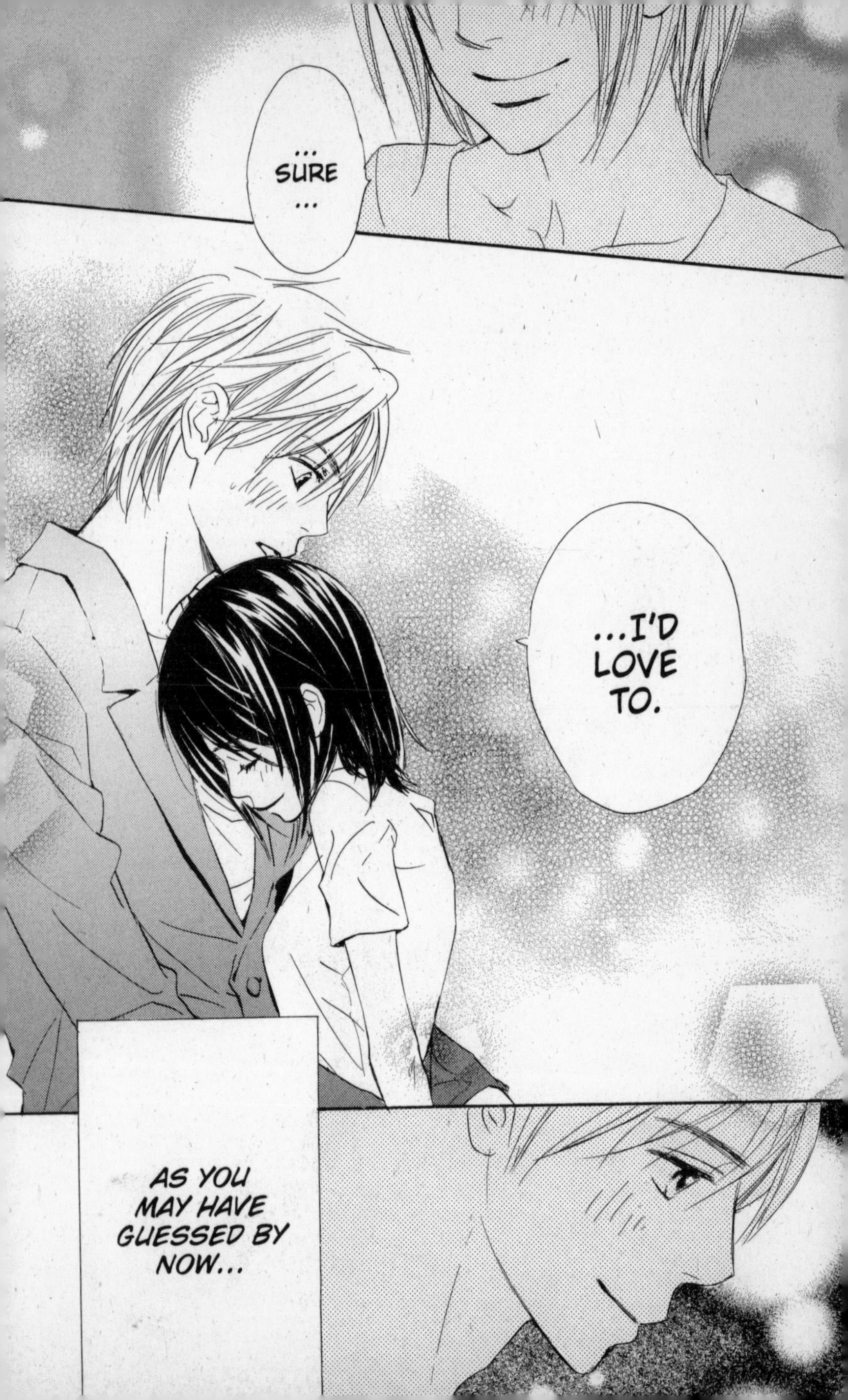

... SURE ...
...I'D LOVE TO.
AS YOU MAY HAVE GUESSED BY NOW...

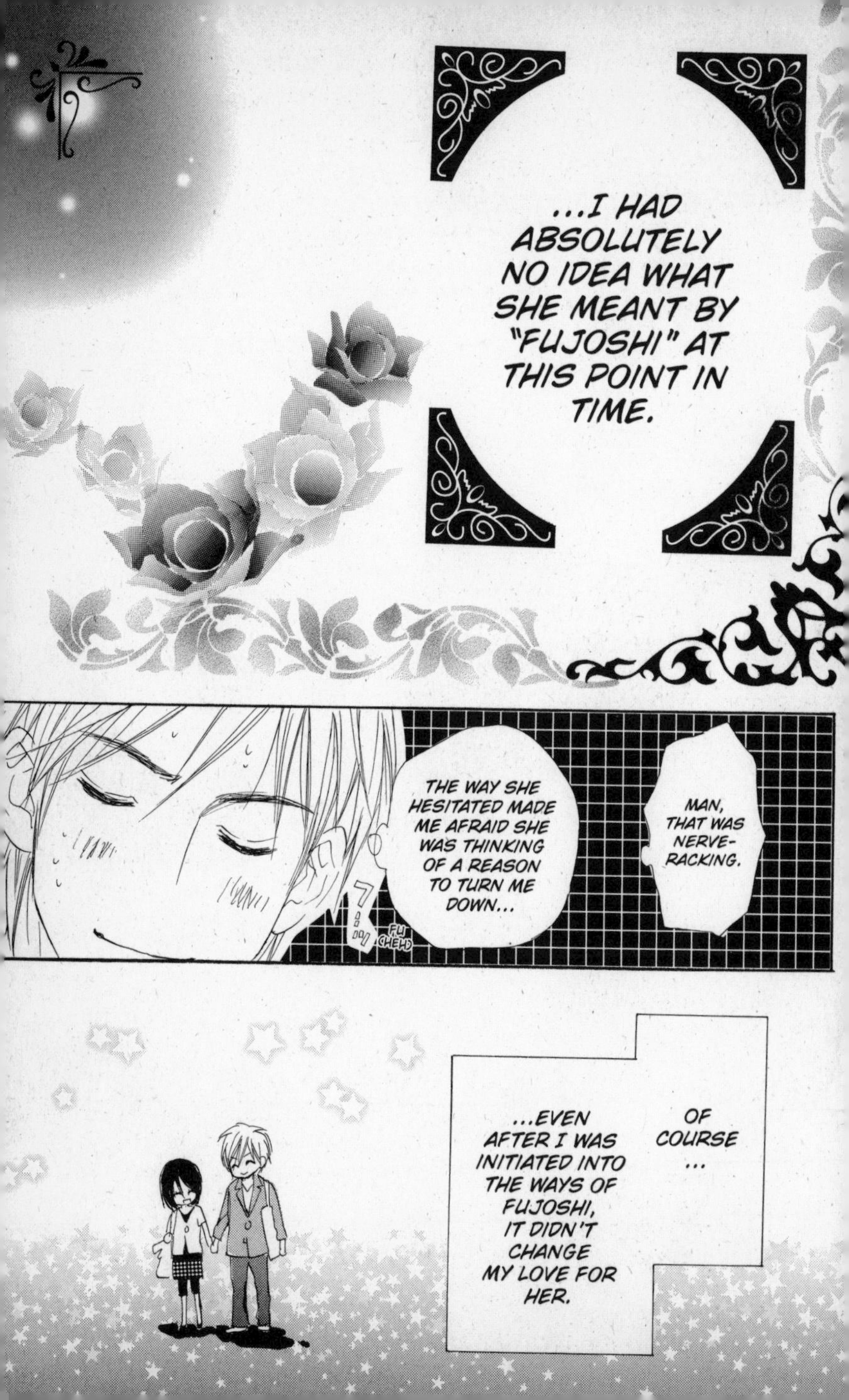
...I HAD ABSOLUTELY NO IDEA WHAT SHE MEANT BY "FUJOSHI" AT THIS POINT IN TIME.
MAN, THAT WAS NERVE-RACKING.
THE WAY SHE HESITATED MADE ME AFRAID SHE WAS THINKING OF A REASON TO TURN ME DOWN...
OF COURSE...
...EVEN AFTER I WAS INITIATED INTO THE WAYS OF FUJOSHI, IT DIDN'T CHANGE MY LOVE FOR HER.

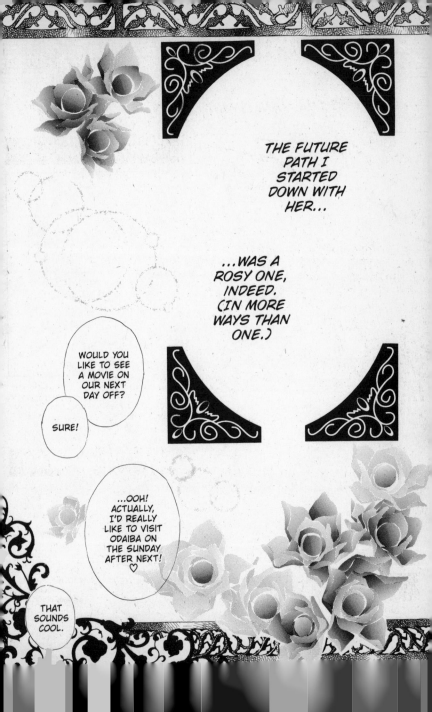

THE FUTURE PATH I STARTED DOWN WITH HER...

...WAS A ROSY ONE, INDEED. (IN MORE WAYS THAN ONE.)

WOULD YOU LIKE TO SEE A MOVIE ON OUR NEXT DAY OFF?

SURE!

...OOH! ACTUALLY, I'D REALLY LIKE TO VISIT ODAIBA ON THE SUNDAY AFTER NEXT! ♡

THAT SOUNDS COOL.

FUJOSHI NEWS vol.02

SECRETS OF "SEPATTE TAKURO" (2)

HERE ARE THE MAIN CHARACTERS OF "SEPATAKU"!!

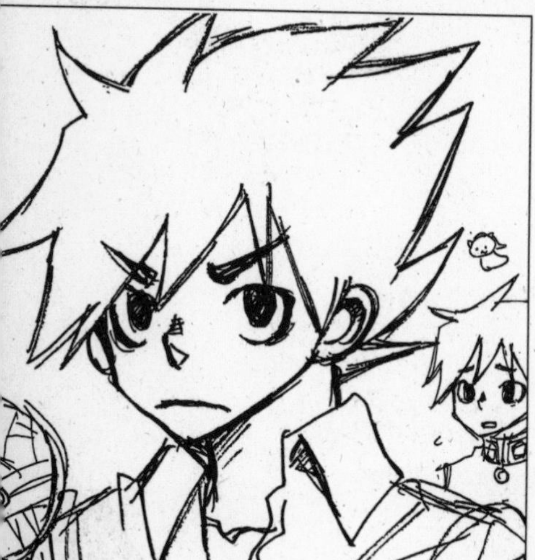

TAKURO SEBA (13)

NORMALLY SHY AND SLIGHTLY GLOOMY, BUT WHEN THE SPIRIT OF SEPAK TAKES OVER HIS BODY, HE BECOMES FIERCE AND FIERY. HE'S NEVER PLAYED SEPAK TAKRAW BEFORE IN HIS LIFE, BUT HE POSSESSES A NATURAL TALENT FOR THE GAME.

YUMA HIBINO (15)

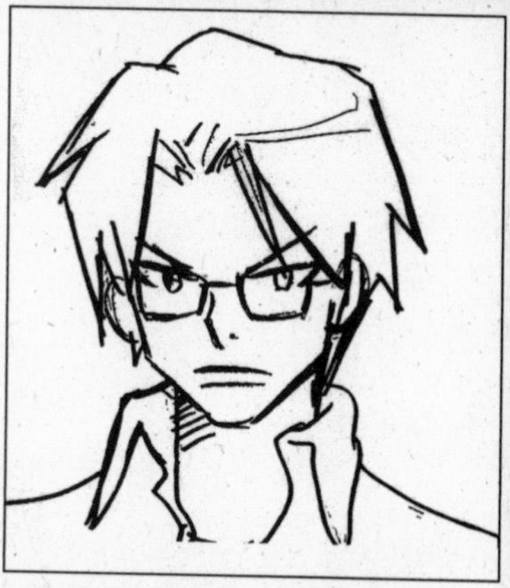

MAYA MIDDLE SCHOOL CLASS PRESIDENT AND SEPAK TAKRAW TEAM CAPTAIN. HE IS VERY SERIOUS AND METHODICAL, AND HAS BEEN PLAYING TAKRAW SINCE HE WAS A LITTLE BOY.

HIKARU HOSHIKAGE (14)

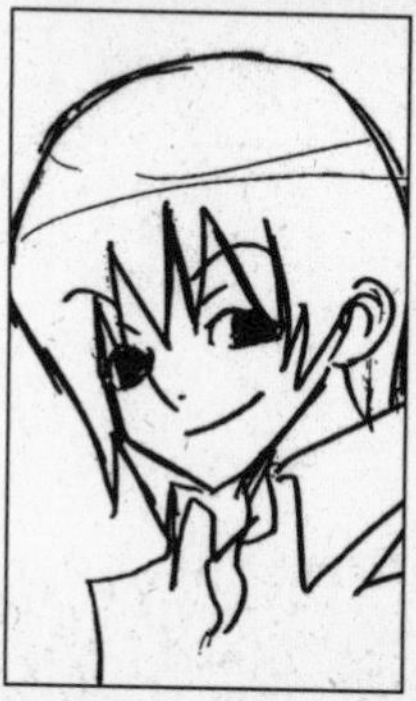

STAR PLAYER OF THE SEPAK TAKRAW TEAM. HE LEADS AN INNOCENT, EASYGOING LIFE. HE WAS BORN WITH A GIFT FOR TAKRAW, AND HIS BRILLIANT PLAY BREAKS ALL BOUNDARIES.

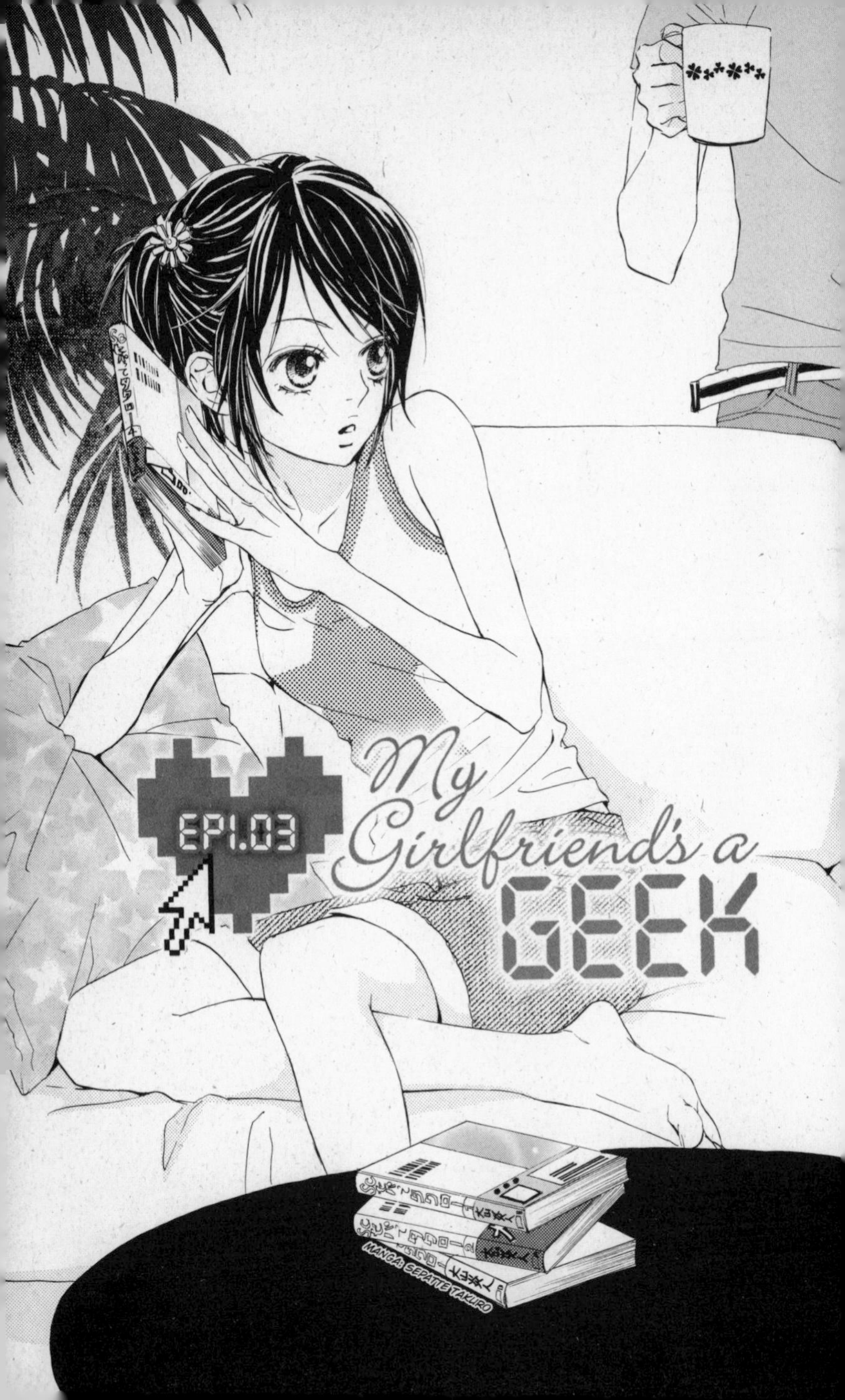
EP1.03
My Girlfriend's a
GEEK
MANGA: SEPATTE TAKURO

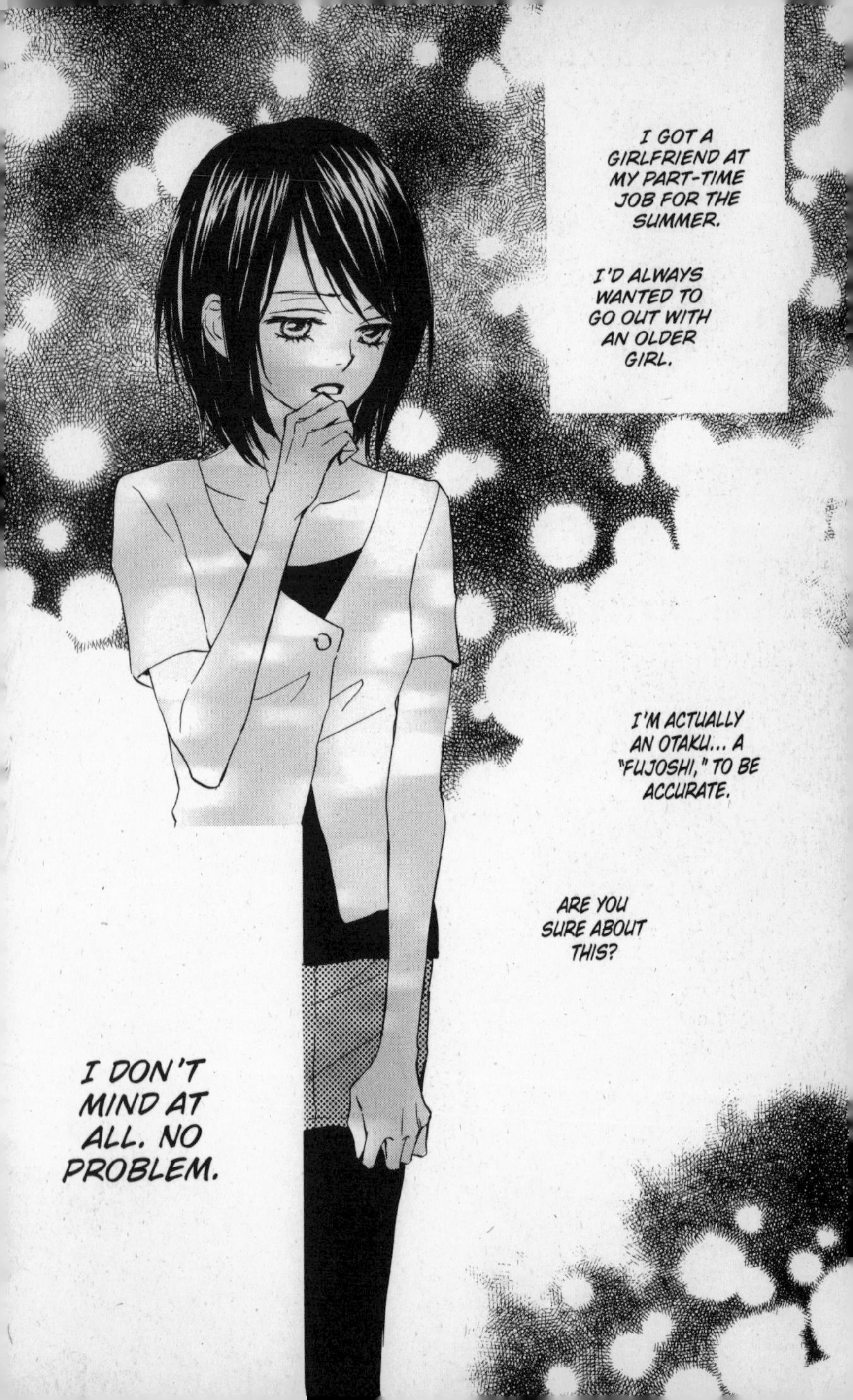
I GOT A GIRLFRIEND AT MY PART-TIME JOB FOR THE SUMMER.
I'D ALWAYS WANTED TO GO OUT WITH AN OLDER GIRL.
I'M ACTUALLY AN OTAKU... A "FUJOSHI," TO BE ACCURATE.
ARE YOU SURE ABOUT THIS?
I DON'T MIND AT ALL. NO PROBLEM.

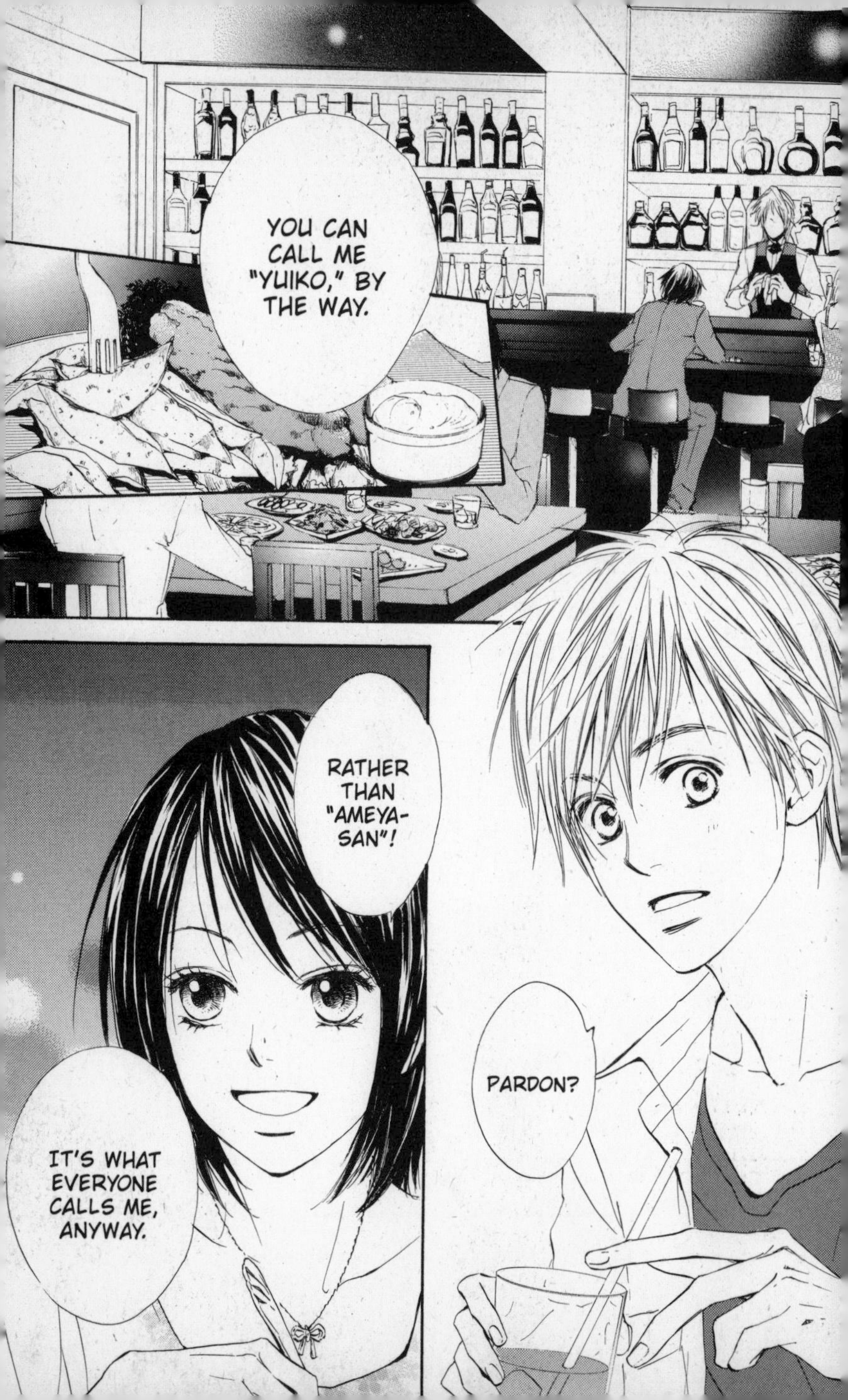
YOU CAN CALL ME "YUIKO," BY THE WAY.
PARDON?
RATHER THAN "AMEYA-SAN"!
IT'S WHAT EVERYONE CALLS ME, ANYWAY.

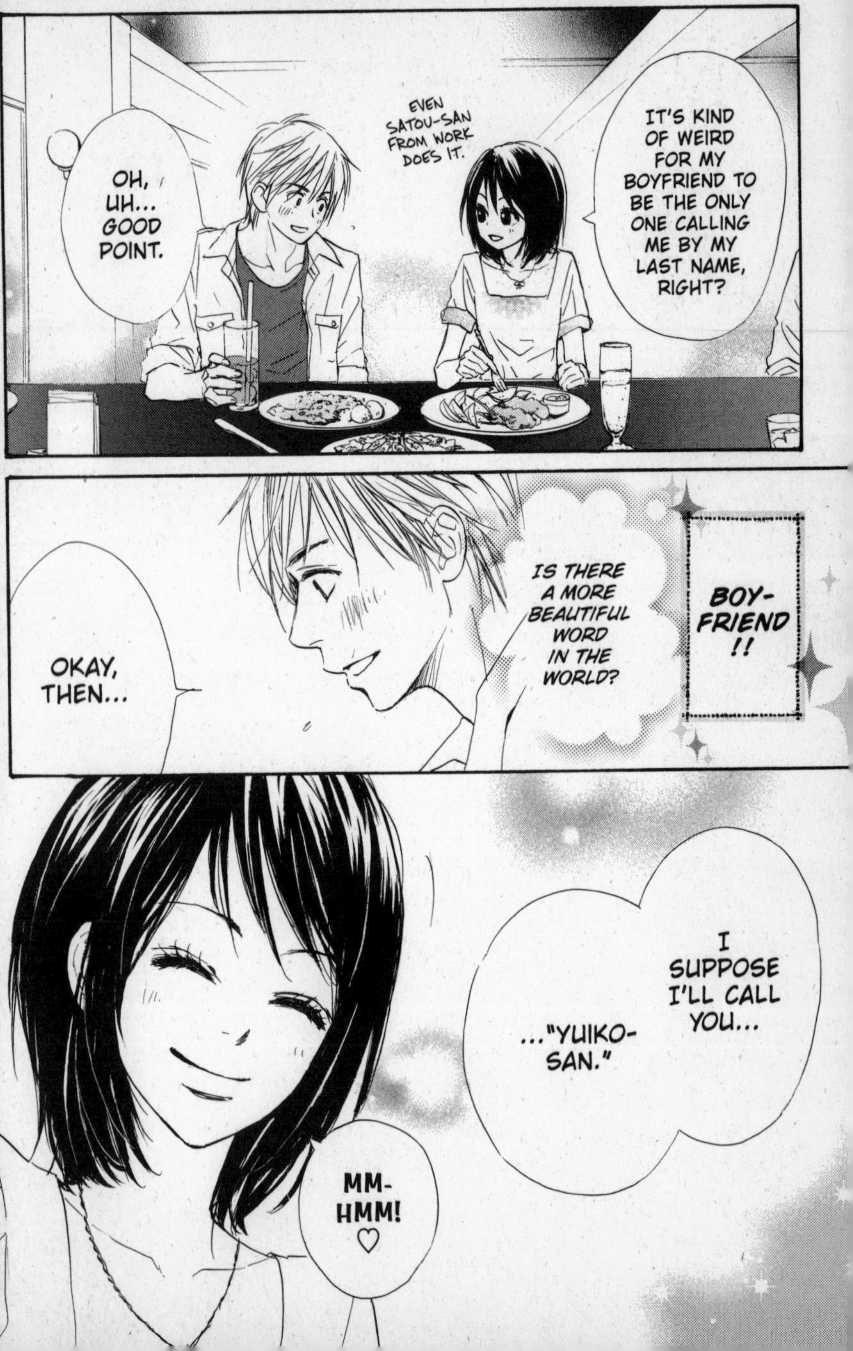
IT'S KIND OF WEIRD FOR MY BOYFRIEND TO BE THE ONLY ONE CALLING ME BY MY LAST NAME, RIGHT?
EVEN SATOU-SAN FROM WORK DOES IT.
OH, UH... GOOD POINT.
BOY-FRIEND!!
IS THERE A MORE BEAUTIFUL WORD IN THE WORLD?
OKAY, THEN...
I SUPPOSE I'LL CALL YOU...
..."YUIKO-SAN."
MM-HMM! ♡

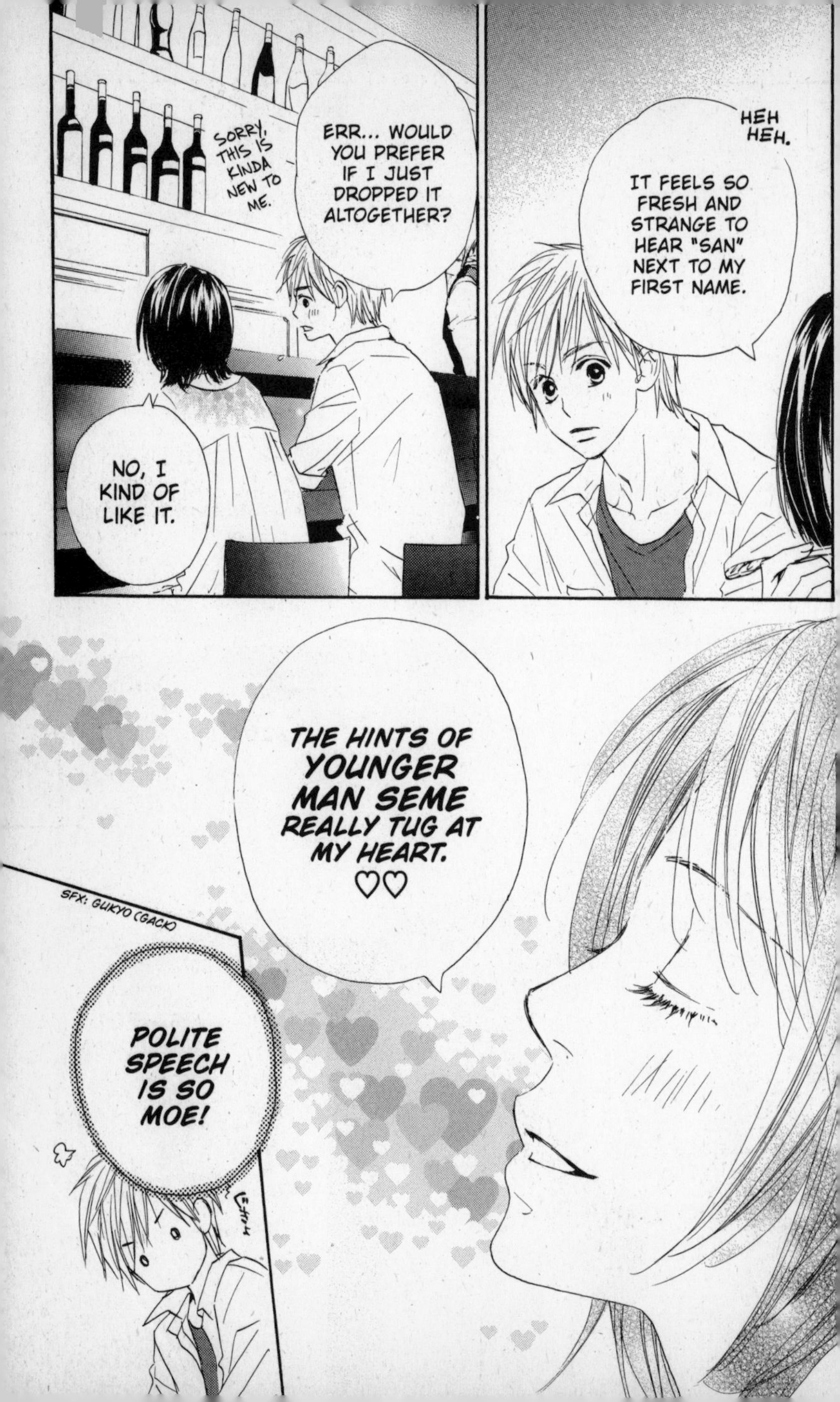
HEH HEH.
IT FEELS SO FRESH AND STRANGE TO HEAR "SAN" NEXT TO MY FIRST NAME.
ERR... WOULD YOU PREFER IF I JUST DROPPED IT ALTOGETHER?
SORRY, THIS IS KINDA NEW TO ME.
NO, I KIND OF LIKE IT.
THE HINTS OF YOUNGER MAN SEME REALLY TUG AT MY HEART. ♡♡
SFX: GUKYO (GACK)
POLITE SPEECH IS SO MOE!

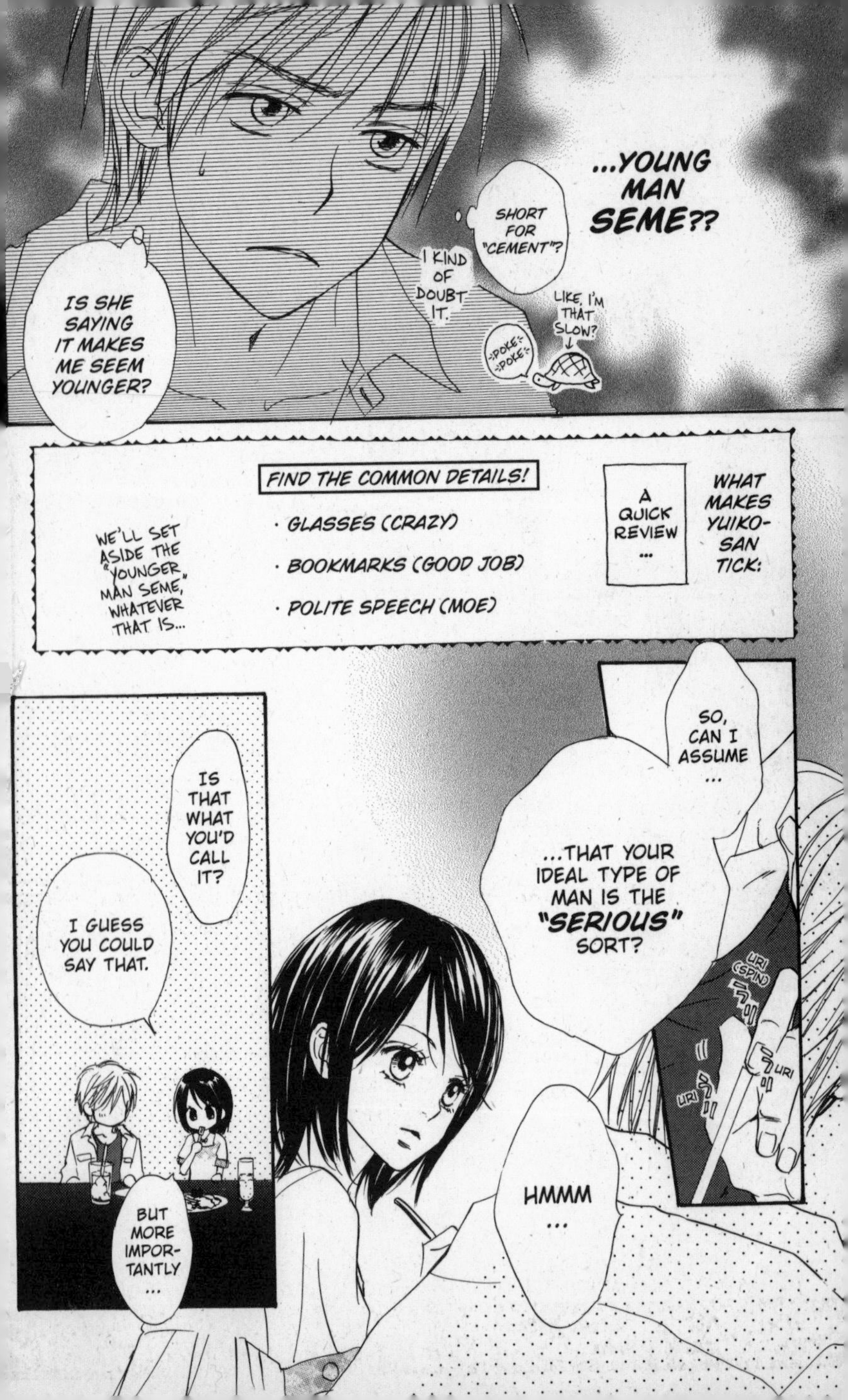
...YOUNG MAN SEME??
SHORT FOR "CEMENT"?
I KIND OF DOUBT IT.
LIKE, I'M THAT SLOW?
POKE POKE
IS SHE SAYING IT MAKES ME SEEM YOUNGER?
WHAT MAKES YUIKO-SAN TICK:
A QUICK REVIEW ...
FIND THE COMMON DETAILS!
· GLASSES (CRAZY)
· BOOKMARKS (GOOD JOB)
· POLITE SPEECH (MOE)
WE'LL SET ASIDE THE "YOUNGER MAN SEME," WHATEVER THAT IS...
SO, CAN I ASSUME ...
...THAT YOUR IDEAL TYPE OF MAN IS THE "SERIOUS" SORT?
URI (SPIN)
URI
URI
HMMM ...
IS THAT WHAT YOU'D CALL IT?
I GUESS YOU COULD SAY THAT.
BUT MORE IMPORTANTLY ...

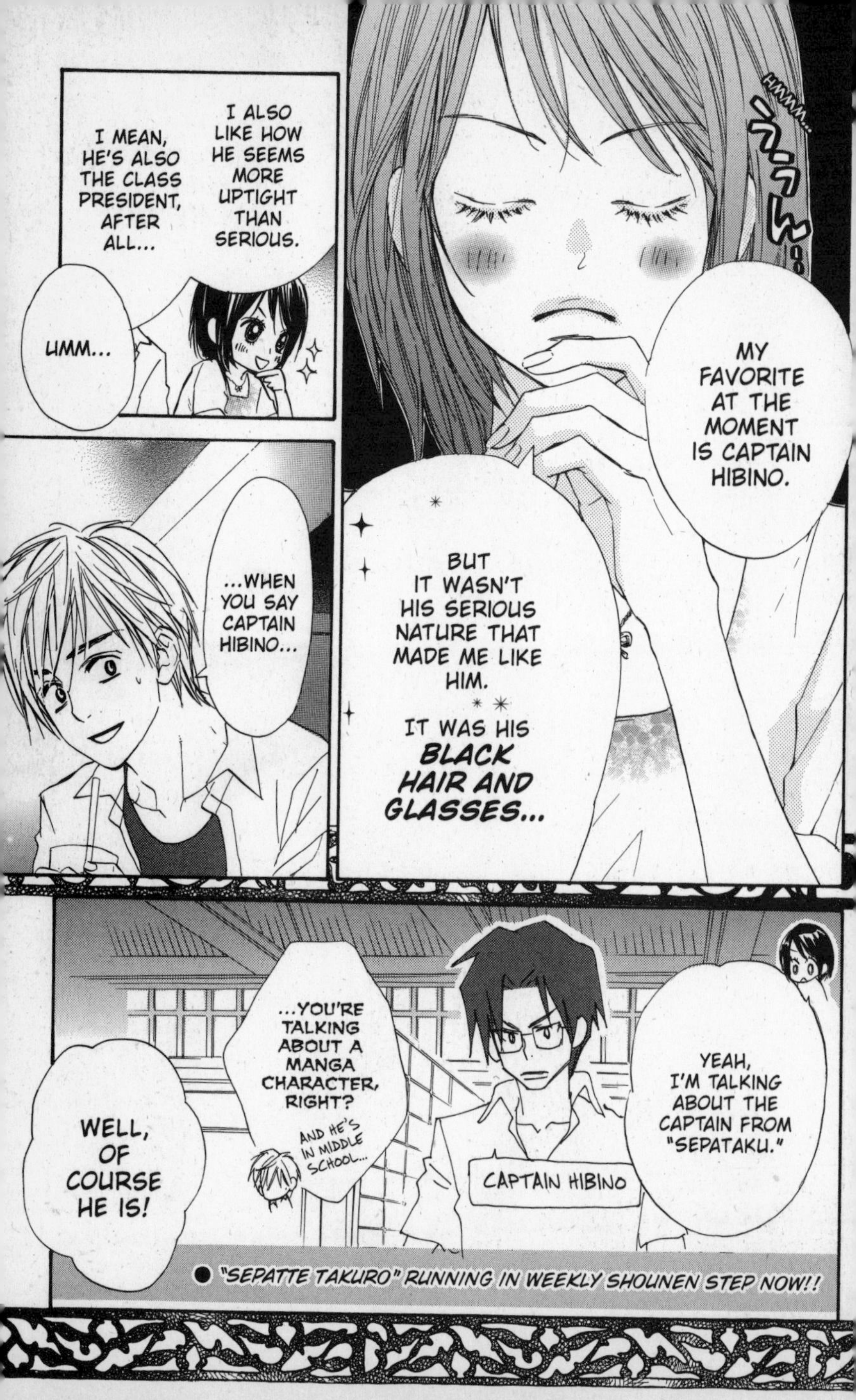
HMMM...
MY FAVORITE AT THE MOMENT IS CAPTAIN HIBINO.
BUT IT WASN'T HIS SERIOUS NATURE THAT MADE ME LIKE HIM.
IT WAS HIS BLACK HAIR AND GLASSES...
I ALSO LIKE HOW HE SEEMS MORE UPTIGHT THAN SERIOUS.
I MEAN, HE'S ALSO THE CLASS PRESIDENT, AFTER ALL...
UMM...
...WHEN YOU SAY CAPTAIN HIBINO...
YEAH, I'M TALKING ABOUT THE CAPTAIN FROM "SEPATAKU."
CAPTAIN HIBINO
...YOU'RE TALKING ABOUT A MANGA CHARACTER, RIGHT?
AND HE'S IN MIDDLE SCHOOL...
WELL, OF COURSE HE IS!
"SEPATTE TAKURO" RUNNING IN WEEKLY SHOUNEN STEP NOW!!

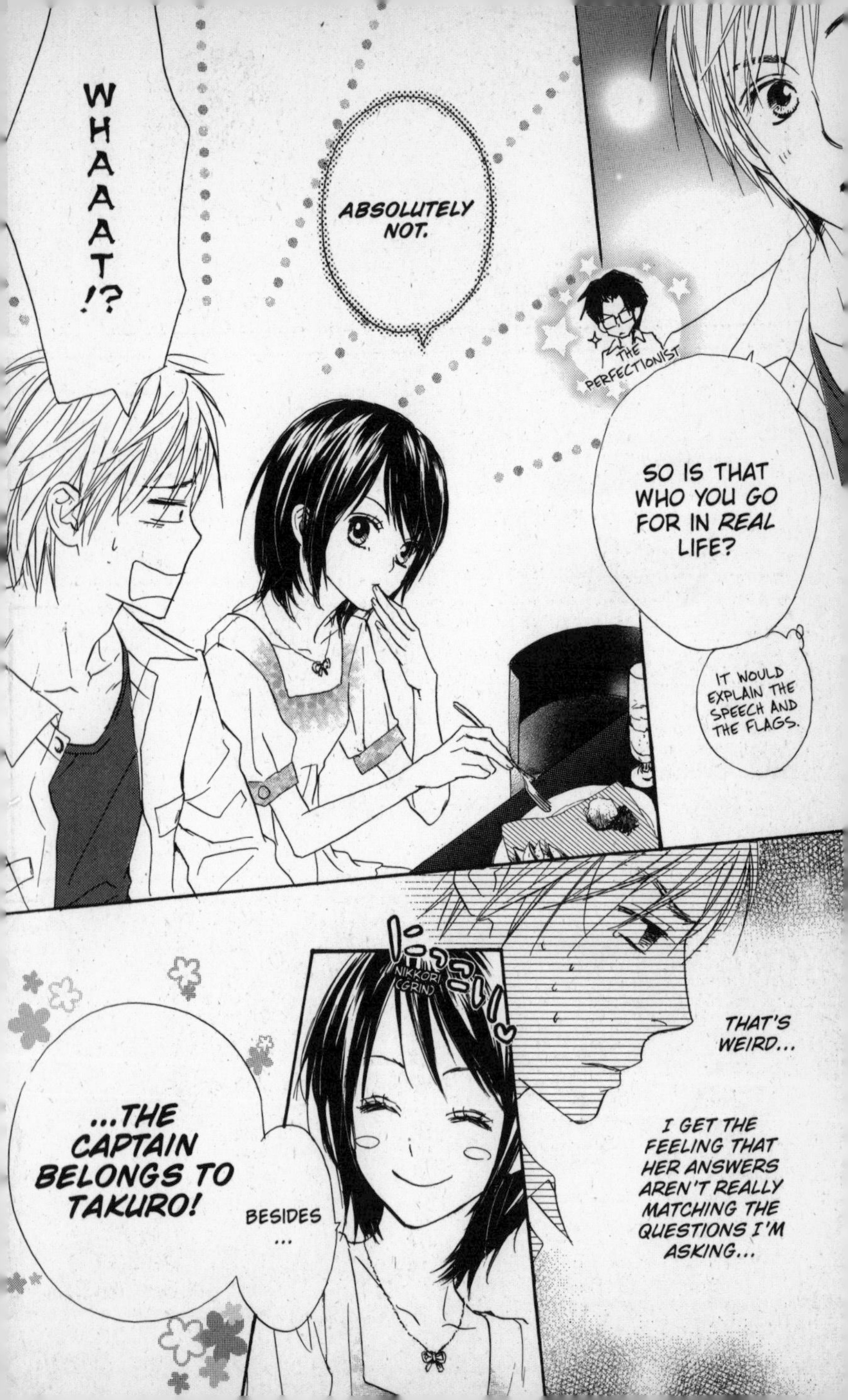
SO IS THAT WHO YOU GO FOR IN REAL LIFE?
IT WOULD EXPLAIN THE SPEECH AND THE FLAGS.
THE PERFECTIONIST
ABSOLUTELY NOT.
WHAAAT!?
THAT'S WEIRD...
I GET THE FEELING THAT HER ANSWERS AREN'T REALLY MATCHING THE QUESTIONS I'M ASKING...
NIKKORI (GRIN)
BESIDES ...
...THE CAPTAIN BELONGS TO TAKURO!

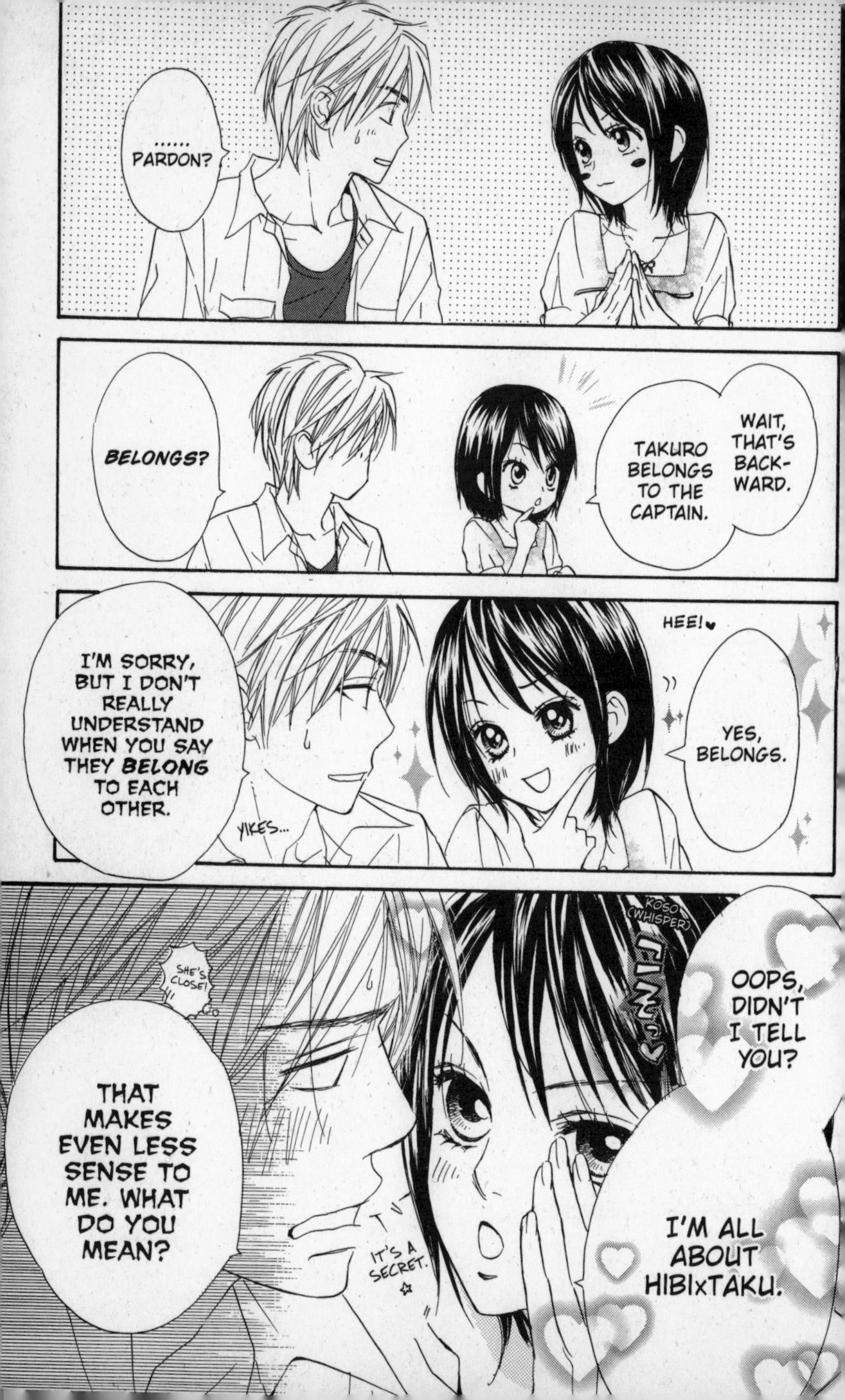

...... PARDON?
WAIT, THAT'S BACKWARD.
TAKURO BELONGS TO THE CAPTAIN.
BELONGS?
HEE!♥
YES, BELONGS.
I'M SORRY, BUT I DON'T REALLY UNDERSTAND WHEN YOU SAY THEY BELONG TO EACH OTHER.
YIKES...
KOSO (WHISPER)
OOPS, DIDN'T I TELL YOU?
I'M ALL ABOUT HIBIxTAKU.
IT'S A SECRET. ☆
SHE'S CLOSE!
THAT MAKES EVEN LESS SENSE TO ME. WHAT DO YOU MEAN?

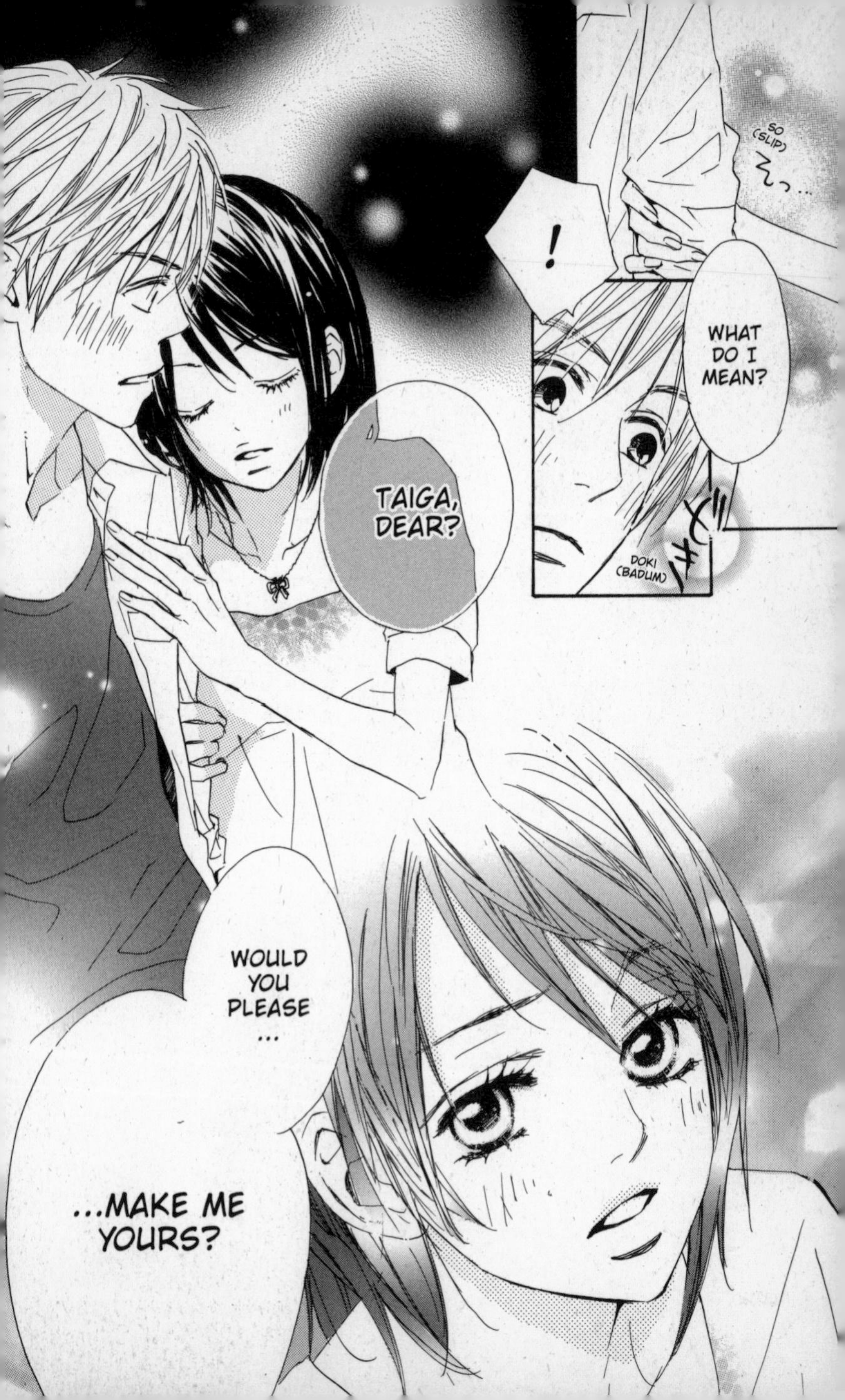
SO (SLIP)
!
WHAT DO I MEAN?
DOKI (BADUM)
TAIGA, DEAR?
WOULD YOU PLEASE ...
...MAKE ME YOURS?

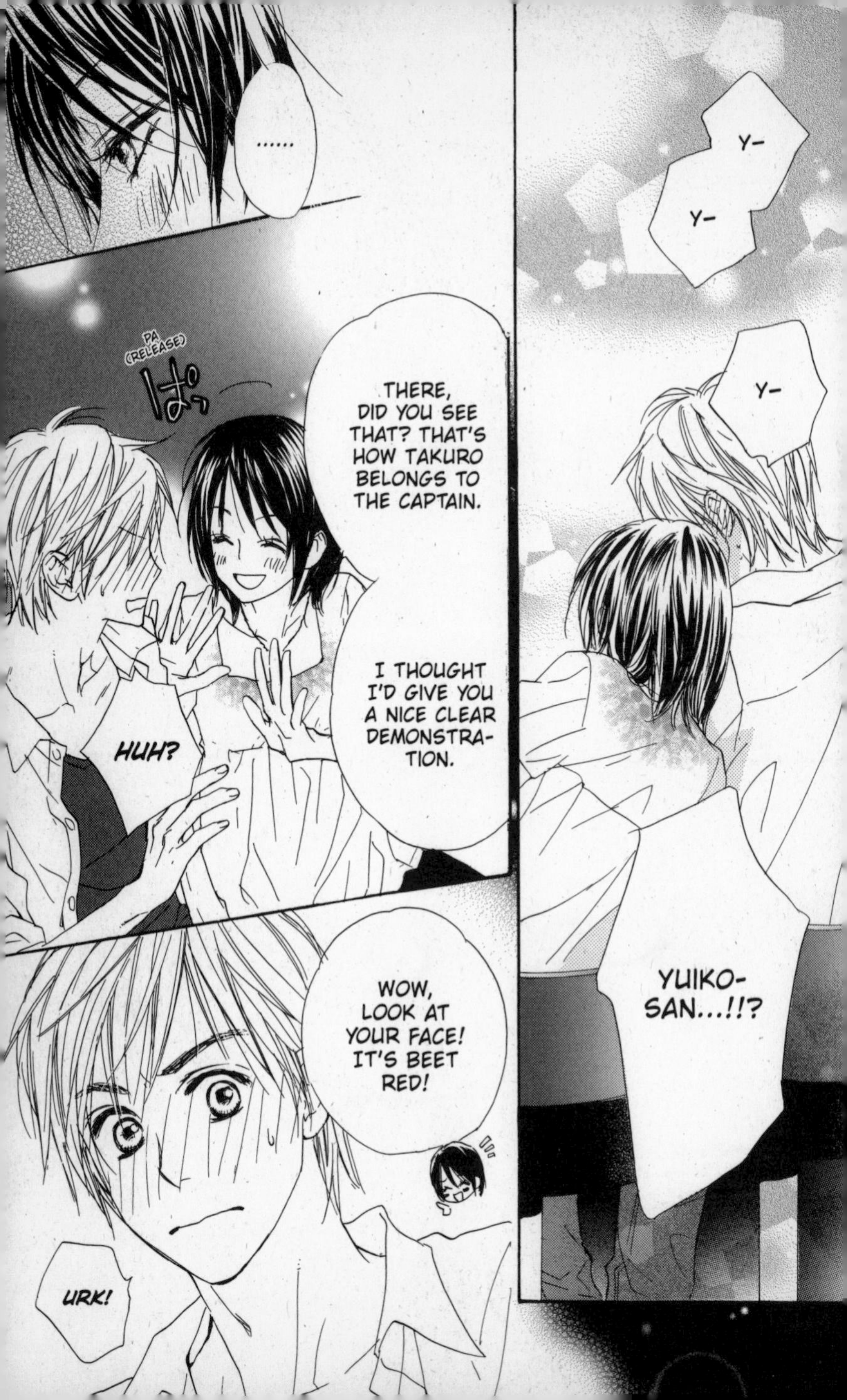
Y-
Y-
Y-
YUIKO-SAN...!!?
......
PA (RELEASE)
ぱっ
THERE, DID YOU SEE THAT? THAT'S HOW TAKURO BELONGS TO THE CAPTAIN.
I THOUGHT I'D GIVE YOU A NICE CLEAR DEMONSTRATION.
HUH?
WOW, LOOK AT YOUR FACE! IT'S BEET RED!
URK!

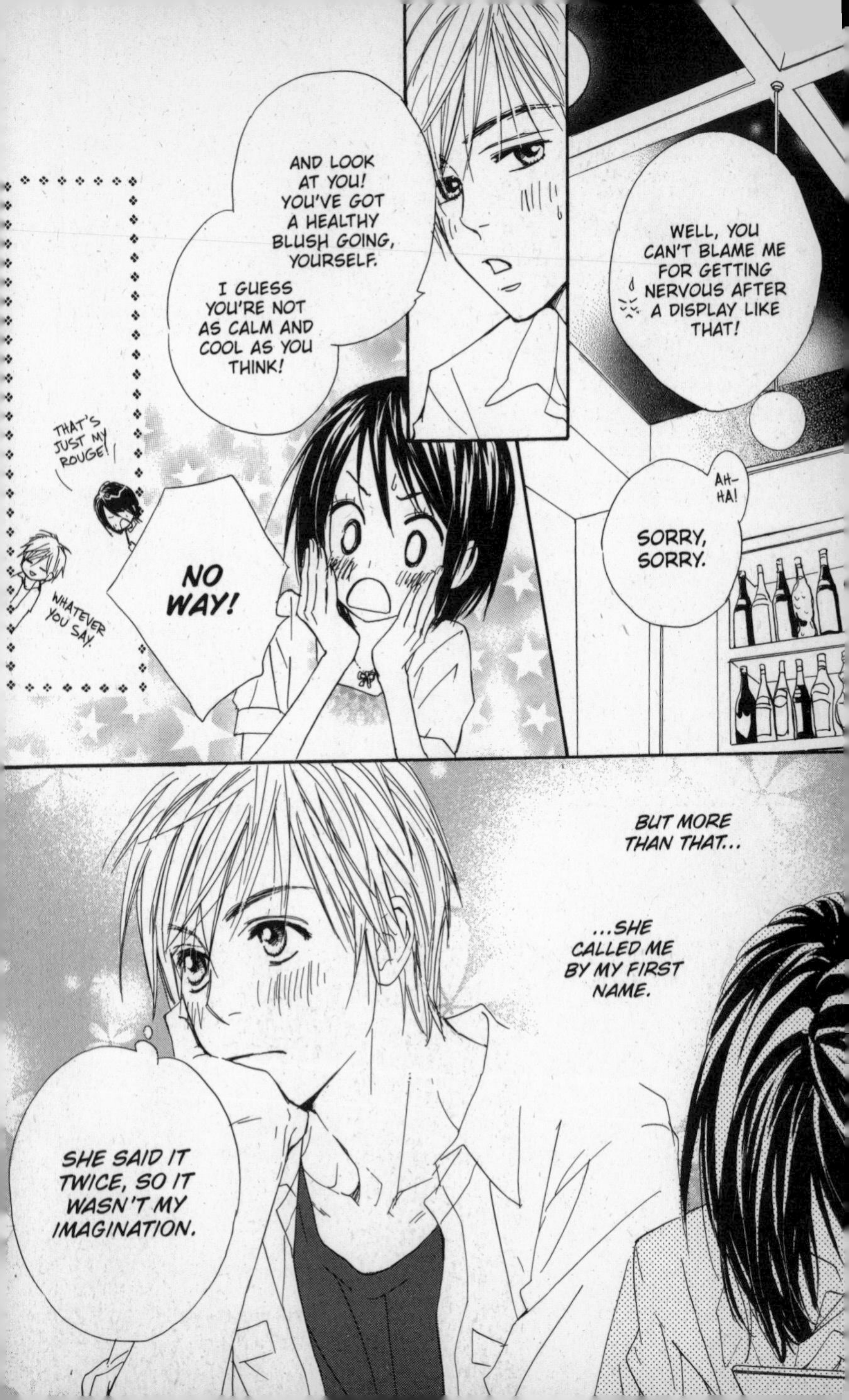
WELL, YOU CAN'T BLAME ME FOR GETTING NERVOUS AFTER A DISPLAY LIKE THAT!
AND LOOK AT YOU! YOU'VE GOT A HEALTHY BLUSH GOING, YOURSELF.
I GUESS YOU'RE NOT AS CALM AND COOL AS YOU THINK!
AH-HA!
SORRY, SORRY.
NO WAY!
THAT'S JUST MY ROUGE!
WHATEVER YOU SAY.
BUT MORE THAN THAT...
...SHE CALLED ME BY MY FIRST NAME.
SHE SAID IT TWICE, SO IT WASN'T MY IMAGINATION.

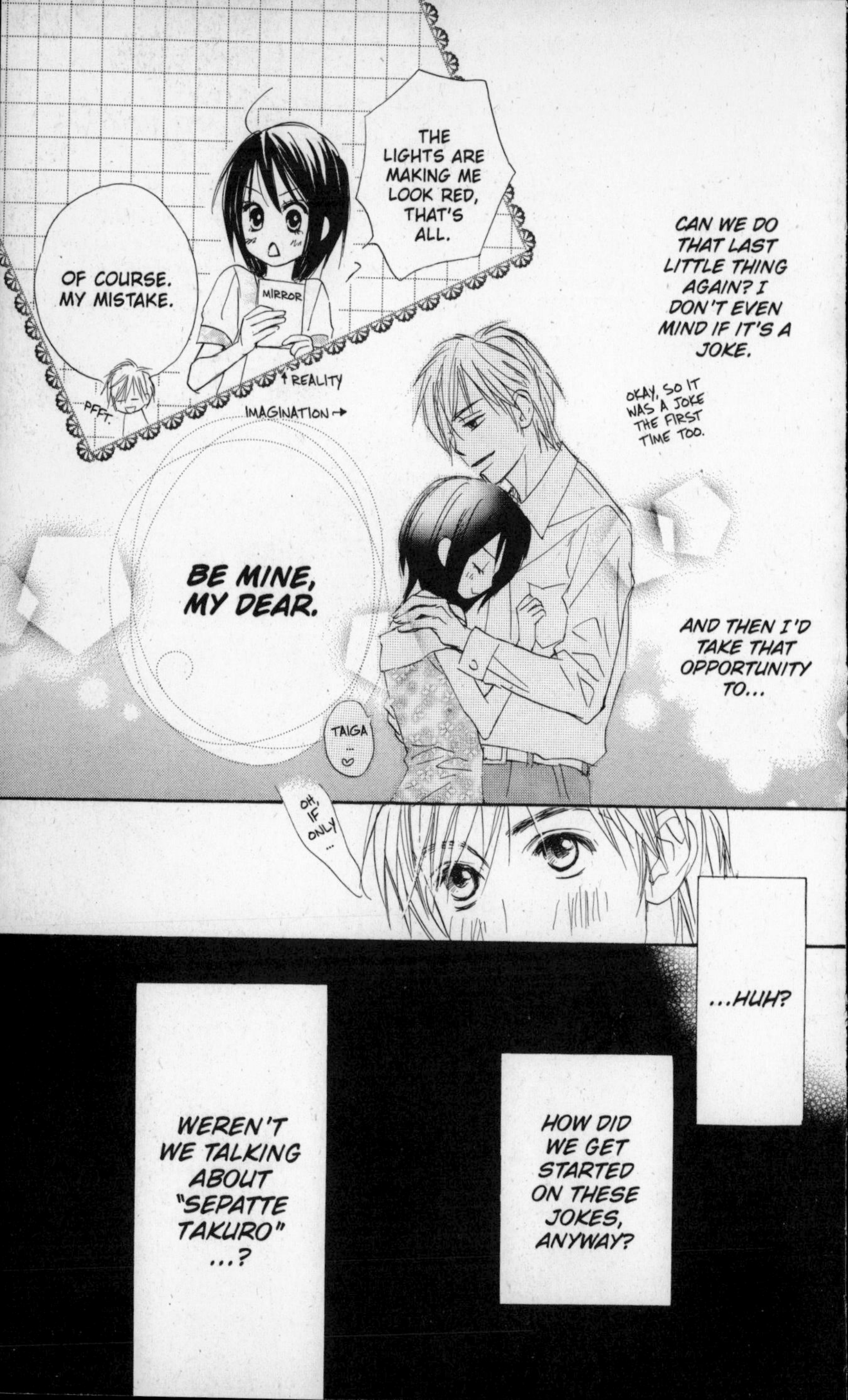
CAN WE DO THAT LAST LITTLE THING AGAIN? I DON'T EVEN MIND IF IT'S A JOKE.
OKAY, SO IT WAS A JOKE THE FIRST TIME TOO.
THE LIGHTS ARE MAKING ME LOOK RED, THAT'S ALL.
MIRROR
↑REALITY
OF COURSE. MY MISTAKE.
PFFT.
IMAGINATION →
AND THEN I'D TAKE THAT OPPORTUNITY TO...
BE MINE, MY DEAR.
TAIGA... ♡
OH, IF ONLY...
...HUH?
HOW DID WE GET STARTED ON THESE JOKES, ANYWAY?
WEREN'T WE TALKING ABOUT "SEPATTE TAKURO"...?

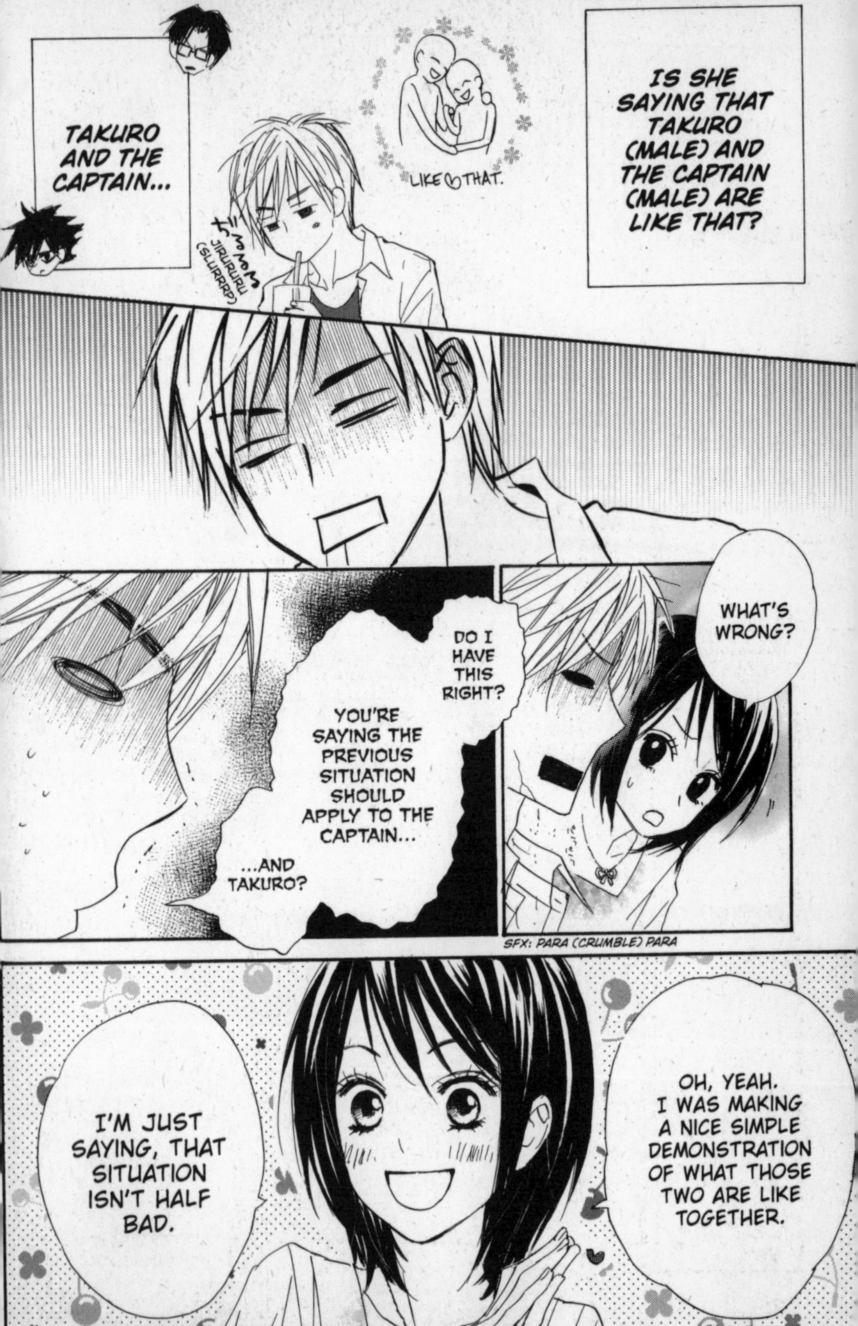
IS SHE SAYING THAT TAKURO (MALE) AND THE CAPTAIN (MALE) ARE LIKE THAT?
LIKE ♡ THAT.
JIRURURU (SLURRP)
TAKURO AND THE CAPTAIN...
WHAT'S WRONG?
DO I HAVE THIS RIGHT?
YOU'RE SAYING THE PREVIOUS SITUATION SHOULD APPLY TO THE CAPTAIN...
...AND TAKURO?
SFX: PARA (CRUMBLE) PARA
OH, YEAH. I WAS MAKING A NICE SIMPLE DEMONSTRATION OF WHAT THOSE TWO ARE LIKE TOGETHER.
I'M JUST SAYING, THAT SITUATION ISN'T HALF BAD.

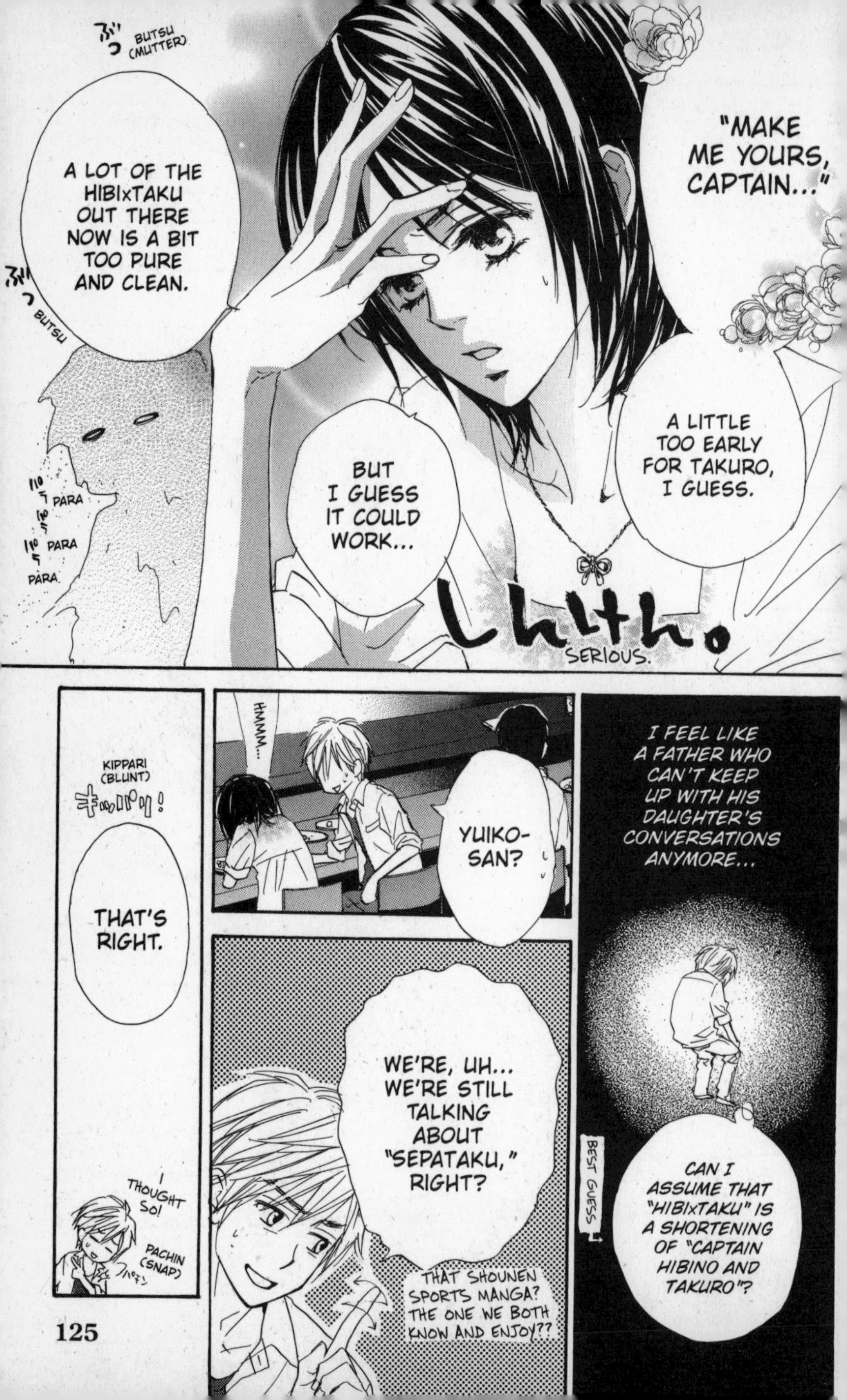
"MAKE ME YOURS, CAPTAIN..."
A LITTLE TOO EARLY FOR TAKURO, I GUESS.
BUT I GUESS IT COULD WORK...
SERIOUS.
BUTSU (MUTTER)
A LOT OF THE HIBIxTAKU OUT THERE NOW IS A BIT TOO PURE AND CLEAN.
BUTSU
PARA
PARA
PARA
I FEEL LIKE A FATHER WHO CAN'T KEEP UP WITH HIS DAUGHTER'S CONVERSATIONS ANYMORE...
BEST GUESS
CAN I ASSUME THAT "HIBIxTAKU" IS A SHORTENING OF "CAPTAIN HIBINO AND TAKURO"?
HMMM...
YUIKO-SAN?
WE'RE, UH... WE'RE STILL TALKING ABOUT "SEPATAKU," RIGHT?
THAT SHOUNEN SPORTS MANGA? THE ONE WE BOTH KNOW AND ENJOY??
I THOUGHT SO!
PACHIN (SNAP)
KIPPARI (BLUNT)
THAT'S RIGHT.

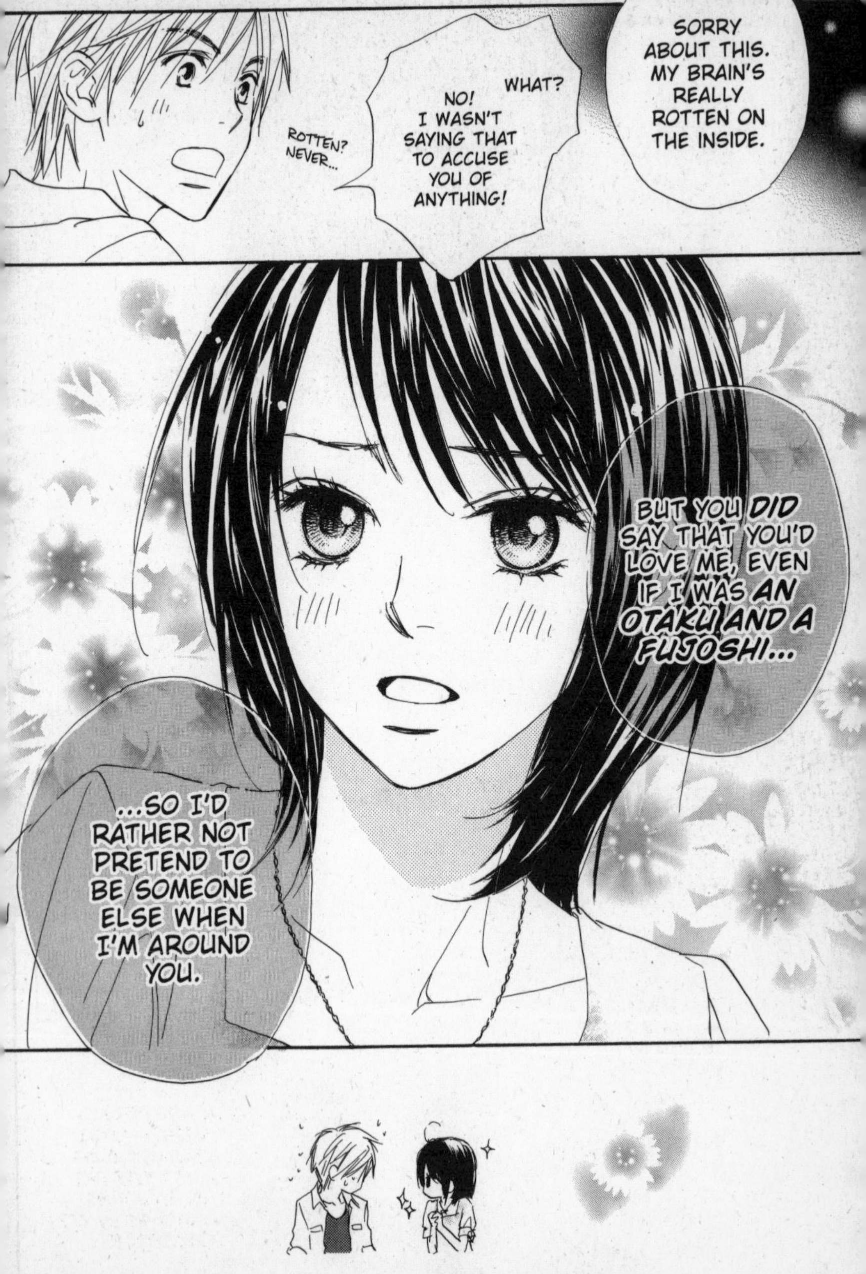
SORRY ABOUT THIS. MY BRAIN'S REALLY ROTTEN ON THE INSIDE.
WHAT?
NO! I WASN'T SAYING THAT TO ACCUSE YOU OF ANYTHING!
ROTTEN? NEVER...
BUT YOU DID SAY THAT YOU'D LOVE ME, EVEN IF I WAS AN OTAKU AND A FUJOSHI...
...SO I'D RATHER NOT PRETEND TO BE SOMEONE ELSE WHEN I'M AROUND YOU.

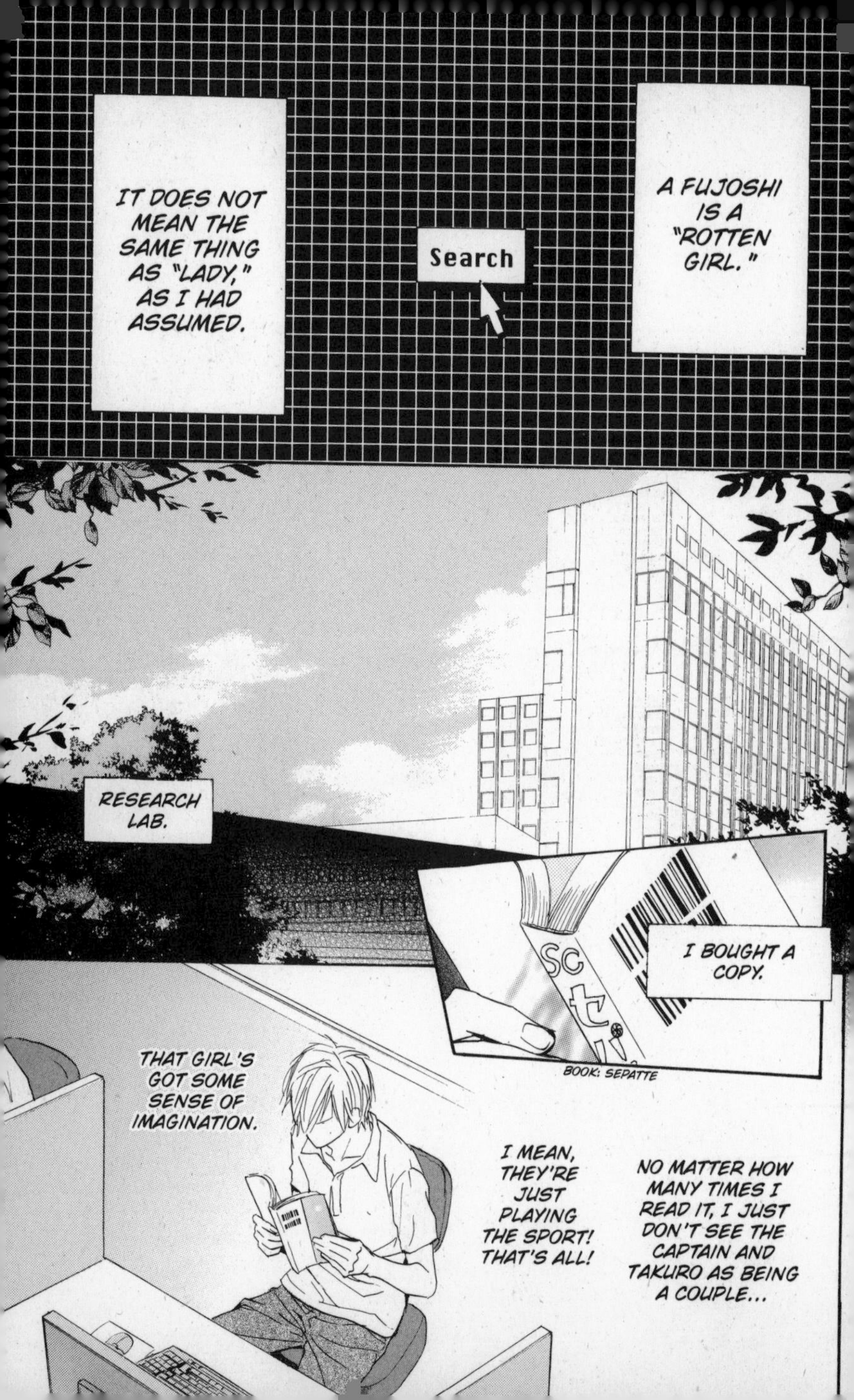
A FUJOSHI IS A "ROTTEN GIRL."
Search
IT DOES NOT MEAN THE SAME THING AS "LADY," AS I HAD ASSUMED.
RESEARCH LAB.
I BOUGHT A COPY.
BOOK: SEPATTE
NO MATTER HOW MANY TIMES I READ IT, I JUST DON'T SEE THE CAPTAIN AND TAKURO AS BEING A COUPLE...
I MEAN, THEY'RE JUST PLAYING THE SPORT! THAT'S ALL!
THAT GIRL'S GOT SOME SENSE OF IMAGINATION.

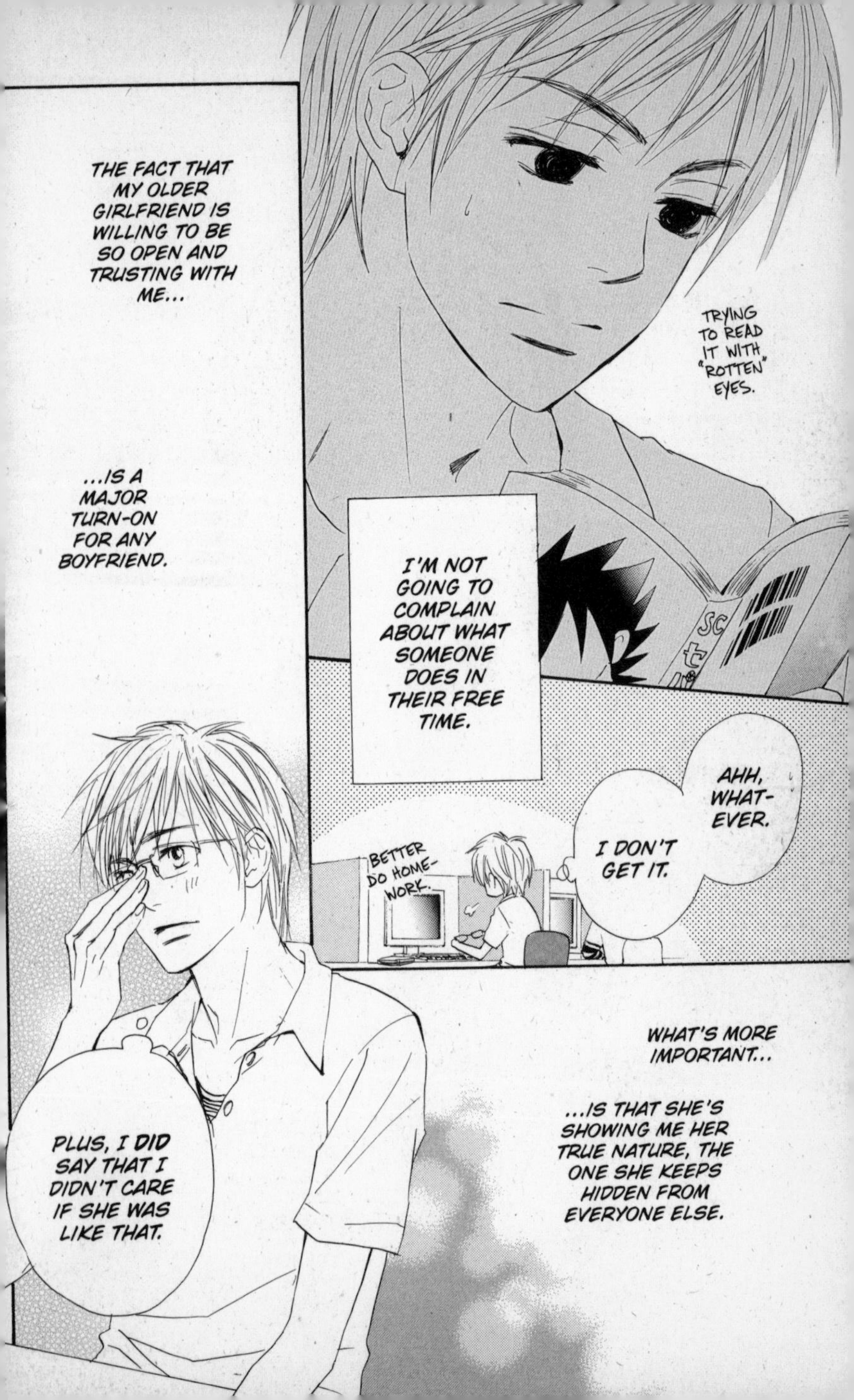

TRYING TO READ IT WITH "ROTTEN" EYES.
THE FACT THAT MY OLDER GIRLFRIEND IS WILLING TO BE SO OPEN AND TRUSTING WITH ME...
...IS A MAJOR TURN-ON FOR ANY BOYFRIEND.
I'M NOT GOING TO COMPLAIN ABOUT WHAT SOMEONE DOES IN THEIR FREE TIME.
AHH, WHAT-EVER.
I DON'T GET IT.
BETTER DO HOME-WORK.
WHAT'S MORE IMPORTANT...
...IS THAT SHE'S SHOWING ME HER TRUE NATURE, THE ONE SHE KEEPS HIDDEN FROM EVERYONE ELSE.
PLUS, I DID SAY THAT I DIDN'T CARE IF SHE WAS LIKE THAT.

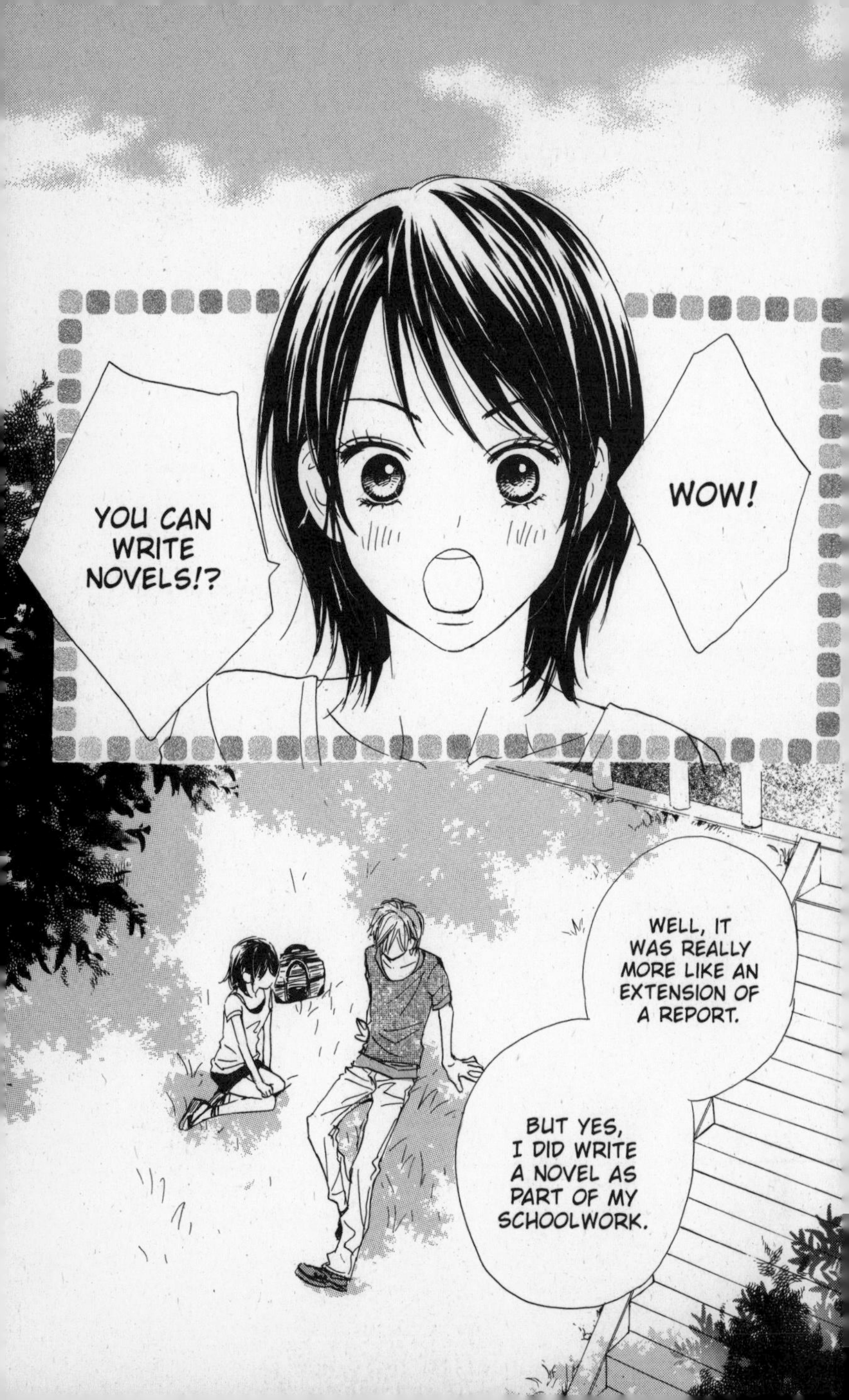
WOW!
YOU CAN WRITE NOVELS!?
WELL, IT WAS REALLY MORE LIKE AN EXTENSION OF A REPORT.
BUT YES, I DID WRITE A NOVEL AS PART OF MY SCHOOLWORK.

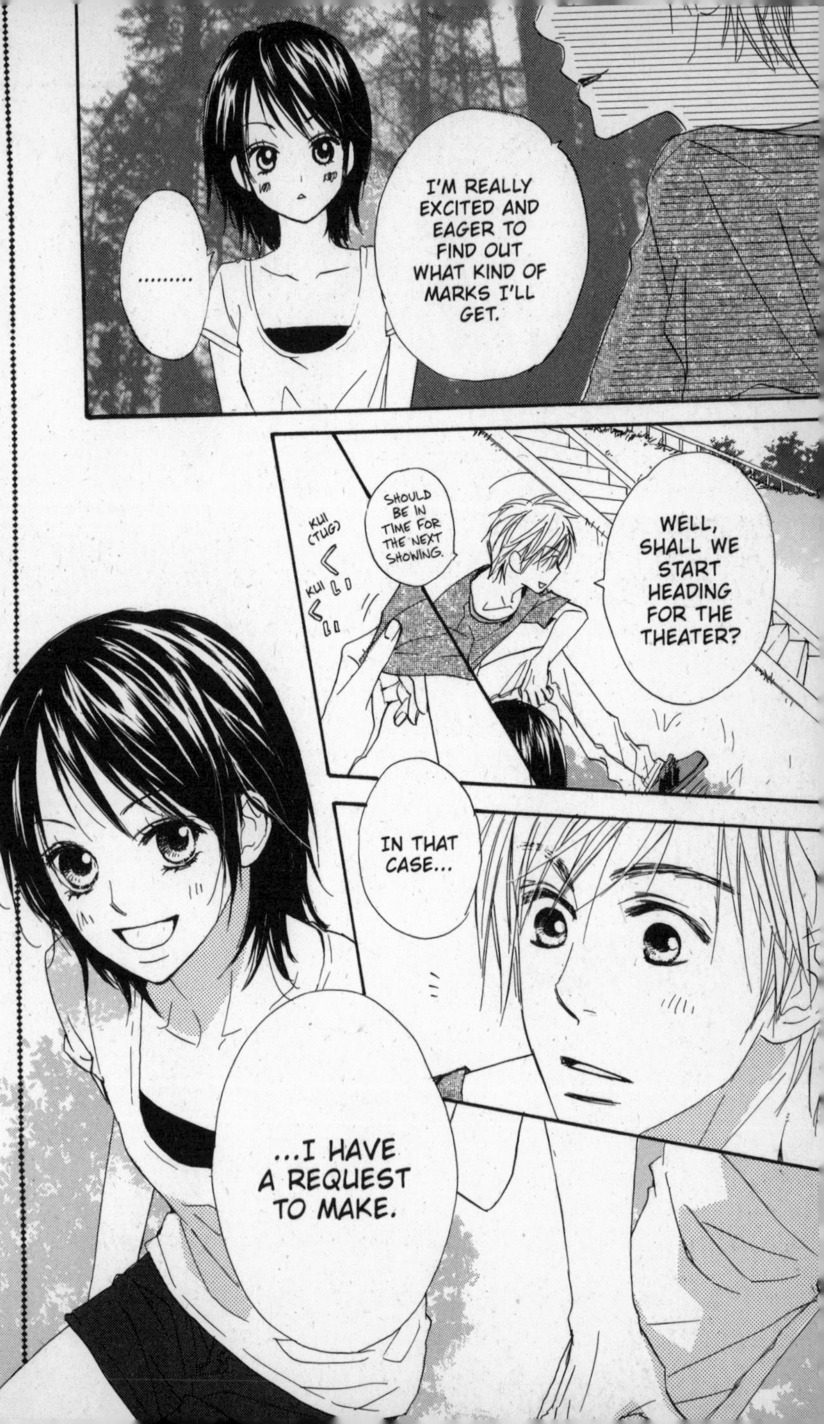
I'M REALLY EXCITED AND EAGER TO FIND OUT WHAT KIND OF MARKS I'LL GET.
....
WELL, SHALL WE START HEADING FOR THE THEATER?
SHOULD BE IN TIME FOR THE NEXT SHOWING.
KUI (TUG)
KUI
IN THAT CASE...
...I HAVE A REQUEST TO MAKE.

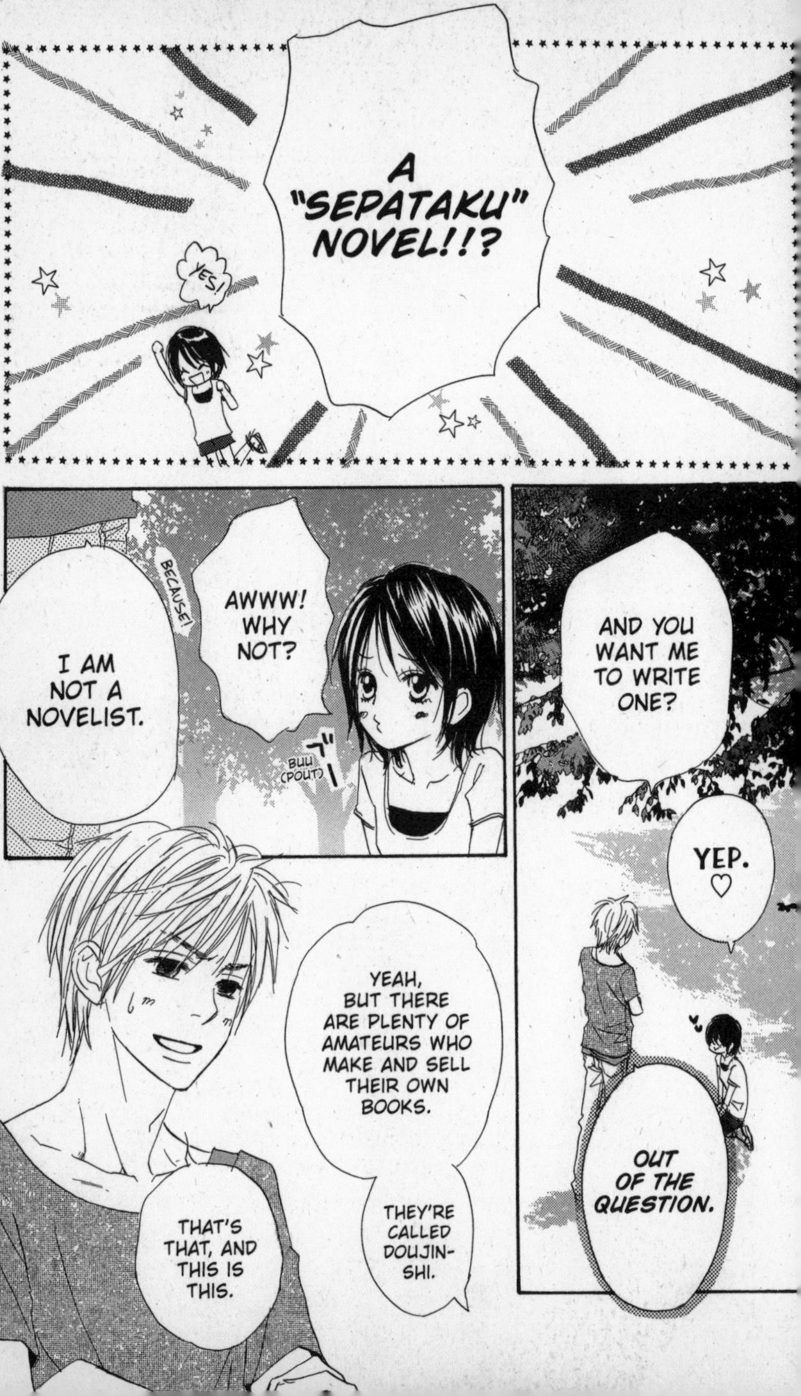
A "SEPATAKU" NOVEL!!?
YES!
AND YOU WANT ME TO WRITE ONE?
YEP. ♡
OUT OF THE QUESTION.
AWWW! WHY NOT?
BECAUSE!
I AM NOT A NOVELIST.
BUU (POUT)
YEAH, BUT THERE ARE PLENTY OF AMATEURS WHO MAKE AND SELL THEIR OWN BOOKS.
THEY'RE CALLED DOUJIN-SHI.
THAT'S THAT, AND THIS IS THIS.

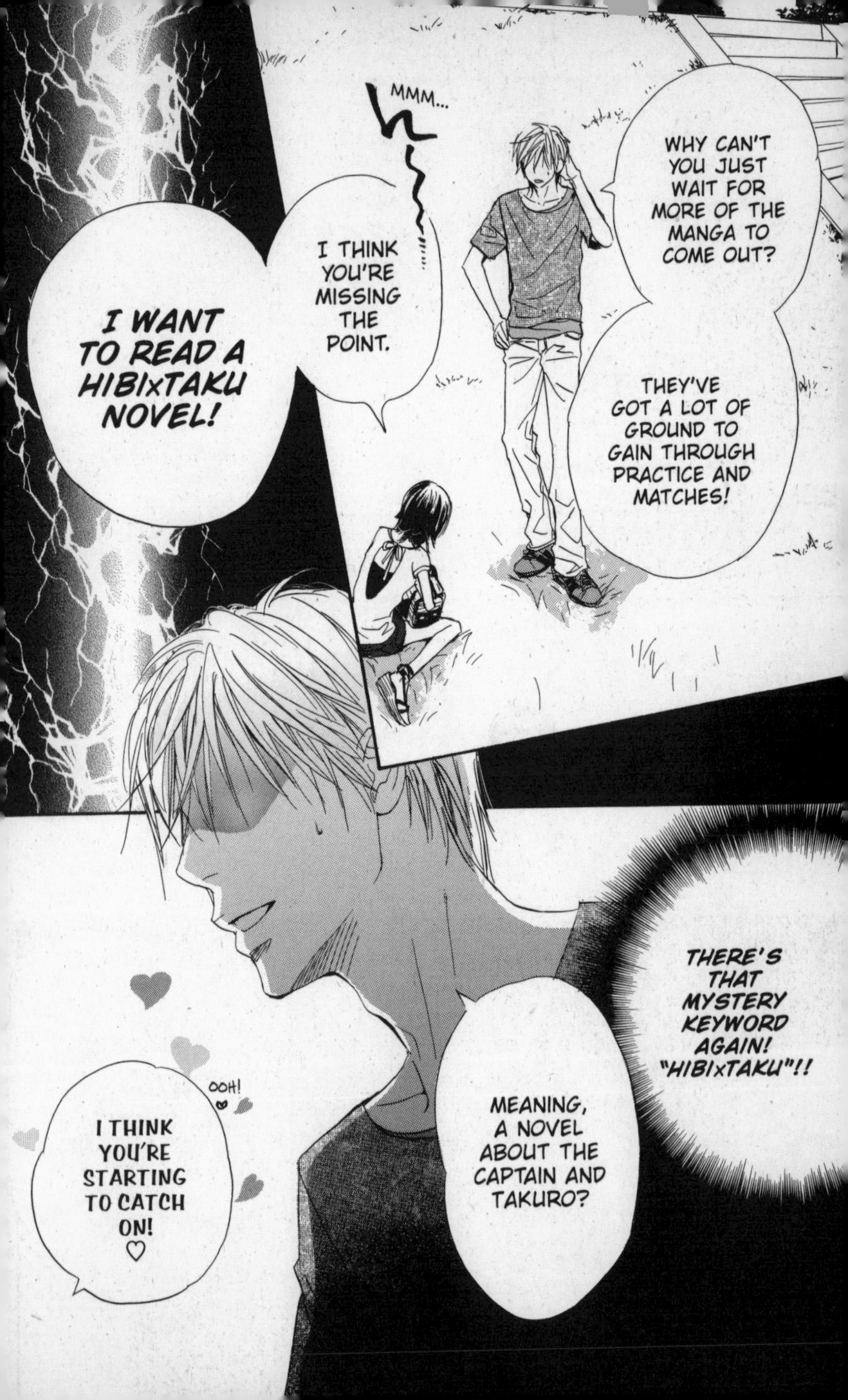
WHY CAN'T YOU JUST WAIT FOR MORE OF THE MANGA TO COME OUT?
THEY'VE GOT A LOT OF GROUND TO GAIN THROUGH PRACTICE AND MATCHES!
MMM...
I THINK YOU'RE MISSING THE POINT.
I WANT TO READ A HIBIxTAKU NOVEL!
THERE'S THAT MYSTERY KEYWORD AGAIN! "HIBIxTAKU"!!
MEANING, A NOVEL ABOUT THE CAPTAIN AND TAKURO?
OOH!
I THINK YOU'RE STARTING TO CATCH ON! ♡

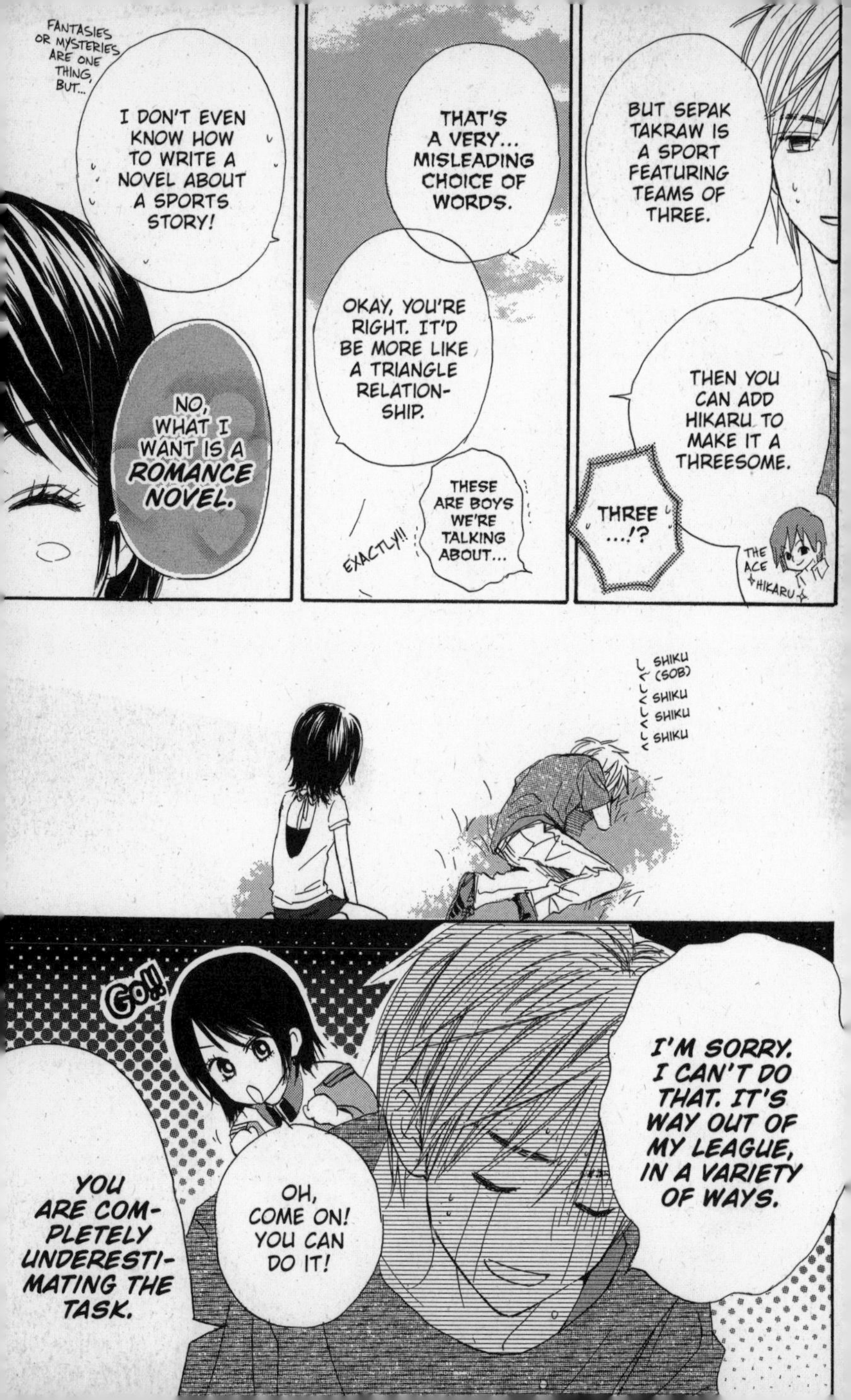
BUT SEPAK TAKRAW IS A SPORT FEATURING TEAMS OF THREE.
THEN YOU CAN ADD HIKARU TO MAKE IT A THREESOME.
THREE ...!?
THE ACE ✧HIKARU✧
THAT'S A VERY... MISLEADING CHOICE OF WORDS.
OKAY, YOU'RE RIGHT. IT'D BE MORE LIKE A TRIANGLE RELATION-SHIP.
THESE ARE BOYS WE'RE TALKING ABOUT...
EXACTLY!!
FANTASIES OR MYSTERIES ARE ONE THING, BUT...
I DON'T EVEN KNOW HOW TO WRITE A NOVEL ABOUT A SPORTS STORY!
NO, WHAT I WANT IS A ROMANCE NOVEL.
SHIKU (SOB) SHIKU SHIKU SHIKU
I'M SORRY. I CAN'T DO THAT. IT'S WAY OUT OF MY LEAGUE, IN A VARIETY OF WAYS.
GO!!
OH, COME ON! YOU CAN DO IT!
YOU ARE COM-PLETELY UNDERESTI-MATING THE TASK.

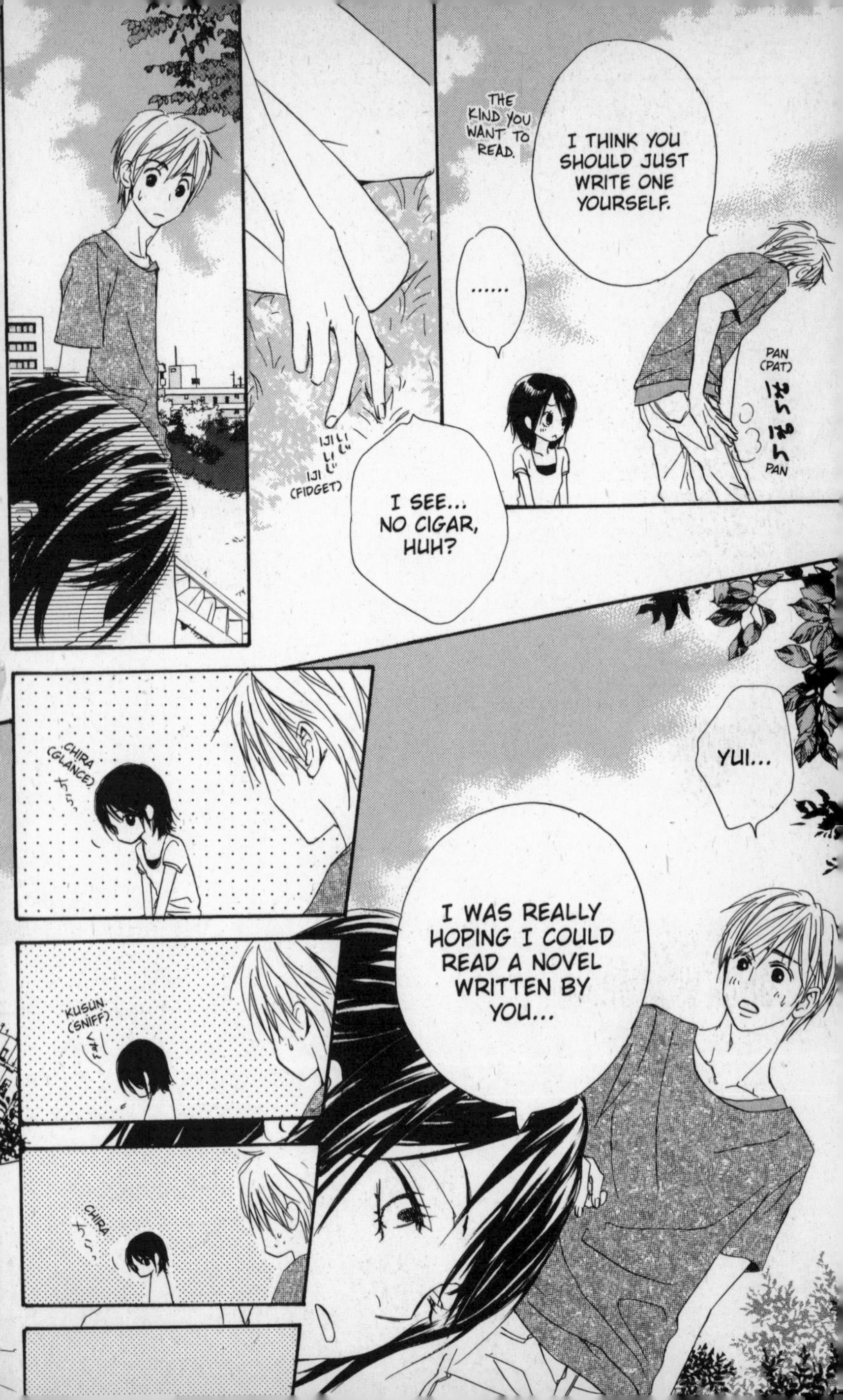
PAN (PAT)
ぱん ぱん
PAN
I THINK YOU SHOULD JUST WRITE ONE YOURSELF.
THE KIND YOU WANT TO READ.
......
IJI IJI (FIDGET)
I SEE... NO CIGAR, HUH?
YUI...
I WAS REALLY HOPING I COULD READ A NOVEL WRITTEN BY YOU...
CHIRA (GLANCE)
KUSUN (SNIFF)
CHIRA

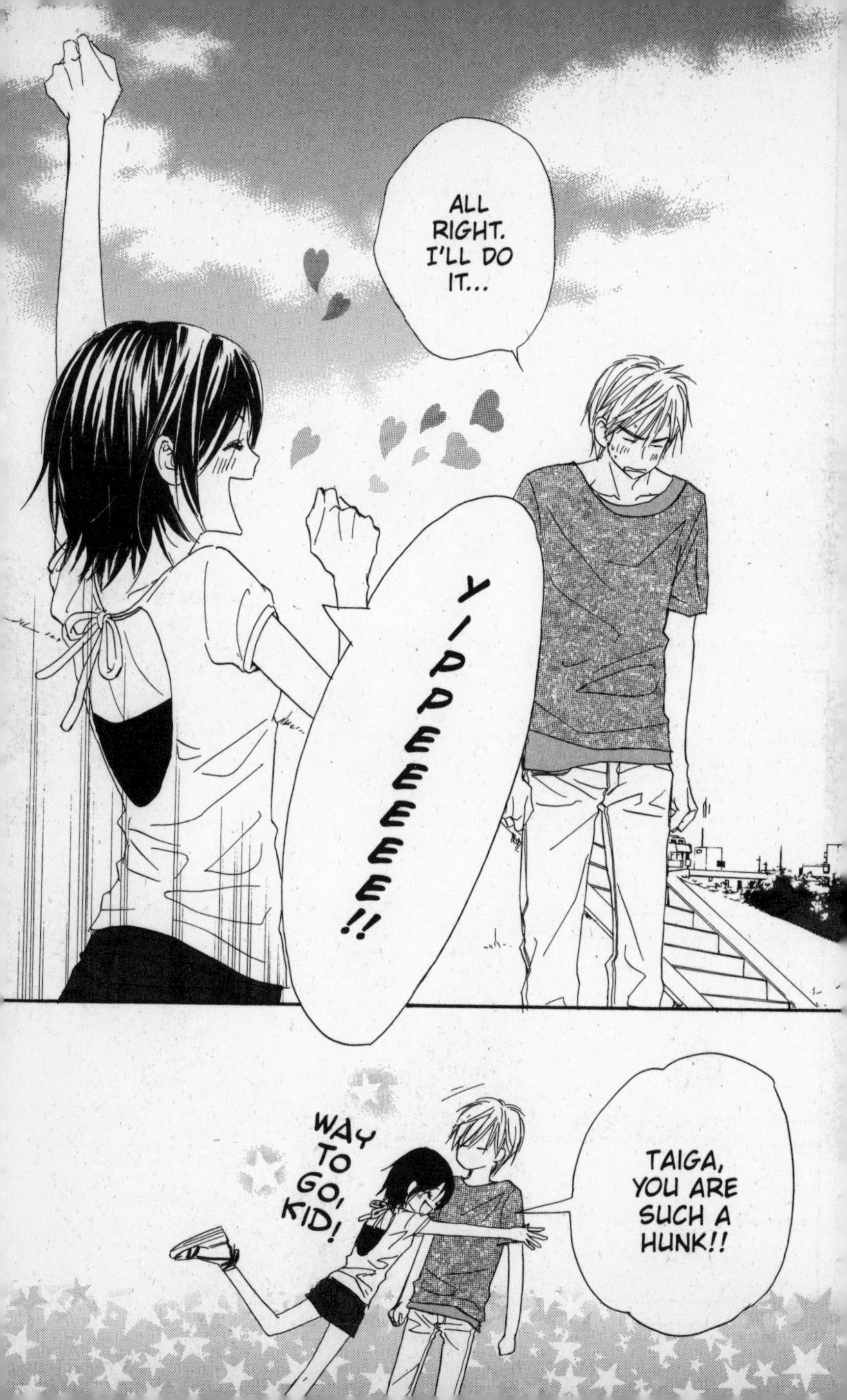
ALL RIGHT. I'LL DO IT...
YIPPEEEEE!!
TAIGA, YOU ARE SUCH A HUNK!!
WAY TO GO, KID!

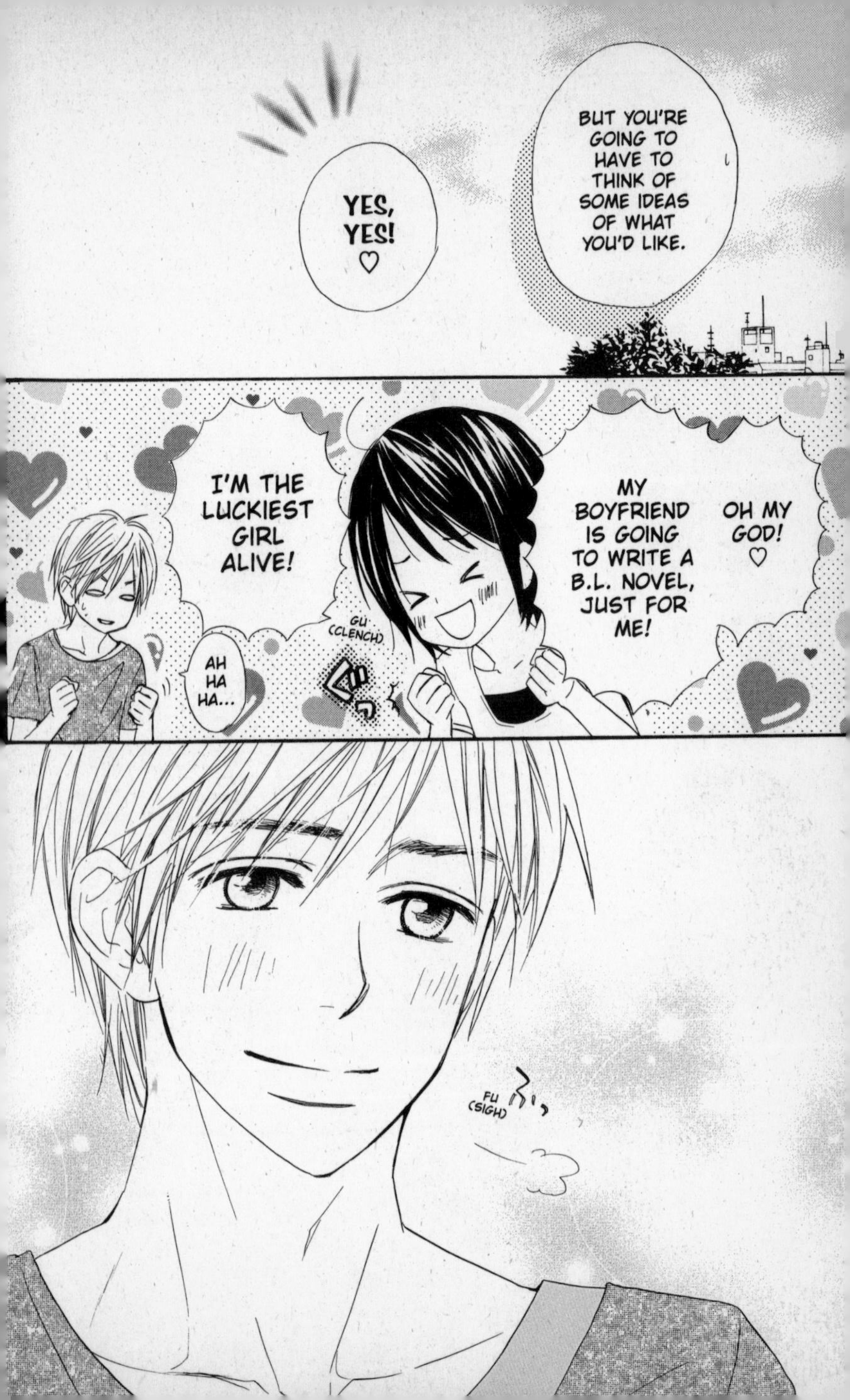
BUT YOU'RE GOING TO HAVE TO THINK OF SOME IDEAS OF WHAT YOU'D LIKE.
YES, YES! ♡
OH MY GOD! ♡
MY BOYFRIEND IS GOING TO WRITE A B.L. NOVEL, JUST FOR ME!
I'M THE LUCKIEST GIRL ALIVE!
GU (CLENCH)
AH HA HA...
FU (SIGH)

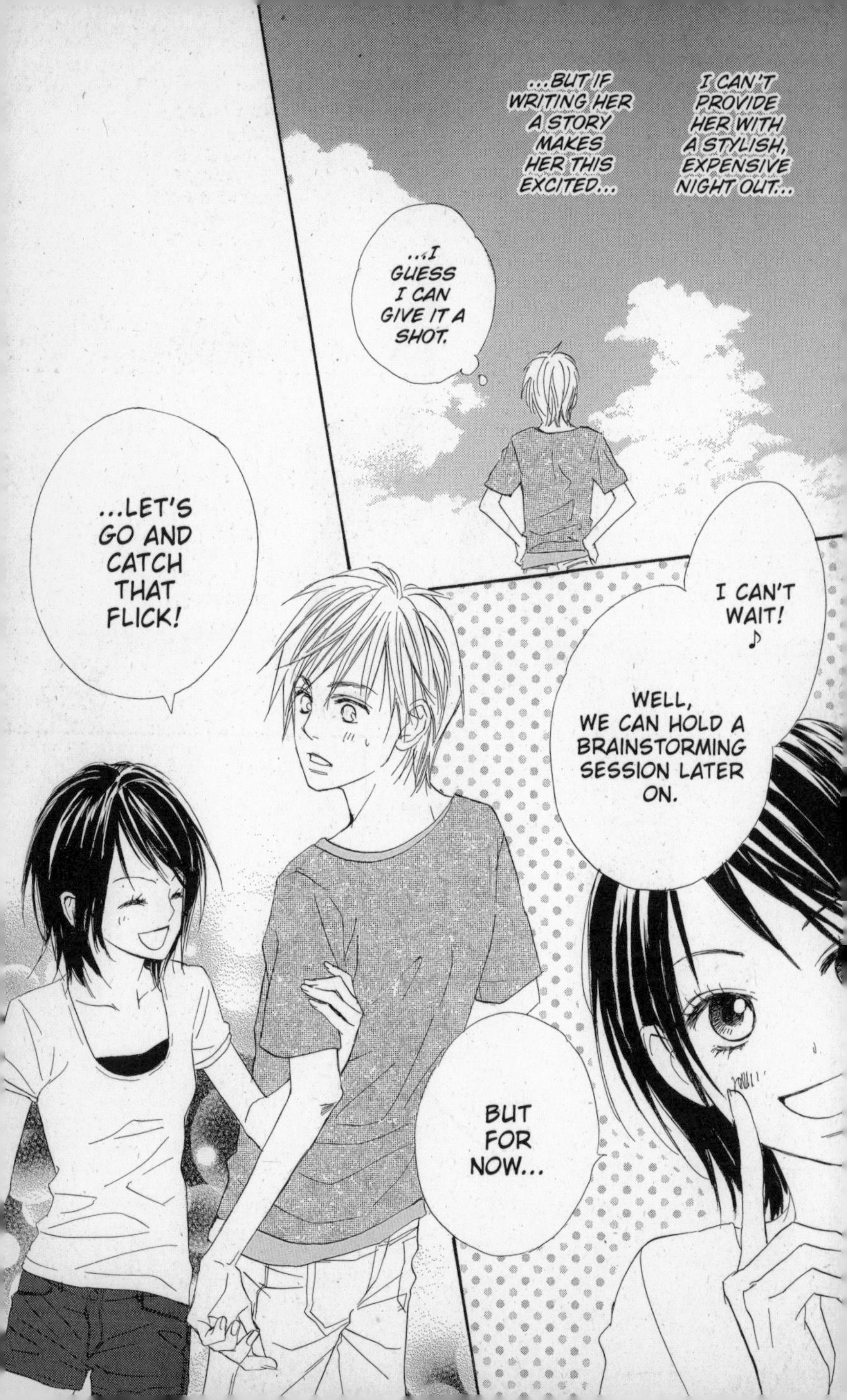
I CAN'T PROVIDE HER WITH A STYLISH, EXPENSIVE NIGHT OUT...
...BUT IF WRITING HER A STORY MAKES HER THIS EXCITED...
...I GUESS I CAN GIVE IT A SHOT.
I CAN'T WAIT! ♪
WELL, WE CAN HOLD A BRAINSTORMING SESSION LATER ON.
BUT FOR NOW...
...LET'S GO AND CATCH THAT FLICK!

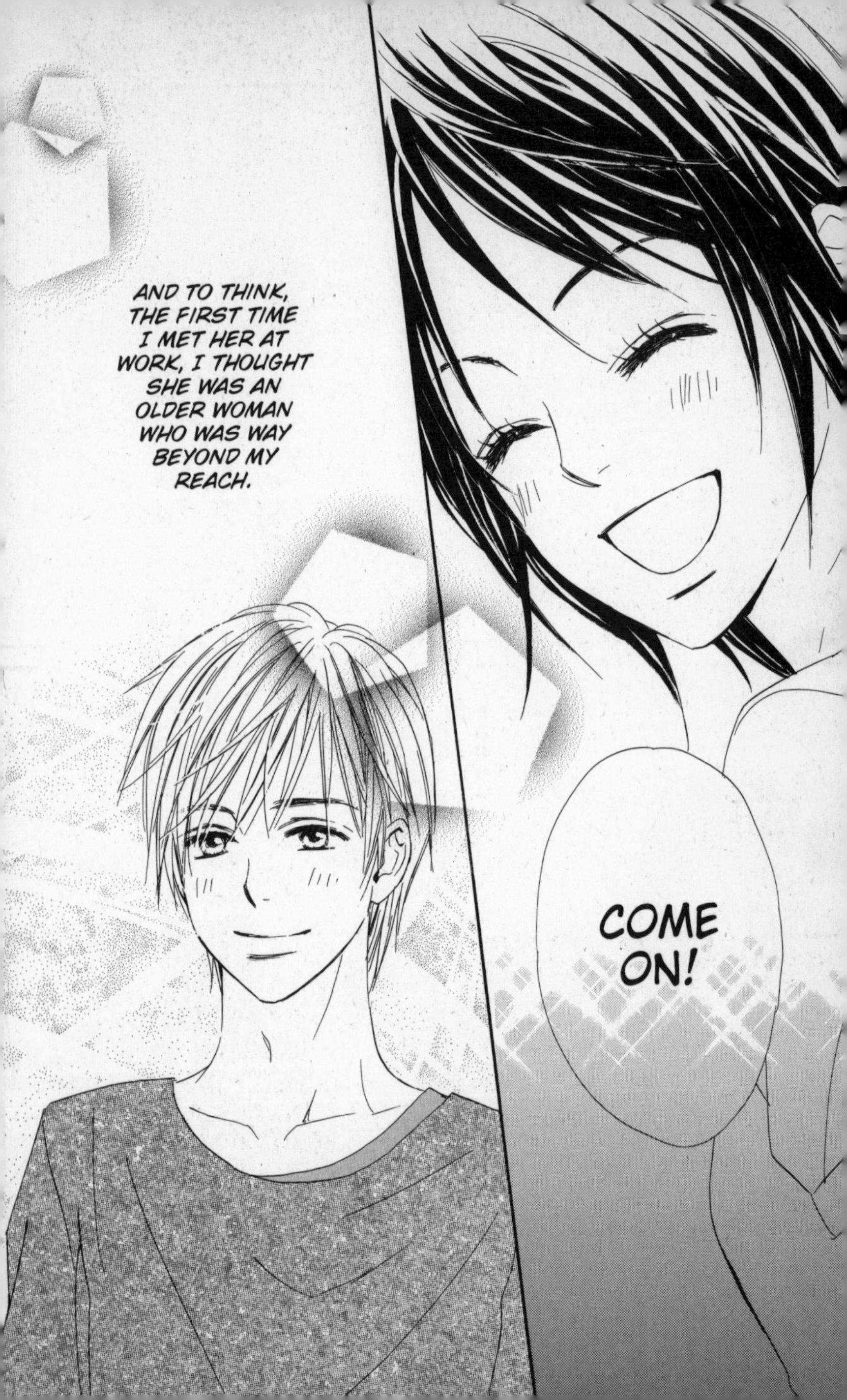
COME ON!
AND TO THINK, THE FIRST TIME I MET HER AT WORK, I THOUGHT SHE WAS AN OLDER WOMAN WHO WAS WAY BEYOND MY REACH.

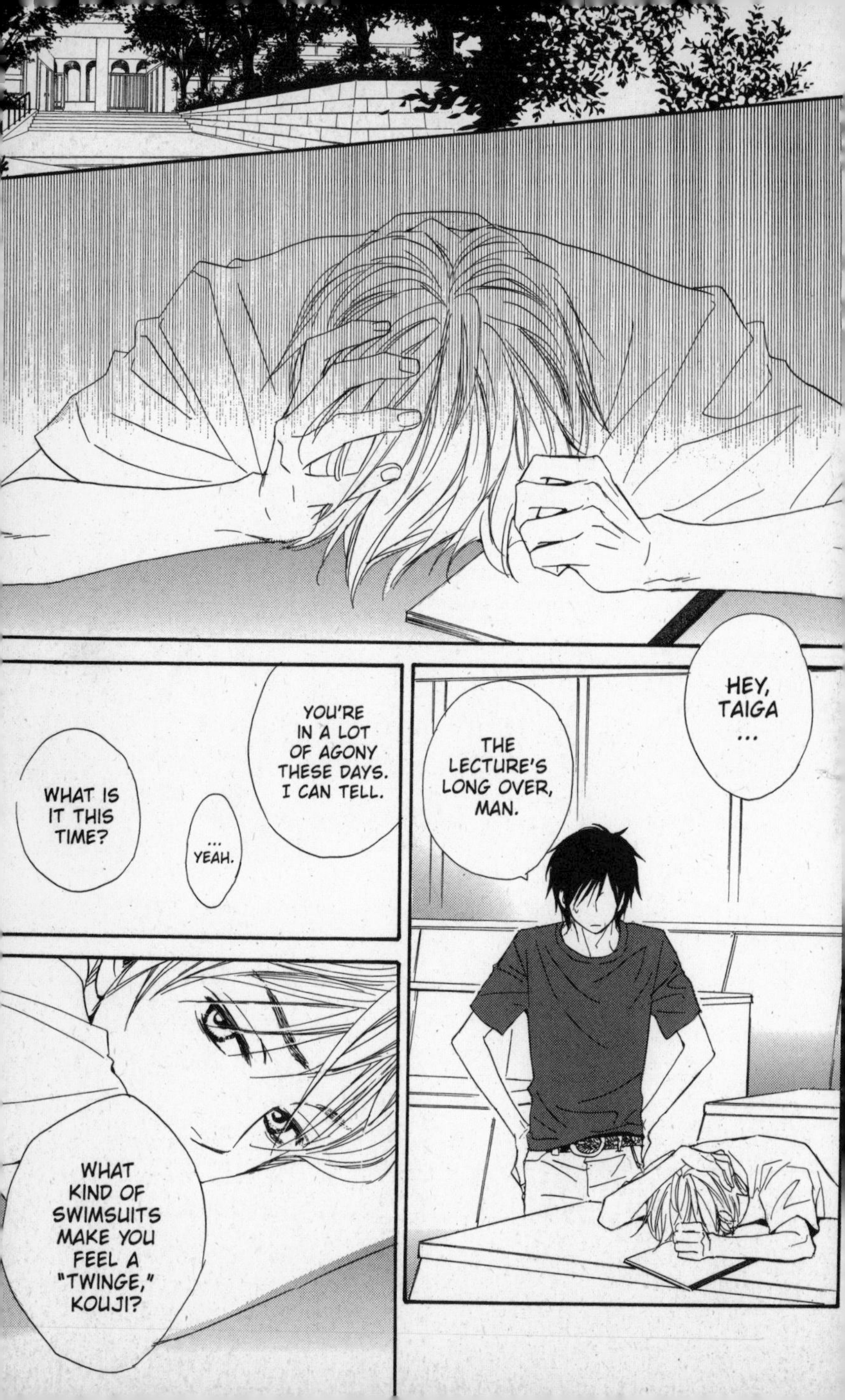
HEY, TAIGA ...
THE LECTURE'S LONG OVER, MAN.
YOU'RE IN A LOT OF AGONY THESE DAYS. I CAN TELL.
... YEAH.
WHAT IS IT THIS TIME?
WHAT KIND OF SWIMSUITS MAKE YOU FEEL A "TWINGE," KOUJI?

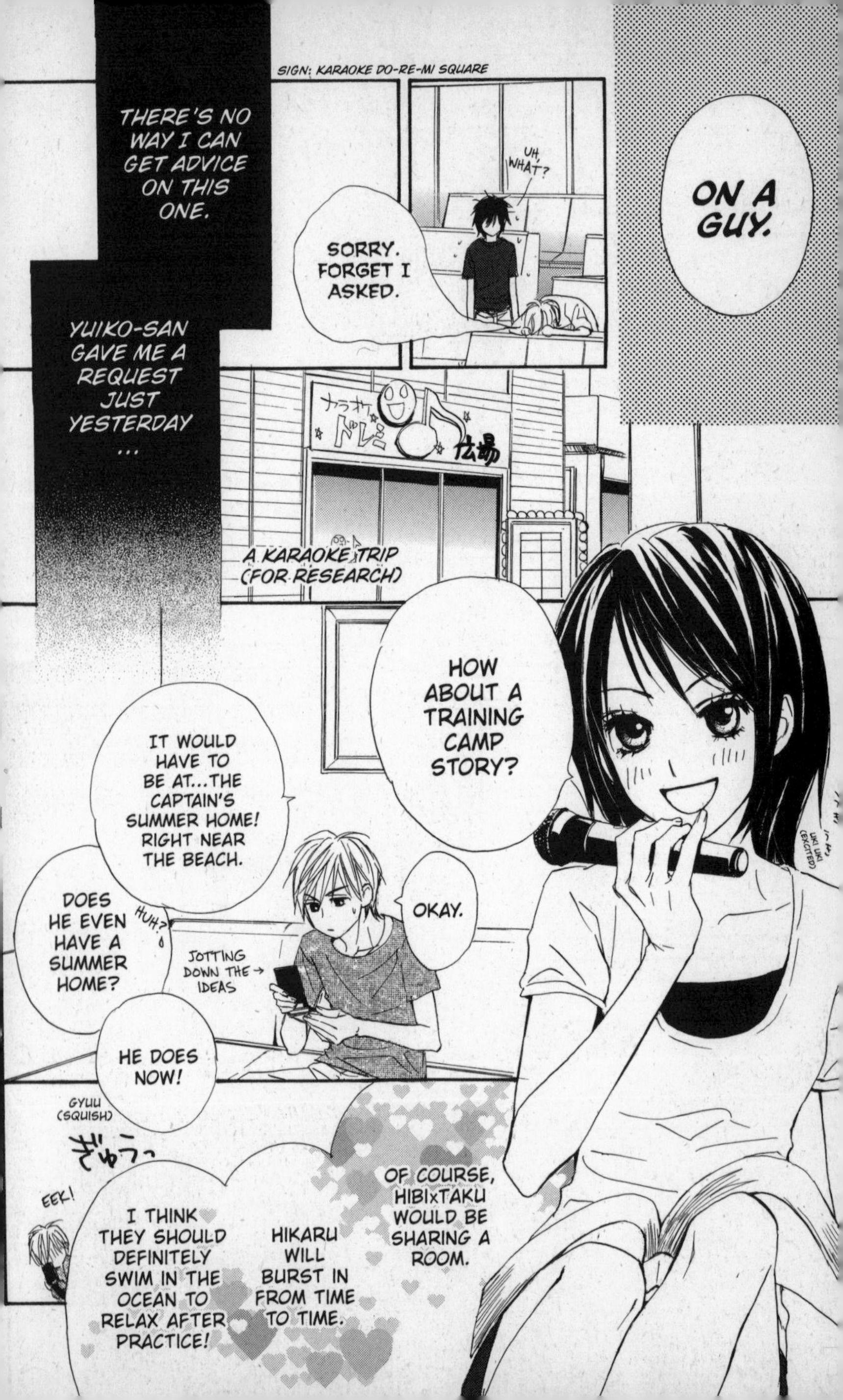

ON A GUY.
SIGN: KARAOKE DO-RE-MI SQUARE
UH, WHAT?
SORRY. FORGET I ASKED.
THERE'S NO WAY I CAN GET ADVICE ON THIS ONE.
カラオケ ドレミ 広場
A KARAOKE TRIP (FOR RESEARCH)
YUIKO-SAN GAVE ME A REQUEST JUST YESTERDAY ...
UKI UKI (EXCITED)
HOW ABOUT A TRAINING CAMP STORY?
OKAY.
IT WOULD HAVE TO BE AT...THE CAPTAIN'S SUMMER HOME! RIGHT NEAR THE BEACH.
HUH?
DOES HE EVEN HAVE A SUMMER HOME?
JOTTING DOWN THE IDEAS
HE DOES NOW!
OF COURSE, HIBIxTAKU WOULD BE SHARING A ROOM.
HIKARU WILL BURST IN FROM TIME TO TIME.
I THINK THEY SHOULD DEFINITELY SWIM IN THE OCEAN TO RELAX AFTER PRACTICE!
GYUU (SQUISH)
ぎゅうっ
EEK!

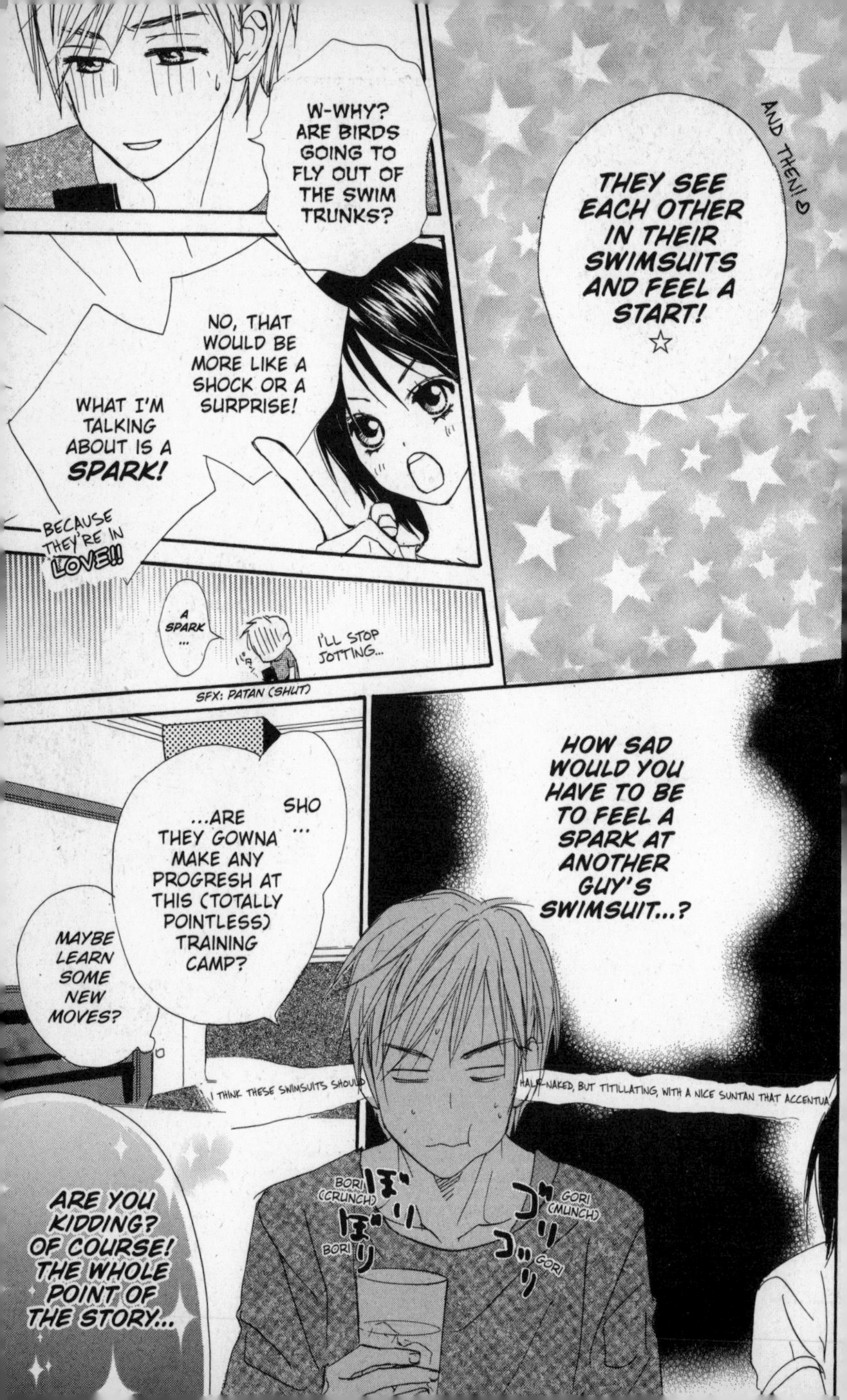
AND THEN!♡
THEY SEE EACH OTHER IN THEIR SWIMSUITS AND FEEL A START! ☆
W-WHY? ARE BIRDS GOING TO FLY OUT OF THE SWIM TRUNKS?
NO, THAT WOULD BE MORE LIKE A SHOCK OR A SURPRISE!
WHAT I'M TALKING ABOUT IS A SPARK!
BECAUSE THEY'RE IN LOVE!!
A SPARK...
I'LL STOP JOTTING...
SFX: PATAN (SHUT)
HOW SAD WOULD YOU HAVE TO BE TO FEEL A SPARK AT ANOTHER GUY'S SWIMSUIT...?
I THINK THESE SWIMSUITS SHOULD
HALF-NAKED, BUT TITILLATING, WITH A NICE SUNTAN THAT ACCENTUA
GORI (MUNCH)
GORI
BORI (CRUNCH)
BORI
SHO...
...ARE THEY GOWNA MAKE ANY PROGRESH AT THIS (TOTALLY POINTLESS) TRAINING CAMP?
MAYBE LEARN SOME NEW MOVES?
ARE YOU KIDDING? OF COURSE! THE WHOLE POINT OF THE STORY...

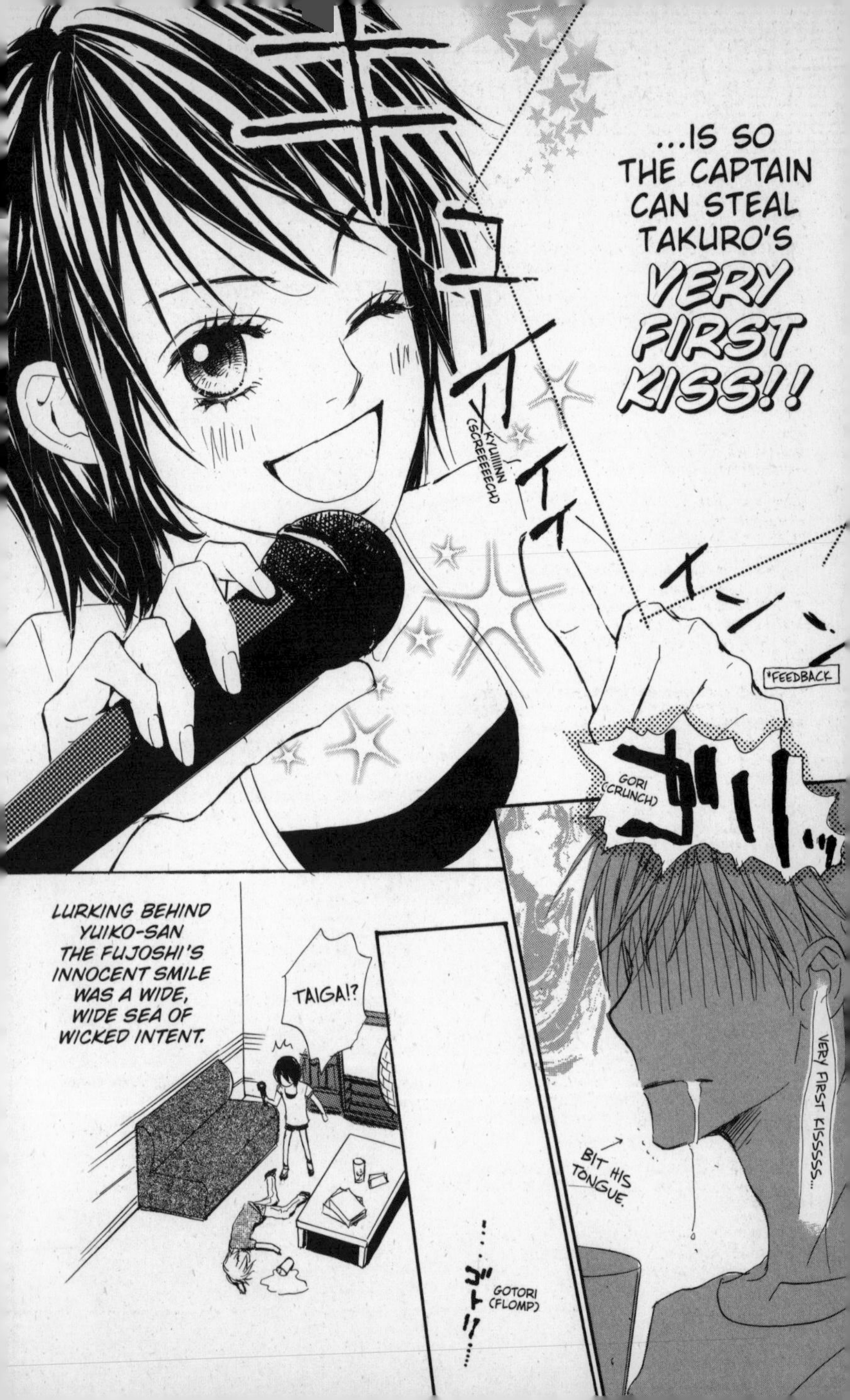
...IS SO THE CAPTAIN CAN STEAL TAKURO'S VERY FIRST KISS!!
KYUIIIINN (SCREEEEECH)
*FEEDBACK
GORI (CRUNCH)
VERY FIRST KISSSSS...
BIT HIS TONGUE.
...
GOTORI (FLOMP)
TAIGA!?
LURKING BEHIND YUIKO-SAN THE FUJOSHI'S INNOCENT SMILE WAS A WIDE, WIDE SEA OF WICKED INTENT.

FUJOSHI NEWS

vol.03

YUIKO-SAN GLOSSARY

AGE GAP COUPLING WHEN THE TOP (SEME) AND BOTTOM (UKE) IN A RELATIONSHIP HAVE A SUBSTANTIAL DIFFERENCE IN AGE.

BESPECTACLED MAN A MAN WHOSE APPEAL IS AUGMENTED BY THE WEARING OF GLASSES.

B.L. AN ABBREVIATION OF "BOYS' LOVE," A GENRE OF NOVELS/MANGA/GAMES BASED UPON LOVE BETWEEN MEN.

BLACK HAIR AND GLASSES THE BLACK HAIR MUST BE LONG AND SILKY, AND THE GLASSES MUST BE GLINTING AND SPARKLING.

BRIDE THE TITLE OF A BRAND-NEW WIFE. SOMETIMES A BOY WILL ATTAIN THIS TITLE INSTEAD OF A YOUNG LADY.

BUTLER CAFÉ A CAFÉ IN WHICH WAITERS DRESSED AS BUTLERS OR FOOTMEN PROVIDE ENTERTAINMENT AND LEISURE.

CONCUBINE A WOMAN WHOM A MARRIED MAN TREATS IN THE SAME WAY AS HIS WIFE. CAN ALSO REFER TO THE THIRD SON OF A DISGRACED NOBLE FAMILY, WHOM AN UNMARRIED MAN TREATS IN THE SAME WAY AS HE WOULD HIS WIFE (IF HE HAD ONE).

DOUJINSHI A PUBLICATION CREATED BY PEOPLE CONNECTED BY THE SAME GOAL OR HOBBY (E.G., A FAVORITE MANGA, A FAVORITE PAIRING).

FOOTMAN MALE SERVANT OF LOW RANK. BUTLER-IN-TRAINING.

FUJOSHI A WOMAN WHO ENJOYS DISSECTING AND REARRANGING THINGS. HEALTHY, INNOCUOUS SPORTS MANGA BECOME ROMANCE MANGA UNDER THEIR SUPERVISION. THE TERM'S RANGE HAS GROWN IN RECENT TIMES, AND CAN NOW APPLY TO WOMEN WHO SIMPLY ENJOY MANGA AND ANIME IN GENERAL.

GAP THE RUSH OF MOE SENSATION THAT RESULTS DUE TO LARGE SHIFTS FROM THE NORM. E.G., PEOPLE WEARING GLASSES WHO DO NOT USUALLY WEAR THEM.

HIBI×TAKU A PAIRING WITHIN "SEPATTE TAKURO" DOUJINSHI FANDOM IN WHICH CAPTAIN HIBINO IS THE SEME AND TAKURO IS THE UKE.

HIBI×TAKU NOVEL A NOVEL PACKED WITH THE EXCITING AND TITILLATING ROMANCE OF HIBI×TAKU.

MAID CAFÉ A CAFÉ OUT OF SOME WONDERFUL DREAM, IN WHICH THE WAITRESSES ARE DRESSED AS MAIDS.

PAIRING COUPLING. IN MOST CASES, CONSISTS OF A SEME AND UKE. OFTEN DESCRIBED WITH AN "×" BETWEEN EACH NAME, E.G., HIBI×TAKU, SEBAS×SHOTA.

POLITE SPEECH CHARACTER A CHARACTER WHO ALWAYS USES THE POLITE JAPANESE LANGUAGE FORM OF "DESU" AND "-MASU." BEHIND THIS GENTLE EXTERIOR OFTEN LIES DARK AMBITION OR FIERCE EMOTION.

POLITE SPEECH MOE TO FIND THE ABOVE CHARACTER ARCHETYPE A TURN-ON.

QUEEN THE KING'S WIFE. CAN ALSO REFER TO A FORMER SALARYMAN WHO WENT ON BUSINESS TRIPS OUT OF THE COUNTRY.

ROTTEN TALK THE CONVERSATION OF FUJOSHI. E.G., "THE CAPTAIN BELONGS TO TAKURO."

SCISSOR ATTACK THE NAME OF A TECHNIQUE IN SEPAK TAKRAW. AFTER JUMPING, THE LEGS ARE CROSSED IN MIDAIR AS THE BALL IS KICKED.

SEBASTIAN A WESTERN NAME. FOR SOME REASON, EVERY BUTLER'S NAME SHOULD BE SEBASTIAN.

SEME TO INCITE BATTLE OR INVADE THE ENEMY'S TERRITORY. ALSO, A ROLE IN A RELATIONSHIP BETWEEN MEN.

SHOTA AN ABBREVIATION OF SHOUTAROU (A YOUNG BOY IN SHORT SHORTS) COMPLEX.

SHOUTAROU SHOUTAROU KANEDA, MAIN CHARACTER OF "TETSUJIN 28." A YOUNG BOY WHO LOOKS GOOD IN SHORT SHORTS.

TASTY A DEVELOPMENT THAT IS "CONVENIENT" TO YUIKO-SAN'S IMAGINATION.

UKE TO ACCEPT SOMETHING THAT HAS BEEN OFFERED. ALSO, A ROLE IN A RELATIONSHIP BETWEEN MEN.

VCR TIMER WHAT YOU USE TO RECORD TV SHOWS. MOST ANIME SHOWS ARE THIRTY MINUTES, SO GETTING THE TIME WRONG BY 15 MINUTES IS LOSING HALF OF THE WEEK'S ENTERTAINMENT.

WEEKLY SHOUNEN STEP YUIKO-SAN'S FAVORITE. A SHOUNEN MANGA MAGAZINE BASED AROUND THE THEMES OF FIGHTING, JUSTICE, AND BRAVERY.

YOUNGER SEME WHEN A YOUNGER CHARACTER PLAYS THE "SEME" ROLE.

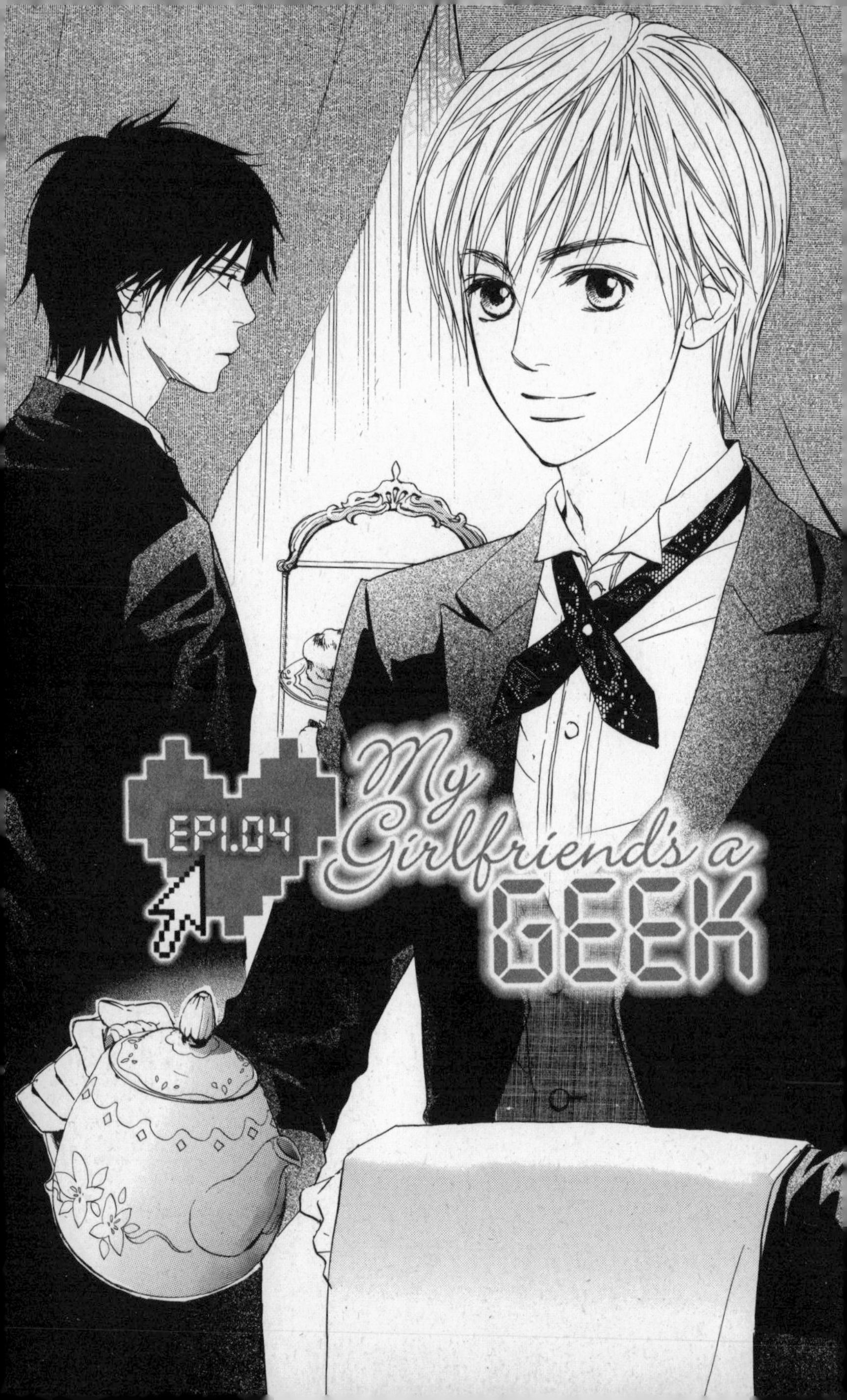
EP1.04
My Girlfriend's a
GEEK

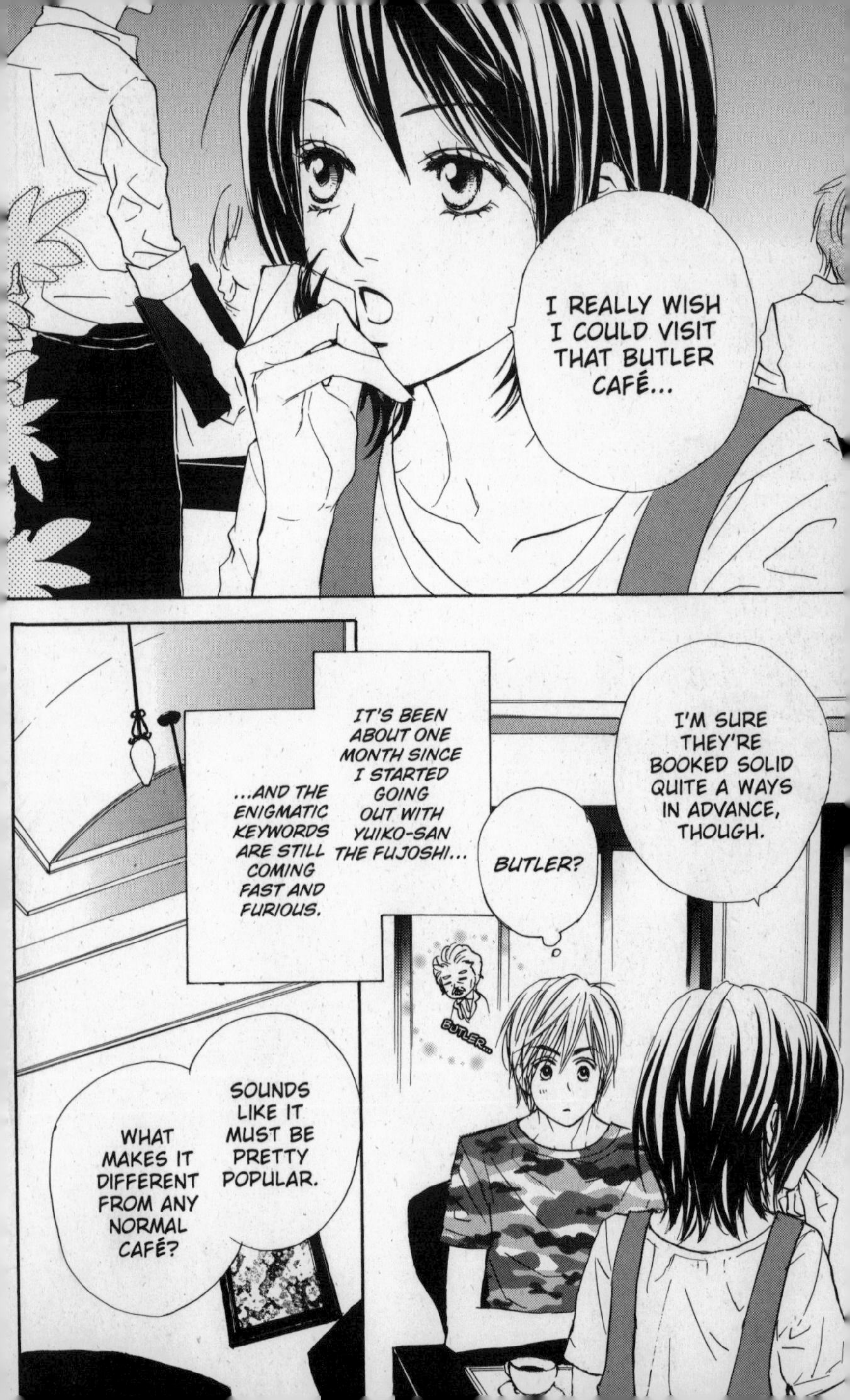
I REALLY WISH I COULD VISIT THAT BUTLER CAFÉ...
I'M SURE THEY'RE BOOKED SOLID QUITE A WAYS IN ADVANCE, THOUGH.
BUTLER?
IT'S BEEN ABOUT ONE MONTH SINCE I STARTED GOING OUT WITH YUIKO-SAN THE FUJOSHI...
...AND THE ENIGMATIC KEYWORDS ARE STILL COMING FAST AND FURIOUS.
BUTLER...
SOUNDS LIKE IT MUST BE PRETTY POPULAR.
WHAT MAKES IT DIFFERENT FROM ANY NORMAL CAFÉ?

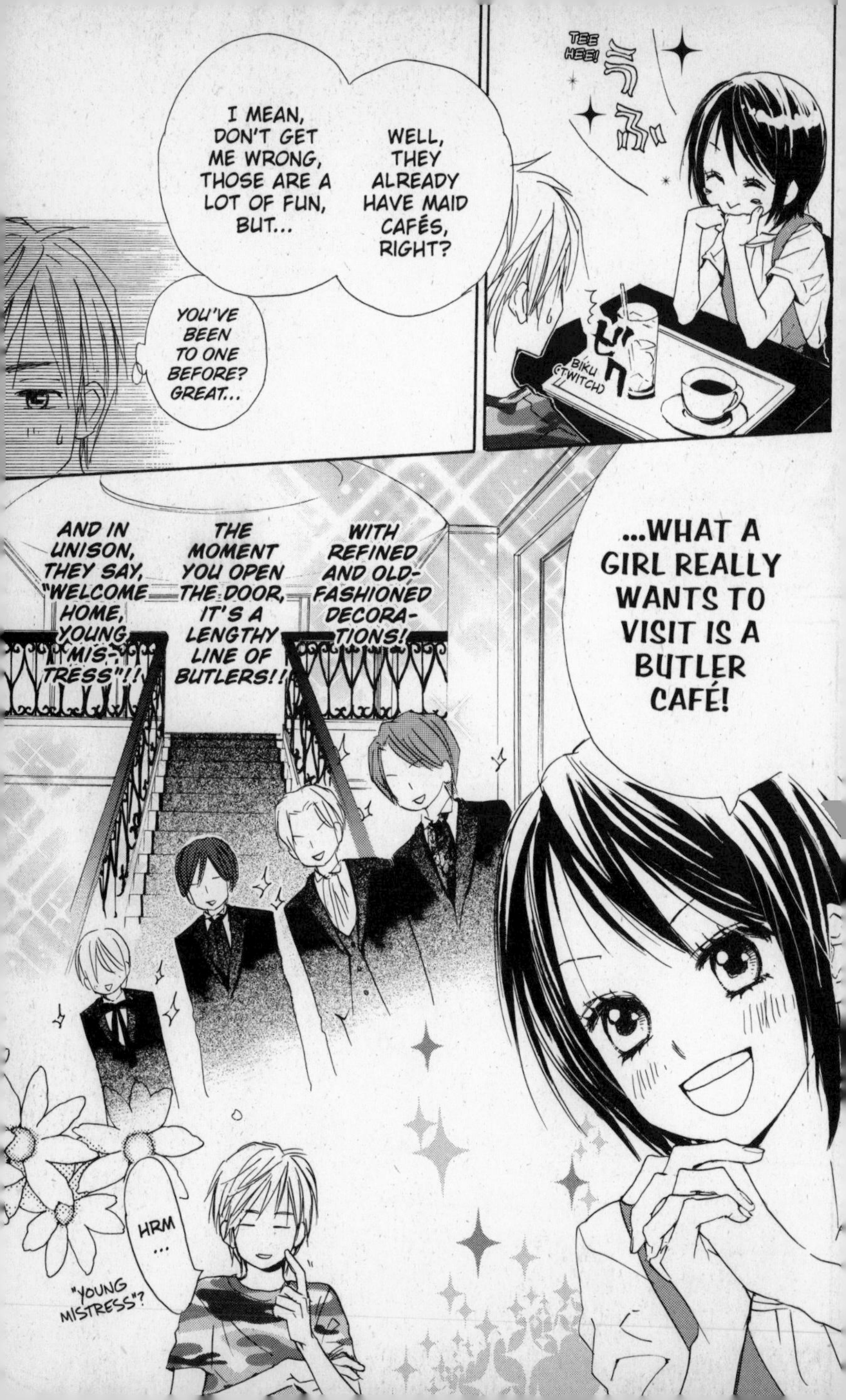
TEE HEE!
BIKU (TWITCH)
WELL, THEY ALREADY HAVE MAID CAFÉS, RIGHT?
I MEAN, DON'T GET ME WRONG, THOSE ARE A LOT OF FUN, BUT...
YOU'VE BEEN TO ONE BEFORE? GREAT...
...WHAT A GIRL REALLY WANTS TO VISIT IS A BUTLER CAFÉ!
WITH REFINED AND OLD-FASHIONED DECORATIONS!
THE MOMENT YOU OPEN THE DOOR, IT'S A LENGTHY LINE OF BUTLERS!!
AND IN UNISON, THEY SAY, "WELCOME HOME, YOUNG MISTRESS"!!
HRM ...
"YOUNG MISTRESS"?

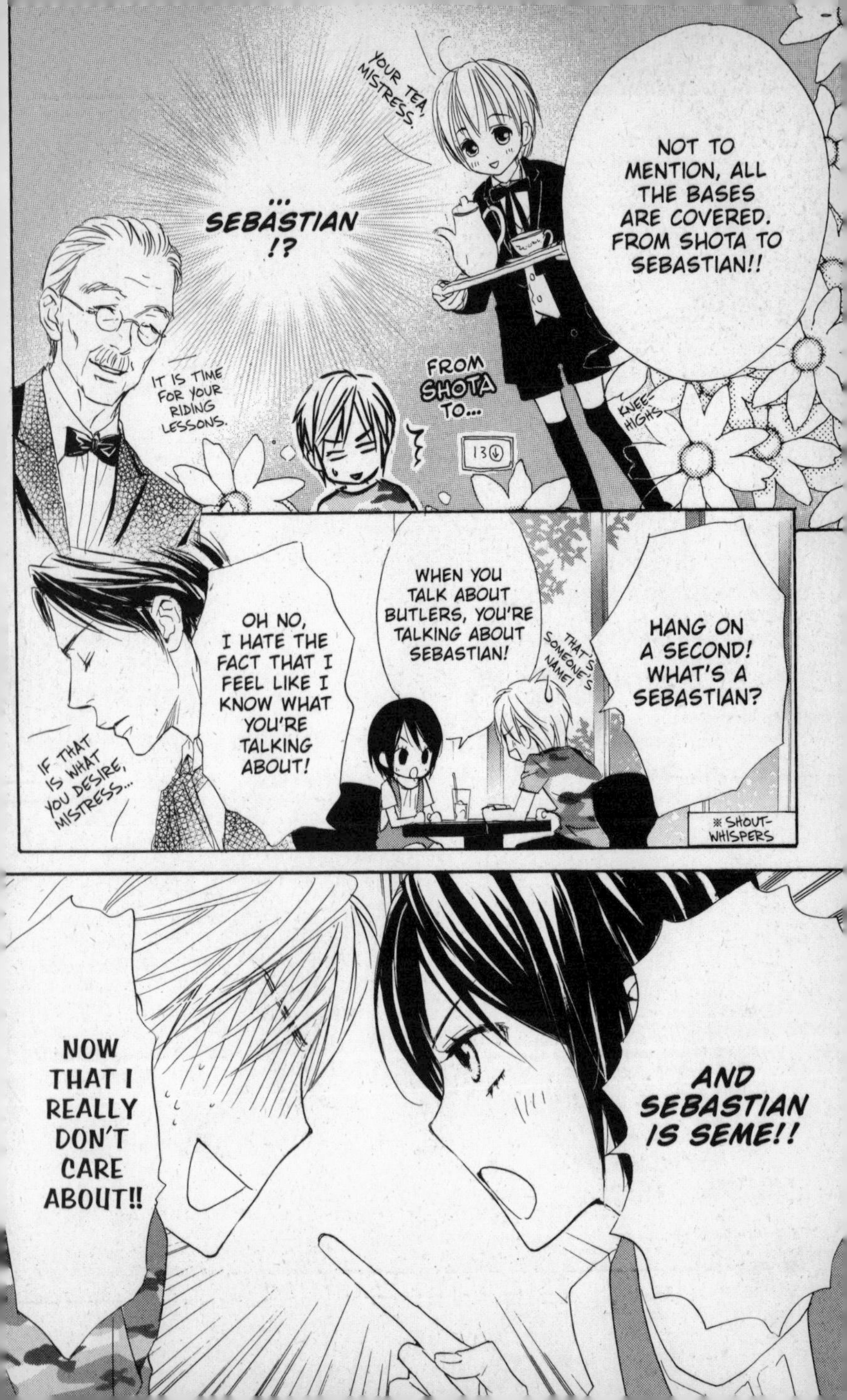
NOT TO MENTION, ALL THE BASES ARE COVERED. FROM SHOTA TO SEBASTIAN!!
YOUR TEA, MISTRESS.
...SEBASTIAN!?
KNEE-HIGHS
FROM SHOTA TO...
13
IT IS TIME FOR YOUR RIDING LESSONS.
HANG ON A SECOND! WHAT'S A SEBASTIAN?
※SHOUT-WHISPERS
THAT'S SOMEONE'S NAME!
WHEN YOU TALK ABOUT BUTLERS, YOU'RE TALKING ABOUT SEBASTIAN!
OH NO, I HATE THE FACT THAT I FEEL LIKE I KNOW WHAT YOU'RE TALKING ABOUT!
IF THAT IS WHAT YOU DESIRE, MISTRESS...
AND SEBASTIAN IS SEME!!
NOW THAT I REALLY DON'T CARE ABOUT!!

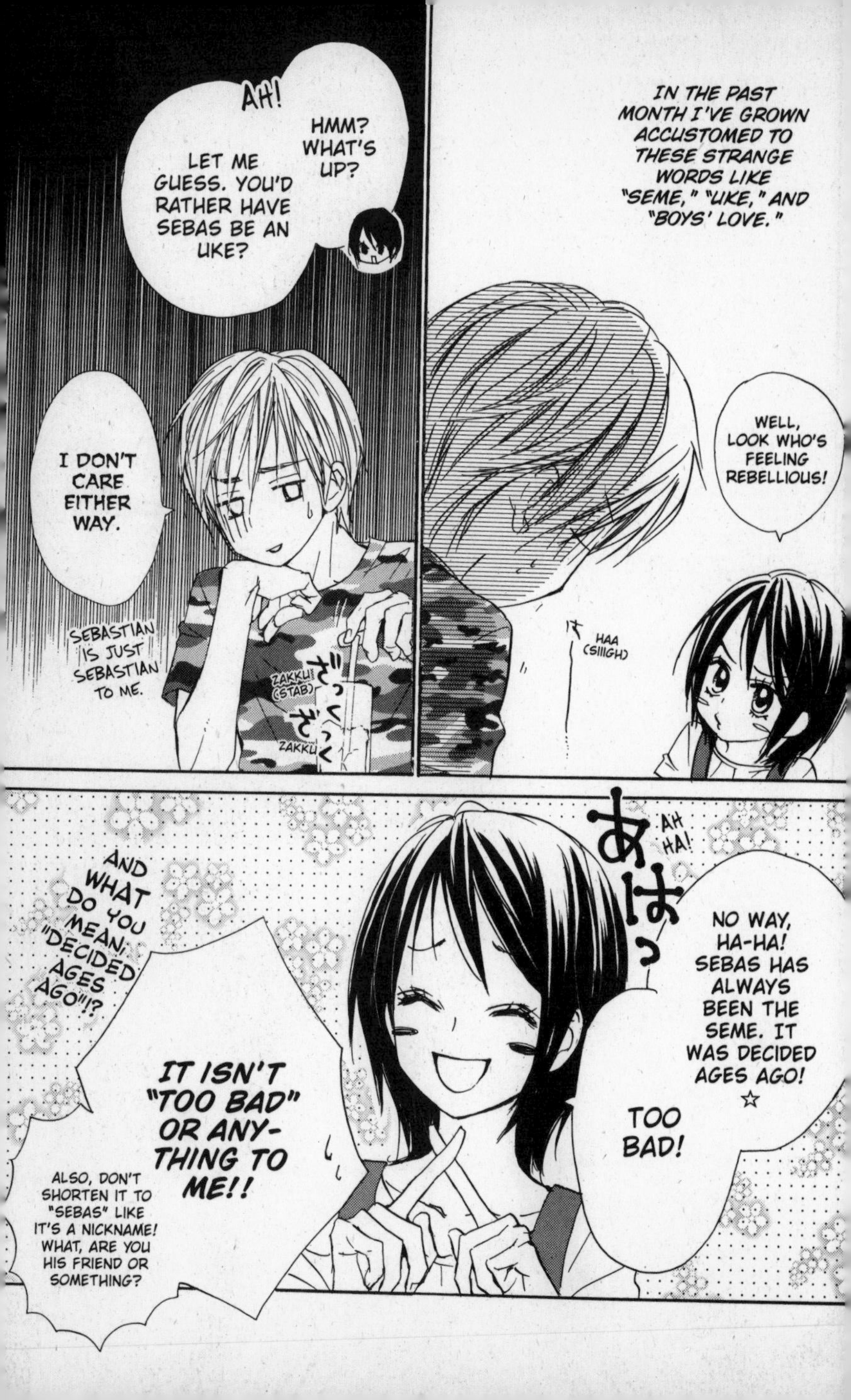
IN THE PAST MONTH I'VE GROWN ACCUSTOMED TO THESE STRANGE WORDS LIKE "SEME," "UKE," AND "BOYS' LOVE."
WELL, LOOK WHO'S FEELING REBELLIOUS!
HAA (SIIIGH)
AH!
HMM? WHAT'S UP?
LET ME GUESS. YOU'D RATHER HAVE SEBAS BE AN UKE?
I DON'T CARE EITHER WAY.
ZAKKU (STAB)
ZAKKU
SEBASTIAN IS JUST SEBASTIAN TO ME.
AH HA!
NO WAY, HA-HA! SEBAS HAS ALWAYS BEEN THE SEME. IT WAS DECIDED AGES AGO! ☆
TOO BAD!
IT ISN'T "TOO BAD" OR ANY-THING TO ME!!
AND WHAT DO YOU MEAN, "DECIDED AGES AGO"!?
ALSO, DON'T SHORTEN IT TO "SEBAS" LIKE IT'S A NICKNAME! WHAT, ARE YOU HIS FRIEND OR SOMETHING?

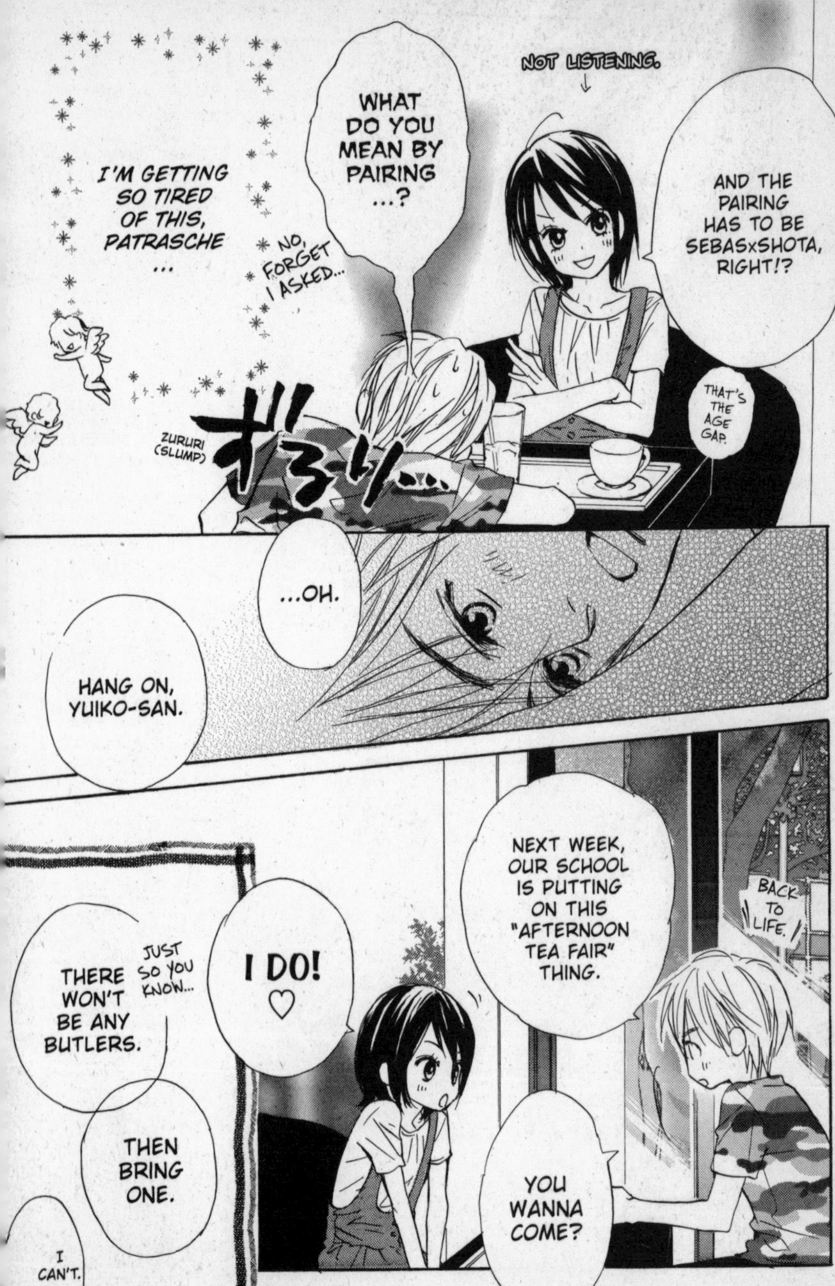
NOT LISTENING.
AND THE PAIRING HAS TO BE SEBASxSHOTA, RIGHT!?
THAT'S THE AGE GAP.
WHAT DO YOU MEAN BY PAIRING ...?
NO, FORGET I ASKED...
I'M GETTING SO TIRED OF THIS, PATRASCHE ...
ZURURI (SLUMP)
...OH.
HANG ON, YUIKO-SAN.
NEXT WEEK, OUR SCHOOL IS PUTTING ON THIS "AFTERNOON TEA FAIR" THING.
BACK TO LIFE.
YOU WANNA COME?
I DO! ♡
JUST SO YOU KNOW...
THERE WON'T BE ANY BUTLERS.
THEN BRING ONE.
I CAN'T.

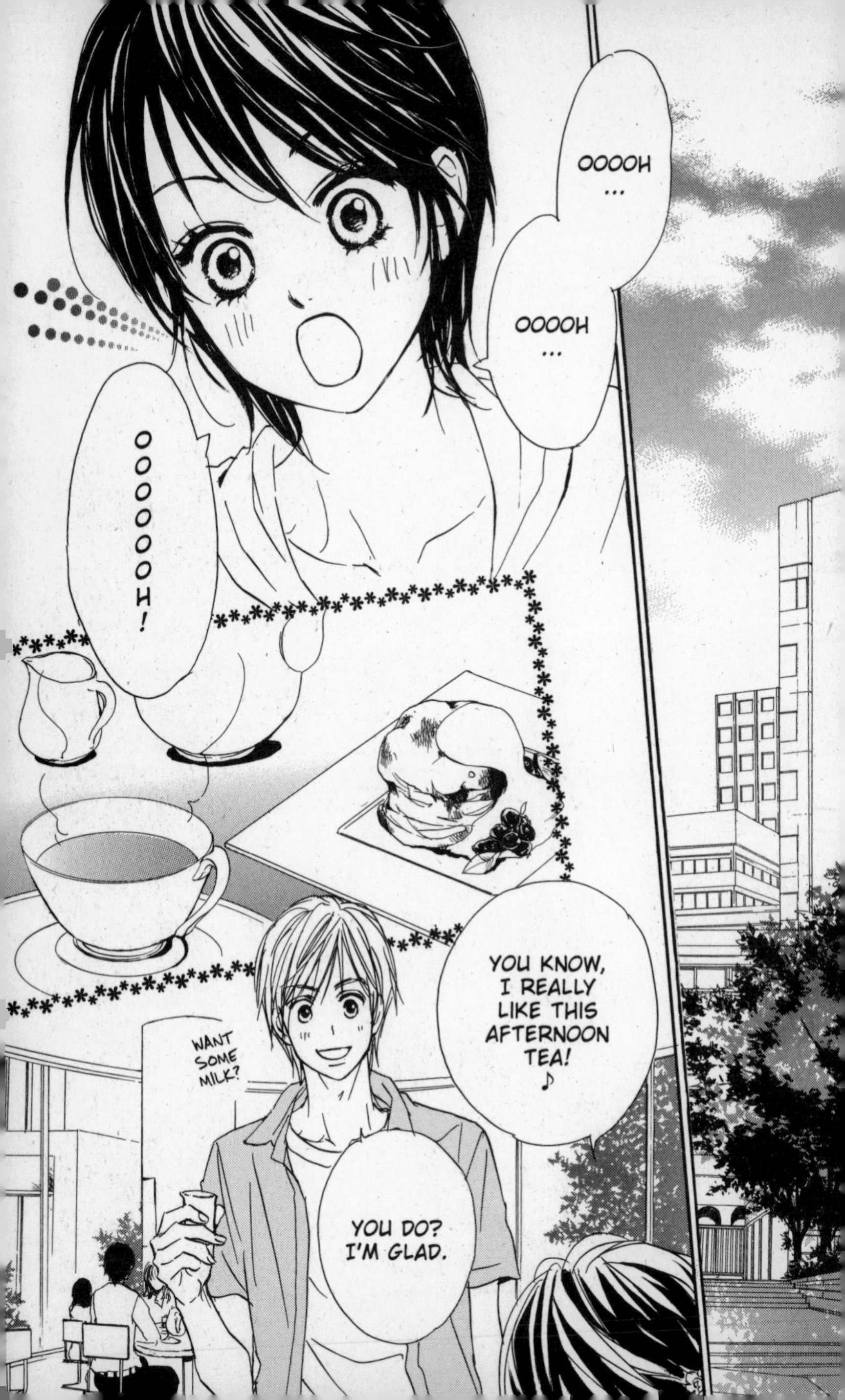
OOOOH ...
OOOOH ...
OOOOOOH!
YOU KNOW, I REALLY LIKE THIS AFTERNOON TEA! ♪
YOU DO? I'M GLAD.
WANT SOME MILK?

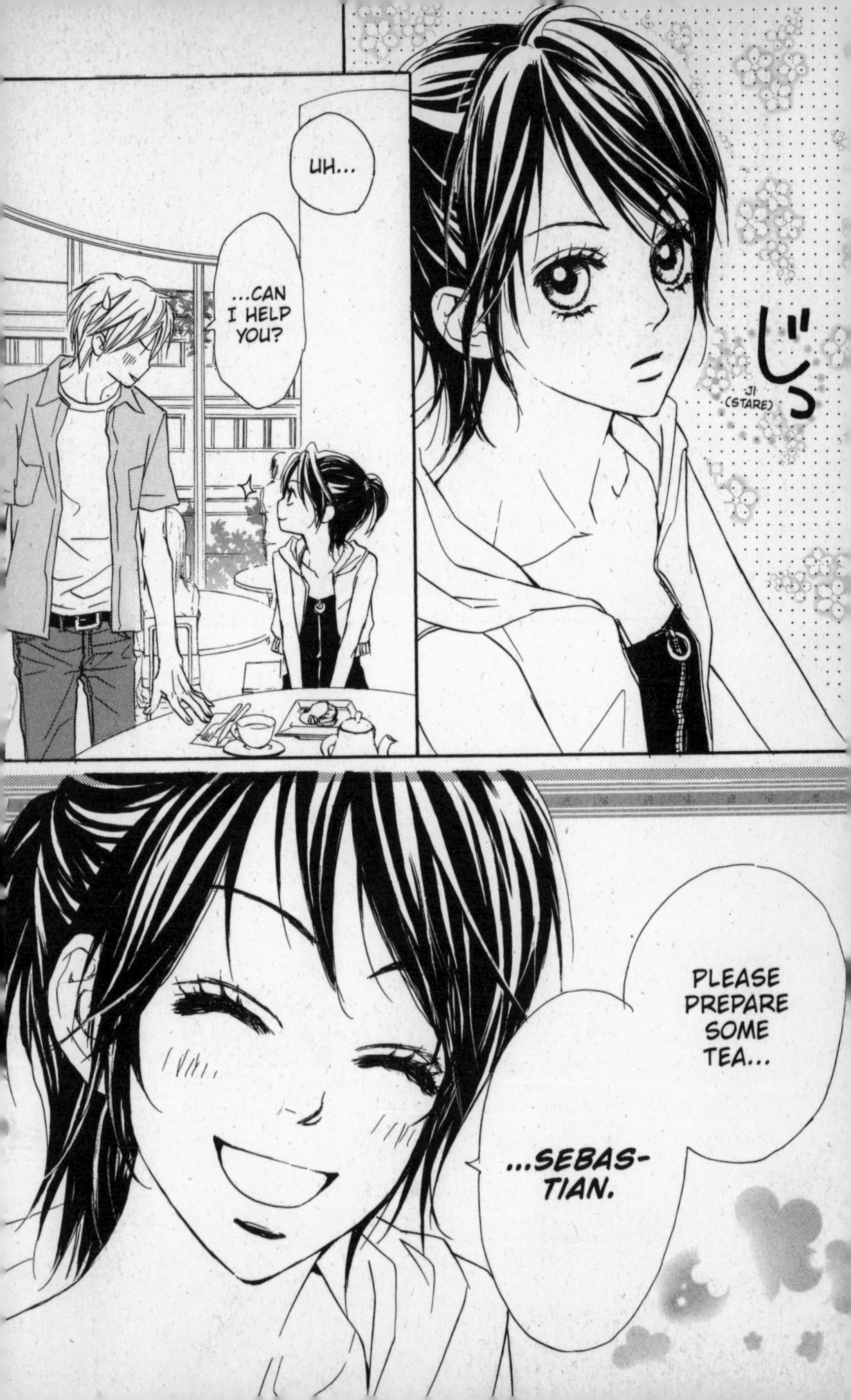
じっ
JI (STARE)
UH...
...CAN I HELP YOU?
PLEASE PREPARE SOME TEA...
...SEBAS-TIAN.

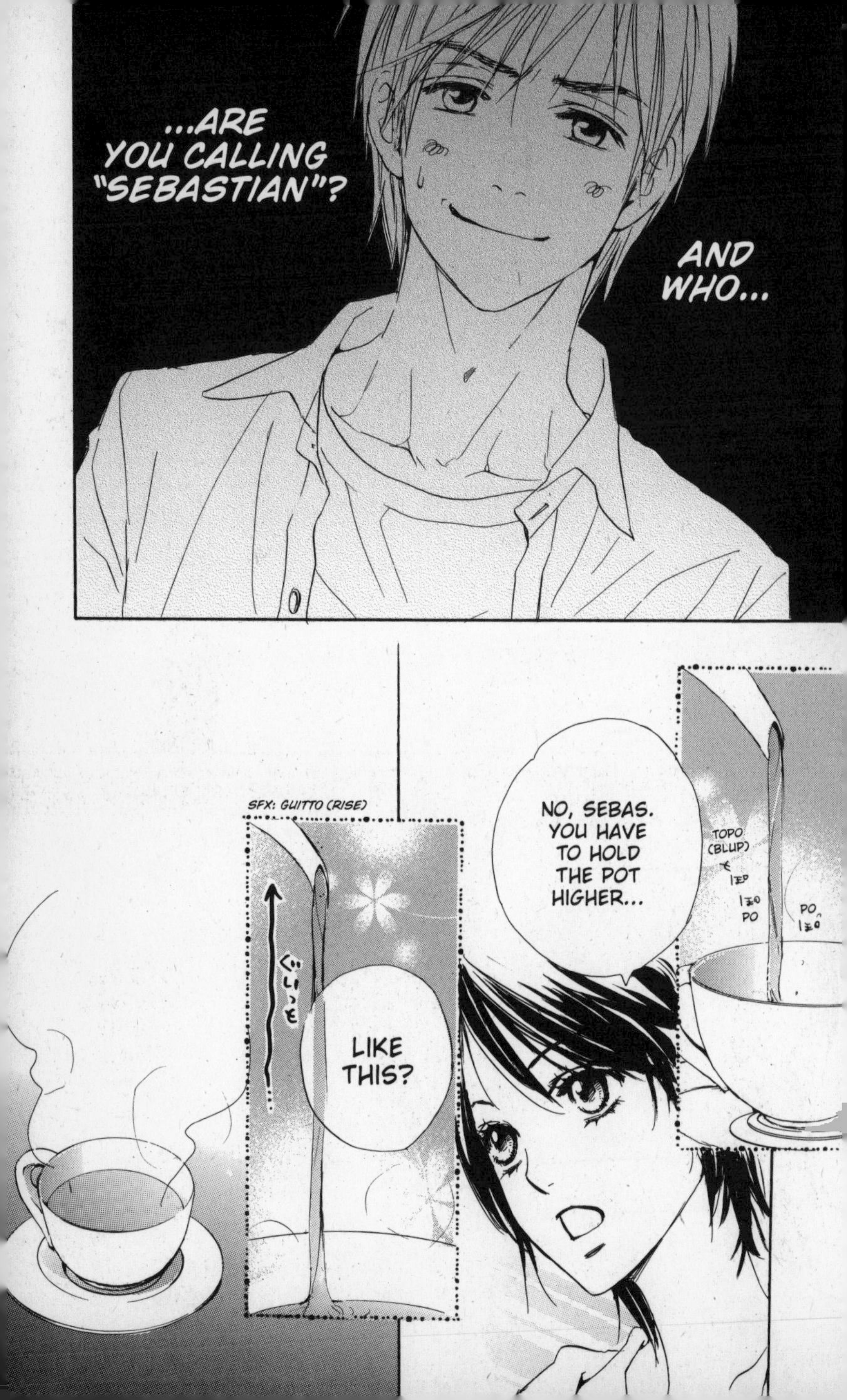
AND WHO...
...ARE YOU CALLING "SEBASTIAN"?
TOPO (BLUP)
PO
PO
NO, SEBAS. YOU HAVE TO HOLD THE POT HIGHER...
SFX: GUITTO (RISE)
LIKE THIS?

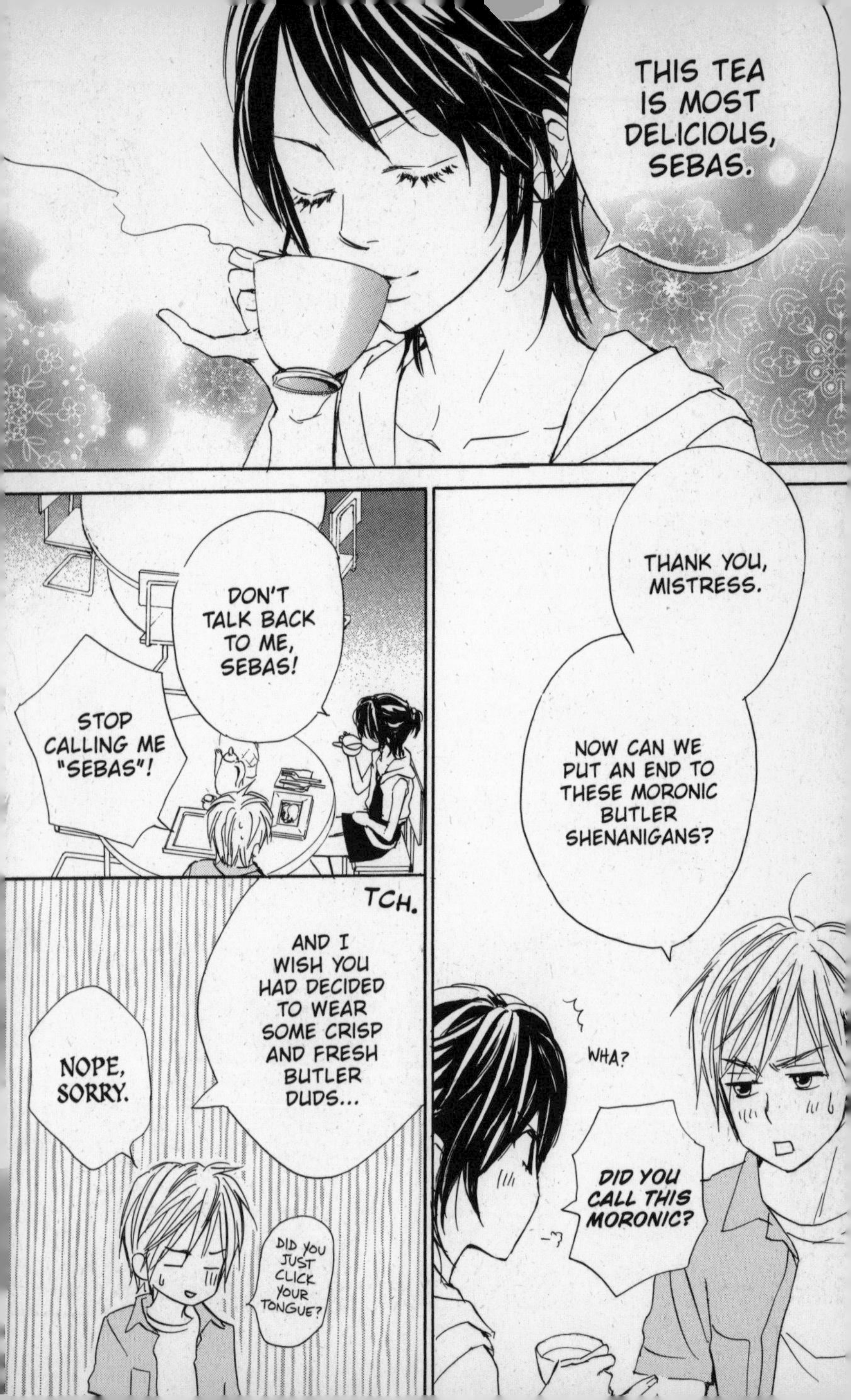
THIS TEA IS MOST DELICIOUS, SEBAS.
THANK YOU, MISTRESS.
NOW CAN WE PUT AN END TO THESE MORONIC BUTLER SHENANIGANS?
WHA?
DID YOU CALL THIS MORONIC?
DON'T TALK BACK TO ME, SEBAS!
STOP CALLING ME "SEBAS"!
TCH.
AND I WISH YOU HAD DECIDED TO WEAR SOME CRISP AND FRESH BUTLER DUDS...
NOPE, SORRY.
DID YOU JUST CLICK YOUR TONGUE?

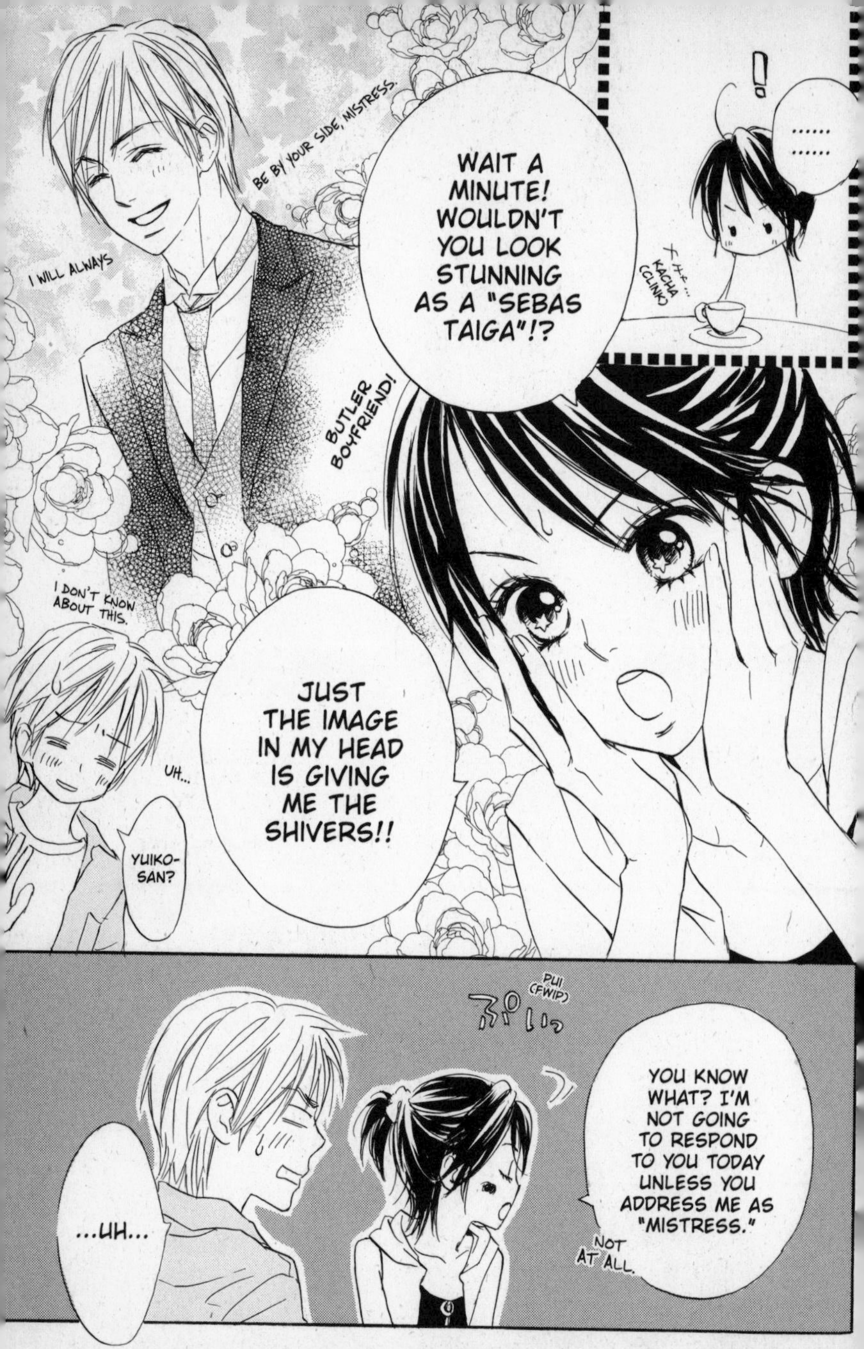

!
......
......
KACHA (CLINK)
WAIT A MINUTE! WOULDN'T YOU LOOK STUNNING AS A "SEBAS TAIGA"!?
BUTLER BOYFRIEND!
I WILL ALWAYS
BE BY YOUR SIDE, MISTRESS.
JUST THE IMAGE IN MY HEAD IS GIVING ME THE SHIVERS!!
I DON'T KNOW ABOUT THIS.
UH...
YUIKO-SAN?
PUI (FWIP)
YOU KNOW WHAT? I'M NOT GOING TO RESPOND TO YOU TODAY UNLESS YOU ADDRESS ME AS "MISTRESS."
NOT AT ALL.
...UH...

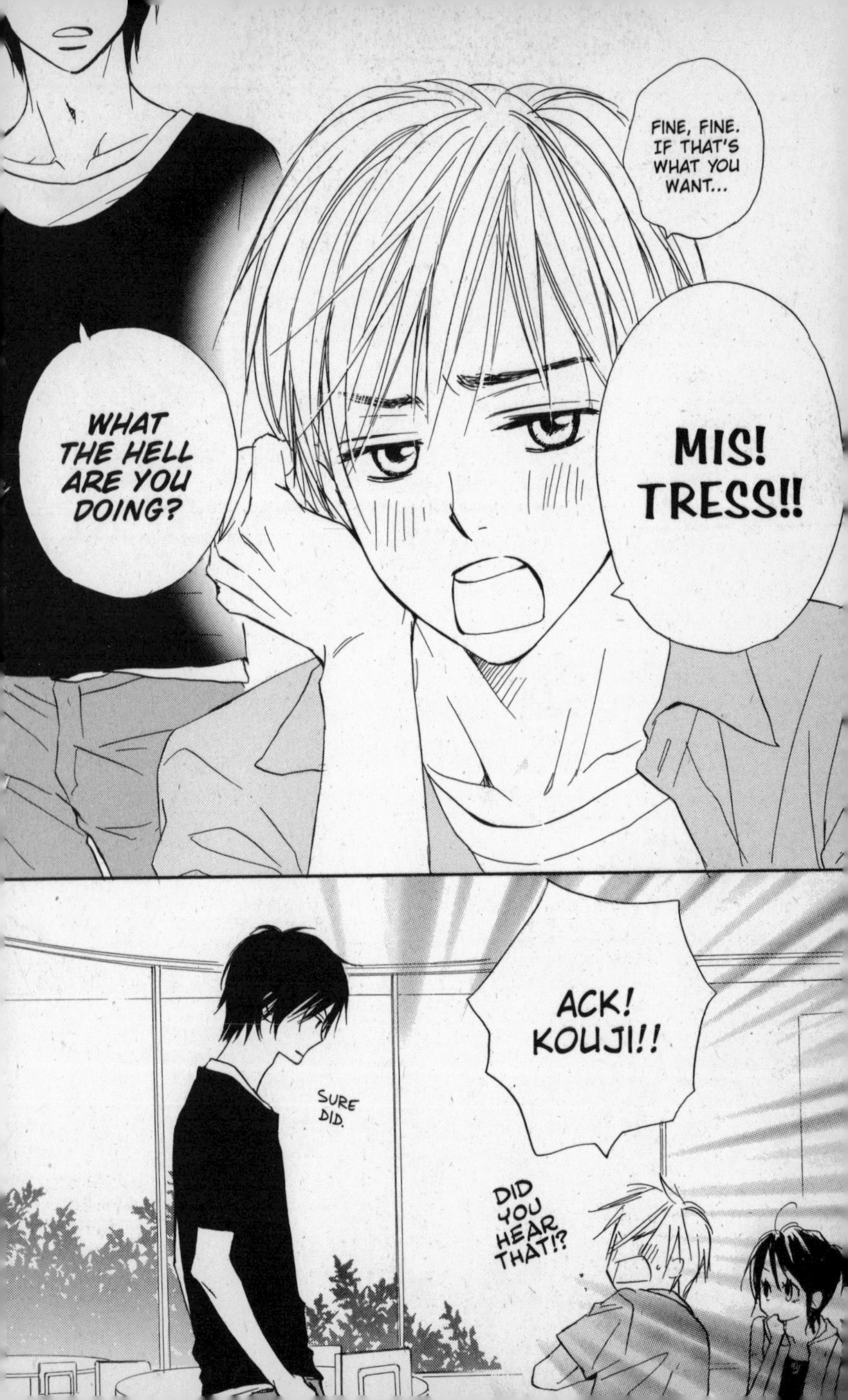
FINE, FINE. IF THAT'S WHAT YOU WANT...
MIS! TRESS!!
WHAT THE HELL ARE YOU DOING?
ACK! KOUJI!!
DID YOU HEAR THAT!?
SURE DID.

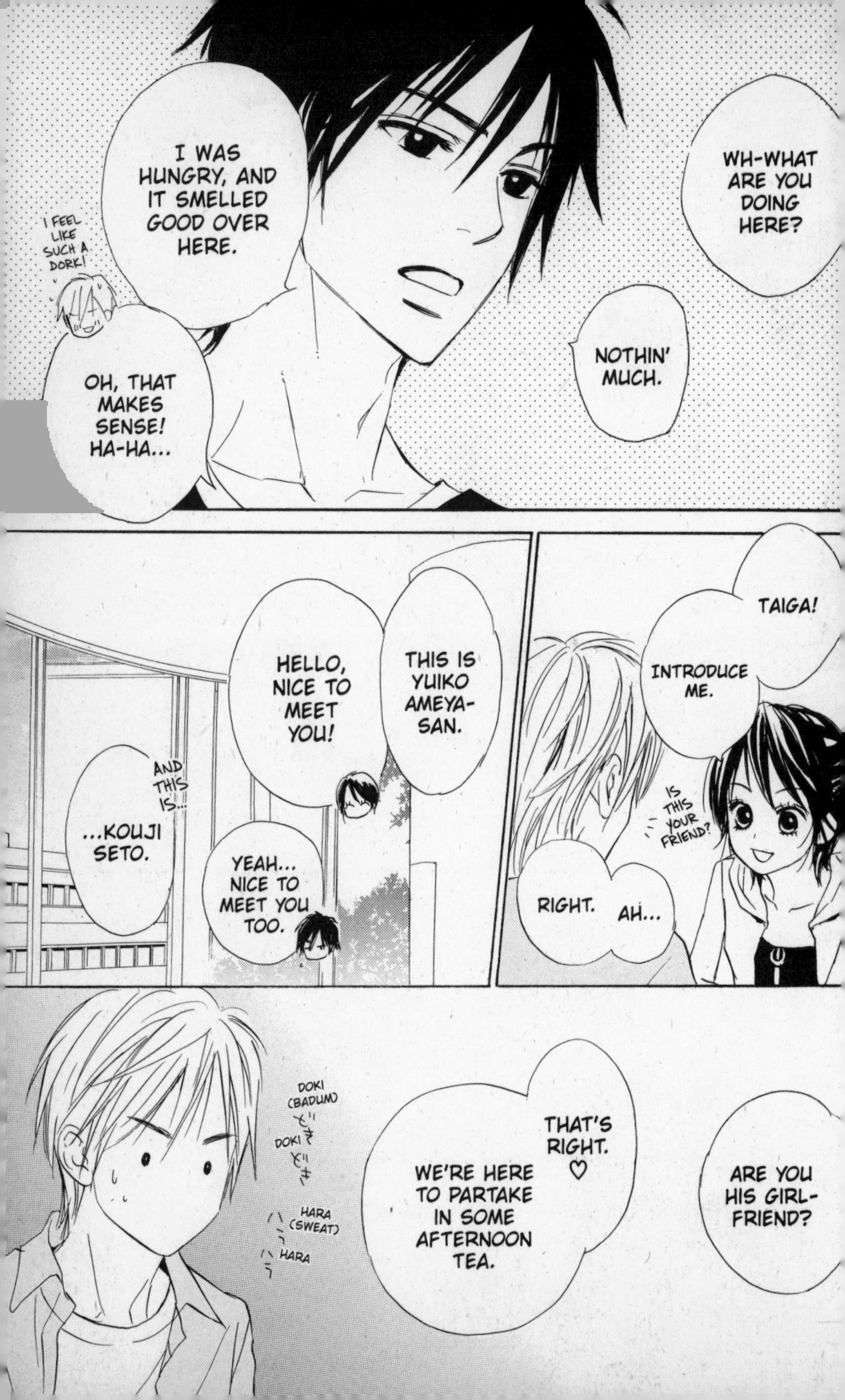
WH-WHAT ARE YOU DOING HERE?
NOTHIN' MUCH.
I WAS HUNGRY, AND IT SMELLED GOOD OVER HERE.
OH, THAT MAKES SENSE! HA-HA...
I FEEL LIKE SUCH A DORK!
TAIGA!
INTRODUCE ME.
IS THIS YOUR FRIEND?
AH...
RIGHT.
THIS IS YUIKO AMEYA-SAN.
HELLO, NICE TO MEET YOU!
AND THIS IS...
...KOUJI SETO.
YEAH... NICE TO MEET YOU TOO.
ARE YOU HIS GIRL-FRIEND?
THAT'S RIGHT. ♡
WE'RE HERE TO PARTAKE IN SOME AFTERNOON TEA.
DOKI (BADUM) DOKI
HARA (SWEAT) HARA

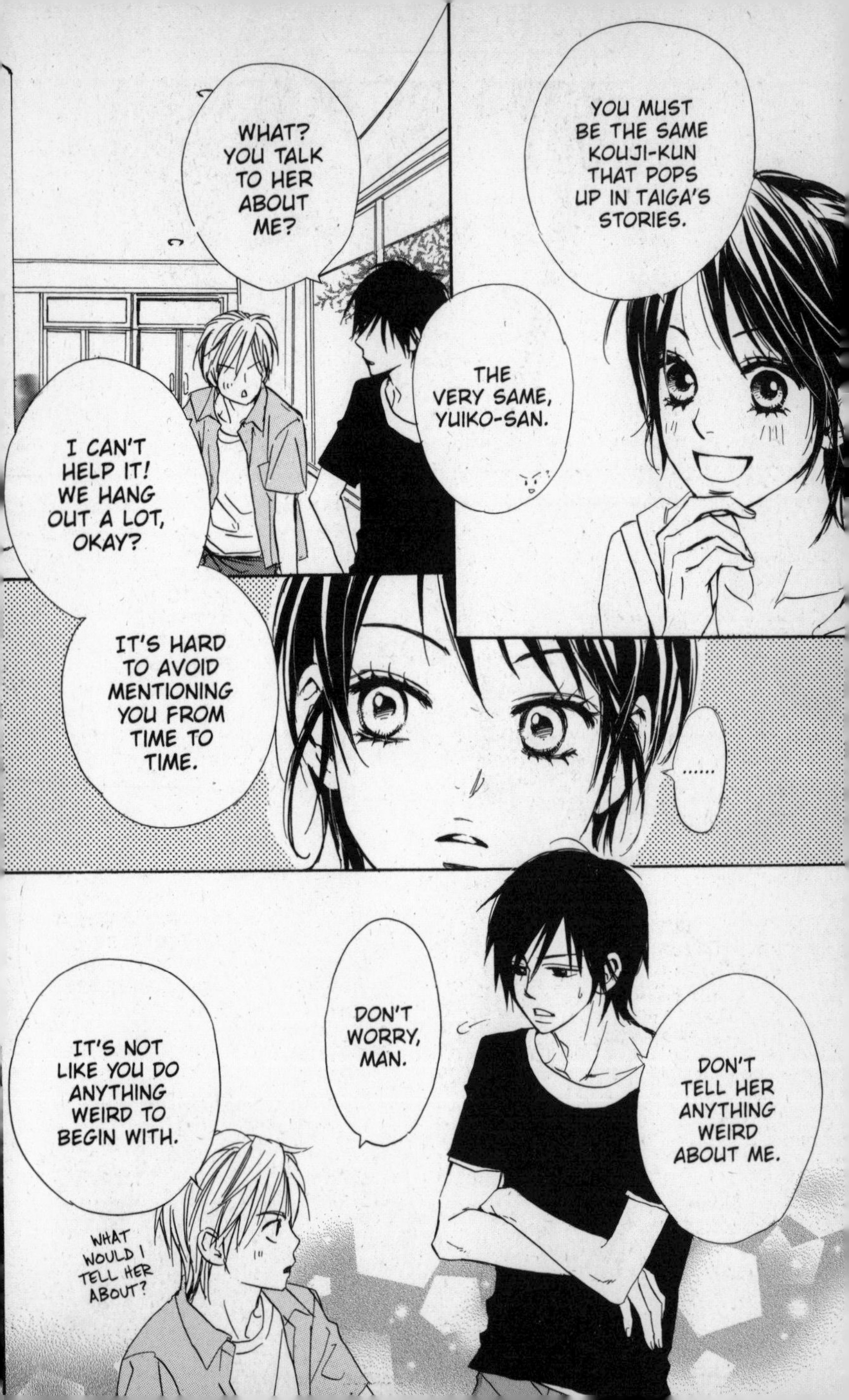
YOU MUST BE THE SAME KOUJI-KUN THAT POPS UP IN TAIGA'S STORIES.
THE VERY SAME, YUIKO-SAN.
WHAT? YOU TALK TO HER ABOUT ME?
I CAN'T HELP IT! WE HANG OUT A LOT, OKAY?
IT'S HARD TO AVOID MENTIONING YOU FROM TIME TO TIME.
......
DON'T TELL HER ANYTHING WEIRD ABOUT ME.
DON'T WORRY, MAN.
IT'S NOT LIKE YOU DO ANYTHING WEIRD TO BEGIN WITH.
WHAT WOULD I TELL HER ABOUT?

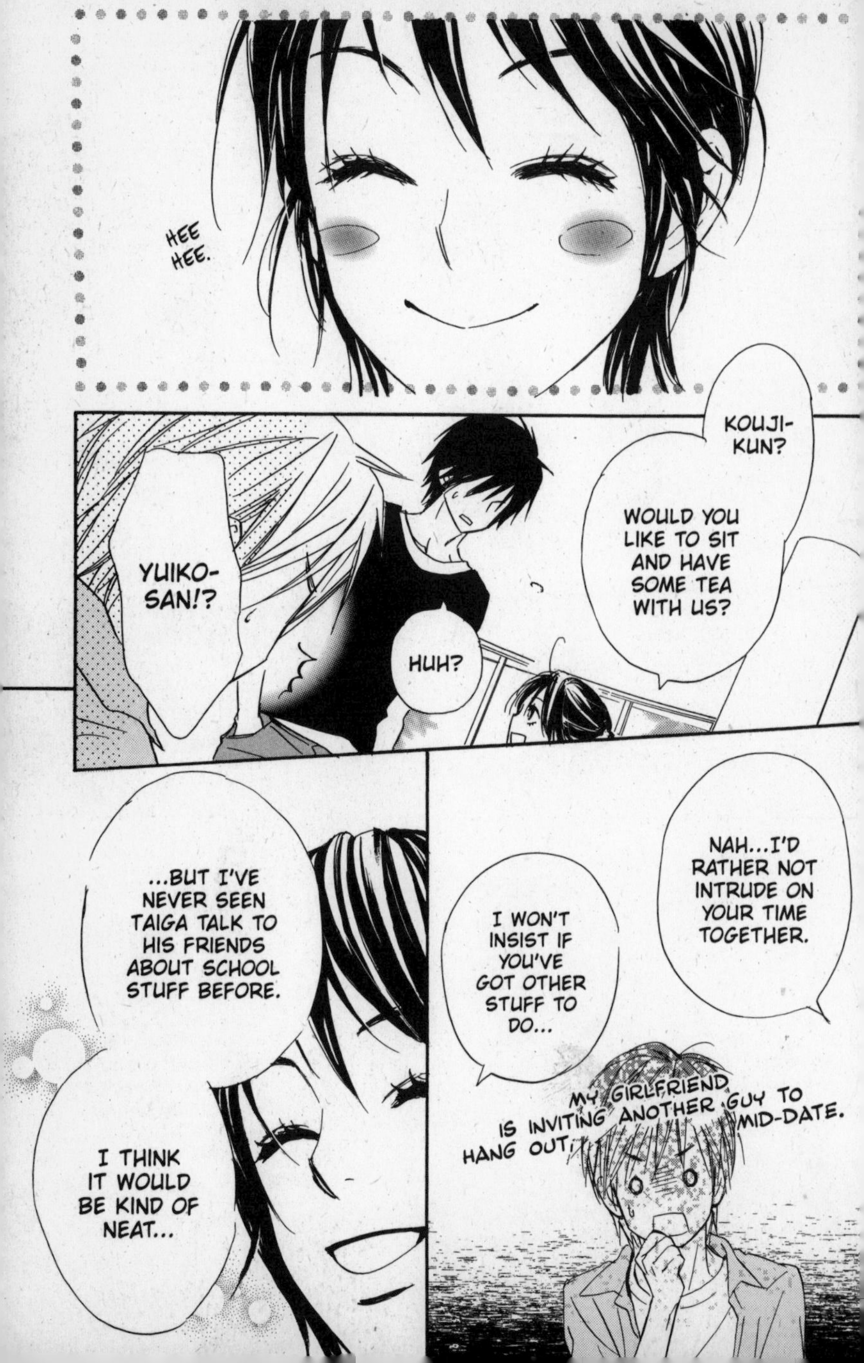
HEE HEE.
KOUJI-KUN?
WOULD YOU LIKE TO SIT AND HAVE SOME TEA WITH US?
HUH?
YUIKO-SAN!?
NAH...I'D RATHER NOT INTRUDE ON YOUR TIME TOGETHER.
I WON'T INSIST IF YOU'VE GOT OTHER STUFF TO DO...
MY GIRLFRIEND IS INVITING ANOTHER GUY TO HANG OUT, MID-DATE.
...BUT I'VE NEVER SEEN TAIGA TALK TO HIS FRIENDS ABOUT SCHOOL STUFF BEFORE.
I THINK IT WOULD BE KIND OF NEAT...

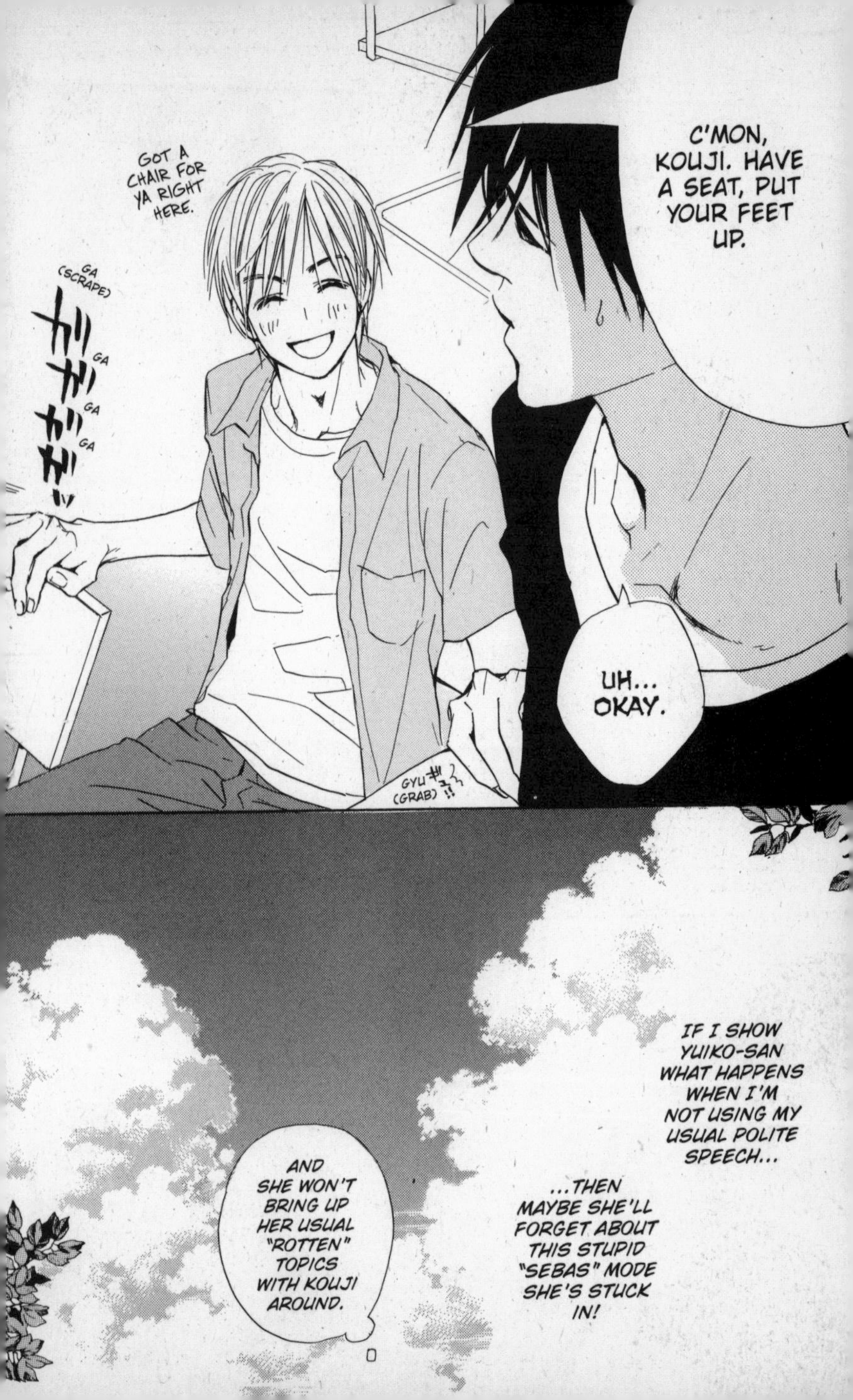
C'MON, KOUJI. HAVE A SEAT, PUT YOUR FEET UP.
GOT A CHAIR FOR YA RIGHT HERE.
GA (SCRAPE)
GA
GA
GA
UH... OKAY.
GYU (GRAB)
IF I SHOW YUIKO-SAN WHAT HAPPENS WHEN I'M NOT USING MY USUAL POLITE SPEECH...
...THEN MAYBE SHE'LL FORGET ABOUT THIS STUPID "SEBAS" MODE SHE'S STUCK IN!
AND SHE WON'T BRING UP HER USUAL "ROTTEN" TOPICS WITH KOUJI AROUND.

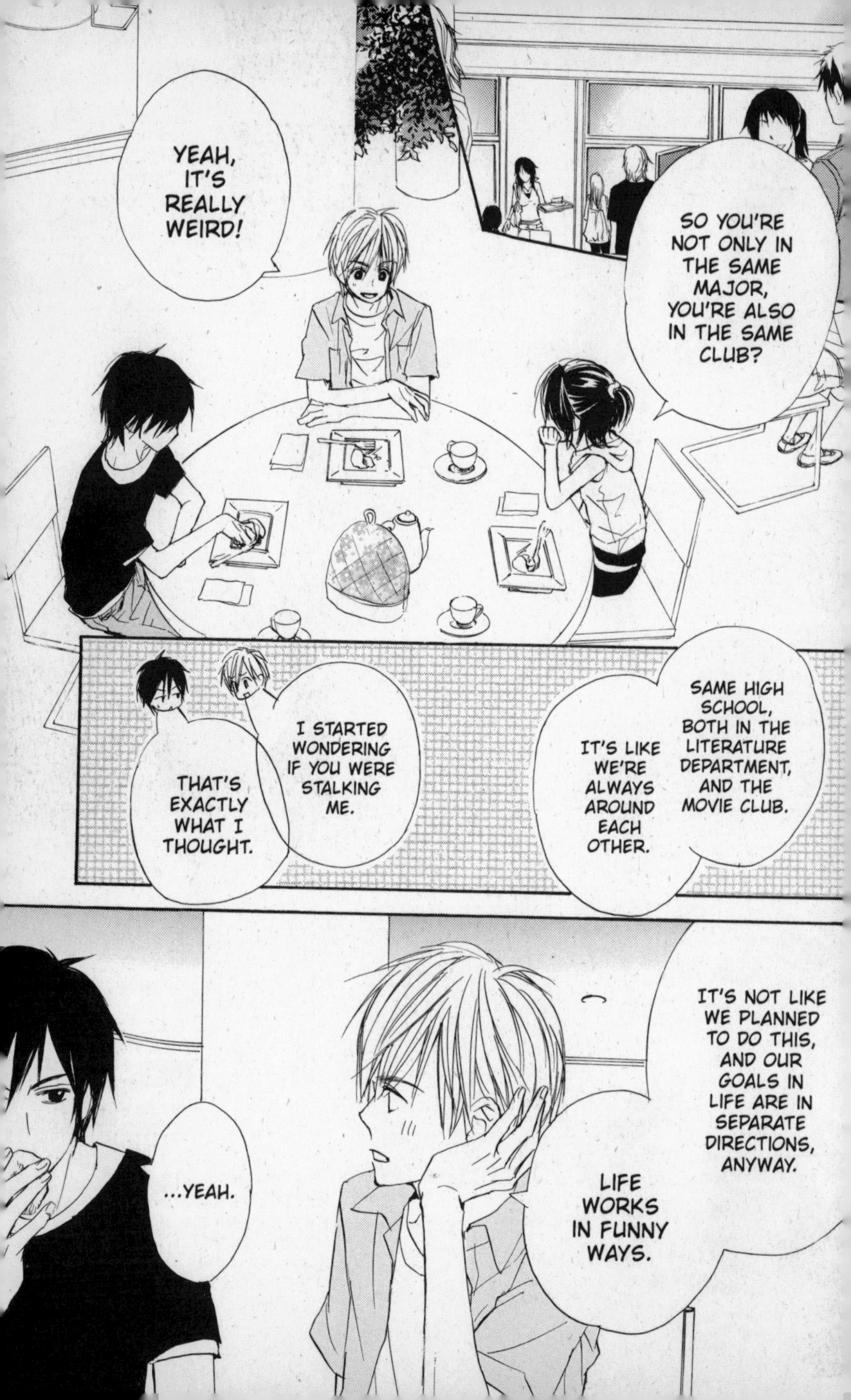
SO YOU'RE NOT ONLY IN THE SAME MAJOR, YOU'RE ALSO IN THE SAME CLUB?
YEAH, IT'S REALLY WEIRD!
SAME HIGH SCHOOL, BOTH IN THE LITERATURE DEPARTMENT, AND THE MOVIE CLUB.
IT'S LIKE WE'RE ALWAYS AROUND EACH OTHER.
I STARTED WONDERING IF YOU WERE STALKING ME.
THAT'S EXACTLY WHAT I THOUGHT.
IT'S NOT LIKE WE PLANNED TO DO THIS, AND OUR GOALS IN LIFE ARE IN SEPARATE DIRECTIONS, ANYWAY.
LIFE WORKS IN FUNNY WAYS.
...YEAH.

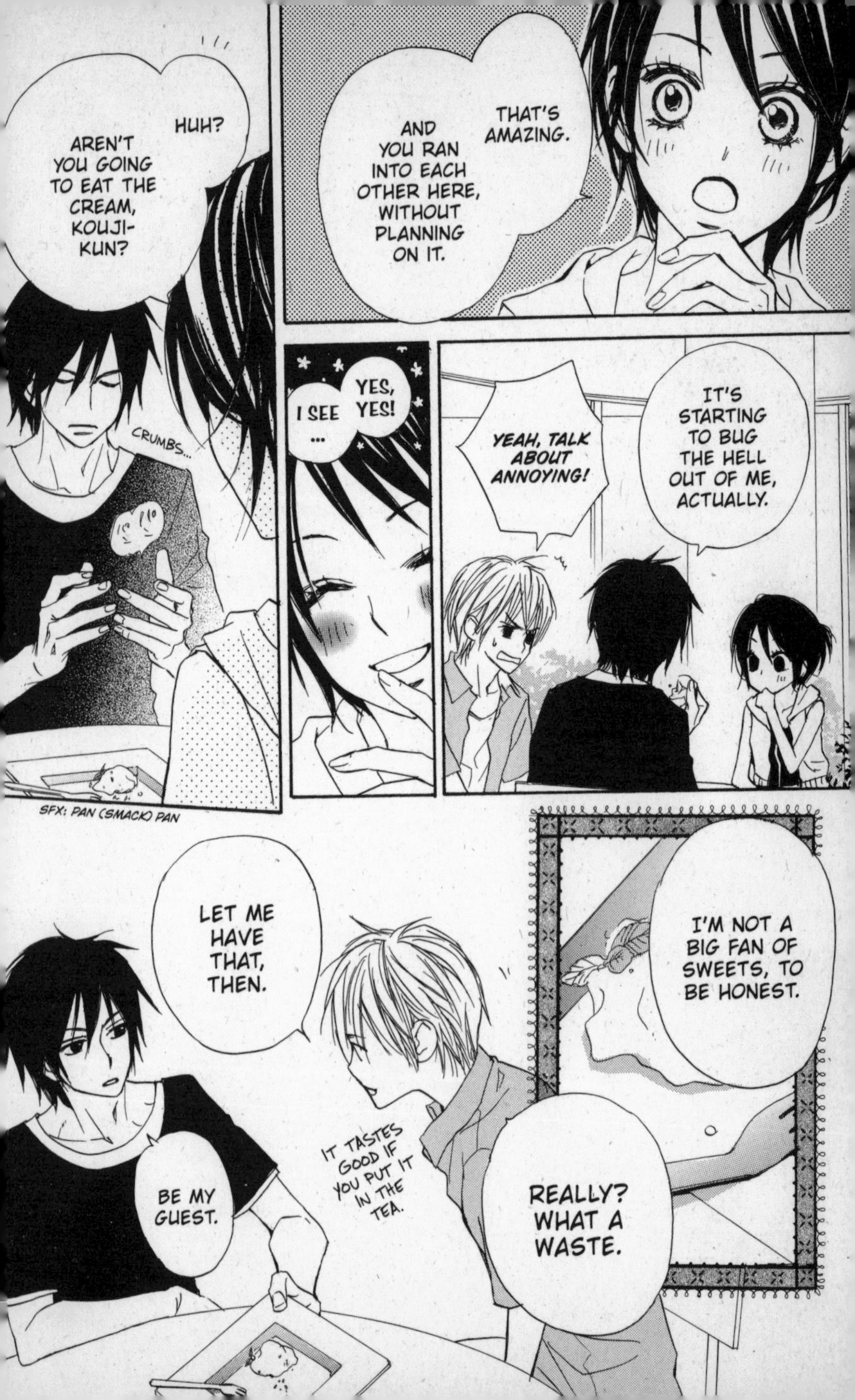
THAT'S AMAZING.
AND YOU RAN INTO EACH OTHER HERE, WITHOUT PLANNING ON IT.
IT'S STARTING TO BUG THE HELL OUT OF ME, ACTUALLY.
YEAH, TALK ABOUT ANNOYING!
YES, YES!
I SEE ...
HUH?
AREN'T YOU GOING TO EAT THE CREAM, KOUJI-KUN?
CRUMBS...
SFX: PAN (SMACK) PAN
I'M NOT A BIG FAN OF SWEETS, TO BE HONEST.
REALLY? WHAT A WASTE.
LET ME HAVE THAT, THEN.
IT TASTES GOOD IF YOU PUT IT IN THE TEA.
BE MY GUEST.

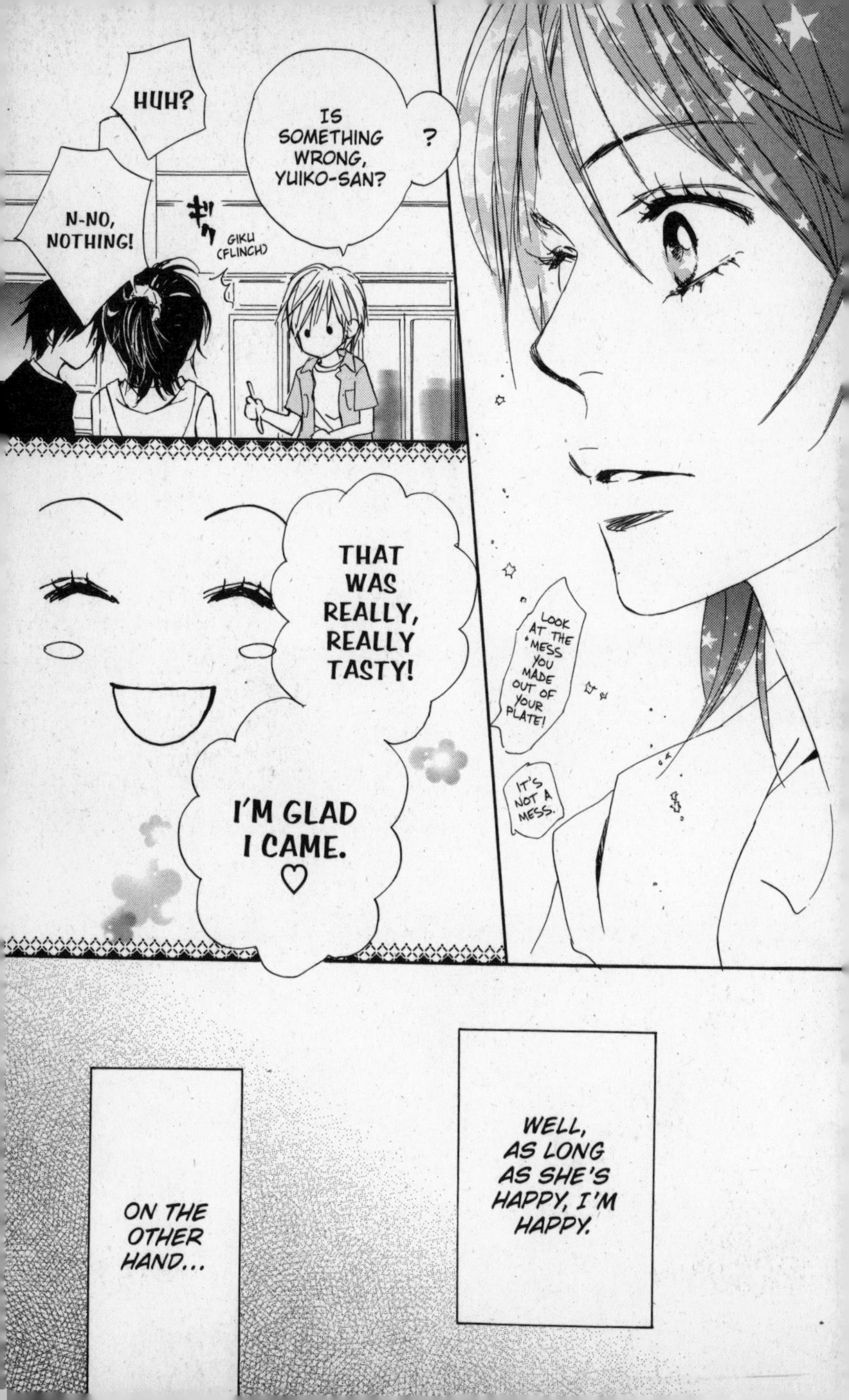
LOOK AT THE MESS YOU MADE OUT OF YOUR PLATE!
IT'S NOT A MESS.
?
IS SOMETHING WRONG, YUIKO-SAN?
HUH?
GIKU (FLINCH)
N-NO, NOTHING!
THAT WAS REALLY, REALLY TASTY!
I'M GLAD I CAME. ♡
WELL, AS LONG AS SHE'S HAPPY, I'M HAPPY.
ON THE OTHER HAND...

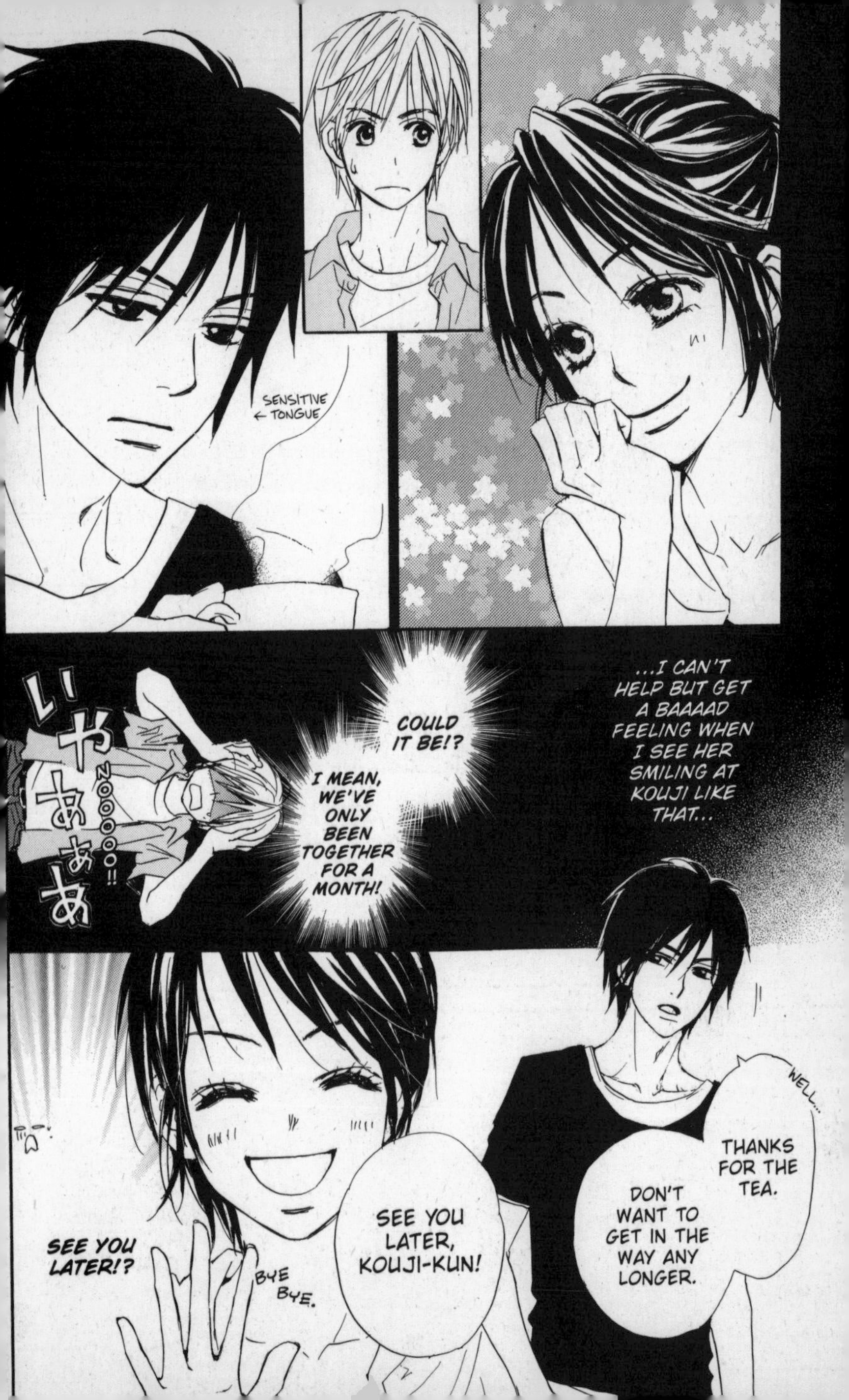
SENSITIVE
← TONGUE
...I CAN'T HELP BUT GET A BAAAAD FEELING WHEN I SEE HER SMILING AT KOUJI LIKE THAT...
COULD IT BE!?
I MEAN, WE'VE ONLY BEEN TOGETHER FOR A MONTH!
いやぁぁぁ
NOOOOOO!!
WELL...
THANKS FOR THE TEA.
DON'T WANT TO GET IN THE WAY ANY LONGER.
SEE YOU LATER, KOUJI-KUN!
BYE BYE.
SEE YOU LATER!?

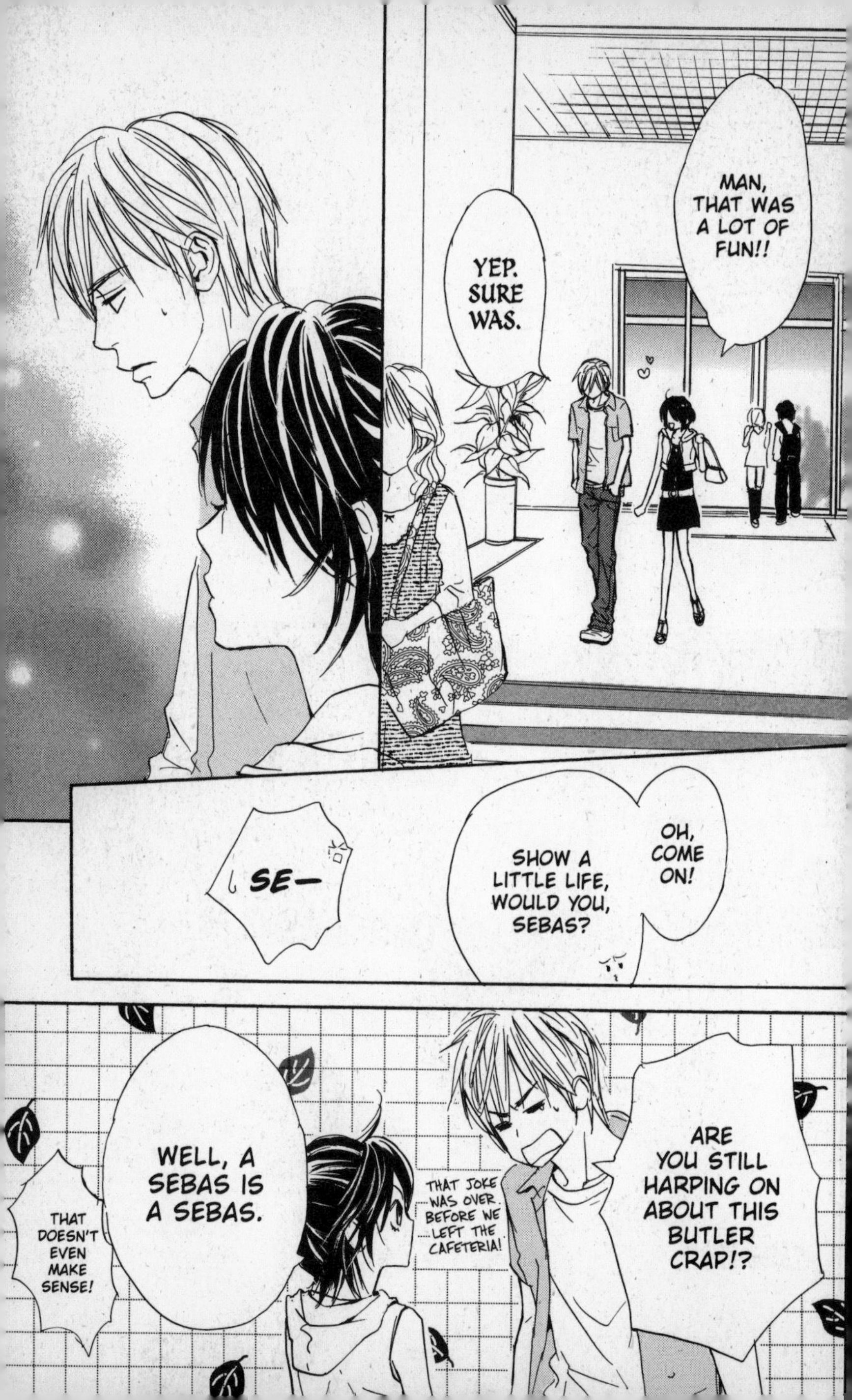
MAN, THAT WAS A LOT OF FUN!!
YEP. SURE WAS.
OH, COME ON!
SHOW A LITTLE LIFE, WOULD YOU, SEBAS?
SE—
ARE YOU STILL HARPING ON ABOUT THIS BUTLER CRAP!?
THAT JOKE WAS OVER BEFORE WE LEFT THE CAFETERIA!
WELL, A SEBAS IS A SEBAS.
THAT DOESN'T EVEN MAKE SENSE!

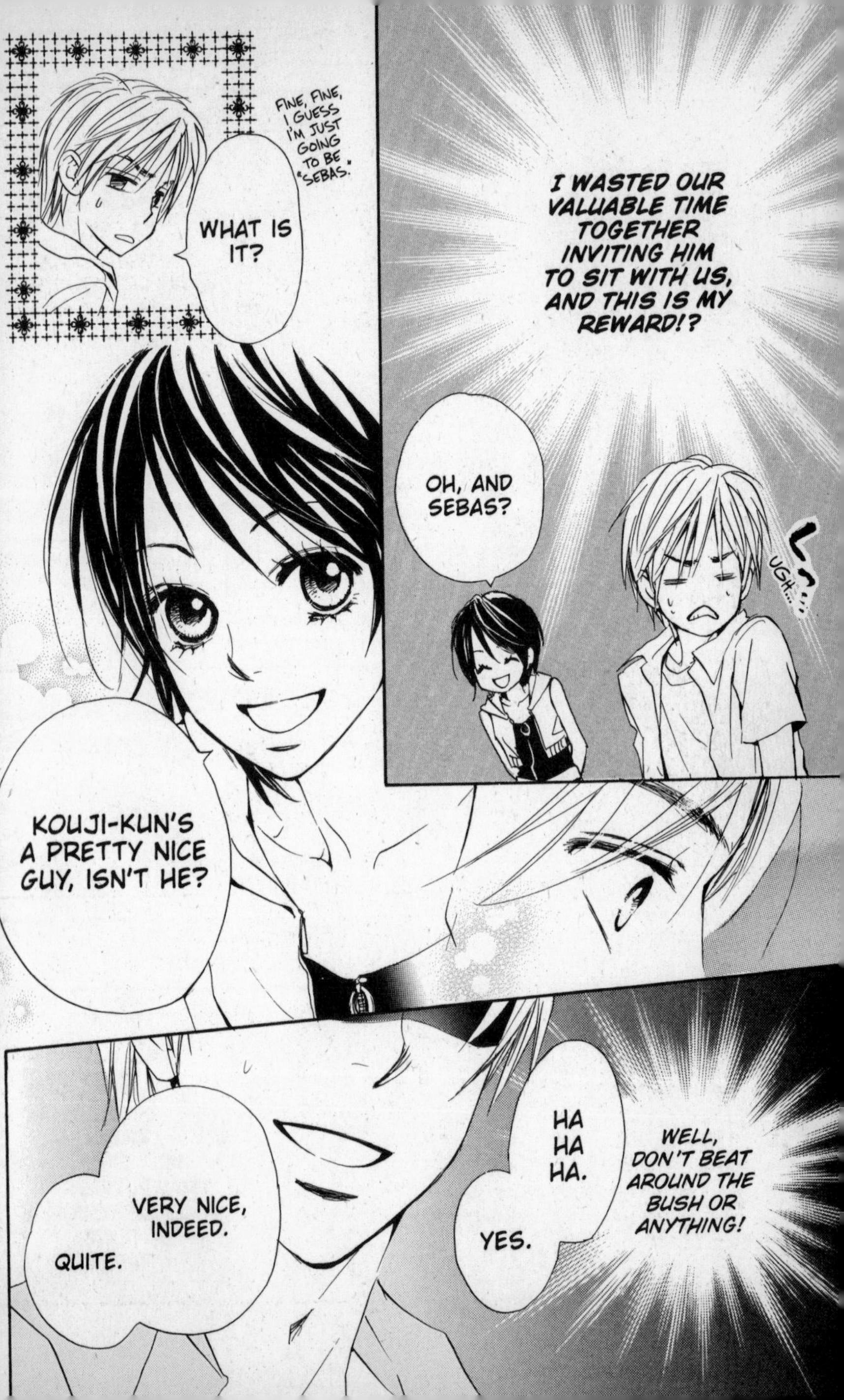
I WASTED OUR VALUABLE TIME TOGETHER INVITING HIM TO SIT WITH US, AND THIS IS MY REWARD!?
OH, AND SEBAS?
UGH...
FINE, FINE, I GUESS I'M JUST GOING TO BE "SEBAS."
WHAT IS IT?
KOUJI-KUN'S A PRETTY NICE GUY, ISN'T HE?
WELL, DON'T BEAT AROUND THE BUSH OR ANYTHING!
HA HA HA.
YES.
VERY NICE, INDEED.
QUITE.

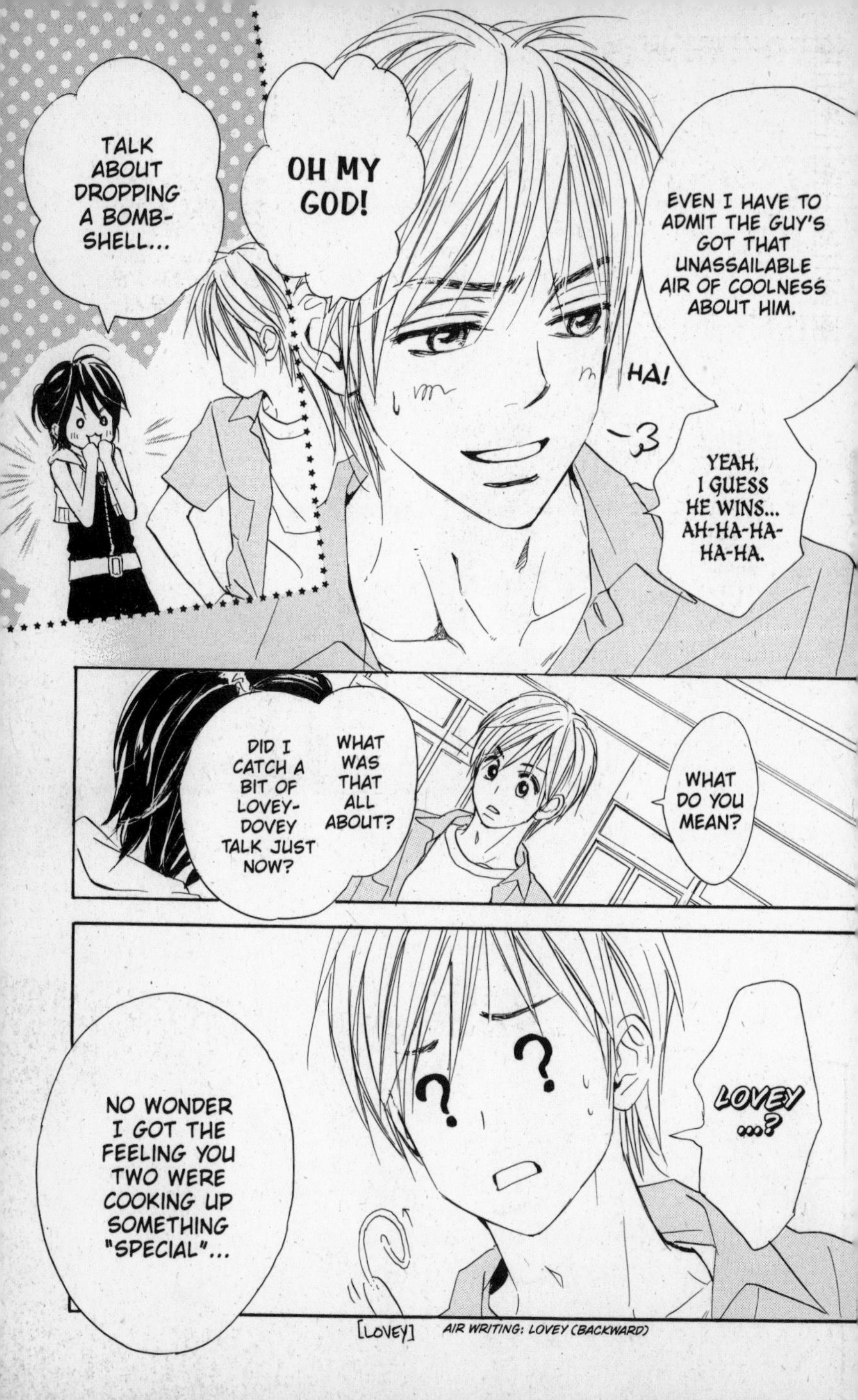
EVEN I HAVE TO ADMIT THE GUY'S GOT THAT UNASSAILABLE AIR OF COOLNESS ABOUT HIM.
HA!
YEAH, I GUESS HE WINS... AH-HA-HA-HA-HA.
OH MY GOD!
TALK ABOUT DROPPING A BOMB-SHELL...
WHAT DO YOU MEAN?
WHAT WAS THAT ALL ABOUT?
DID I CATCH A BIT OF LOVEY-DOVEY TALK JUST NOW?
LOVEY ...?
NO WONDER I GOT THE FEELING YOU TWO WERE COOKING UP SOMETHING "SPECIAL"...

[LOVEY] AIR WRITING: LOVEY (BACKWARD)

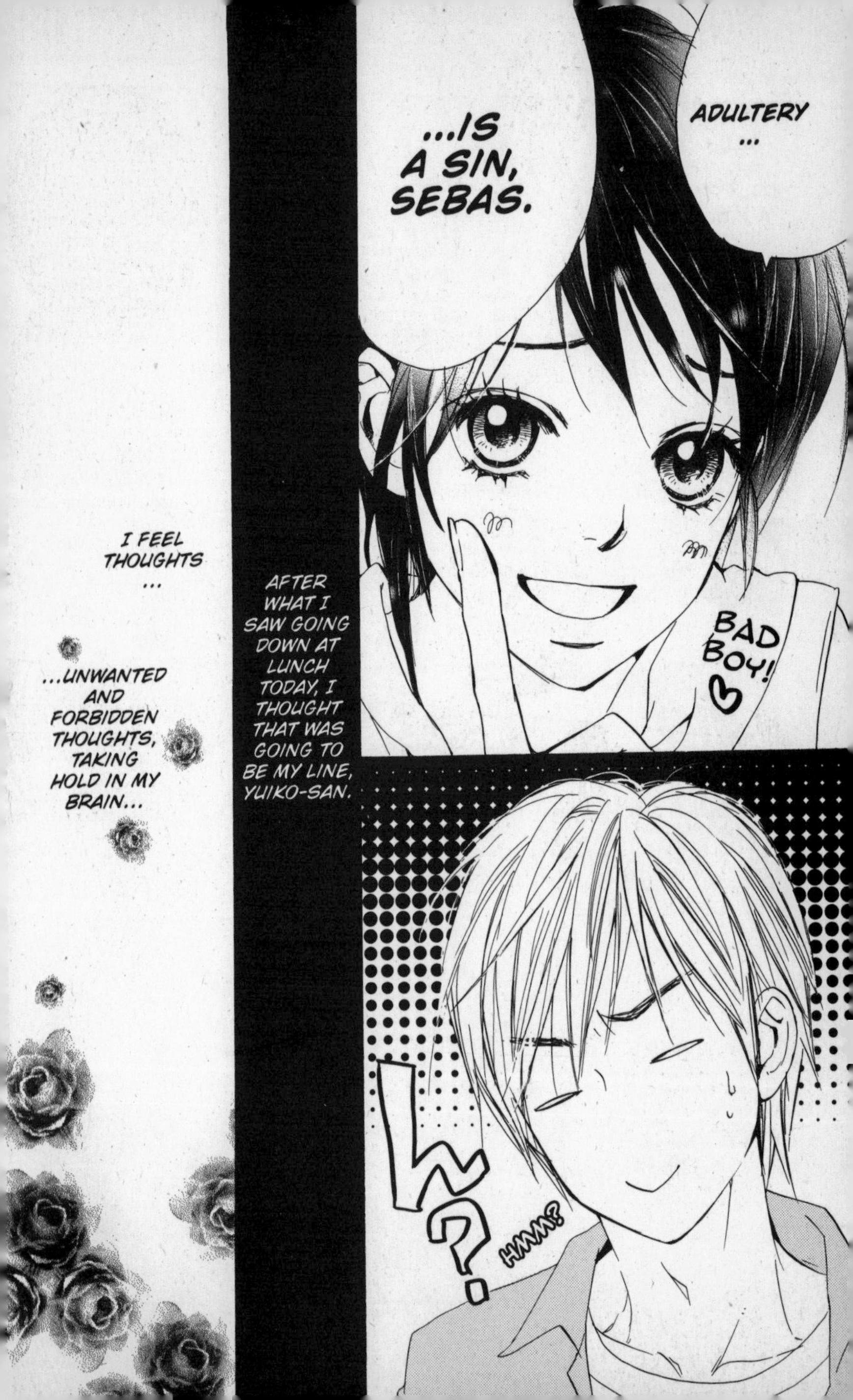
ADULTERY ...
...IS A SIN, SEBAS.
BAD BOY!
HMM?
AFTER WHAT I SAW GOING DOWN AT LUNCH TODAY, I THOUGHT THAT WAS GOING TO BE MY LINE, YUIKO-SAN.
I FEEL THOUGHTS ...
...UNWANTED AND FORBIDDEN THOUGHTS, TAKING HOLD IN MY BRAIN...

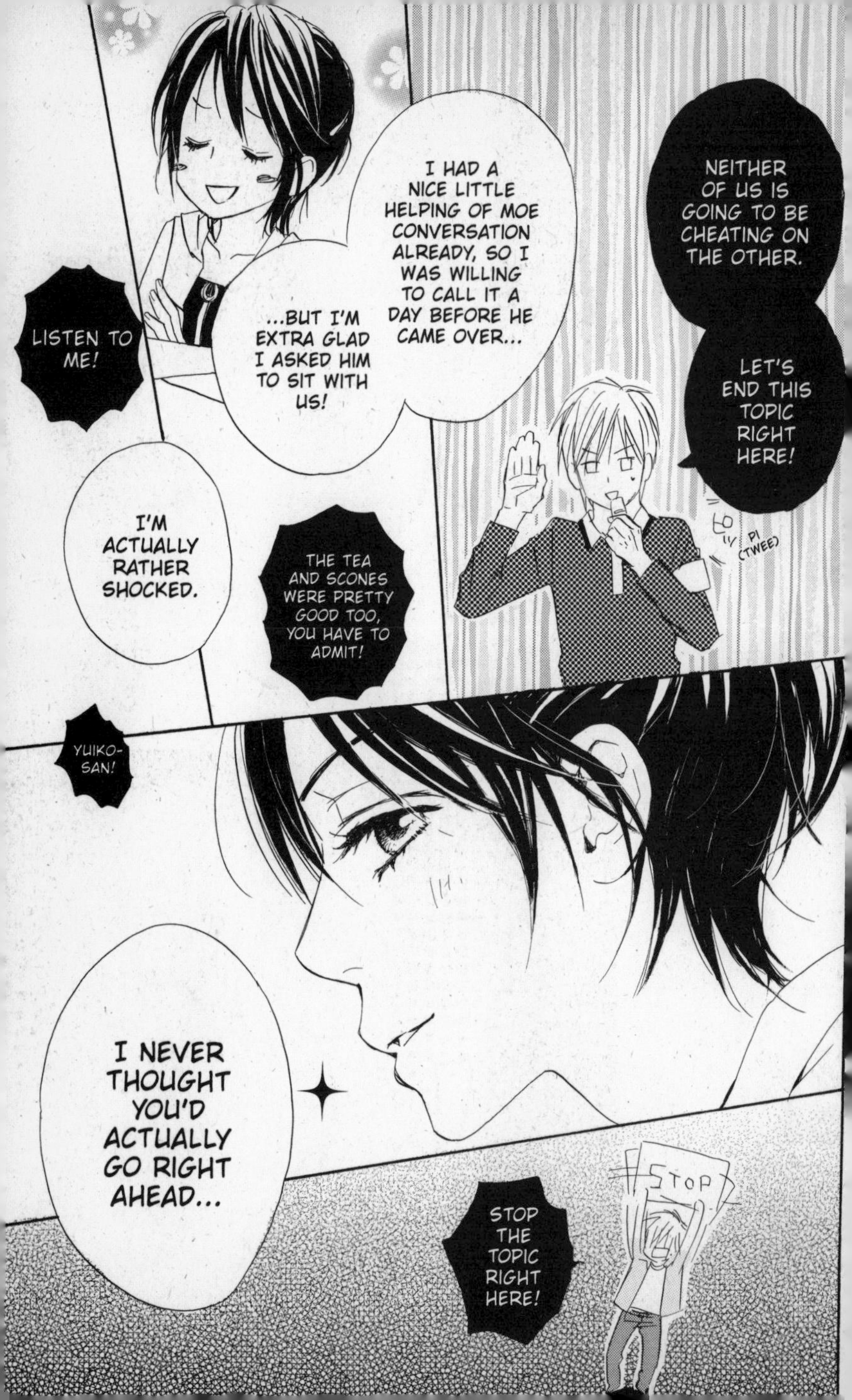
NEITHER OF US IS GOING TO BE CHEATING ON THE OTHER.
LET'S END THIS TOPIC RIGHT HERE!
PI (TWEE)
I HAD A NICE LITTLE HELPING OF MOE CONVERSATION ALREADY, SO I WAS WILLING TO CALL IT A DAY BEFORE HE CAME OVER...
...BUT I'M EXTRA GLAD I ASKED HIM TO SIT WITH US!
LISTEN TO ME!
I'M ACTUALLY RATHER SHOCKED.
THE TEA AND SCONES WERE PRETTY GOOD TOO, YOU HAVE TO ADMIT!
YUIKO-SAN!
I NEVER THOUGHT YOU'D ACTUALLY GO RIGHT AHEAD...
STOP
STOP THE TOPIC RIGHT HERE!

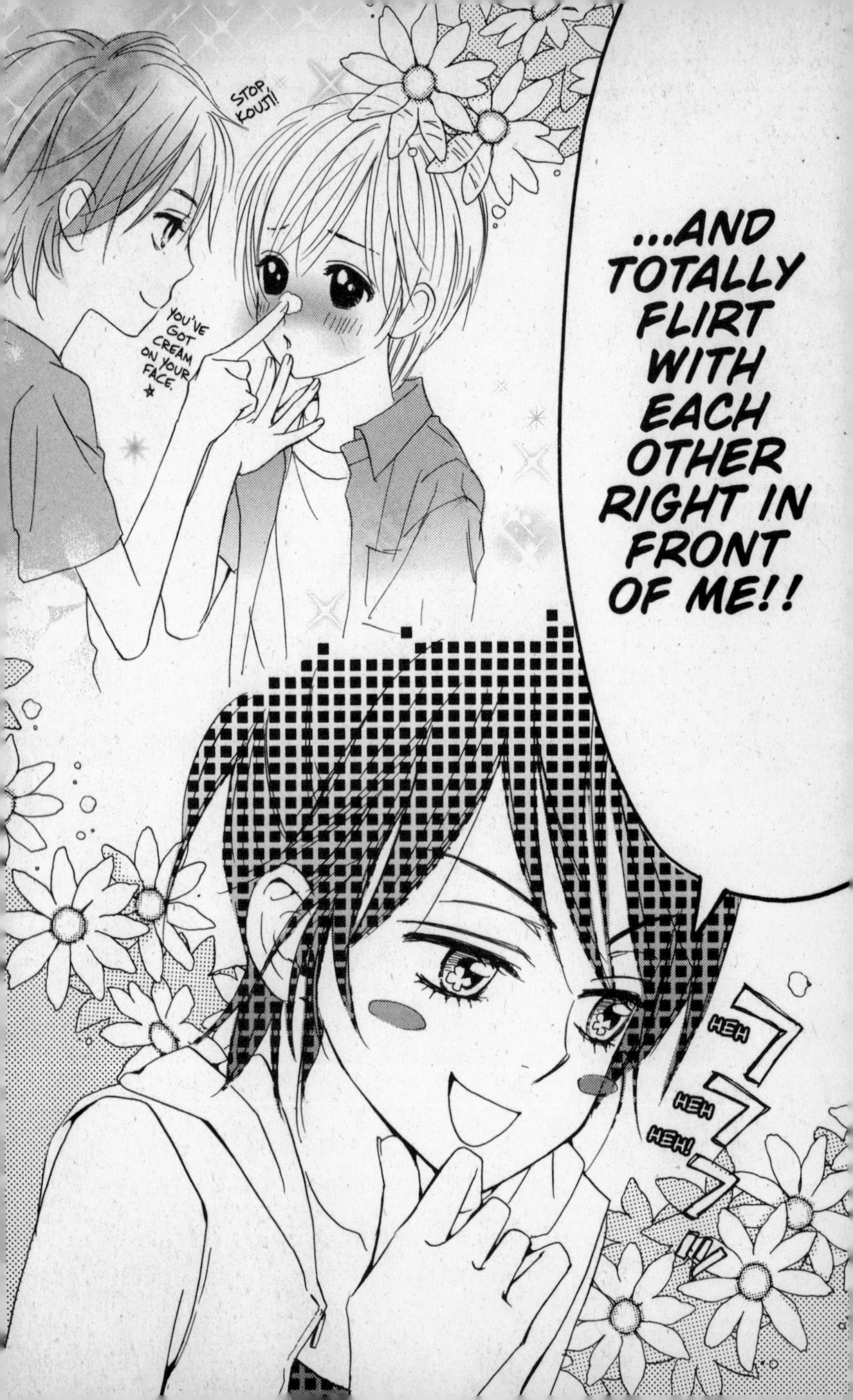

...AND TOTALLY FLIRT WITH EACH OTHER RIGHT IN FRONT OF ME!!
STOP, KOUJI!
YOU'VE GOT CREAM ON YOUR FACE. ☆
HEH HEH HEH!

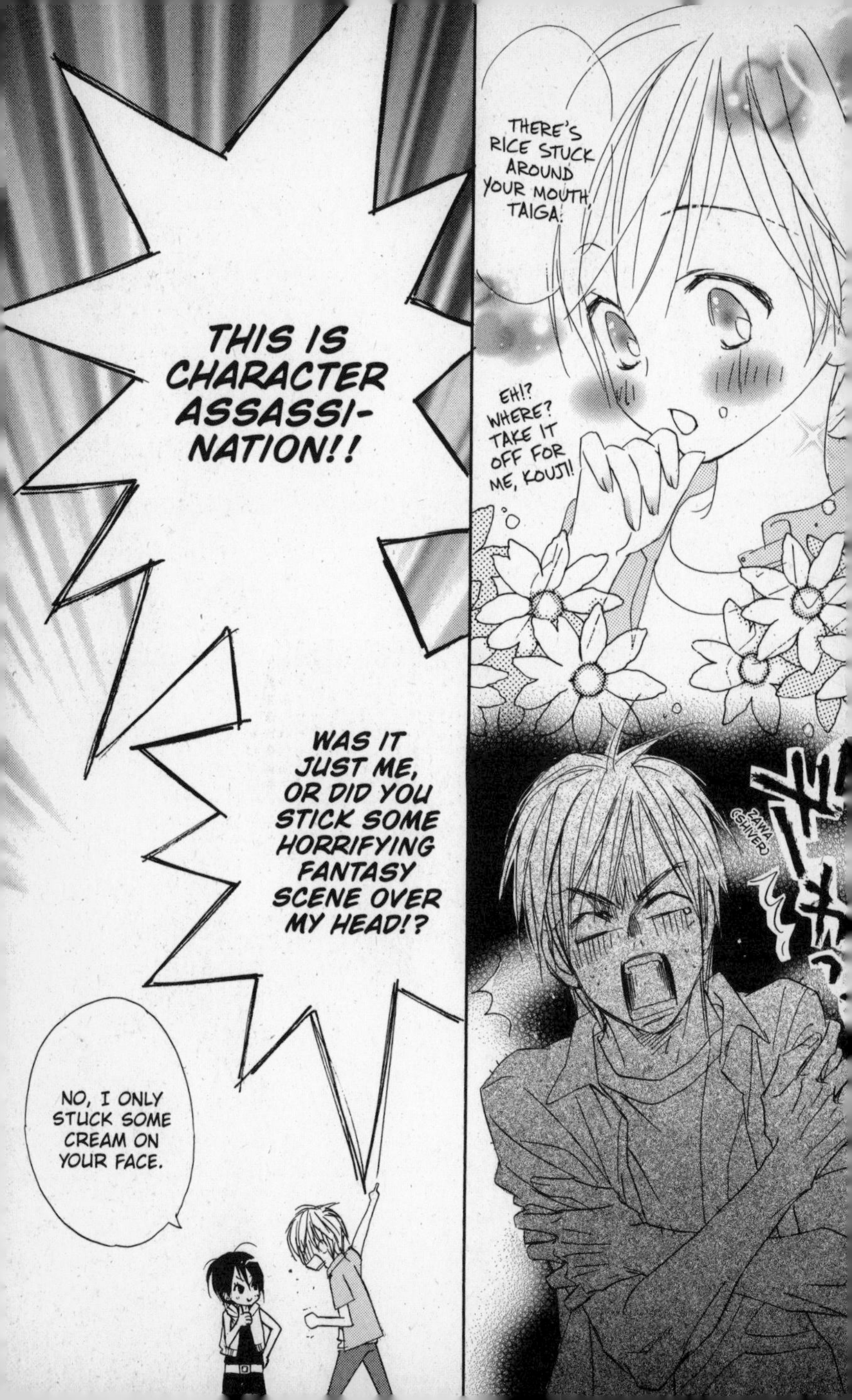

THERE'S RICE STUCK AROUND YOUR MOUTH, TAIGA!
EH!? WHERE? TAKE IT OFF FOR ME, KOUJI!
ZAWA (SHIVER)
THIS IS CHARACTER ASSASSI-NATION!!
WAS IT JUST ME, OR DID YOU STICK SOME HORRIFYING FANTASY SCENE OVER MY HEAD!?
NO, I ONLY STUCK SOME CREAM ON YOUR FACE.

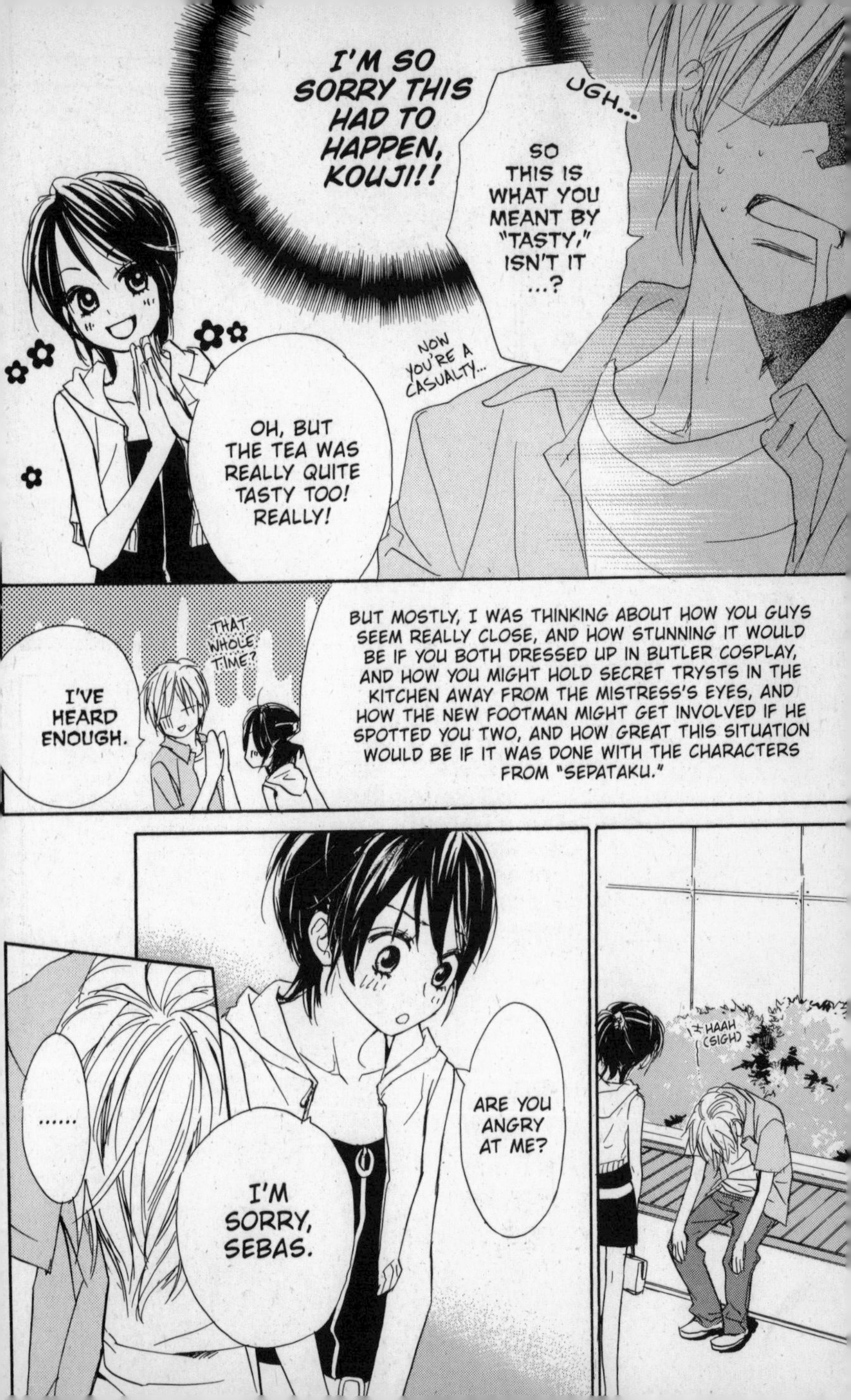
UGH...
SO THIS IS WHAT YOU MEANT BY "TASTY," ISN'T IT ...?
I'M SO SORRY THIS HAD TO HAPPEN, KOUJI!!
NOW YOU'RE A CASUALTY...
OH, BUT THE TEA WAS REALLY QUITE TASTY TOO! REALLY!
BUT MOSTLY, I WAS THINKING ABOUT HOW YOU GUYS SEEM REALLY CLOSE, AND HOW STUNNING IT WOULD BE IF YOU BOTH DRESSED UP IN BUTLER COSPLAY, AND HOW YOU MIGHT HOLD SECRET TRYSTS IN THE KITCHEN AWAY FROM THE MISTRESS'S EYES, AND HOW THE NEW FOOTMAN MIGHT GET INVOLVED IF HE SPOTTED YOU TWO, AND HOW GREAT THIS SITUATION WOULD BE IF IT WAS DONE WITH THE CHARACTERS FROM "SEPATAKU."
THAT WHOLE TIME?
I'VE HEARD ENOUGH.
HAAH (SIGH)
ARE YOU ANGRY AT ME?
I'M SORRY, SEBAS.
......

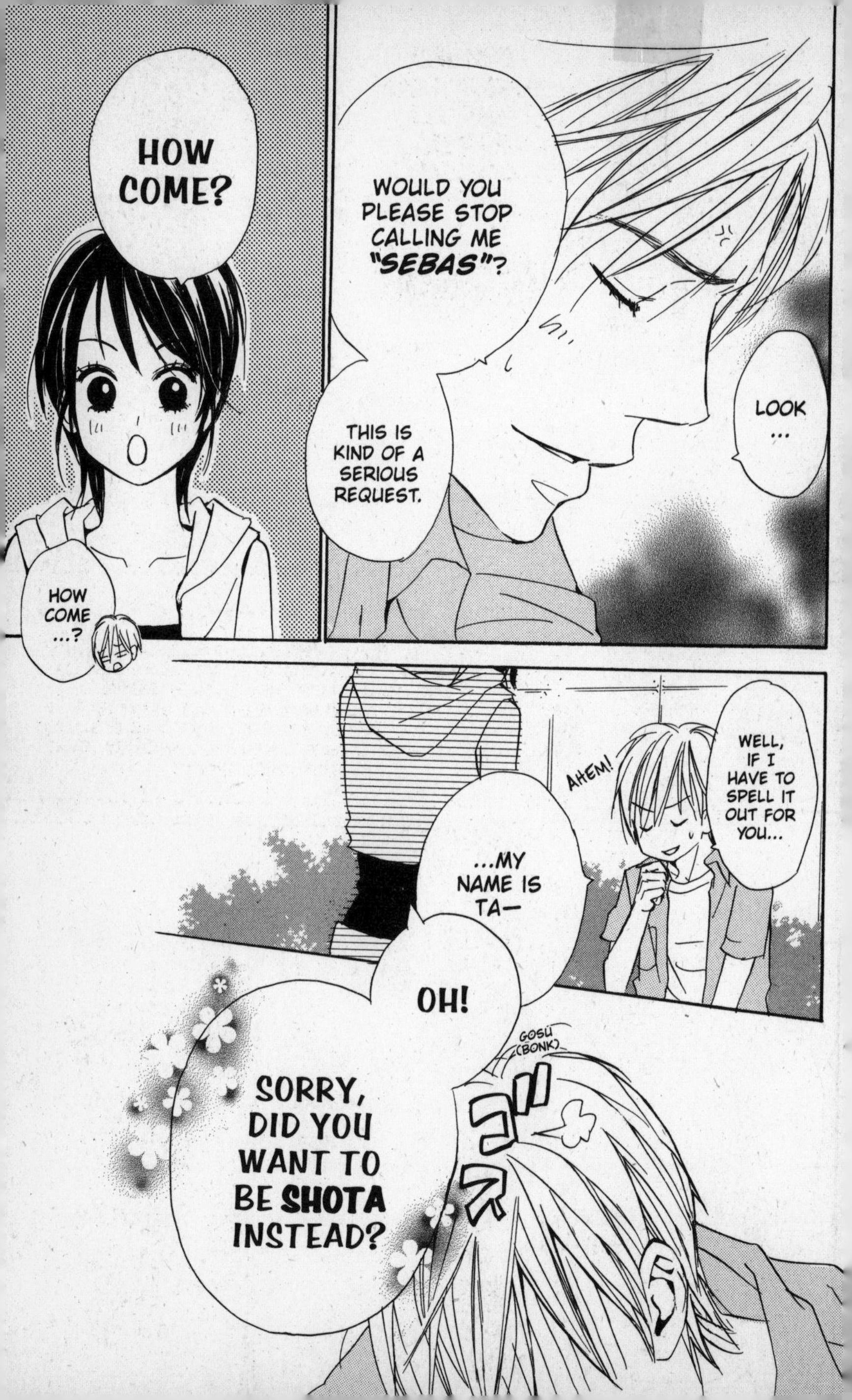
LOOK...
WOULD YOU PLEASE STOP CALLING ME "SEBAS"?
THIS IS KIND OF A SERIOUS REQUEST.
HOW COME?
HOW COME...?
WELL, IF I HAVE TO SPELL IT OUT FOR YOU...
AHEM!
...MY NAME IS TA—
OH!
SORRY, DID YOU WANT TO BE SHOTA INSTEAD?
GOSU (BONK)

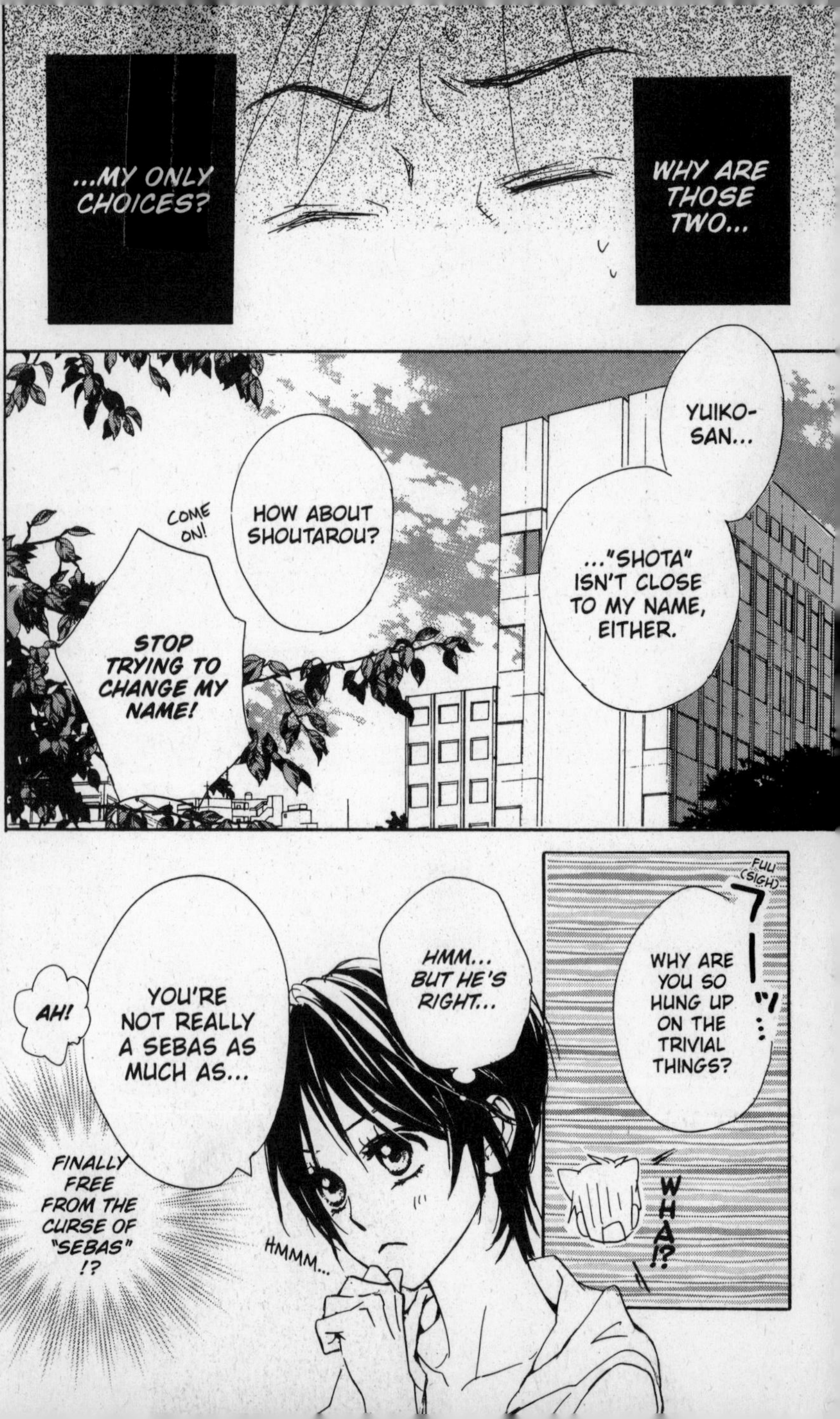
WHY ARE THOSE TWO...
...MY ONLY CHOICES?
YUIKO-SAN...
..."SHOTA" ISN'T CLOSE TO MY NAME, EITHER.
HOW ABOUT SHOUTAROU?
COME ON!
STOP TRYING TO CHANGE MY NAME!
FUU (SIGH)
WHY ARE YOU SO HUNG UP ON THE TRIVIAL THINGS?
WHA!?
HMM... BUT HE'S RIGHT...
HMMM...
YOU'RE NOT REALLY A SEBAS AS MUCH AS...
AH!
FINALLY FREE FROM THE CURSE OF "SEBAS" !?

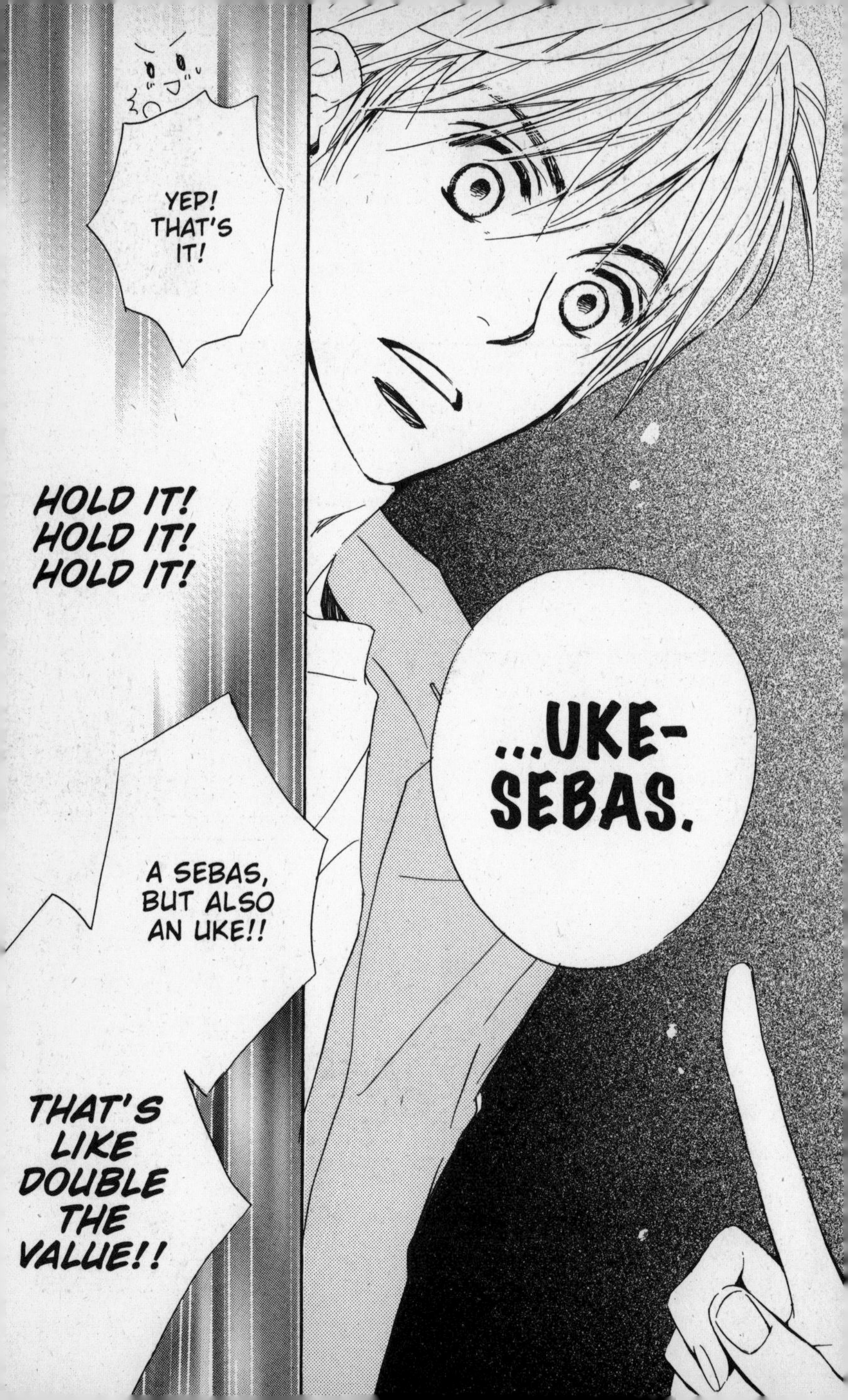
...UKE-SEBAS.
YEP! THAT'S IT!
HOLD IT! HOLD IT! HOLD IT!
A SEBAS, BUT ALSO AN UKE!!
THAT'S LIKE DOUBLE THE VALUE!!

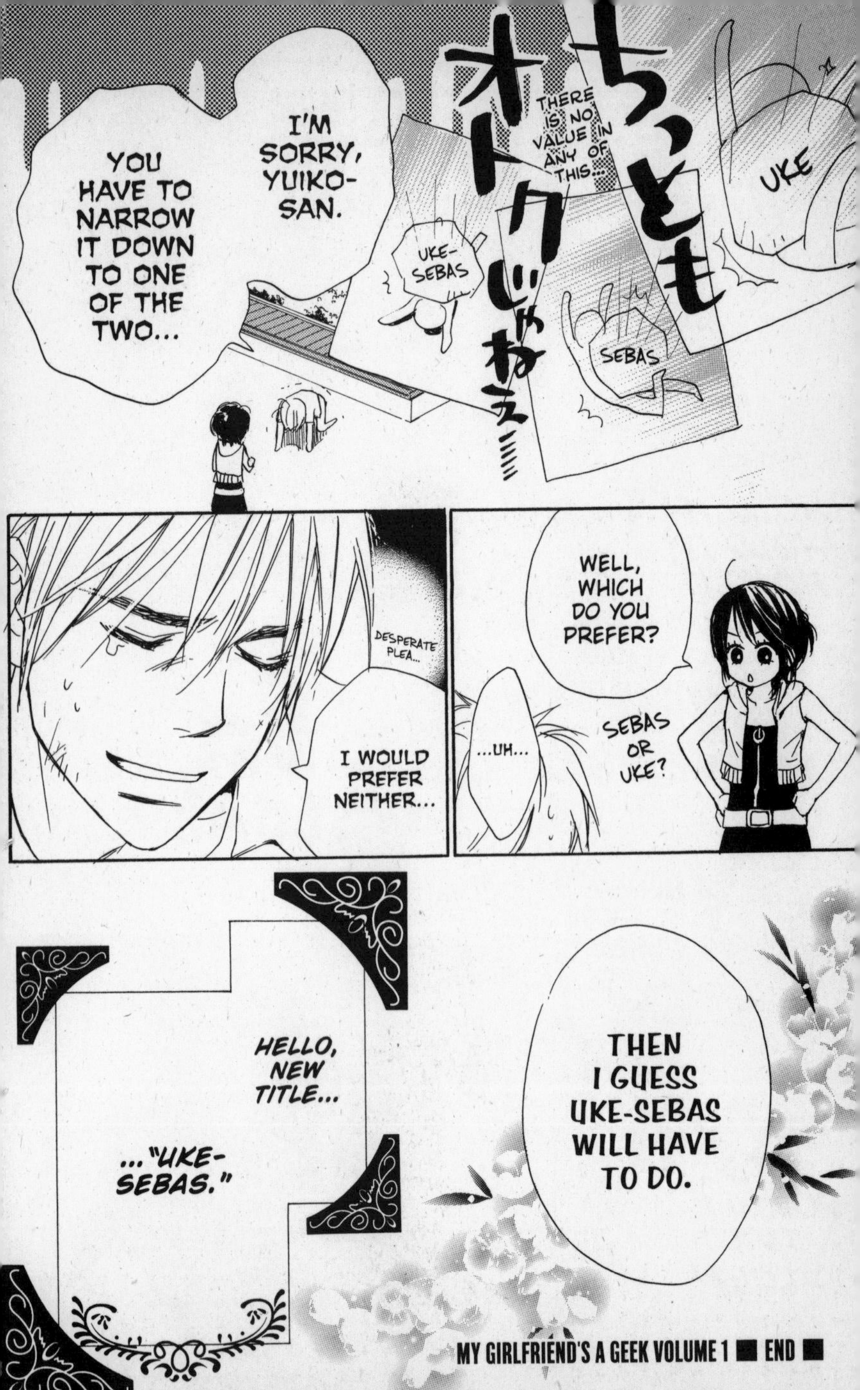
UKE
ちっとも
オトクじゃねェ!!!!
THERE IS NO VALUE IN ANY OF THIS...
SEBAS
UKE-SEBAS
I'M SORRY, YUIKO-SAN.
YOU HAVE TO NARROW IT DOWN TO ONE OF THE TWO...
WELL, WHICH DO YOU PREFER?
SEBAS OR UKE?
...UH...
DESPERATE PLEA...
I WOULD PREFER NEITHER...
THEN I GUESS UKE-SEBAS WILL HAVE TO DO.
HELLO, NEW TITLE...
..."UKE-SEBAS."

MY GIRLFRIEND'S A GEEK VOLUME 1 ■ END ■

AFTERWORD ESSAY
PENTABU

ME, MY GIRLFRIEND, AND "MY GIRLFRIEND'S A GEEK."

Y-ko   "Ooh… Look at Taiga-kun getting pushed around again this chapter!"

Me   "………"

Y-ko   "Aww, I love how cute he is when he's super-deformed!"

Me   "……Umm…"

Y-ko   "What? Ooh, I need to get an outfit like the one Yuiko-san is wearing."

Me   "……You're kind of close."

Y-ko   "Huh? Yes, because I'm hugging you.
        Come on, now! Turn the page! Turn, turn, turn!"

Me   "…Yes, ma'am."

So.

In my hands I hold the latest issue of Comic B's-Log, in which Shinba-sensei's manga version of *My Girlfriend's a Geek* is being serialized.

And leaning on my back, staring over my shoulders like a baby in a sling, is Y-ko.

………

I stopped turning the page, and looked at her.

Seeing me turn my head, Y-ko looks at me, puzzled.

Y-ko   "Hmm? What's wrong?"

Me   "Nothing…"

Y-ko   "Oh, is having me holding you from behind causing your heart to beat like crazy?

        You little **pervert**!"

Me   "…No, it's not that."

Y-ko   "Well, what is it?"

Me   "You feel heavy… **Have you gained weight?**"

Y-ko   "Yah!"

Me   "Gff!!"

With that kinda cute cry of "yah!" she reached around and put me into…

…a sleeper hold.

...H-hang on...Uncle...Uncle...

Y-ko	"Whew!"
Me	"You know, after a vicious, nearly fatal attack like that, I don't think you have the right to sit back and breathe out that **'job well done'** kind of satisfied sigh..."
Y-ko	"Heh-heh! But in the front of the book, there's that illustration of Yuiko-san putting Taiga in a sleeper hold, so I wanted to try it too."
Me	"We get such a moving, adorable illustration to grace our book, and that's all you can say about it?"
Y-ko	"Bah! Big words coming from a guy whose first impressions of the manga were, **'I like how the collarbone and hand bones are drawn.'** I'll call you **Sebas Collarbone-fetish Mutou!**"
Me	"Don't give me that ridiculous middle name! Plus, my name is not Sebas! That isn't a real name, it's just a nickname you saddled me with!"
Y-ko	"Hrmph... Fine... **Taiga Mutou Collarbonesky!**"
Me	"What!? Okay, that one at least sounds a bit more like an actual name!"
Y-ko	"Heh heh! Doesn't it? I've been getting into really long names since I watched the **new Gundam show.**"
Me	"Long names? Great, another weird hobby..."
Y-ko	"Oh, whatever! Turn the page, Collarbonesky."
Me	"Don't call me that!!"
Y-ko	"Why not? Doesn't it sound really regal and cool, like Dostoyevsky?"
Me	"Actually, now that you mention it...no, it doesn't!" The only impression it gives off is that its owner must be a **really weird person!**"
Y-ko	"Oh, it does? Darn... How about, **Taiga Mutou Boyslovesky?**"
Me	"BL-sky? What do I have to do with BL!?"
Y-ko	"Well, I tried to give you a name about something you actually like with Collarbonesky, and you didn't want it! That means you only have one choice: You have to match my name, **Yuiko Boyslovesky**!!"
Me	"Why is that my only choice? I only get two options!? Plus, if you're supposed to be a secret fujoshi, why would you announce it right in your name!? Then you're telling everyone your secret!"

(continued)

So,

as you know, Rize Shinba-sensei has turned my life with a fujoshi girlfriend into a manga. It was amazing enough when my blog was packaged into a book, but to have an amazing manga adaptation too... It's too much for words.

I would like to express my heartful thanks to everyone who supported this story, Shinba-sensei, and everyone at the publishing companies.

Thank you so, so, so much.

Y-ko and I are both excitedly looking forward to our story being told through Shinba-sensei's talented pen. I hope that you will too.

December 2007

Pentabu,
who learned to love collarbones through Shinba-sensei's art.
Y-ko
who thinks that Shinba-sensei's Yuiko-san is the ideal woman.

TRANSLATION NOTES

PAGE 38
Sepatte Takuro A bit of a pun based on the Japanese pronunciation of sepak takraw ("sepa takuro"). Translated, it means something like "Play Sepak, Takuro." It seems that readers like to shorten the title to "Sepataku."
The sport of takraw itself is like kick volleyball, in which two teams of three have to keep a small ball made of woven rattan airborne without touching the floor on their side of the net. It's played primarily in Southeast Asian countries like Thailand, Malaysia, and Laos.

PAGE 104
Fujoshi A self-deprecating term referring to female fans of *yaoi* (aka., "Boys' Love"/"B.L."). The word is a homophone of the Japanese word for "respectable lady," but with the character for "woman" replaced with the character for "rotten," thus forming a word that means "rotten girl." This refers to the supposedly "rotten" thoughts and fantasies that *fujoshi* have about characters or people in gay relationships that would not normally occur. In recent years, the term's definition has been loosened slightly to sometimes include female otaku without a strong predilection for B.L.

PAGE 108
Rosy future In Japan, gay subculture is sometimes described using the word *bara* ("rose"). This term has a particular meaning within B.L./*yaoi* to indicate gay comics or stories that are strictly created by and for gay men, as opposed to most B.L. (which is made by and for women). In a general sense, however, the word "rose" can be understood to simply correspond to gay culture as a whole.

Odaiba An artificial island in Tokyo Bay that features many entertainment, leisure and shopping destinations.

PAGE 150
Patrasche The name of the dog in the novel *A Dog of Flanders*, which was made into a popular anime series in the 1970s.

MY GIRLFRIEND'S A GEEK ①
RIZE SHINBA
PENTABU

Translation: **Stephen Paul**   •   Lettering: **Alexis Eckerman**

FUJYOSHI KANOJO Vol. 1 © 2007 RIZE SHINBA © 2006, 2007 PENTABU. All rights reserved. First published in Japan in 2007 by ENTERBRAIN, INC., Tokyo. English translation rights arranged with ENTERBRAIN, INC. through Tuttle-Mori Agency, Inc., Tokyo.

Translation © 2010 by Hachette Book Group, Inc.

Yen Press
Hachette Book Group
237 Park Avenue, New York, NY 10017

www.HachetteBookGroup.com
www.YenPress.com

Yen Press is an imprint of Hachette Book Group, Inc. The Yen Press name and logo are trademarks of Hachette Book Group, Inc.

First Yen Press Edition: May 2010

ISBN: 978-0-7595-3173-4

10 9 8 7 6 5 4 3 2

BVG

Printed in the United States of America

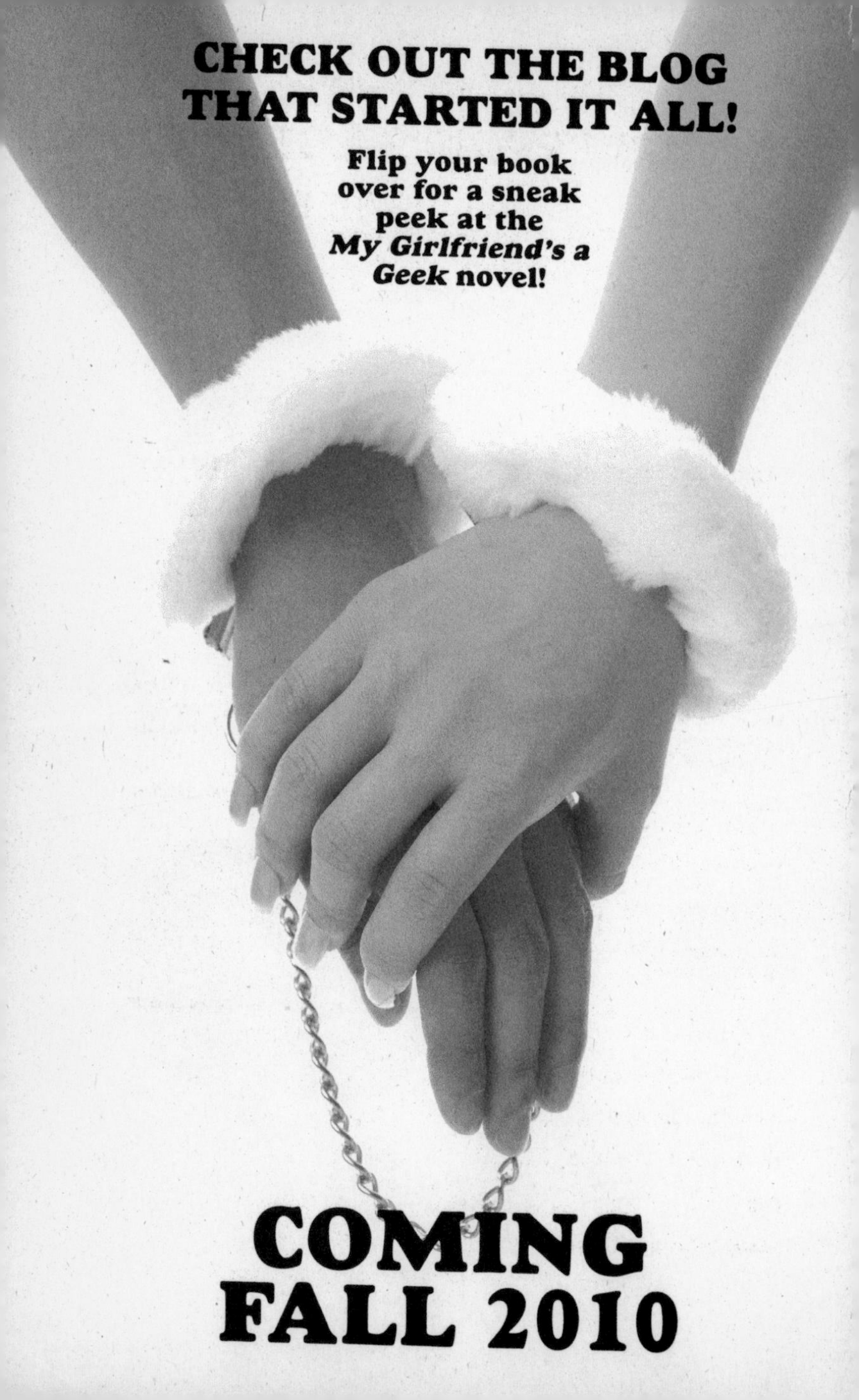
CHECK OUT THE BLOG THAT STARTED IT ALL!
Flip your book over for a sneak peek at the *My Girlfriend's a Geek* novel!
COMING FALL 2010

Apparently, this game has been turned into an anime.
Apparently, it's not really that erotic...
Apparently, it's actually very popular...
I have learned something today.

Read more about
Pentabu's travails in
Yen Press's edition of
My Girlfriend's a Geek,
Vol. 1 coming to a store
near you in Fall 2010!!

I don't know why she denied it the first time.
At any rate, it was one hell of a roar.
I'm sure it must have upset the neighbors.

And, of course, it just had to be "it is an eroge" that I screamed so loud.
I can practically see the neighbors pointing at the back of my head tomorrow.

...Someone, anyone, **save me.**

...Whew. Well, that earth-shaking bellow helped calm me down.
I'm okay. I'm still hanging in there. I can still fight.
I got into a boxing stance within my mind,
and I delivered a withering smack down to local fujoshi, Y-ko.

Me: Ahem. And why, pray tell, did you buy this eroge?

I couldn't help but frame the question politely. You are *so* weak, me!
But I just can't help it. She's older than me.
It's my personal motto to always speak politely to my elders.

Y-ko: Huh? Because I wanted it.

...Well, that makes sense.
However, I can't back down yet.
I've got to get answers to *all* of my questions.

Me: ...And why did you have to use *my* account? Why not use your own?
Y-ko: What? Because it would be **embarrassing** to buy an eroge
         with mine.

She looked at me with an expression like *can't you even understand that?*
Yes, yes, I do.
It is indeed embarrassing.
I know because I am feeling it in real time.
...I know it so well it hurts.

I mean...

...there are limits to injustice.

I hesitantly approached my girlfriend,
who was lying in my room, reading *Love Celeb*
and sporting a grin, the type of which no human being should ever sport.

Me: Y-ko, did you buy anything from Amazon using my computer?
Y-ko: Oh yeah, I did.

I knew it.

And with an "Oh, it arrived," she grabbed the package from my hands.
She began tearing directly through the cardboard.
Most people would neatly cut through or rip off the tape on the lid,
but my girlfriend does not bother herself with methods that involve more than
one step.

And what should emerge from the shattered, torn carcass of this cardboard
box, but…a smaller box. Judging from the packaging, it was some kind of
game.
And it didn't look like a PlayStation game.
Therefore, it was most likely a game to be played on the PC.
A sudden possibility popped into my head, and I asked my girlfriend a
question.

Me: I hate to even consider this possibility…
         …but that wouldn't happen to be what they call an **eroge**,
         would it…?

I really hope it's not the case.
That is another world that I really don't want to get involved in, for entirely
different reasons.
Not least of which is the fact that she's buying it under *my* name.
This was her answer.

Y-ko: No!! It's not an eroge!!
Me: Oh, then that's okay. But you don't need to shout about…
Y-ko: It's a **world-famous** eroge!!

Ah, I see. It must be *very* erotic, then.

Me: So **it is an eroge, then!!**
It was a scream emitted from my entire body and soul.

of sexy hooks and twists. It also has that, uh, whatchamacallit (great, so much for this definition!) where characters from Mayu Shinjo's other series *Sensual Phrase* show up. Anyway, if you're interested, you should borrow it from a friend or go read it at a manga café. By the way, it's apparently quite successful and has even been popular in several other countries around the world.

So...
Uhh...
...Why am I being punished this way?

It's like **my world is coming to an end.**

I just want to cry.

EROGE.
2005/11/15 17:56

So, I got a package the other day.
It was from Amazon.
I don't remember ordering anything,
but the package is clearly addressed to me from Amazon.

I scrawled off a hasty signature like a celebrity
and took the box back into my room.

I looked multiple times to confirm that it was indeed *my* name on the package,
but I still couldn't remember buying anything.
In this case, there could be only one answer...

It was clearly **my girlfriend's doing.**

Where are you trying to take me?

FUJOSHI-ISH LINES.

My girlfriend occasionally...no, *frequently*, acts in strange ways.
Let's call it...fujoshi-itis.
I think she's coming down with another bad bout of it.

Y-ko: Hey, try saying a line like something out of a manga.
Me: ....Like what?
Y-ko: Umm, like something that will make that *Speed Wagon* guy want to
           call you **"Idiot!"** and slap you upside the head.

As usual, a **completely absurd and impossible request** out of the blue.

Despite my better judgment, however, I decided to ask.
It wouldn't do to upset my girlfriend, after all.

Me: Errr... Can you give me an example?
Y-ko: Okay... Like something from this manga.

"This" manga turned out to be *Love Celeb*.

Great. **Mayu Shinjo!!**

Love Celeb: Gin's grandfather is the prime minister of Japan, and his father
is the head of an elite business conglomerate. Gin himself is the heir to the
"Fujiwara group." Instead of following his predetermined fate, however, he
falls in love with the unsuccessful teen idol Kirara in this shōjo manga full

FUJOSHI @ MAID CAFÉ.

Before maid cafés were known and open to the general public,
when they were only frequented by real life otaku,
I visited one with some college friends.

Or should I say, overwhelmed by the incredible line
and the procession of bespectacled, backpack-hauling warriors,
we were intimidated and left before ever setting foot within the building.
When I regaled my girlfriend with this tale,
she blithely replied —

Y-ko: Too bad. **They're fun.**

You mean...

You've been to one before?!

Y-ko: Hmm? Yeah, they say, **"Welcome home, my lady."**

So, uh, what's your point?

Y-ko: Yeah, I thought it was **really moe.**
Me: What?! Girls are allowed to get moe over other girls?!

...There is something seriously wrong with this lady.
But I just can't bring myself to care anymore...
I must be reaching the end.

Y-ko: Hey, would you want to go together?
Me: ...Huh? Where?
Y-ko: A totally over-the-top maid café. You'd think it was really moe.
          I guarantee it.

Uh, Y-ko...
The following question has several different meanings:

times as fast as the unit it was based upon. By the way, this anime series was originally aired...

...in 1979 and 1980.

That's right, **before we were born.**

Where did you learn *that* one?
My friend was desperately trying to contain his laughter.
His hands were trembling on the steering wheel.
My friend's girlfriend appeared to have no idea what it meant.
She sat in the passenger seat, looking puzzled.
They already knew the dirty secret that my girlfriend was a fujoshi, by the way, so they probably decided that they didn't need to ask.

Next, my girlfriend said this.

Y-ko: Oh wait, ○○ (Friend's GF) doesn't know about Gundam, does she? Well, the next time you come over...

...you can borrow it!!

...Please, it's one thing to drag *me* into your world, but leave my friend's girlfriend out of this.

Don't do it.

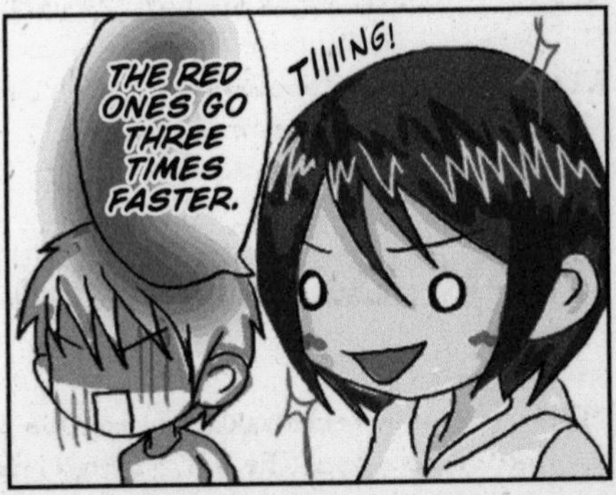
THE RED ONES GO THREE TIMES FASTER.
TIIIING!

And even worse,

I'm starting to enjoy it.

...So, umm, where is my life headed?

MY GIRLFRIEND.
`2005/11/10 15:35`

My girlfriend is one of those popular (?) fujoshi.
And she's not just any fujoshi.
She's a very high-level specimen, a spectacular example of otaku-ology.
She will quite often blurt out unbelievable things.
For example, when we went out on a double date with another couple, we had rented a car and were on our way to the beach.
As we sat at a traffic light, we saw a red truck (one of those shipping company vehicles) pass by.

Friend A: So why are all delivery vehicles, even the post office's, colored red?

Friend B: So that they stand out?

As I sat half-listening to their conversation, my girlfriend spoke up from right next to me.

Y-ko: **"The red ones go three times faster."**

The car was absolutely silent for a moment.
You know what to say next, everyone.
Ready, set...

You mean Char's Zaku?!

*Char's Zaku: A vehicle that appeared in *Mobile Suit Gundam*. It was known as Char's personal mobile suit. Painted bright red, it was said to move three

GREETINGS.

2005/11/08 22:14

Greetings.
My name is Pentabu.
One year ago, I began a relationship with my girlfriend.
I had always wanted to go out with an older woman. It was all very thrilling.
The problem is…

…she was a fujoshi.

A serious one!!

…Every ongoing day is a battle.

In this blog, I hope to track the many trials and travails of our relationship.

ABOUT ME.

2005/11/08 22:28

Well, I'd better start telling you about my girlfriend!!
The girlfriend that I met at a part-time job and worked hard enough to get
romantically involved with!!

…She's a big-time fujoshi…

Huh? "As long as she's cute," you say? Yes, you've got a point there.
But you see… there's just one problem.
Through some sequence of events that I have yet to understand…

I'm…

…being forced to write a *Seed* novel…

(*Seed = Gundam SEED)

This blog is a record of battle as dictated
by a man with a fujoshi girlfriend.

Okay, that was a lie. I'm not fighting at all.

The war is purely one-sided. Each day I am dragged
farther and farther into the world of otaku.

I cannot be held responsible for any
damages incurred by reading this blog and
falling into the same predicament.

There is much otaku talk contained within,
so please follow your directions carefully and
do not exceed your recommended dosage.

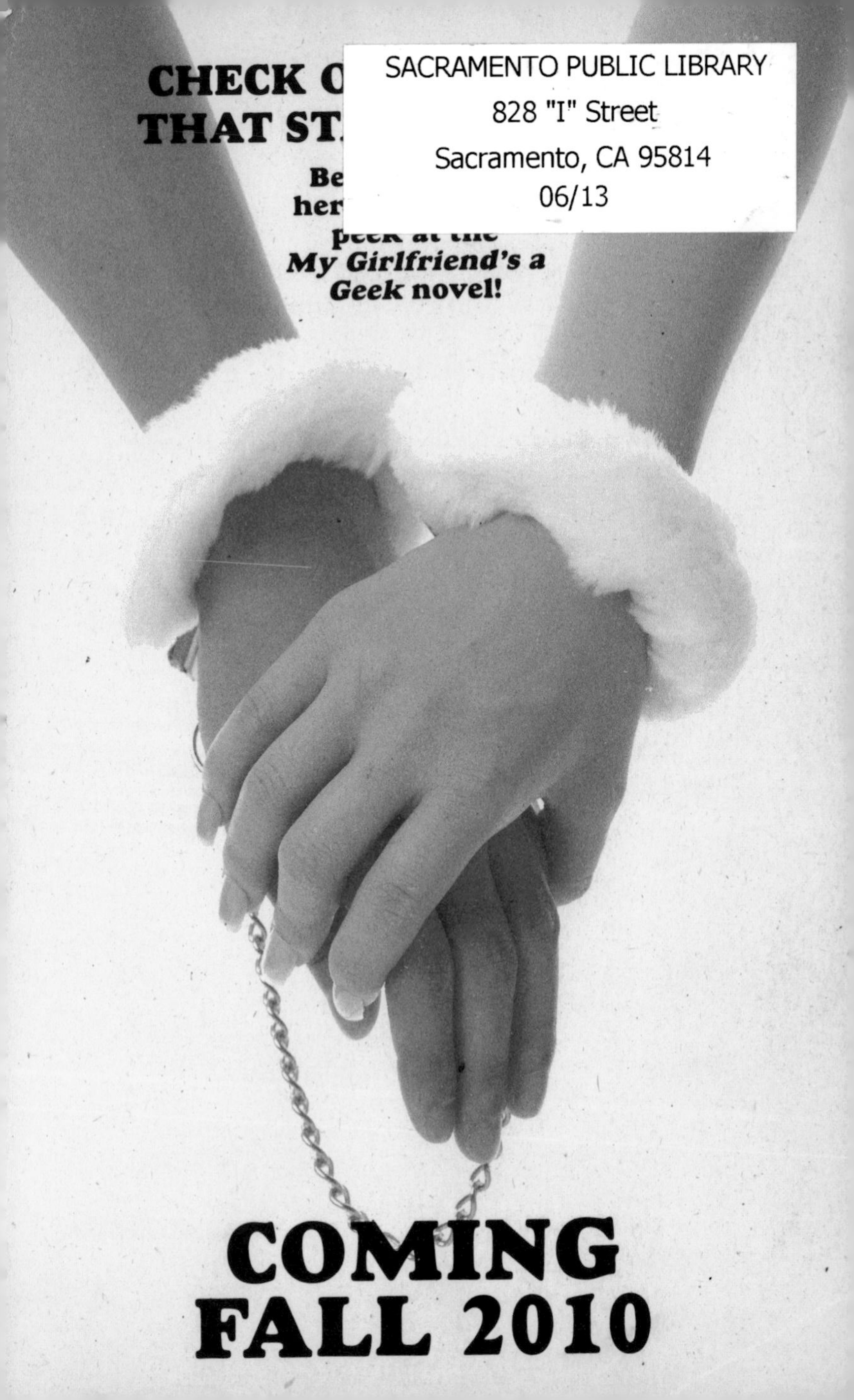
CHECK O
THAT ST
Be
her
My Girlfriend's a
Geek novel!
COMING
FALL 2010